W9-AGU-185

LEIBNIZ'
UNIVERSAL
JURISPRUDENCE

LEIBNIZ'
UNIVERSAL
JURISPRUDENCE

Justice as the Charity of the Wise

PATRICK RILEY

HARVARD UNIVERSITY PRESS

Cambridge, Massachusetts   London, England   1996

For Samuel H. Beer

Vir bonus qui amat omnes

Library of Congress Cataloging-in-Publication Data

Riley, Patrick, 1941–
    Leibniz' universal jurisprudence : justice as the charity of the
wise / Patrick Riley.
        p.   cm.
    Includes bibliographical references and index.
    ISBN 0-674-52407-1 (alk. paper)
    1. Leibniz, Gottfried Wilhelm, Freiherr von, 1646–1716.
2. Justice (Philosophy)—History—17th century.   3. Love.
4. Ethics, Modern—17th century.   5. Law—Philosophy—
History—17th century.   I. Title.
B2599.J8R55   1996
172'.2'092—dc20   96-8903

Contents

Acknowledgments

I owe my entire career as a Leibniz scholar to Harvard University, and more particularly to two of its greatest intellectual lights, Judith N. Shklar and Samuel H. Beer. It was Dita Shklar who, in 1969, persuaded me to prepare and publish my *Political Writings of Leibniz* and who urged me, up until her premature death in 1992, to write a book to be called *Ancient and Modern Idealism: Plato, Leibniz, Kant.* What I have now produced is not too far from that topic, and I hope that she would have been pleased by the present volume. But it would never have come into existence at all had not my old friend Sam Beer welcomed me back to Cambridge with constant encouragement (and the generous gift of his own office for my work). It is a pleasure to dedicate this book to him; the dedication, *Vir bonus qui amat omnes,* "a good man who loves everyone," applies to him with special aptness, and is an adaptation of Leibniz' definition of the "just man" in his ethical writings from the 1670s forward. A third Harvard connection should be mentioned as well: Aida Donald, Editor-in-Chief of Harvard University Press, who shepherded my earlier *Will and Political Legitimacy* through the Press, has also generously encouraged *Leibniz' Universal Jurisprudence.* I am grateful to my old university, and to my friends who sustain it, for making a career of Leibniz scholarship possible and now for giving it a permanent written form. For it seems to me evident that if Leibniz' highest moral ideal—the perfect governance of all human relations through "wise charity" and "universal benevolence"—were realized, the world would be infinitely better off than it ever has been (or, lamentably, ever will be).

Large books do not get written without leisure time and financial support, and I gratefully acknowledge the aid of the National Endowment for the Humanities and the American Philosophical Society; both were encouraged to support me by letters from my teacher John Rawls and my colleague Quentin Skinner, who exaggerated my merits—though nothing can exaggerate my debt to them. Without a travel grant from the Leibniz-Gesellschaft I could never have visited Hanover in the summer of 1994—where I wrote the passage on "the identity of indiscernibles" in the Herrenhausen gardens where Leibniz first demonstrated that principle to members of the Hanoverian court. But I owe most of all to the unstinting financial (and other) help of my parents, who liberally underwrote most of my project; whoever thinks that Renaissance patronage is dead has not met them.

I am also grateful to Columbia University, and more particularly to Julian Franklin, for inviting me to speak on Leibniz' theory of justice as "wise charity" in December 1993; I gave more or less the same talk at Harvard in April 1994 (at the generous invitation of Pratap Mehta) and benefited from the provocative questions of Professor Mehta himself, as well as of Harvey Mansfield and Seyla Benhabib. I presented part of this paper at Oxford University in May 1994, and there received helpful comments from the venerable Leibniz scholar W. H. Barber—as well as from Sir Isaiah Berlin, who told me everything about Ernst Cassirer's doomed effort to teach the *Theodicy* in German at Oxford in 1938–39. When I gave an enlarged and elaborated version of this lecture at the VI Leibniz-Kongress in Hanover in July 1994, I received valuable criticism and kind encouragement from Herbert Breger, Thomas Gil, Emily Grossholz, André Robinet, Heinrich Schepers, H. P. Schneider, Robert Sleigh, Jr., Gerda Utermöhlen, and Charles-Yves Zarka.

Gerda Utermöhlen recently retired from the Leibniz-Archiv of the Niedersächsische Landesbibliothek in Hanover, but it was she (together with the late, lamented Albert Heinekamp) who always welcomed me back to the archive for more than twenty years, and who facilitated work on unpublished manuscripts of Leibniz; it was they, too, who kindly gave me permission to publish three of those manuscripts in the 1970s and 1980s. It was Drs. Utermöhlen and Heinekamp who made work in Hanover such a pleasure; fortunately their colleague Wilhelm Totok is still there, to help old and new Leibniz scholars. Though my largest archival debt is to the Leibniz-Archiv, I have also been given much appreciated help, for twenty-five years, by the Austrian National Library (Vienna), the Vatican Library (Rome), the Biblioteca Nazionale (Florence), the British Library (London), the Bodleian Library (Oxford), the Correr Library (Venice), and the Houghton Library (Harvard).

I also owe an important debt to Jerome Schneewind of Johns Hopkins University; his own reflections on Leibniz' natural law theory have helped me greatly, but he gives credit for most of his insights to René Sève of the Sorbonne, Paris—and I must say that Sève's two books on Leibniz from 1989 and 1994 have stimulated me more than any recent ones (even if I am sometimes inspired to oppose him). Certainly my own views have been sharpened and clarified by his vigorous and mainly sympathetic interpretation of Leibniz' "universal jurisprudence." And I have derived confidence and consolation from the thought that my own interpretations are not too far removed from those of André Robinet, *doyen* of French Leibniz scholars, in his magisterial new *G. W. Leibniz: Le meilleur des mondes par la balance de l'Europe*—a copy of which he generously gave me in Hanover in July 1994. (But Sève and Robinet would unite to remind me that the greatest of all French Leibnizians was Gaston Grua, who died just after completing his magnificent *Jurisprudence universelle et théodicée selon Leibniz*—that work from 1953 which has remained a model for all later Leibniz students, and a constant inspiration to me.)

After the manuscript of this book was substantially completed, I was invited to participate in the editing of what will become Volume IV of Leibniz' *Politische Schriften* (in the Akademie-Ausgabe of the Prussian Academy); while working at this editorial task in Berlin and Potsdam I was privileged to present a (very compressed) version of my work to the newly reconstituted Berlin-Brandenburg Academy. For this invitation to Berlin and Potsdam in February 1995 I am most grateful to Hartmut Rudolph, leader of the Leibniz edition in Berlin; for probing questions at the meeting of the Berlin-Brandenburg Academy I am indebted to Ursula Goldenbaum of the Humboldt-Universität.

There are also three younger Leibniz scholars to thank. Mark Larrimore of the Department of Religion at Princeton University, whose dissertation on Leibniz' religious and political thought was so insightful, has generously commented on my Leibniz research during trips to Cambridge and in letters; and my old students Sankar Muthuchidambaram and Jason Cooper—now both at Harvard University—have listened patiently to my attempts to explicate Leibniz' political and moral thought. Jason Cooper has also read many pages of this book in draft, and offered valuable comments. One needs the encouragement of younger people with fresh, undogmatic views, and that I have received in generous measure.

I would like to thank the *Journal of the History of Philosophy* for permitting me to reuse (heavily rewritten) portions of two of my Leibniz articles from the 1970s: "An Unpublished MS of Leibniz on the Allegiance Due to Sovereign Powers," 11, no. 3 (July 1973), and "An Unpublished MS of Leibniz on the Greeks as Founders of Rational Theology," 13, no. 4 (October 1976). I would also like to thank the *Journal of the History of Ideas* for allowing me to reuse rewritten portions of my article " 'New' Political Writings of Leibniz," 54, no. 1 (1994). And I would like to express my gratitude to the former and present directors of the Leibniz-Archiv in Hanover, Drs. Albert Heinekamp and Herbert Breger, for their generous permission to publish portions of two Leibniz manuscripts: "De Bono Unitatis et Malis Schismatis" (LH 1, 7, 1, BL. 1–2), and an untitled piece on Franco-German relations from 1711 (LH XI, 5, BL. 61). Penultimately I want to thank Elizabeth Gretz at Harvard University Press, who edited my book with wonderfully sympathetic understanding (even while rigorously weeding countless Teutonisms out of my English prose).

Last—but how could it be least?—the constant support of my wife, Joan A. Riley, has made this (and all my other work for thirty years) possible; she knows well that without her devoted efforts I would never accomplish anything. And my son John Riley (Christ Church, Oxford) has been most generous in helping me with classical (particularly Roman) citations; since Leibniz thought that a Christianized Roman jurisprudence was the heart of "universal justice," that help has been crucial.

Despite so much generous and sympathetic aid from so many quarters, and over so many years, there will still be faults and lapses in *Leibniz' Universal Jurisprudence;* for those I alone am responsible.

Thanks to the generous invitation of the Saxon Academy of Sciences in Leipzig, I was able to participate in the commemorations marking the 350th anniversary of the birth of Leibniz (born in Leipzig on July 1, 1646). Only a trip to Leipzig could have shown me conclusively what I ought to have suspected: that Leibniz' synthesis of Christian and Greek thought—not least in his definition of justice as "the charity of the wise or universal benevolence"—was in part suggested by his Leipzig education. For Leibniz, however autodidactic he may have been, was nevertheless a student at the Nikolaischule in Leipzig; and a recent restoration (1994) of the Aula (assembly hall) of this venerable school revealed that the young Leibniz sat, from 1653 to 1661, under inscriptions from the Old and New Testaments and from Greek philosophy which were hand-lettered on the walls. Fragmentary and ruined as these inscriptions now are, two which survive fairly clearly foreshadow mature "Leibnizian" themes: a Latinized line from Isocrates insists that "only immortal wisdom [*sapientia*] should govern our choice," while a famous plea of King David's from the Psalms, "Create a pure heart in me, O Lord, and an upright spirit," is emblazoned in foot-high letters from one end of the Aula of the Nikolaischule to the other. (This psalm, number 51, begins with David's hope for mercy through God's "loving kindness.") While nothing can diminish the highly original way in which Leibniz combines Judaeo-Christian love or "charity" with Greek (especially Platonic) "wisdom," it is fascinating to see that Leibniz' Christian Platonism was not just "in the air" but (literally) on the walls that surrounded him from the age of seven.

During the 350th birthday festivities, the city of Leipzig mounted an exhibit called "The Young Leibniz and Leipzig"—and here the revelation was that of seeing Leibniz' student marginalia (written while he was an adolescent) on his own copy of the *Philosophia Practica* (Leipzig, 1661) of his philosophy teacher, Jacob Thomasius (1622–1684). I had thought that Thomasius taught Leibniz only a (fairly) orthodox version of scholasticized Aristotelianism; but in the marginalia to the chapter of the *Philosophia Practica* called "De Amiticia" (On Friendship), Cicero's title, the young Leibniz underscored the phrase *Amicitia est benevolentia*, "friendship is benevolence," and then wrote the word *Amor* in the page margin—an astonishing anticipation of his mature insistence that justice is the charity or love "of the wise, that is, *benevolentia universalis*."

Cambridge, Massachusetts
Hanover, Berlin-Charlottenburg, Leipzig, Germany
September 1993–April 1996

Note on Leibniz
Translations

It is perhaps customary to note that translations not otherwise identified in the notes are my own, but in the case of Leibniz, further comment is called for. Since Leibniz' political thought is still so little known in the English-speaking world—even the enlarged Cambridge University Press edition of the *Political Writings* (1988) contains only a few key works—it seems reasonable to weave into the present book a number of passages which have never seen the light of day in English. Thus in Chapter 1 the "Unvorgreiffliches Bedencken" of c. 1698–1701—which makes Leibniz' moral-political debt to Plato's *Euthyphro* transparent—is extensively quoted; in Chapter 2 Leibniz' theory of "substance" (monadology) is illuminated by translations of portions of "Double Infinity in Pascal and the Monad" (c. 1695–1697) and of "Conversation sur la liberté" (c. 1699–1700)—Leibniz' most striking brief defense of his version of human freedom; in Chapter 3 Leibniz' idea of theodicy as "universal jurisprudence" is amplified with fragments of the "Theodicy or Apology for the Justice of God" (c. 1707), with substantial parts of Leibniz' letter to the Jesuit Grimaldi elevating practical "charity" over speculative "grace," and with paragraphs from the "Notes on Bayle" (c. 1706), which served as the basis of the *Theodicy*. And near the end of Chapter 3 there is not just a first translation but a first publication of key parts of a small but significant Leibniz manuscript from c. 1691, "De Bono Unitatis et Malis Schismatis," in which it is urged that the "precept" of Christian social unity is *caritas summum*, the "highest charity," and that without such wise love, society will be afflicted by Hobbesian horrors: "hatred and diffidence," "internecine war," "infidelity succeeded by impiety," and "libertinism."

But it is in Chapter 4 that passages from a whole series of little-known and never-translated writings are given: Leibniz' 1697 letter to Electress Sophie of Hanover urging that Friedrich Spee's *Güldenes Tugendbuch* is the main modern work which correctly raises charity above faith and hope; his letters to Andreas Morrell (1697–98) making the same moral point; his notes on William Penn (1695) praising charity, "disinterested" love, and scientific enlightenment; his *Dialogue sur des sujets de réligion* (1679) praising the same virtues in an even more eloquent way; and finally "True Piety" from 1710, drawing together all of Leibniz' thoughts on charity as the "first" of the Christian virtues.

In Chapter 5, which shows how much of Leibniz' political thought was (increasingly) anti-Hobbesian, there is a translation of a crucial 1671 letter to Lambert von Velthuysen of Utrecht (in which Leibniz' doubts about Hobbes begin to surface), a translation of important interpretations of Hobbes from the 1680s (published within the last fifteen years in the so-called *Voraus Edition* at the University of Münster), a translation of noteworthy passages of the 1700 *Observations on the Principles of Justice* (with its criticism of "Lockeanism" as well as Hobbism), and—above all—a translation of large fragments of the *Grundriss* (the remarkable work which Leibniz produced at the age of twenty-five, and which reveals that his social theory resting on charity, toleration, and enlightenment was essentially in place in 1671). Chapter 5 also contains translations of the key paragraphs of Leibniz' *Lettre sur l'éducation d'un prince* (1685, revised 1710), and of his extraordinary *Elements of Perpetual Justice* (1695), with its equation of Roman jurisprudence with eternity, nature, and divinity.

In Chapter 6, there are translations of Leibniz' 1697 letter to Bossuet's colleague Mme. de Brinon (jokingly urging that France give up Catholicism for Lutheranism), of fragments of the *Consilium Aegyptiacum* (1671), which Leibniz tried to press on Louis XIV, and of most of an untitled manuscript from 1711 urging the Protestant powers of Northern Europe to resist French imperialism more strongly.

In addition to these translations of large fragments of works which enrich our understanding of Leibniz' political and moral philosophy, there are scattered throughout the book dozens of phrases and sentences which have never been rendered into English before. In a writer who left nine-tenths of his work unpublished, the translation of unknown (and sometimes unpublished) fragments, large and small, is especially important.

# Introduction

Gottfried Wilhelm Leibniz, the son of a Leipzig University professor, was born in 1646, two years before the end of the Thirty Years' War.[1] He was thoroughly educated—largely through his own voracious reading—in Scholastic philosophy and in jurisprudence, including especially the Roman law (which was later to be crucial to his notion of justice as a steady ascent from "refraining from harm" to "living honorably" or charitably).[2] At an early age he attempted a correspondence with Hobbes, whom he was later to see as his principal philosophical antagonist among the moderns; but Hobbes never replied, in part, perhaps, because of Leibniz' left-handed compliments ("certain men are . . . wrong in ascribing license and impiety to your hypotheses").[3] After receiving his doctorate of law in 1666, he published in the following year a treatise entitled *New Method [Nova Methodus] of Learning and Teaching Jurisprudence*—a work which brought him to the attention of the Elector of Mainz, Prince-Bishop Johann Philipp von Schönborn, then the most powerful figure in the Holy Roman Empire.[4] Following a few years' service to the Elector, Leibniz went to Paris in 1672—ostensibly to present to Louis XIV his *Consilium Aegyptiacum* (urging that French wars against the Dutch be diverted to the Levant, and that the Holy Land be wrested from the Ottoman Empire).[5] Leibniz remained in Paris until 1676—with an excursion to London in 1673, where he was made a member of the Royal Society.[6] In Paris he became a brilliant mathematician (initially through the help of Huygens),[7] and made a number of important permanent friendships—above all with Malebranche (who was attempting a synthesis of Cartesianism and Augustinianism)[8] and with Arnauld (the great Jansenist theologian and colleague of Pascal).[9] Unable to secure the diplomatic post he hoped for, Leibniz rather reluctantly attached himself to the house of Brunswick-Lüneburg, rulers of the (soon-to-be) Electorate of Hanover, and became the official apologist for and historian-librarian of this principality.[10] He arrived at Hanover in 1676 (after meeting with Spinoza in The Hague),[11] and lived there until the end of his life forty years later—though he made many scholarly and diplomatic visits to Berlin, Vienna, Rome, Florence, and Venice.[12] By 1677, his first full year in Hanover, he had begun to define justice as "the charity of the wise" *(caritas sapientis)*—the definition he clung to for the next four decades.[13] At about this same time he made free but remarkable translations of Plato's *Phaedo* and *Theaetetus*.[14]

At Hanover Leibniz, in addition to his official duties (which soon included those of a judge)[15] and his philosophical efforts, carried on a wide range of political activities and correspondence. He entered into a letter exchange with Bossuet (the most powerful French ecclesiastic of the Grand Siècle) concerning the reunification of Christendom; this became his life-long passion, as it had been that of his favorite modern political theorist, Grotius.[16] Officially a Lutheran, Leibniz nonetheless became the defender of a reformed and truly universal Catholic Church (though he apparently turned down the Librarianship of the Vatican during his trip to Rome in 1689);[17] at the same time he vigorously defended the Conciliar movement of the fifteenth century, believing that if it had succeeded, the Reformation would have been unnecessary and the "universal" authorities (Pope and Holy Roman Emperor) would still be viable as co-heads of a Dantean *respublica christiana*.[18] To produce the desired reconciliation, Leibniz recommended toleration, charity, and compromise; and this, of course, made all parties suspicious of him. Though he was the last thinker of great stature to defend the Empire as something more than a vestigial Gothic oddity, he was also a frequent apologist for the rights of the imperial electors and princes, and tried to strike a balance between the *majestas* of the Empire and the sovereignty of the princes. "Sovereignty," for him, meant simply internal control and "influence" in European affairs, but did not exclude ultimate allegiance to a universal "Christian Republic."[19] His efforts to recast sovereignty led to a broad attack on Hobbes and Pufendorf and, ultimately, to a more general critique of legal positivism. That critique was at its most striking in two works from the early 1700s which defined justice through the charity of the wise and demi-Platonic "eternal moral verities," not through the authorized commands of sovereigns—the "Meditation on the Common Concept of Justice" (c. 1703), and the *Opinion on the Principles of Pufendorf* (1706).[20]

If those works were overtly political, a kind of tacit politics was contained even in Leibniz' works of "pure" philosophy. In the "Discourse on Metaphysics" (1686), usually taken to be the first full statement of Leibniz' mature thought, a central question is whether Julius Caesar "had" to cross the Rubicon and subvert the Roman Republic—whether Caesar's "complete concept," eternally imbedded in the mind of God, "determined" his historical activity.[21] The *New Essays Concerning Human Understanding* (1704), which so impressed Kant upon their posthumous publication in 1765, criticized Locke's moral, political, and religious thought from what Leibniz called a "Platonic" perspective.[22] The *Theodicy* (1710) is an account of divine justice in the "best" possible world, and is developed through a critique of Hobbes, Spinoza, and Cartesianism;[23] the celebrated *Monadology* (1714) ends with an account of perfect universal justice in "the City of God."[24]

In the *Codex Iuris Gentium* (1693), Leibniz first published his argument that justice is "wise love" or "universal benevolence";[25] he extended and elaborated this view during the great quarrel over "disinterested" love and quietism which turned Bossuet and Fénelon into bitter enemies in the closing years of the seventeenth century.[26]

In later years, while keeping up his interest in the reunification of the *respublica christiana* and in the refutation of "Hobbism," Leibniz devoted considerable time to justifying the Hanoverian succession to the British throne, arguing that a Stuart restoration would make France the absolute and arbitrary arbiter of Europe.[27] On behalf of the Empire, he wrote large tracts attacking French seizure of imperial territories; against Louis XIV's devastations, he argued that charity and benevolence were the proper virtues for an enlightened prince, and was instrumental in trying to set up academies of arts and sciences, as well as economic and educational councils, in Berlin and Vienna—and, at the behest of Peter the Great, in Russia.[28] He was the founder and first president of the Prussian Academy in Berlin (1701).[29]

At the end of his life—marked by acrimonious exchanges with the Newton-surrogate Samuel Clarke, and by a happy correspondence concerning Plato with the French Platonist Remond[30]—Leibniz gave up somewhat on his plans for reviving a *respublica christiana,* but still insisted that his Dantean scheme would be better than a system of independent "Hobbesian" states and religious fragmentation; the tone of his last political letters is resigned, elegiac, and ironic.[31] When he died in 1716, famous in an astounding variety of subjects, the rationalized and purified medieval system (resting on *caritas sapientis*) which he had tried to sustain had largely disappeared.

"When one considers oneself and compares one's talents with those of a

Leibniz," Diderot wrote in the *Encyclopédie* (that Leibnizian project *par excellence*), "one is tempted to throw books away and seek some hidden corner of the world where one may die in peace. This man's mind was the foe of disorder: the most entangled things fell into order when they entered it. He combined two great qualities which are almost incompatible with each other—the spirit of discovery and that of method; and the most determined and varied study, through which he accumulated knowledge of the most widely differing kinds, weakened neither the one quality nor the other. In the fullest meaning these words can bear, he was a philosopher and a mathematician."[32]

The central idea of Leibniz' "universal jurisprudence," which aims to find quasi-geometrical eternal moral verities equally valid for all rational beings, human or divine, is that justice is "the charity of the wise *(caritas sapientis)*"[33]—that it is not mere conformity to sovereign-ordained "positive" law given *ex plenitudo potestatis* (in the manner of Hobbes), nor mere "refraining from harm" or even "rendering what is due" (the *neminem laedere* and *suum cuique tribuere* of Roman law).[34] The equal stress on "charity" and on "wisdom" suggests that Leibniz' practical thought is a kind of fusing of Platonism—in which the wise know the eternal truths such as absolute goodness (*Phaedo* 75d), which the gods themselves also know and love (*Euthyphro* 9e–10e), and therefore deserve to rule (*Republic* 443d–e)[35]—and of Pauline Christianity, whose key moral idea is that charity or love is the first of the virtues ("though I speak with the tongues of men and of angels, and have not charity, I am become as sounding brass, or a tinkling cymbal").[36] There is, historically, nothing remarkable in trying to fuse Platonism and Christianity; for Augustine's thought (particularly the early *De Libero Arbitrio*) is just such a fusion.[37] But Leibniz was the last of the great Christian Platonists, and left the world just as Hume, Rousseau, and Kant were about to transform and "secularize" it: Hume by converting morality into psychology ("sentiments" of approval and disapproval disjointed from "reason"),[38] Rousseau by reverting to pre-Christian antiquity (the "Spartan mother" with a radically civic "general will"),[39] and Kant by rethinking Aristotelian *telos* (in order to respect persons as "ends" who ought never to be treated merely as "means," and in order to define morality as "pure practical teleology").[40]

But if justice rightly understood is wise charity (or universal benevolence), three main questions arise: (1) Where does Leibniz find this novel notion of justice? (2) Can an infinite Being be said to be restricted by timeless moral ideas which he finds "imbedded" in his own understanding and does not create in time (ideas which he then follows in fashioning a fully justifiable "best" of all possible worlds from a range of logically possible ones?), and (3) Can finite beings, for example human beings in the "human forum," actually act with greater wise charity, if their sheer finitude and limitation— what Leibniz calls their "metaphysical evil"—keeps them from knowing and therefore willing the right and the good?[41]

The first question is mainly historical: if one decomposes *caritas sapientis* into its parts, charity and wisdom, the provenance of both elements is clear enough—charity or love is the very heart of Christian ethics (St. Paul's "the greatest of these is charity" or St. John's "a new commandment I give unto you, that ye love one another");[42] and the notion that justice requires the rule of the wise is famously Platonic. How charity and wisdom relate, how they might modify each other, is not just a historical but a philosophical problem— since love is "affective," wisdom "cognitive"; but the really grave difficulties in Leibniz' universal jurisprudence relate to questions (2) and (3). For it is not clear that a wisely charitable God would create a world which, though it may be "best," is not simply good; an *être infiniment parfait* might sooner contemplate his own perfection, *ad infinitum*.[43] And whether Judas or Pontius Pilate could have acted better, been more benevolent, is notoriously problematical given Leibniz' ideas of "substance" (or monad) and of preestablished harmony. (Since, however, Leibniz is a supremely architectonic thinker who wants to relate everything to "first philosophy," one cannot just cordon off his moral and political thought from his metaphysics and theology: that is precisely what he himself did not do.)

The essential thing, then, in a philosopher of Leibniz' stature—and he was not just a political theorist, but one of the three or four greatest general thinkers of the seventeenth century—is to relate his central moral and political ideas to the structural principles of his first philosophy. The celebrated *Monadology*, for example, is Leibniz' theory of "substance"—but for him a (rational) substance or monad is a person, a mind, a "citizen" of the City of God governed by "eternal moral verities" and by moral memory;[44] in short the *Monadology* is a theory of personality on which all further Leibnizian convictions about morality and justice are based. (Indeed one does not have to strain or force in order to read the *Monadology* as a theory of justice.) And the *Theodicy* is a theory of the perfect justice of a divine "person" or mind who brings about what is "best," and who "justifies himself against complaints."[45] Leibniz is always a moralist thinking of what is justifiable, even when he seems to be a metaphysician or a theologian: "theology is the highest point in knowledge of those things which concern the mind, and includes in some way good morals and good politics."[46] (That statement about what is "highest" should give pause to those who view Leibniz mainly as a mathematician and logician—as should his insistence that "the most important and the most serious matters in life" are "justice, the quiet and the good of the state, human health, and even religion.")[47]

What is crucial, then, is to see how Leibniz' central moral-political convictions flow reasonably, and possibly irresistibly, from his "pure philosophy." The radically fundamental question in Leibniz is: "Why is there something rather than nothing?" (*Principles of Nature and Grace*, 1714);[48] but to that he also returns a moral-political answer, or set of answers: God is there, *ex necessitatis*, because perfection (which includes moral perfection above all) entails automatic existence, and then that necessary being creates everything and everyone else in time by the moral principle of what is "best."[49] The whole of Leibnizianism is one huge "theodicy," one vast "universal jurisprudence"—but theodicy is an account of what ought to be, what deserves to be, what has "sufficient reason" for being. To state it another way, it hardly matters whether one calls Leibniz a "theodicist" or a "monadologist," because God as creator of the "best" world is the just monarch of substances or persons or monads. At bottom Leibniz, like all the greatest philosophers, is a moralist.[50]

Certainly this view would be (generally) endorsed by Kant—a good authority on German philosophy before his own. Indeed in his 1790 essay *Über eine Entdeckung*, designed to meet the Wolffian charge that the Kantian "critical philosophy" was just "a degenerate product of Leibnizian thought,"[51] Kant argues that, while he is no Leibnizian, nonetheless the thought of Leibniz "contains these three great original principles: (1) the principle of sufficient reason . . . ; (2) the monadology; (3) the doctrine of pre-established harmony."[52] But Leibniz' God as just monarch creates the "best" world for the "sufficient reason" that it is best, and serves as wisely charitable ruler of rational monads whose moral relations constitute a branch of "preestablished harmony." For Kant, these Leibnizian strands hang together coherently, in a mutually supporting way—which is not to say that the "system" they constitute is thereby (knowably) true. Indeed for Kant Leibnizianism was a "dogmatism" which "said more than it knew"[53]—but it was the most subtle, careful, and refined form of dogmatism known to him.

Given the fact that Leibniz' "universal jurisprudence" is equally a theodicy and a monadology—since God is conceived as "the sovereign substance

[who] immutably maintains justice" for all other rational substances in the best world[54]—it is singularly perverse of Luc Ferry, in his much-discussed *Homo Aestheticus* (1993), to go out of his way to praise Heidegger's bizarre reading of the *Monadology* (which is certainly Leibniz' best-known account of radically individual substances which are fully autonomous, not mere "modes" of an all-engulfing divinity, *à la* Spinoza). Paraphrasing Heidegger, Ferry urges that "Nietzsche = Leibniz, less harmony, less God, where god is understood as the monad of monads who brings into accord the different individual monads' multiple perspectives so that they may form a world, a universe, meaning a coherent totality and not, as in Nietzsche, a radically chaotic multiplicity. One could hardly put it better."[55]

In truth one could hardly put it worse: Leibniz minus preestablished harmony between substances and minus God leaves zero, not Nietzsche, since for Leibniz the monads must be "imbedded" (as logically possible eternal ideas) in the mind of God before they are "translated" into existence as parts of a compossible harmonious order—the "best" world. Without the mind of God, Caesar and Cicero are not "there." To describe Nietzschean aestheticizing individualism as "Leibnizian" less the very principles that constitute Leibnizianism is nothing but a fashionable trick: one might as well say that an atheist is really St. Anselm "less" the ontological proof of the existence of God. And given that Leibniz' central moral-political idea, *caritas sapientis,* is equally Christian and Platonic, it is mistaken even to relate Leibniz to the Nietzsche for whom Platonism was an escape into an imaginary Beyond ("how the true world finally became a fable")[56] and for whom Christian egalitarianism was "the revolt of everything that crawls against everything that has height."[57] It must be possible to do better than this.

An important reason for studying Leibniz' practical (moral, political, legal, religious) thought in close connection to his "first philosophy" is suggested by J. B. Schneewind in his illuminating article "Kant and Natural Law Ethics" (1993).

> The perfectionists, among whom I include Spinoza, Malebranche, Leibniz, and Wolff, believe that objective knowledge of the human good is available to at least some people. They also believe that the universe in which we live is divinely ordered and therefore harmonious, and that if a sufficient number of people knew the basic truth about the universe, harmony among human beings would also arise. Although each of us, on their view, seeks primarily his own perfection, the perfection and

therefore the good of one person cannot in the end be in conflict with the perfection of others. As Leibniz puts it: "It is most true that one cannot know God without loving one's brother, that one cannot have virtue without having charity . . . , and that one even advances one's own good in working for that of others: for it is an eternal law of reason and the harmony of things . . . that our duty must also be our happiness." Conflict, therefore, is due to metaphysical ignorance. Metaphysics shows us the ultimate nature of things.[58]

Setting aside the fact that Leibniz himself increasingly took Spinoza to be a radical "Cartesian" voluntarist worse than Hobbes,[59] it is certainly the case that Leibniz was a "perfectionist" in ethics and politics as well as in metaphysics and theology: he took over and refined the Anselmian argument that a perfect being exists necessarily;[60] he argued that that divine being creates the most nearly perfect ("best") world that is possible;[61] he urged that essences have a "claim" to exist in proportion to the degree of their perfection;[62] he said that love is a "feeling of perfection" in others, and that charity should be regulated by wisdom (which shows how much each person deserves to be loved because of his perfection)—and this notion of wise charity or *caritas sapientis* then becomes Leibniz' definition of justice itself: *justitia est caritas sapientis seu benevolentia universalis* ("justice is the charity of the wise, that is, universal benevolence).[63] Indeed for Leibniz the most general of all moral notions, "the good," is defined through perfection in his most important contribution to political philosophy, the "Meditation on the Common Concept of Justice": "One may ask what the true good is. I answer that it is nothing else than that which serves in the perfection of intelligent substances: from which it is clear that order, contentment, joy, wisdom, goodness and virtue are good things essentially, and can never be evil."[64] Moreover Leibnizian wisely charitable rulers should "perfect" the state (and their subjects) by alleviating poverty and misery ("the mother of crimes"), by improving education through the founding of academies of arts and sciences, and by avoiding war.[65]

Leibniz' moral and political perfectionism, then, flows from (or at least is congruent with) his metaphysical and theological perfectionism: there is no gap between the theoretical and the practical—whereas by contrast in Kant finite rational beings know "the moral law" as an "apodeictic certainty" (the "fact of reason") but will never attain scientific knowledge of "things in themselves" (hence the primacy of "practical" over theoretical reason in

Kant).[66] (It is not surprising, then, that Kant should urge in the *Tugendlehre* that we have a knowable duty to advance "our own perfection," even while he thought that the ontological argument deducing God's real existence from his "perfection" was indemonstrable and that the alleged "perfection" of the cosmos remained inaccessible to finite beings.)[67]

To be sure, it is a little exaggerated to say, as Schneewind does, that for Leibniz human conflict is "due to metaphysical ignorance" *simpliciter*, for Leibniz at least strives to operate with an "Augustinian" notion of "bad will" (male-volence); but since that bad will often collapses into sheer ignorance ("metaphysical" limitation or evil), it is not clear that Leibniz successfully maintains his stated, insisted-on distinction between bad will ("moral evil") and mere finite ignorance ("metaphysical evil").[68] He may, that is, unwillingly approach the Spinozist notion that evil is ignorance[69]—despite his constant animadversions against the great Dutch thinker. But this will be taken up with care in Chapter 2, in connection with Leibniz' effort to show that Judas Iscariot and Pontius Pilate are blameworthy and reprehensible for their un-wise and uncharitable treatment of Christ, for their failure to be good willing.

The point, still, is that Schneewind is right to insist on Leibniz' "perfec-tionism" as something that links every facet of his thought: metaphysical, theological, moral, political, psychological. Leibniz at least aims at a harmo-nious unity in his own thinking, theoretical and practical, and sees it as an echo of the *harmonia rerum*. The proof that this view is right, indeed, can be found in Leibniz' own words, in the *Memoir for Enlightened Persons of Good Intention* from 1710: "I put forward the great principle of metaphysics as well as of morality, that the world is governed by the most perfect intelligence which is possible, which means that one must consider it as a universal monarchy."[70] There perfection both describes what is and prescribes what ought to be.

This practical perfectionism emerges most plainly in Leibniz' *Observationes de Principio Iuris* from 1700, in which the claim that "God is the supremely perfect Being, and the supremely perfect distributor of goods" glides into the moral-political assertion that "the intrinsic perfection or badness of acts, rather than the will of God, is the cause of justice," and that "the basis on which a certain action is by its nature better than another comes simply from the fact that a certain other action is by its nature worse, such that it destroys perfection, or produces imperfection."[71]

Not the smallest reason to attend to Leibniz as a political-moral philoso-pher is that he is unique: he brings together an incomparable knowledge of modern science and mathematics (making him the only plausible rival to Newton)[72] with an ethical position which is in some sense "ancient" (fusing Pauline charity, Platonic wisdom and eternal verities, and Augustinian good will). In the great seventeenth-century "quarrel between the ancients and the moderns," Leibniz does not really take sides definitively: in a typical passage he may move easily from ardent enthusiasm for the latest scientific discoveries of Leeuwenhoek or van Helmont to a defense of Plato and Parmenides against the "excesses" of Descartes and Hobbes (but without wholly embracing the ancient pair or wholly rejecting the modern).[73] To put it somewhat too crudely, he tilts toward modernity in the sciences and toward antiquity in morals and politics: his enthusiasm for an intelligently resuscitated *respublica christiana* under universal "wise charity" could have flourished in the age of Dante or Ficino,[74] but his theoretical speculations were as advanced as (and in mathematical logic more advanced than) the best seventeenth-century accomplishments. One gets some sense of this from Leibniz' account of his own thought in the *New Essays* (1704):

> This system appears to combine Plato with Democritus, Aristotle with Descartes, the Scholastics with the moderns, theology and ethics with reason. It seems to take the best from all sides, and then to go further than anyone has yet gone . . . I see now what Plato meant when he regarded matter as an imperfect and transitory thing; what Aristotle intended by his entelechy [or substance]; what is that promise of another life, which Democritus himself made, according to Pliny; how far the Skeptics were right in crying against the senses; . . . how a rational explanation [through monadology] is to be given of the views of those who attribute life and perception to all things.[75]

And in a parallel passage in a letter of 1698 to Basnage de Beauval, in which Leibniz synthetically draws together "the Platonic and Pythagorean reduction of everything to harmonies, numbers, and ideas," the substances "of Aristotle and the Scholastics," and "the mechanical explanation of all particular phenomena according to Democritus and the moderns," he goes on to describe truly inclusive and synthetic philosophy (his own!) in roughly the same language that he uses to describe the "best" of all possible worlds created by God: these ancient and modern philosophies "are all considered together as in a center of perspective, viewed from which the object (confused from every other point of view) reveals its regularity and the harmony of its parts."[76] And if we fail to "accomplish" this overview, Leibniz complains, it is because of the same limited, limiting sectarianism which keeps the "schism" of the West from being overcome and the *respublica christiana* charitably restored: "We have failed to accomplish this [truly synthetic philosophy] by our sectarian spirit, limiting ourselves by rejecting others."[77] Here Leibniz' theory and practice are one: narrow, limited sectarianism defeats both philosophical completeness and good morals.

How, then, should Leibniz the "political theorist" be viewed? To be sure, as a court official, diplomat and official historian he produced a great deal of "political thought"—hundreds of pages, for example, on the War of the Spanish Succession alone (1701–1714).[78] And since he was a man of supreme gifts even his workaday productions (like Mozart's) are of superior quality.

But what matters for Leibniz the philosopher is not dozens of occasional pieces and *Flugschriften*, however accomplished: what matters is the metaphysics and theology of "perfectionism." And his moral-political philosophy is a crucial part of that perfectionism: God exists because perfection entails necessary existence, and the one necessary Being creates a best world justly—where justice itself is "wise love," and love in its turn is a "feeling of perfection." So Leibniz' universal jurisprudence of *caritas sapientis* is an integral part of his first philosophy; his political and moral ideas are not just a collection of *disjecta membra*, but true members of a philosophical *corpus* of weight and substance.

Certainly Leibniz understood himself to be a moralist above all, and was willing to say so in the *New Essays* of 1704: "You [Locke] were more conversant with speculative philosophers, and I was more inclined toward ethics."[79] Reflecting on this passage, Robert Mulvaney correctly reminds us that "Leibniz' legal training, his preference for a career in the world rather than in the academy, his anxiety over the direction of European history, and, above all, his conviction, in the Platonic tradition, that broadly moral principles have ontological primacy, should have led scholars all along to appreciate the central moral animation of Leibniz' effort."[80]

It is that central moral animation which matters most of all, and it is therefore what will be stressed here: first philosophy, leading to moral philosophy, leading to universal jurisprudence. The occasional pieces, however fine and finished, will be treated only as they bear on what is essential in Leibniz as one of the half-dozen greatest philosophers of the seventeenth century, who is rivaled only by Descartes, Spinoza, Malebranche, Hobbes, and Locke.

A final prefatory word may be helpful. From our perspective—post-Humean, post-Kantian—Leibniz politicizes theology and theologizes politics: he politicizes theology because God is conceived as the just monarch of a "best" world, and he theologizes politics because justice is Christian "charity" regulated by wisdom. As Robert Merrihew Adams argues in his remarkable *Leibniz: Determinist, Theist, Idealist* (1994), "Leibniz clearly thought that jurisprudence is important for theology. In his *New Method of Learning and Teaching Jurisprudence*, published in 1667, he states that 'Theology is a certain species of jurisprudence (the latter being taken universally), for it deals with the [system of] Justice and Laws obtaining in the Republic, or rather Kingdom, of God over human beings.' "[81] If Leibniz could say that at the age of twenty-one and if he could maintain that position into full maturity—repeating the language of the *Nova Methodus* almost verbatim in a letter to the jurisconsult Placcius in 1697, and criticizing Pascal's *Pensées* (the greatest religious work of the seventeenth century) for its supposed neglect of jurisprudence[82]—that means that Leibniz viewed philosophical theology and "theories of justice" as the same thing under different labels. Or, to put it even more strongly, if "theology is a certain *species* of jurisprudence" (as the *Nova Methodus* asserts) then *justitia* must be the *genus* of which theology is the species: what then matters most about God is that he be just, not only an omnipotent first cause. If God is the necessary being, and justice is the necessary attribute of that being, then theology is indeed a mere species of the jurisprudential *genus*.

Leibniz will remain incomprehensibly strange, will perhaps even be thought guilty of "category mistakes," if one fails to see that for him theory and practice, God and men, theology and justice, are welded together by perfection: the perfect Being, who exists *ex necessitatis*, must govern his created world as well as is possible (in the "best" way), and we (finite) beings must recognize and indeed feel that perfection (which leads to love as a feeling of perfection), and that love or *caritas* spreads from the perfect Being to those finite creatures whom he had "sufficient reason" to translate into existence. This incredibly ambitious universal jurisprudence, valid for any "mind" in any logically possible universe, must seem extravagant in our present moral-political world—in which a Rorty argues that political principles have (and can have) no metaphysical-theological "foundations"[83] and in which a Rawls wants to use only "thin" and widely shared assumptions to underpin his theory of justice.[84] Leibniz' universal jurisprudence is, by contrast, "thick": it aims to deduce moral-political perfectionism from metaphysical-theological perfectionism. It aims to present earthly justice as an outgrowth of universal justice, as the limb of a tree is the outgrowth of the trunk.

No living moral philosopher would venture to offer such a universal juris-prudence now; such a project may indeed be doomed in its origins—but to see it brilliantly attempted by one of the supreme intellects of early modernity is something of great value. For it is possible, if admittedly not very likely, that Leibniz is simply right.

Foundations

It was characteristic of Leibniz to try to reconcile apparently conflicting ideas, to take from each kind of thought that which was soundest and to synthesize it with the seemingly incommensurable truths of other systems;[1] thus he struggled throughout his life to fuse Platonism, Cartesianism, Augustinian voluntarism, Christian charity, Scholasticism, Hobbesian mechanistic materialism, and a number of other doctrines into a plausible whole whose apex would be a rational theology (Leibniz used God with a relatively sparing hand, and was contemptuous of philosophers who drew him in at the first sign of intellectual difficulty).[2] Given this desire for reconciliation, for harmony, for synthesis—which he applied to political and moral philosophy as much as to any other philosophical question—it should come as no surprise that Leibniz wanted to establish, or rather discover, a "universal jurisprudence," a system of justice and law common to God and man (and generally to any rational "substances");[3] anticipating Kant, Leibniz urged that justice and injustice "do not depend solely on human nature," but on "the nature of intelligent substance in general."[4] As substances linked by intelligence, God and man exist for Leibniz in a "society or universal republic of spirits" which is "the noblest part of the universe," a moral realm within physical nature, a realm in which "universal right is the same for God and for men."[5] As early as 1671, in a letter to Hermann Conring, Leibniz urged that God as a "very wise mind" wishes that which "is most congruent with the harmony of things, with the universal good, with (so to speak) the universal republic; for there is only a single and uniform doctrine of natural law and of the best universal commonwealth."[6] Or, as Leibniz put it near the end of his life, in the *Monadology:*

. . . the totality of all spirits must compose the City of God, that is to say, the most perfect state that is possible, under the most perfect of monarchs.

This City of God, this truly universal monarchy, is a moral world in the natural world, and is the most exalted among the works of God.[7]

For Leibniz, the difference between divine and human justice was one of degree, not kind; God's justice is simply infinitely more perfect than men's, and "to say . . . that God's justice is different from men's is like saying that the arithmetic or the geometry of men is false in heaven."[8] It is erroneous, Leibniz insisted, to say that we must not judge God in terms of the "common concept" of justice, for it must be the case that one has "an idea or a notion of justice when one says that God is just, otherwise one would only attribute a word to him."[9] Just as the arithmetic and geometry of men and of God differ only in the degree of their perfection, so too "natural jurisprudence and every other truth is the same in heaven and on earth."[10] "As for the order of justice," Leibniz wrote in 1696, "I believe that there are universal rules which must be valid as much with respect to God as with respect to intelligent creatures." Intelligible truths "are universal, and what is true here below with respect to us is also such for the angels and for God himself." The eternal truths "are the fixed and immutable point on which everything turns," such as "the truths of numbers, of arithmetic, and those of motion or weight in mechanics and in astronomy." And for that reason it is "correctly said" (in the Wisdom of Solomon) that God "does everything through numbers, by measure and by weight."[11] (Here Scripture is acceptable because it is "mathematical.")

This stress on the universal, quasi-geometrical necessity of justice was not an original inspiration on Leibniz' part; Duns Scotus, inter alia, had argued that "every inquiry regarding God is based on the supposition that the [divine] intellect has the same univocal concept which is obtained from creatures," that if one wanted to say that God is wise but that his wisdom has no relation to the "formal notion" of wisdom "in itself and absolutely," one could say nothing at all about God.[12] And closer to Leibniz' own time, Galileo had argued in his *Dialogo sopra i due Massimi Sistemi del Mondo* that "to be sure, the divine intellect knows . . . truths in infinitely greater fullness than does ours, for it knows them all; but of the few which the human intellect grasps, I believe that the knowledge of them is equal to the divine knowledge in objective certainty, since men can see their necessity, and there can be no higher degree of certainty than that."[13] But Leibniz used the notion of objectively certain "eternal verities" politically and morally to attack the idea of justice as bare superior power; the "formal notion" of justice, he observed in a commentary on Hobbes, has nothing to do with the mere "sovereign" command of authorities: "it does not depend on the arbitrary laws of superiors, but on the eternal rules of wisdom and goodness, in men as well as in God."[14]

For Leibniz it was merely an empiricist prejudice to see justice as "unreal" if it did not consist of tangible commands backed by power and threats. "The qualities of mind are not less real than those of body," he wrote in a Platonizing passage in the *New Essays*. "It is true that you do not see justice as you see a horse, but you understand it no less, or rather you understand it better; it is no less in actions than directness or obliqueness is in motions."[15] And if justice were simply derivative from the possession of power, "all powerful persons would be just, each in proportion to his power"; if an "evil genius" somehow seized supreme universal power, Leibniz insisted, he would not cease to be "wicked and unjust and tyrannical" simply because he could not be successfully "resisted."[16] Those who derive justice from irresistible power, he thought—and here Thrasymachus, Callicles, and Hobbes make up an unholy trinity—simply confuse "right" and "law": the concept of right cannot (by definition) be unjust, but law can be because it is "given and maintained by power"; only in God is there an absolute coincidence of right and power which produces just law.[17]

Perhaps the finest mature statement of Leibniz' view is contained in the *Opinion on the Principles of Pufendorf* (1706), which gained a European reputation through Barbeyrac's translation:

> Neither the norm of conduct itself, nor the essence of the just, depends on [God's] free decision, but rather on eternal truths, objects of the divine intellect . . . Justice follows certain rules of equality and of proportion which are no less founded in the immutable nature of things, and in the divine ideas, than are the principles of arithmetic and of geometry. . . . Divine justice and human justice have common rules which can be reduced to a system; and they must be taught in universal jurisprudence.[18]

Pufendorf himself, in Leibniz' view, failed to appreciate this *jurisprudence universelle;* it was that failure which made him "not much of a lawyer and even less of a philosopher." For Pufendorf, Leibniz lamented, defended the "absurd" view that justice comes *non aeternis veritates et rerum naturae, sed voluntati et arbitrio nudo Dei legislatoris* ("not from the eternal truths and natures of things, but from the naked will and choice of God as legislator"). And the result is *"despotismus."*[19]

THE PLACE OF GOD IN LEIBNIZ' UNIVERSAL JURISPRUDENCE

All of this suggests (what Leibniz apparently believed) that God is not just a first cause or an "imaginary metaphysical being, incapable of thought, will and action," but that he is "a definite substance, a person, a mind."[20] "I should rather be for those who recognize in God, as in every other mind [*esprit*], three primordial elements: force, knowledge, and will," Leibniz wrote in 1698. "For every action of a mind requires *posse, scire, velle.*"

> The original essence of every substance consists in *force;* it is this force which makes it the case that God necessarily is, and that all which exists must emanate from him. Next comes *light* or wisdom, which includes all the possible ideas and all the eternal verities. The last factor is *love* or will, which chooses between the possibles that which is best, and is the origin of contingent truths and of the present world. Thus the will is born when force is determined by enlightenment.[21]

"This trinity" of divine attributes (as Leibniz does not hesitate to call it) "is much more distinct and solid, in my opinion, than that of salt, sulphur, and mercury." And in the definitive *Monadology,* Leibniz urges that in God "there is power, which is the source of all, also knowledge, whose content is the variety of the ideas, and finally will, which makes changes or products according to the principle of the best."[22] God, then, like men, has knowledge, will, and power, but Leibniz wanted to be certain that justice is not deduced out of the last two attributes alone; God will act, perfectly (as men will act, though imperfectly) in a way such that just action is the issue of knowledge and volition combined. "Wisdom," he argued in the "Meditation on the Common Concept of Justice," "is in the understanding, and goodness is in the will. And justice as a result is in both. Power is another matter, but if it is added it transforms right into fact."[23]

It is precisely because Leibniz usually conceived of moral activity, for both God and men, in terms of voluntary and rational action that he could not reduce justice simply to a Platonic proportion or a fixed harmony; an action, rationally chosen, had to be involved. And this is why Leibniz always defined justice as "the charity of the wise."[24] "The proper treatment of justice and that of charity cannot be separated," he urged in one of his earliest writings. "Neither Moses, nor Christ, nor the Apostles nor the ancient Christians regulated justice otherwise than according to charity . . . [and] I, too, after having tried countless definitions of justice, finally felt myself satisfied only by this one; it alone I have found universal and reciprocal."[25] Charity is "a universal benevolence, which the wise man carries into execution in conformity with the measures of reason, to the end of obtaining the greatest good."[26] Charity, a "habit of loving" (with love defined as a "feeling of perfection" in others), necessitated voluntary action; it was to be regulated by wisdom, which could provide a knowledge of what men deserved through their "perfections."[27] (In Leibniz' philosophy, "perfection" is both the cause of love and the reason which regulates that love—as will be seen more fully in Chapter 4.)

Leibniz' view of justice as charity tempered by a knowledge of what is deserved obviously suggests a more generous and benevolent idea of the just than that entertained by many philosophers; but since his full view of charity can be more happily taken up at a later point, it will perhaps be sufficient to say for the moment that he had at least three excellent reasons for conceiving justice as *caritas sapientis*. First, in a universal jurisprudence, the same rules must apply to God and man. But the traditional (Roman) definition of justice, resting on the idea that something is owed or due, cannot be applied to God, who can owe no duties. God can, however, love, and wisdom will show how much each rational being deserves to be loved. Since this idea can apply to men as well as to God, it is the perfect foundation for a universal jurisprudence. Second, if charity is the essence of justice, then mere power or mere command cannot be. Adopting such a universal solution is the best antidote to all legal-positivist views of justice, such as Hobbes'.[28] And finally, charity presupposes not merely a *ius strictum* (forbearance from violence against others), and not merely rendering what is due, but an active benevolence; and Leibniz believed that if one tried to make the happiness of others one's own, not only would ordinary life be happier, but disasters such as the disintegration of Christendom after the Reformation could be healed. True charity, he thought, could overcome doctrinal differences; "charity must prevail over all other considerations in the world."[29]

Despite the attractiveness of this view, Leibniz sometimes did try to define justice simply in terms of harmony, of proportion, of ratios as precise as any in mathematics. One of his more extreme "Platonic" statements in this vein (1696) urged that the

> eternal truths are the fixed and immutable point on which everything turns. Such is the truth of numbers in arithmetic, and of figures in geometry.
>
> That postulated, it is well to consider that order and harmony are also something mathematical and which consist in certain proportions: and that justice being nothing else than the order which is observed with regard to the good and evil of intelligent creatures, it follows that God, who is the sovereign substance, immutably maintains justice and the most perfect order which can be observed.[30]

Throughout his life Leibniz was tempted to assert that principles of justice, as "eternal verities," had the same logical status as A = A or 2 + 2 = 4, and for an obvious reason: one of his great hopes was that of reducing all complex propositions to their simplest form, to primary and irreducible concepts whose "predicates" were clearly contained in their subjects, to a "universal symbolistic" in which argument would be replaced by the use of a universal language.[31] Certainly differences over the character of justice could be obviated if, as Leibniz hoped, "justice follows certain rules of equality and of proportion which are no less founded in the immutable nature of things, and in the ideas of the divine understanding, than the principles of arithmetic and geometry."[32]

The reason that Leibniz could not and did not consistently maintain this idea of justice is that there is no voluntary act in it; a justice of harmony and proportion alone presupposes a kind of aesthetic passivity which fails to take Christian voluntarism into account. In most Christian thought, justice is not simply a proportion but an action; and Leibniz, who grew up reading the Scholastics, was aware of the transformation made in the idea of justice by philosophers such as Thomas Aquinas:

> Now justice does not aim at directing an act of the cognitive power, for we are not said to be just through knowing something aright . . . but since we are said to be just through doing something aright, justice must needs be in some [rational] appetitive power.[33]

That Leibniz (usually) favored this view—originally suggested by Aristotle's *Ethics* and much elaborated by medieval philosophy after Augustine[34]—is perfectly clear: in an important early work he insisted that Christian virtues "consist not only in talking and in thinking, but in thinking practically, that is, in acting";[35] and in a late letter (1706) he described justice and injustice in terms of the "moral goodness or badness of actions."[36] Justice, then, cannot be a simple proportion or harmony in Leibniz: harmony may be the product of justice, but it cannot be the whole of it. (It must be granted, however, that there is a certain tension in Leibniz' thought which is caused by his working with two kinds of premises—Christian voluntarism ("good will") and Platonic rationalism—simultaneously; sometimes he tilts toward Christ, sometimes Plato, even if an equilibrium between those world views was what he aimed at.)[37]

If Leibniz was, as a Christian, unavoidably a voluntarist, that does not mean that justice for him was founded on pure will alone: for Leibniz there is a crucial difference between voluntarism (having a "good will" as one's motive) and "radical voluntarism"—the notion that will alone creates or constructs moral norms, à la Nietzsche or Sartre. A good act must be voluntary, but will does not "make" that goodness *ex nihilo*.[38] But a kind of radical voluntarism was what Leibniz thought he saw in Hobbes (as a latter-day Thrasymachus); and he asserted again and again that to say *stat pro ratione voluntas*, let will take the place of reason, is properly the motto of a tyrant.[39] If will were uppermost, indeed creative of right, there would be as many kinds of justice as there were arbitrary commands; if the justice of God were invented by fiat, there would be no sufficient reason to praise him.

> For why praise him for what he has done if he would be equally praiseworthy in doing exactly the opposite? Where will his justice and his wisdom be found if nothing is left but a certain despotic power, if will takes the place of reason, and if, according to the definition of tyrants, that which is pleasing to the most powerful is by that very fact just?[40]

It is important to recall that, for Leibniz, God operates within limits; he chooses the best among possibilities, but he does not create ideas or essences himself. "Wisdom and justice have their eternal theorems," he observed, and "God does not establish them at all by his will; but he discovers them in his essence, he follows them."[41] In an act of justice (divine or human), knowledge and volition, though separate faculties, must work together—knowledge providing the eternal standard of what ought to be done, and will providing the temporal element of choice. "To will is nothing but the striving which arises from thought, or to strive for something which our thinking recognizes."[42] Reason, or thought, or knowledge alone is not sufficient for a moral action; if it were, intellectual error would be equal to moral evil. The will must be "conformed" to reason, must choose "the best."[43]

Clearly, then, Leibnizian justice requires a voluntary act of charity. For Leibniz, as will be seen fully in Chapter 4, makes "wise charity" and universal "benevolence"—good willing—interchangeable.[44] But if God and men are to be just, by the same standard though in differing degrees, whence evil, particularly moral evil? If God is just, why is the world full of imperfection and pain and sin (as Leibniz grants)?[45] If men are unjust because they are less perfect than God, how can they be fully responsible for their actions—if evil turns out to be mere finite limitation? In short, can both God and men be just (or, more generally, good) by the same standard—since the point of a universal jurisprudence is its equal applicability to all minds? That Leibniz was aware of these difficulties is perfectly evident throughout his work, but particularly in his most famous book, the *Theodicy*, whose subtitle suggests that the author will reconcile three apparently irreconcilable problems—the justice of God, the moral freedom of men, and the origin of evil.[46] Leibniz was unwilling to define his ideas of right and justice in narrow terms; and precisely because his notion of justice is so universal, so little political in any restricted sense, an excursion into his metaphysics and theology is essential. A narrower treatment, leaving his "first philosophy" to one side, would inevitably ignore what is most distinctive in his political thought. To be sure, Leibniz sometimes appears to define politics in an extremely restricted sense: "the science of the pleasant is medicine, that of the useful is politics, and that of the just is ethics."[47] But this is not his usual view; and indeed it would be more accurate to say that Leibniz tried to develop a metaphysics of perfection, of which the pleasant, the useful, and the just would simply be different aspects. (After all, if one is seeking the eternal jurisprudence of "the republic of the universe," one has not confined himself to a Machiavellian politics of getting and keeping earthly power. That much is clear in a letter which Leibniz wrote to his old teacher Jacob Thomasius in 1669: "Moral philosophy—that is to say, practical or political philosophy, which is one and the same science, as you taught me—treats the end [purpose] of things, that is to say, the good.")[48] Some effort, then, must be made to show how and why "perfectionism" is the thread which leads from metaphysics and theology to ethics and psychology (and then to justice) in Leibniz' thought.

Divine Justice and Human Responsibility

Leibniz makes human justice turn on divine justice to avoid arbitrariness and the equation of justice with power; but he must then explain the justice of God, given a visible world full of evil, not all of it apparently deserved, but all of it allowed, if not positively willed, by God.[49] To understand the place of evil in the "best" universe which Leibniz' God creates, a general understanding of God's mode of operation is required. The eternal verities and all essences (all possible non-self-contradictory beings) are in his understanding, not in his will or power. "Does the will of God form the ideas which are in his understanding?" No, Leibniz says; this would involve an infinite regress of causality and would "confuse understanding and will."[50] In every intelligent being, he insists, "the acts of the will are of their nature posterior to the acts of the understanding . . . the eternal truths are in the divine understanding. It does not follow, however, that there is anything before God, but only that the acts of the divine understanding are prior to the acts of the divine will." And therefore "the essences of things are co-eternal with God."[51]

Leibniz goes on to argue that it is essential to God's moral freedom that he choose the best from a range of possibles; if this were not the case—if essence were equal to existence—then the universe would exist by a blind necessity (of the sort that Leibniz feared in Spinoza). "If we wished absolutely to destroy such pure possibles," he observed in a letter to Arnauld, "we should destroy contingency and freedom, for if nothing is possible except what God has actually created, whatever God has created would be necessary."[52] God's power only translates a portion of essence into existence; but the best is not determined by power. Now, God need not create the universe: eternal truths do not have a merely temporal reality, and essences can remain just that. But if God does create a universe he is restricted by the eternal verities and by logical possibilities: the essence of a circle is round, and it cannot have a square existence; that the sum of the angles of a triangle is equal to 180° is a function of God's understanding, not of his will. Nor does God create the essences of particular possible substances. "God was able to create matter, a man, a circle, or leave them in nothingness, but he was not able to produce them without giving them their essential properties. He had of necessity to make man a rational animal and to give the round shape to a circle."[53] On this point Leibniz parted company with the Cartesians, who founded even the character of truth itself on the omnipotent will of God—a kind of cosmic sovereignty. As Descartes wrote in his *Reply to the Six Objections,*

It is self-contradictory that the will of God should not have been from eternity indifferent to all that has come to pass or that will ever occur, because we can form no conception of anything good or true . . . the idea of which existed in the divine understanding before God's will determined him to act. . . . Thus, to illustrate, God did not will . . . the three angles of a triangle to be equal to two right angles because he knew that they could not be otherwise. On the contrary . . . it is because he willed the three angles of a triangle to be necessarily equal to two right angles that this is true and cannot be otherwise.[54]

One of the most consistent things in Leibniz' philosophical development was his hostility to such hyper-creationist notions, as an early (1677) letter of his shows: "I know that it is the opinion of Descartes that the truth of things depends on the divine will. This has always seemed absurd to me. . . . Who would say that A is not non-A because God has decreed it?"[55]

In the history of philosophy the idea that the concept of justice, as an "eternal verity," is not a mere adjunct of power, that it is an idea whose necessary truth is at least analogous to the truths of mathematics and logic, is commonly associated with Plato.[56] Now while it is not true that Leibniz was a Platonist in any doctrinaire sense—his clinging to Pauline charity and to Augustinian good will would have made that difficult—nonetheless he did agree with Plato on many points of fundamental importance. "I have always been quite content, since my youth," he wrote to Remond in 1715, "with the moral philosophy of Plato, and even in a way with his metaphysics; for those two sciences accompany each other, like mathematics and physics."[57] Leibniz, indeed, was Platonic not only in the way he conceived the concept of justice, but even in some of his more practical political opinions: he always urged, for example, that "following natural reason, government belongs to the wisest."[58]

With the possible exception of the *Republic,* the Platonic work which Leibniz admired most—at least for use in moral and political philosophy—was the *Euthyphro,* which he paraphrased almost literally in his most important work on justice, the "Meditation on the Common Concept of Justice." In the *Euthyphro,* which deals with the question whether "the rules of goodness and of justice are anterior to the decrees of God" (in Leibniz' words), Plato "makes Socrates uphold the truth on that point."[59] And that truth is, as Ernst Cassirer puts it, that the good and the just are "not the product but the objective aim and the motive of his will."[60] That Leibniz was much affected by Plato's formulation of this point is evident in a bare comparison of their words. In the *Euthyphro* (10d–e):

> Socrates: Then what are we to say about the holy [or the just], Euthyphro? . . . Is it not loved by all the gods?
>
> Euthyphro: Yes.
>
> Socrates: Because it is holy, or for some other reason?
>
> Euthyphro: No, it is for that reason.
>
> Socrates: And so it is because it is holy that it is loved; it is not holy because it is loved.
>
> Euthyphro: So it seems.

The opening lines of Leibniz' "Meditation" on justice merely convert Platonic dialogue into straightforward prose:

> It is agreed that whatever God wills is good and just. But there remains the question whether it is good and just because God wills it or whether God wills it because it is good and just: in other words, whether justice and goodness are arbitrary, or whether they belong to the necessary and eternal truths about the nature of things, as do numbers and proportions.[61]

Leibniz' devotion to the doctrine of Plato's *Euthyphro* is clear not just in the "Meditation on the Common Concept of Justice" and in the *Theodicy*, but in the slightly earlier "Unvorgreiffliches Bedencken" (c. 1698–1701), which he wrote partly to counter the extreme Calvinist view that God creates everything *ex nihilo* through his "fullness of power" (*plenitudo potestatis*) and creative "will" alone. One must consider, Leibniz now says, "whether the will of God really makes right [*das Recht*], and whether something is good and right simply because God wills it, or whether God wills it because it is good and right in itself [*an sich gut und recht ist*]."[62] The radical voluntarist view of justice as a divine "product" Leibniz ascribes to a number of now-obscure Calvinist theologians, but also to those Cartesians "who teach that two times two makes four and three times three makes nine, for no other reason [*Ursach*] than that God wills it."[63] (To lump Descartes with second-hand Calvinists was a rather uncharitable joke, given that Descartes offered his creationist voluntarism as a kind of evidence of orthodoxy: what greater sacrifice could a philosopher make than to concede that God makes truth?)[64]

But such a radically voluntarist position, for Leibniz, is as calamitous morally as it is mathematically: for on such a view "the *aeternae veritates* would have no certainty in themselves, and even the *bonitas et justitia dei* would be only extrinsic denominations, and in fact would be groundless, if their truth derived from God's will alone. *Si tantum staret pro ratione voluntas.*" Those who say, Leibniz adds, that "God wills the evil of punishment without regard to the evil of sin," that he wills to "eternally damn" men even before "any of their sins come into play," forget that such a view "in no way abides with God's justice, goodness, and charity."[65] (The last clause is a conscious re-working of 1 Corinthians 13, "Now abideth faith, hope, charity, these three;" Leibniz replaces "faith" and "hope" with two additional *moral* virtues.)[66] For if God's decree were "quite absolute, and had no *causam impulsivam* whatsoever, then God would be an acceptor of persons, through election, and would deal with men as a tyrant with his underlings . . . for no other reason than *sic volo sic jubeo.*" (This phrase from Juvenal's *Satire* VI, line 223, continues with another phrase which had great weight with Leibniz: the whole sentence reads *Hoc volo, sic jubeo, sit pro ratione voluntas,* and was understood by Leibniz to say, "Thus I will do, thus I ordain, my will takes the place of reason.")[67]

Leibniz goes on to say, in the "Unvorgreiffliches Bedencken," that "the eternal truths of goodness and justice, of ratio and proportion," as well as all other "necessary truths," have "their ground in the eternal being of God himself: not, however, in his free decree." And finally he plays the "ontological proof" trump card: if all truths were divinely caused *ex nihilo*, then the truth about the necessary existence of God himself (as revealed by St. Anselm) would be "a product of the free will of God, which is absurd in the highest degree [*absurdissimum*]."[68] In that passage, Plato triumphs over Euthyphro-Thrasymachus-Descartes-Hobbes one last time.

LEIBNIZ' PLATONISM: A FULLER CONSIDERATION

Given Leibniz' visible devotion to Plato and Platonism, which runs like a red thread through his whole moral and political philosophy, early and late,[69] it is worthwhile to consider a little more fully the exact sense in which Leibniz was (and was not) a Platonist. For among Leibniz' intellectual ancestors, the one who comes closest to the Leibnizian project of establishing a universal jurisprudence which is (like mathematics) equally valid for finite and infinite "minds" in any logically possible cosmos is surely Plato—but more nearly in the *Euthyphro, Phaedo,* and *Meno* than in the *Republic.* For in the *Euthyphro* (9e–10e), Socrates makes it clear that even the gods themselves revere (and do not arbitrarily create or change) the eternal and necessary moral truths; and at *Phaedo* 75d it is urged that even finite minds can know (or rather recall) the "absolute ideas"—whether of mathematics or of ethics—which the gods also "see" and which cannot be derived from the observation of phenomena.[70]

It is a standard Platonic method (and one much appreciated by Leibniz) to throw light on morally problematical and elusive notions, such as "justice" and "virtue," by attempting to relate them to (or sometimes indeed to equate them with) the "necessary" truths of mathematics and geometry which all rational beings see in the mind's eye. That is clearest in *Phaedo*, where all "absolute" ideas are placed on a footing of logical equality: "absolute goodness," "absolute beauty," and "absolute [mathematical] equality" are mentioned in one single breath.

> If we obtained [knowledge] before our birth, and possessed it when we were born, we had knowledge, both before and at the moment of birth, not only of equality and of relative magnitudes, but of all absolute standards . . . [such as] absolute beauty, goodness, uprightness, holiness, and, as I maintain, all those characteristics which we designate in our discussion by the term "absolute."[71]

But in some ways the most striking example of the Platonic method is in the *Meno*, where a discussion between Socrates and Meno over the nature of "virtue" gets bogged down until Socrates takes aside Meno's utterly uneducated slave and shows (in effect) that any rational being has within him what we would now call *a priori* knowledge of mathematical and geometrical truth which cannot be "learned," but which can be drawn out and brought to full consciousness by Socratic probing.

> Socrates: What do you think, Meno? . . . These [geometrical] opinions were somewhere in him, were they not?
>
> Meno: Yes.
>
> Socrates: . . . At present these opinions, being newly aroused, have a dreamlike quality. But if the same questions are put to him on many occasions and in different ways, you can see that in the end he will have a knowledge on the subject as accurate as anybody's. . . . This knowledge will not come from teaching but from questioning. He will recover it for himself.[72]

After Socrates draws this pure rational knowledge from Meno's slave—the boy will no longer be barred by the Platonic saying, "let no one ignorant of geometry enter here"[73]—the conversation turns from geometry back to virtue;

and we now learn (*Meno* 89a ff.) that "virtue is knowledge"—much as mathematics and geometry are knowledge. The structure of the *Meno*—first virtue, then geometry, then virtue again—makes no sense at all unless Plato is trying to suggest that moral knowledge is logically like mathematical-geometrical knowledge: necessary, universal, eternal, not subject to Heraclitean flux, loved by the gods (who do not "cause" it in time), and so on.[74] And if the first of the virtues is justice, and if justice is a psychic-cosmic "harmony" or equilibrium, and if harmony is (in effect) "mathematics made audible," then justice will be a kind of "participation" in the beautiful mathematical order which links the well-tuned, consonant *psyche* to an equally non-dissonant *polis* (or *psyche* "writ large"), and then to "the harmony of the spheres"—as in *Republic* 443d–e:[75]

> Justice . . . means that a man must not suffer the principles in his soul to do each the work of some other and interfere and meddle with one another, but that . . . having first attained to self-mastery and beautiful order within himself, and having harmonized these three principles [reason, spirit, appetite], the notes or intervals of three terms quite literally the lowest, the highest and the mean, and having . . . made of himself a unit, one man instead of many, self-controlled and in unison, he should then and only then turn to practice . . . believing and naming the unjust action to be that which ever tends to overthrow this spiritual constitution, and brutish ignorance to be the opinion that presides over this.

Leibniz' "Platonism"—his tendency to say, in the manner of the *Phaedo*, that all "absolute ideas" are on a plane of logical equality (reason-provided, universal, changeless)—is clear from the earliest period of his life to the latest; it is evident, for example, in the *Elements of Law and Equity* which he wrote in 1669–70 (at the age of twenty-three).

> The doctrine of law belongs to those sciences that are not built on experiments but on definitions, not on the senses but on demonstrations according to reason; it deals with questions, as we say, of law and not of fact [*juris non facti*]. Since justice consists in a certain harmony and proportion, its meaning remains independent of whether anybody actually does justice to others, or conversely, is treated justly. The same holds for numerical relationships. . . . Hence it is not surprising that the proportions of these sciences possess eternal truth.[76]

And these mathematical and jurisprudential "sciences," he adds, "also do not take their point of departure from the senses, but from a clear and distinct intuition or, as Plato called it, *Idea*, a word which itself signifies discernment or definition."[77]

This notion of an intellectual "intuition" which yields ethics as well as mathematics Leibniz traces not just to *Phaedo* (and *Euthyphro*), but to *Meno* as well; and he makes it plain in proposition 26 of the "Discourse on Metaphysics" (1686) that the doctrine of *Meno* is fundamentally correct if that dialogue is purged of certain "Pythagorean" extravagances.

> The mind at every moment expresses all its future thoughts and already thinks confusedly of all that of which it will ever think distinctly. Nothing can be taught us of which we have not already in our minds the idea. This idea is as it were the material out of which the thought will form itself. This is what Plato has excellently brought out in his doctrine of reminiscence, a doctrine which contains a great deal of truth, provided that it is properly understood and purged of the error of preexistence, and provided that one does not conceive of the soul as having distinctly known at some other time what it learns and thinks now.[78]

Plato, Leibniz goes on to say, has confirmed what is true in his position by "a beautiful experiment": he introduces a boy, Meno's slave, "whom he leads by short steps to extremely difficult truths of geometry bearing on incommensurables, all this without teaching the boy anything, merely drawing out replies by a well-arranged series of questions." A purged and chastened version of the *Meno* shows, Leibniz concludes, "that the soul virtually knows those things, and needs only to be reminded (animadverted) to recognize the truths."[79]

Leibniz' devotion to this kind of chastened Platonic rationalism is nowhere clearer than in his critique of King's *The Origin of Evil*, which he gave great prominence by appending it to the *Theodicy* in 1710. In Leibniz' treatment of King there is a *Meno*-like movement from morality to mathematics, then back to morality; obviously Leibniz wants to say that if one grants the necessity, universality and eternity of mathematics (which even a Pyrrhonist skeptic might), one must then make the same concession with respect to "moral necessity," even in the case of God.

> How is it possible for it to be said that there is no good or evil in the ideas before the operation of God's will? Does the will of God form

the ideas which are in his understanding? . . . Indeed, is it by the will of God, for example, or is it not rather by the nature of numbers . . . that of all equal bodies the sphere has the least surface, [or that] certain lines are incommensurable and consequently ill-adapted for harmony? Do we not see that all these advantages or disadvantages spring from the idea of the thing, and that the contrary would imply contradiction? Can it be thought that the pain and discomfort of sentient creatures, and above all the happiness and unhappiness of intelligent substances, are a matter of indifference to God? And what shall be said of his justice? Is it also something arbitrary, and would he have acted wisely and justly if he had resolved to condemn the innocent?[80]

In this defense of divine justice Leibniz turns back the notion that God's rightfulness is arbitrary by invoking mathematical and geometrical truth: he uses the same rhetorical devices ("do we not see," "can it be thought") to repulse those who would deny a sphere of necessary truths which even God does not create in time by "absolute" genesis. The method is utterly, purely Platonic: to relate problematical and contested ethical notions to the necessary mathematical truth that even a Humean skeptic will not deny.

In his *Art of Discovery* (1685), to be sure, Leibniz laments, demi-Platonically, that reason and truth are not as triumphant in ethics and jurisprudence as they are in mathematics and geometry: "the reason why we make mistakes so easily outside of mathematics (where geometers are so felicitous in their reasonings) is only because in geometry and the other parts of abstract mathematics," we can submit to tests or trials "not only the conclusion but also, at any moment, each step made from the premises, by reducing the whole to numbers." But in "metaphysics and ethics" matters are "much worse" because we can test conclusions only in "a very vague manner."[81]

The only way to "rectify our reasonings" in the practical sphere, Leibniz then suggests, is to make them "as tangible as those of mathematics," so that "we can simply say: let us calculate, without further ado, to see who is right." Such a procedure could work "if words were constructed according to a device that I see as possible"—namely, using "characters," as mathematicians do, to "fix our ideas" by "adding to them a numerical proof."

For by this means, after reducing reasoning in ethics . . . to these terms or characters, we shall be able at any moment to introduce the numerical test in such a way that it will be impossible to make a mistake except willfully.[82]

How could this *calculemus* work best in "ethics"? Plainly if the gap between ethics and mathematics were as small as possible, or even successfully bridged: if (for example) justice were a matter of "proportion," "order," and (mathematics-based) "harmony"—as in Leibniz 1696 letter cited earlier—or if at least our love, the basis of *caritas sapientis*, were truly "proportional" to the degree of perfection found (and felt) in the loved object/subject.[83] Hence Leibniz uses the mathematical language of degree and proportion whenever he can, and bemoans the fact—in the *True Method in Philosophy and Theology* (1686)—that others do not do so as well.

> Geometry clarifies configurations and motions; as a result we have discovered the geography of lands and the course of the stars, and machines have been made which overcome great burdens, whence civilization and the distinction between civilized and barbaric people. But the science which distinguishes the just man from the unjust . . . is neglected. We have demonstrations about the circle, but only conjectures about the soul. . . . The source of human misery lies in the fact that man devotes more thought to everything but the highest good in life.[84]

Why, then, given so much "Platonism," should Leibniz' wise love or *caritas sapientis* (as the core of universal jurisprudence) not be purely and simply Platonic? Why should Leibniz not be, more than any other early-modern philosopher, simply a "footnote to Plato"?[85] After all, there is a striking notion of "wise" love in Plato's *Phaedrus*, in which an upright lover tears himself away from an overtly sexual encounter—described with all the warmth and ardor that Plato could summon up—at the literally climactic moment, and transfers the available quantum of erotic energy from orgasm to love of *philo-sophia* and "eternal verity." (This is "sublimation" in the full and literal sense, since the sublime becomes the only permitted object of an *eros* which has been violently wrenched away from sexuality.)

> [The lover] continues in this converse and society, and comes close to his lover in the gymnasium and elsewhere, and that flowing stream which Zeus as the lover of Ganymede called "the flood of passion" pours in upon him. And part of it is absorbed within him, but when he can contain no more the rest flows away outside him. . . . The soul of the beloved, in its turn, is filled with love. . . . So when they lie side by side . . . he is minded not to refuse to do his part in gratifying his

lover's entreaties; yet his yokefellow [the good steed in the psyche] in turn, being moved by reverence and heedfulness, joins with the driver in resisting. And so, if the victory be won by the higher elements of the mind guiding them into the ordered rule of the philosophical life . . . they have won self-mastery and inward peace.[86]

Since Leibniz also operates with a Platonic idea of love for "eternal verities," à la Euthyphro, why not just style Leibniz a "practical Platonist"?""

Partly because Leibniz almost always speaks of *caritas sapientis*, "wise charity," not *amor sapientis*, "wise love";[87] partly because there is not much full-blooded *eros* in Leibniz which stands in need of "sublimation"; but above all (as was hinted earlier) because Leibniz makes *caritas sapientis* and "universal benevolence" (universal good willing) exactly equivalent, and there is simply no place for early Augustinian "good will" *(benevolentia)* in Plato's rationalism. For Plato makes it clear at 352b in the *Protagoras* that an independent, extra-cognitive faculty of so-called will is not philosophically acceptable.

> Uncover another part of your mind, Protagoras. What is your attitude to knowledge? Do you share the common view . . . that it is nothing strong, no leading or ruling element? [Most people] hold that it is not the knowledge that a man possesses which governs him, but something else—now passion, now pleasure, now pain, sometimes love, and frequently fear. They just think of knowledge as a slave, pushed around by all the other affections. Is this your view, too, or would you not rather say that knowledge is a fine thing quite capable of ruling a man, and that if he can distinguish good from evil, nothing will force him to act otherwise than as knowledge dictates, since wisdom is all the reinforcement he needs?[88]

And Socrates answers his own rhetorical question by insisting that while some people imagine that "there are many who recognize the best but are unwilling to act on it," they are wrong and "what they say is false" (353a).[89]

Leibniz, as a Christian descended partly from Augustine, needs to place *bona voluntas* somewhere in his universal jurisprudence; not only does he "place" it, however, he makes it equal to wise charity itself. And a pure Platonist would never equate sublimated *eros* (which wisely ascends to *philosophia*) with "will," whether "good" or not.[90] There are simply parts of Leibnizian ethics that Platonism cannot accommodate at all; for *caritas sapientis* contains Plato and St. Paul, Athens and Jerusalem. If one makes the notions

of wise charity and of general or universal "benevolence" absolutely equivalent—as Leibniz constantly does, in his correspondence with Arnauld and
Malebranche and then in the *Codex Iuris Gentium* ("charity is universal benevolence")[91]—then *bene-volentia*, good willing, is interchangeable with "the charity
of the wise." This interchangeability is perfectly clear, for example, in Leibniz'
"De Abstractis" (c. 1686), in which he writes, "justitia est benevolentia," then
strikes out benevolence in favor of "justitia est caritas ad normam sapientis":
plainly these notions were viewed by him as morally synonymous.[92] And it is
equally clear in the still-unpublished "De Bono Unitatis et Malis Schismatis"
(c. 1691), in which "the perfection of the will" *(perfectio voluntatis)* is equated
with "the perfection of charity."[93]

A stress on "good willing," of course, is in no way extraordinary in a
Christian thinker (partly) descended from Augustine—given the insistence of
that principal father of the Church that "the only unqualifiedly good thing
on earth is a good will." (That familiar phrase is repeated verbatim in Kant's
Grundlegung of 1785.)[94] And such a voluntarist stress is also characteristic of
the thought of Thomas Aquinas, whose doctrine Leibniz sometimes virtually
paraphrases, for example in the *Causa Dei* which he appended to the *Theodicy*:
"Two things are necessary in order that an action may be virtuous or vicious,
namely that we know and that we will what we do, and that we ourselves can
also abstain from the sin which we are in the course of committing, if only
we bring a sufficient zeal to it."[95] (For Plato it would be enough "that we
know": knowledge immediately generates good conduct.)

To be sure, Leibniz often enough, Plato-like, tries to reduce "will" to a
function of understanding; and here his *Thoughts on the Principles of Descartes*
echoes Plato's magnification of knowledge in the *Protagoras*: "Since our will is
not drawn to obtain or avoid anything, except as the understanding presents
it to the will as something good or bad, it will suffice that we should always
judge rightly, in order that we always act rightly."[96] Here there is no gap
whatever between right knowing and right doing, so that the famous phrase
from Ovid's *Metamorphoses*, "I see the good and I approve it, but I follow the
worse,"[97] becomes unintelligible—if one truly "sees" one (quasi-automat-
ically) "does." But it is Leibniz himself who shows that "always judging
rightly" is beyond our power: if "understanding" presents the perception of
good and bad to "the will," and if understanding itself is unavoidably radically defective in a finite, created "substance," then "will" can be no better
than understanding itself. Good will is limited by bad understanding. And

that is a grave problem for a universal jurisprudence in which *caritas sapientis* and *benevolentia universalis* are convertible terms.[98]

Given Leibniz' Augustinian voluntarist deviations (wavering as these sometimes are) from pure Platonism, it is not at all surprising that in the 1693 *Codex Iuris Gentium*—his first published work to assert that *justitia est caritas sapientis*—there is no talk of sublimating *eros* (viewed as a kind of detachable, transferable quantum of psychic energy which can be moved from "low" to "high"); rather the charity of the wise is defined in terms of philanthropy. "Justice, therefore, which is the virtue governing that disposition of mind [*affectus*] which the Greeks call φιλανθρωπία will . . . be most fittingly defined as the charity of the wise man [*caritas sapientis*], that is to say, charity in obedience to the dictates of wisdom."[99] This is why Leibniz can go on to equate *caritas sapientis* with *benevolentia universalis:* a benevolence which is general or universal is precisely not "particular," not primarily an individual affection for another individual.[100] Generalization transforms emotion into policy. It is not like the case of the upright lover in the *Phaedrus,* who detaches himself from a reclining lover for the ascent to *philosophia*. The carefully chosen terms "philanthropy" and "benevolence" set the Leibnizian tone: this is love from which *eros* barely needs to be expelled. In a sense—indeed in every sense—Plato is much more radical than Leibniz: in the *Phaedrus* a very passionate erotism is wrenched away from sexual love and lifted up to embrace the realm of ideas; Augustine reflects and preserves this sheer erotic ardor in the *Confessions;*[101] but Leibnizian philanthropic benevolence is closer to policy than to passion. (This will become clearer in Chapter 4.)

Nevertheless Leibniz' thought is quite inconceivable without its almost-dominant Platonic component: he does insist, after all, that "the doctrine of Plato concerning metaphysics and morality . . . is holy and just," and that "everything he says about truth and the eternal ideas is truly admirable."[102] If Pauline charity and Augustinian *bona voluntas* are also crucial (not to mention the whole of modern science and mathematics), that just helps to prove the synthetic quality of Leibniz' thought (which he himself insisted on).

It is not, of course, the case that Leibniz was single-handedly responsible for reviving the Platonic notion of justice in the modern world (following centuries of Aristotle-colored Scholasticism): that had been done by Grotius, whom Leibniz always called "the incomparable," and who had urged in *De Jure Belli ac Pacis* that "measureless as is the power of God, nonetheless it can be said that there are certain things over which that power does not extend

. . . just as even God cannot cause that two times two should not make four, so he cannot cause that which is intrinsically evil, to be not evil."[103] And Leibniz always cited this passage with approval. But for all of his upholding of Platonism on this point, Leibniz did not go as far as Kant was later to go, and hold not only that God is not the "cause" of goodness and justice, but that the idea of God is merely deduced, as a "necessary hypothesis," out of the concept of moral perfection. Kant, indeed, became the extreme term in what Plato had begun in the *Euthyphro*, when he argued in the *Critique of Pure Reason* that the reality of moral laws and their "inner practical necessity" has led men to the "postulate" of a wise ruler of the world as a being who gives "effect" to those laws; that such laws cannot be regarded as "accidental" and as "derived from the mere will of the ruler"; that (and here Platonism is clearest) "we shall not look upon actions as obligatory because they are the commands of God, but shall regard them as divine commands because we have an inward obligation to them."[104] This goes beyond what Leibniz could allow, in that it treats God as a "postulate" whose objective reality is indemonstrable, who is only "practically" necessary. For Leibniz "all reality must be founded on something existent,"[105] and even the eternal verities of ethics and mathematics must be co-eternal with an actual God who "finds" those verities in his essence. This makes God necessary for, though not the cause of, the truth of the eternal verities; as Leibniz said in his *Notes on Spinoza's Ethics,*

> Even if we concede that the essence of things cannot be conceived without God . . . it does not therefore follow that God is the cause of the essence of things . . . for a circle cannot be conceived without a center, a line without a point, but the center is not the cause of the circle nor the point the cause of the line.[106]

Whatever their differences, however, Plato, Grotius, Leibniz, and Kant could agree that (in Leibniz' words), "Not the will but the wisdom of God is the final rule of justice [*non voluntas sed sapientia Dei justitiae regula ultima est*]."[107] What this means, among other things, is that Jean Barbeyrac was not careful enough, in his refutation of Leibniz' *Opinion on the Principles of Pufendorf,* when he said that Leibniz makes moral-legal obligation "absolutely independent of the divinity and founded solely on the nature of things;"[108] for Leibniz God is the necessary ground, though not the efficient cause, of moral truth: the *aeternae veritates* of goodness and justice "have their ground" in the eternal divine mind, "not however in his free decree [*nicht aber in den liberis decretis*]."[109]

GOD'S EXISTENCE AND MORAL TRUTH

If, for Leibniz, God is the ground (though not the cause) of the eternal verities of justice and goodness, if practical truth "cannot be conceived without God," then the demonstrable existence of that supreme (and only necessary) being is central to universal jurisprudence itself, to the possibility of wise charity. For it is God who must not just "ground" moral (and all other) truth, but also give to each rational substance what his actions are worth in an immortal afterlife. "If God did not exist," Leibniz grants, "the wise would not be obligated to charity beyond their own utility, nor to honorability, unless it is for their own perfection, of which sufficient account cannot be taken in the brevity of this life."[110] And Leibniz adds in the *New Essays* that "I grant that there is no [moral] precept which one would be indispensably obligated to, if there were not a God who leaves no crime unpunished nor any good action without recompense."[111] God, then, for Leibniz, though not the cause of morality and justice, is nonetheless the guarantor of right's efficacy—even on earth, in the "human forum," in which self-love might not expand sufficiently to inspire charitable treatment of others "as oneself."[112]

Of the traditional proofs of God's existence, the one which Leibniz strove the hardest to perfect was the "ontological" one of St. Anselm—though the "physico-theological" proof (the argument from "design") also appealed strongly to him, as will be seen in Chapter 3. Leibniz had worries about Descartes' recent version of the ontological proof of the existence of God—the Anselmian argument that a perfect being exists of necessity, since he would otherwise lack one perfection, namely existence.[113] Leibniz had long thought Descartes' re-working of Anselm's proof to be "incomplete," as is clear in an important passage from *Meditationes de Cognitione, Veritate, et Ideis* (1684).

The only logical conclusion [of Descartes' version of Anselm] is: "If God is possible, it follows that he exists." For we cannot use definitions safely in order to reach a conclusion, unless we know that these definitions are real or that they involve no contradiction. The reason for this is that from notions which involve a contradiction opposite conclusions may be drawn at the same time, which is absurd. To illustrate this I usually take the instance of the swiftest possible motion, which involves an absurdity. For, suppose a wheel to revolve with the swiftest possible motion, is it not evident, that if any spoke of the wheel be made longer its extremity will move more swiftly than a nail on the circumference of the wheel; wherefore the motion of the circumference is not the swiftest possible, as was supposed by the hypothesis.[114]

And yet "at first sight it may appear that we have an idea of the swiftest possible motion," Leibniz continues, "for we seem to understand what we are saying"—but really we have no such understanding, since "we have no idea of impossible things." What Descartes failed to consider, in Leibniz' view, is whether the idea of "the perfect being" (God) is the idea of an "impossible thing," such as "the swiftest possible motion"; fortunately, Leibniz thinks, Descartes' argument is merely incomplete, since the idea of a perfect being involves no contradiction whatever. Leibniz completed this argument, thirty years later, with section 45 of the *Monadology:* "God alone (or the necessary being) has this prerogative, that he must necessarily exist, if he is possible. And as nothing can interfere with the possibility of that which involves no limits, no negation, and consequently no contradiction, this is sufficient of itself to make known a priori the existence of God."[115]

With these passages from familiar Leibnizian works in mind, one can turn for a moment to the key paragraph of Leibniz' unpublished 1711 manuscript on the Abbé Bucquoi's *Pensées sur l'existence de Dieu*[116]—stopping only to notice that he departs from well-known theological terminology through a striking and original use of the political notion of "sovereignty" in connection with "the greatest perfection." For the Abbé Bucquoi's version of a "sovereign" God to work, Leibniz insists, it would be necessary to prove two things which "are true, but which are not immediately evident."

(1) That a being which has its existence through itself is sovereignly perfect . . . [and] (2) that it is impossible that there be several sovereignly perfect beings. But one could say for example that on the surface of a sphere there are several routes from one pole to the other which are equally the shortest, namely all those which do not have meridians, of which one can find an infinity. And on the same surface there is an infinity of circles which are all *circuli maximi*, that is to say, the greatest, and consequently equal to each other.[117]

And therefore, Leibniz concludes, "the final degree [*le dernier degré*] does not always require that the subject endowed with it be unique." Thus it would be necessary "to prove that this consequence is valid in the case of the greatest perfection"—the case of God.[118] As one knows from the *Monadology* and other works, however, Leibniz did think that "the greatest perfection" is both a logically possible idea and one that entails automatic existence—while "the greatest number" of equal circles is not a possible idea at all. And so in the unpublished 1711 manuscript Leibniz confirms what he had established in the "Discourse on Metaphysics" from 1686:

> The conception of God which is the most common and the most full of meaning is expressed well enough in the words: God is an absolutely perfect being. . . . The nature of numbers or of figures does not permit of perfection. This is because the number which is greatest of all . . . and likewise the greatest of all figures, imply contradictions. The greatest knowledge, however, and omnipotence, contain no impossibility. Consequently power and knowledge do admit of perfection, and insofar as they pertain to God they have no limits.[119]

But God's perfect power is not what Leibniz wants to stress most in the "Discourse"; rather he ends by insisting that "God, who possesses supreme and infinite wisdom, acts in the most perfect manner not only metaphysically but also from the moral standpoint."[120] And that last line reminds us that Leibniz liked to emphasize not merely the limitlessness of God's power (in the manner of Hobbes), but still more the limitlessness of his wisdom and goodness. Complaining of Hobbes' notion that it is thanks to "irresistible power" that "the kingdom over men . . . belongeth naturally to God almighty,"[121] Leibniz says in the "Meditation on the Common Concept of Justice" that "Hobbes . . . wants God to have the right to do everything, because he is all-powerful. This is a failure to distinguish between right and fact. For what one can do is one thing, what one should do, another." If power "were the formal reason of justice, all powerful persons would be just, each in proportion to his power; which is contrary to experience."[122] And this led Leibniz to argue that all "spirits" or minds inhabit a divinely ruled Kingdom of Grace regulated by the charity of the wise. What matters is that while one can think of "the greatest" or limitless perfection (or knowledge, or charity), one cannot really think of "the greatest velocity" or "the greatest number." That careful distinction sets a limit to Leibniz' "Platonism": for if the greatest power or the greatest "wise charity" is both logically possible and (in God) actual, while "the greatest number" is neither possible nor actual, then Plato was not quite careful enough when he insisted in the *Phaedo* that we have equally certain pre-natal knowledge of absolute mathematical equality and

of "all those characteristics [beauty, goodness, uprightness] which we desig-
nate in our discussion by the term 'absolute.' "[123]

For Leibniz, *Phaedo*-lover that he was, this assimilates all "absolutes" a little
too smoothly: absolute knowledge or absolute *caritas* can be conceived; "absolute magnitude" cannot. And while "absolute power"—sovereignty in
Bodin's or Hobbes' sense—can be conceived as a (logically unproblematical)
divine attribute, Leibniz' dread of cosmic despotism led him to subordinate
omnipotence to omniscience and moral perfection. Absolute power cannot
corrupt an absolute being, but Leibniz clearly preferred a Platonic truth-
loving God to a Hobbesian "irresistible" one. And that is why he described
God as "sovereignly wise":[124] sovereignty is transformed into a mere adverbial
modification of being knowledgeable.

GOD'S CREATION OF A JUSTIFIABLE BEST WORLD

God as sovereignly wise "mind" (whose will and power are ruled by knowledge and charity) chooses for translation into existence that configuration of
essences which will guarantee the greatest total perfection, preadjusting all
substances and all of their possible relations in advance (in a preestablished
harmony);[125] the most nearly perfect essences have the greatest "claim" to real
existence, since "all possible things . . . tend toward existence in proportion
to the quantity of essence or reality, or to the degree of perfection which they
involve."[126]

Critics of Leibniz have pointed out that this principle—that the most
nearly perfect essences have the greatest claim to real existence—seems to
contradict another fundamental Leibnizian doctrine, namely, that the universe is a *plenum*, a *continuum* with no "gaps" or "vacuum of forms," in which
one of everything exists and is separated from the substances immediately
above and below it by the smallest possible degree of difference.[127] (This last
principle rests on the so-called identity of indiscernibles, which holds that no
two substances can be precisely alike, since, if they were, God would have no
sufficient reason to create either in preference to the other, and hence would
create neither.)[128] If the most nearly perfect essences have the greatest claim
to existence, then only those essences least inferior to God should be created;
but Leibniz wanted to account for the whole range of existence, from next-
to-nothing to God.

However that may be, Leibniz insists that there must be a "sufficient
reason" for God's choice of a particular universe, and that reason must be

"the best": why the best, and not perfection itself, must be settled for, is dictated (apparently) by the fact that there can be only one God, and that everything else must be imperfect compared with him. "God could not give the creature all without making of it a God."[129] God acts by a moral necessity (the "best") which restricts him but leaves him free in the sense that he could (conceivably) have chosen otherwise (though not as well): this is the famous distinction between metaphysical necessity, whose opposite is inconceivable, and moral necessity, whose opposite is conceivable but less good, and which "inclines without necessitating." "Metaphysical necessity . . . admits of no choice, presenting only one object as possible . . . [but] moral necessity . . . constrains the wisest to choose the best."[130] What leads to the rejection of an alternative course of action, Leibniz notes in the "Discourse on Metaphysics," "is not its impossibility but its imperfection."[131] Within the realm of morality, moral necessity is absolute in the sense that one cannot choose the lesser good and still be right; only the possibility of failing to choose the best is necessary for freedom (for God and men alike: God is wholly free because he always chooses the real best, while men choose the apparent best).[132] God chooses that universe which is best on the whole—it is, after all, the best of possible *worlds* which is translated into existence; but since, for Leibniz, the simultaneous co-existence of all possibles is not itself a possibility, God will produce the best "compossible" (compatible and possible) universe. (The propositions "Caesar crosses the Rubicon" and "Caesar halts at the Rubicon" are equally logically possible; but since both "stories" cannot take place in the single "best" divinely chosen world, the stories are not temporally compatible— hence not com-possible.)[133] It follows that while the whole is as nearly perfect as it can be, each individual part (including particular human beings) might be better in itself, if not considered in its relation to the entire system. The universe, once settled on, has a "hypothetical" necessity: other ones are still conceivable, but in the one actually chosen everything is "certain" and "determined," and has a "moral necessity."[134]

Now Leibniz must account for the existence of three kinds of evil—moral (sin), metaphysical (imperfection or limitation), and physical (pain)[135]—in terms of the divine mode of operation just described, and in a way which will leave both God's justice and men's moral responsibility intact (since all minds must be capable of wise charity). It is absolutely essential that he be able to distinguish between moral and metaphysical evil, if the idea of moral responsibility is to be maintained; if all evil is purely metaphysical (a consequence of limitation or "privation" alone) then sin will be involuntary—

caused, in fact, and not chosen—and thereby not a sin. Justice, as a charitable action, would be impossible for men; "Spinozism" would reign. Generally, Leibniz avoids making God the creator of evil by giving it the same ontological status as goodness: both are "ideas," parts of the divine understanding—and, as will be recalled, God does not create his own understanding. "Evil springs," Leibniz says in the *Theodicy*, ". . . from the forms themselves in their detached state, that is, from the ideas which God has not produced by an act of his will, any more than he has produced numbers and figures, and all possible essences which one must regard as eternal and necessary, for they are in the ideal region of the possibles, that is, in the divine understanding."[136] And this is a question of the justice of the best world: "Since God is just," Leibniz urges in *De Libertate Creaturae et Electione divina*, "he is thus not the cause of evil."[137] Leibniz insisted that God wills the good of each creature substance by an "antecedent" will (borrowing that term from Aquinas and Suarez),[138] but that the non-compossibility of all substances led to adjustments in which the overall perfection of the total scheme is uppermost; as a result, God wills "antecedently the good and consequently the best."[139] Since this means that some evil had to be admitted, including evil actual men, a great strain is put on the doctrine of compossibility: the unproblematical assertion that all logically possible essences cannot enjoy simultaneous historical existence is used to make the highly problematical claim that Caligula and Attila the Hun are unavoidable in the "best" world. And it was this, perhaps, which led to Hegel's acid remark in the *Lectures on the History of Philosophy:* "If I have some goods brought to me in the market, at some town, and say that they are certainly not perfect, but are the best that are to be got, this is quite a good reason why I should content myself with them. But comprehension is a very different thing from this."[140]

It will be recalled that the distinctions between moral and metaphysical necessity, and between moral and metaphysical evil, are of capital importance to Leibniz; the first is the guarantor of moral freedom, the second of moral responsibility. He was certainly not prepared to do away with the latter, particularly since he sometimes admitted (albeit a little reluctantly) the idea of eternal damnation, a punishment he wanted to characterize as (sometimes) justifiable.[141] But there is a serious question whether he really succeeded in upholding the distinction between moral and metaphysical evil; in the *Monadology* he claims that "creatures receive their perfections from the influence of God but . . . their imperfections are due to their own nature, which is incapable of being limitless,"[142] and in the *Theodicy* he insists that

God could not give men "all" without making them divine. If men are unavoidably imperfect, "metaphysically evil," in what sense (or to what degree) can they be held responsible for moral actions, including acts of justice or wise charity? Assigning evil to the status of a "privation" not created by God saves him from the charge of voluntarily manufacturing evil; but it not only virtually destroys moral responsibility in human beings (who are only essences translated into existence, or substances), it also raises the question: why, if an actual universe could not be perfect throughout (a multiplication of divinity), and if the admission of evil was the *conditio sine qua non* of the existence of a world which is (at best) "best," did God create real existence? Referring to the admission of evil into the universe, Leibniz found himself constrained to say that "we can judge by the event (or *à posteriori*) that the permission was indispensable . . . sin made its way into the world; God was therefore unable to prevent it without detriment to his perfections. . . . In God this conclusion holds good: he did this, therefore he did it well."[144] A morally perfect being must have acted in a justifiable way, even if our limited "perspective" presently keeps us from seeing that justice.[145] (The difficulties inherent in this view will be fully treated in Chapter 3.)

Oddly enough, Leibniz makes very little use of the early Augustinian idea that moral evil is inevitable if free will is to be an attribute of finite beings[146]—though he does say that without sin neither Christ nor grace would be possible.[147] His more usual argument is that evil is necessary to the "best" universal plan, though men (because of their limited point of view) cannot know in this life why this is so. ("I do not believe at all that a world without evil, preferable to our own in order, is possible, otherwise it would have been preferred," Leibniz wrote to Bourguet in 1714. "One must believe that the admixture of evil has made the good greater: otherwise evil would not have been admitted at all.")[148] Since God is all good, all just, there must be a sufficient reason which constrained him to admit evil into existence; this is enough. By contrast Malebranche—who, like Leibniz, also had to account for the origin of justifiable evil—urged in his *Dialogues on Metaphysics* that "the world as saved by Jesus Christ is of greater worth than the same universe as at first constructed, otherwise God would never have allowed his work to become corrupted."[149] This is an interesting argument, but it is too specifically Christocentric for Leibniz, who made a very sparing theological use of Christ—even as he made an unsparing moral use of Christian "charity" modified by Platonic "wisdom." (But this will be seen more clearly in Chapter Three, where Leibniz makes Christ the voice of reason and of "natural religion" in the *Theodicy,* and all but collapses revelation into *la raison.*) Leibniz might, however, have done well to consider the advice which Theodore gives to Aristes in Malebranche's ninth *Dialogue:*

> Man, Aristes, is a sinner, he is not such as God made him. God, then, has allowed his work to become corrupt. Harmonize this with his wisdom, and his power, save yourself from the difficulty without the aid of the man-God, without admitting a mediator, without granting that God had mainly in view the Incarnation of his son. I defy you to do it even with the principles of the best philosophy.[150]

Leibniz' problem is fairly clear, and it casts doubt not only on his own work, but on any universal jurisprudence which tries to reconcile universal justice, evil, and human freedom. He was aware that "an inevitable necessity . . . would destroy the freedom of the will, so necessary to the morality of actions: for justice and injustice, praise and blame, cannot attach to [metaphysically] necessary actions."[151] His idea of moral freedom ought to have made meritorious actions and good intentions, wise charity and general benevolence, important; but his account of evil—which "saves" God sooner than men—made this very problematical. Sometimes he makes evil (and evil men) the condition of a compossible "best" whole, in which case men are part of a metaphysical compromise, but not free, as in section 335 of the *Theodicy:* "When a wicked man exists, God must have found in the region of the possibles the idea of such a man forming that sequence of things the choice of which was demanded by the greatest perfection of the universe, and in which errors and sins are not only punished but even repaired to greater advantage, so that they contribute to the greatest good."[152] (But true "errors" are only corrected, not "punished"—unless evil *is* error, which Leibniz cannot afford to say.) Sometimes evil men serve to "heighten" the good of the rest, as dissonance heightens consonance in music ("the glory and the perfection of the blessed may be incomparably greater than the misery and imperfection of the damned, and . . . here the excellence of the total good in the smaller number may exceed the total evil which is in the greater number");[153] but this is only a defense of the justice of pre-destination in terms of a cosmological utilitarian calculus. And sometimes (and most important) men are simply imperfect—their existences, which can be no more nearly perfect than their essences, ensure that their mistakes ("errors") are the result of essential limitations of their possible knowledge of the good and the just, not of evil will, pure *malevolentia.* The whole crucial distinction between metaphysical and moral evil thus appears to break down. As a result, Leibniz is forced into a position which is not very persuasive: "free will is the proximate cause of the evil of guilt, and consequently of the evil of punishment; although it is true that the original imperfection of creatures, which is already presented in the eternal ideas, is the first and most remote cause."[154] (Leibniz' honesty kept him from suppressing either half of that tortured formulation from the *Theodicy*—a formulation he would scarcely have kept if his object had been royalty-pleasing edification, as Bertrand Russell imagined.)[155]

That statement from the *Theodicy* is late (1710), but Leibniz had struggled throughout his philosophical career with this problem, as a letter of 1671 makes clear: "Pilate is condemned. Why? Because he lacks faith. Why does he lack it? Because he lacks the will to attention. Why this? Because he has not understood the necessity of the matter. . . . Why has he not understood it? Because the causes of understanding were lacking"[156]—that is, his metaphysical imperfection made his moral perfection impossible. And fifteen years later, in the "Discourse on Metaphysics," Leibniz had still not resolved the difficulty (as indeed he never did):

> God foresees from all time that there will be a certain Judas, whose idea or concept which God has contains this future free act [of betraying Christ]. There remains then only this question: Why does a Judas, a traitor, who is merely possible in the ideas of God, actually exist? But to this question no answer can be expected here on earth, except the general one that, since God has found it good that he should exist in spite of the sin which God foresaw, this evil must be compensated for with interest in the universe and that God will draw a greater good from it and that it will turn out that this sequence of events including the existence of this sinner, is the most perfect among all other possible kinds.[157]

But even if this is true for the whole, for the best "world," Judas is sacrificed "from all time": how then could he have begun to act with wise charity—by returning the thirty pieces of silver, by repenting and being forgiven? Still no one can say that Leibniz is making things easy for himself: Judas betrays Christ, but Christ is the giver of the "new law" of charity, and "wise charity" is justice itself, universally. Judas thus betrays *caritas sapientis*, but Leibniz must justify the existence of this man who is unjust (uncharitable) *in excelsis*.

These difficulties emerge even more painfully in the "Dialogue on Liberty" (1695, but not published until 1948), in which Leibniz urges that "before all sin, there is an original imperfection in all the creatures, which comes from their limitation." And Leibniz, demi-Platonically, presses a geometrical analogy into service: "As it is impossible that there be an infinite circle, since every circle is terminated by its circumference, it is also impossible that there be an absolutely perfect creature, and this is why it is believed that Holy Scripture wished to speak of the angels themselves, when it intimated that among the ministers of God there is none without defect."[158] He then moves to the most problematical part of his claim: "There was no positive evil in creatures at the beginning, but they were always lacking many perfections. Thus through lack of attention the first man was able to turn away from the sovereign good, and to limit himself to some creature, and thereby he fell into sin: that is to say, from an imperfection which at the beginning was only privative, he fell into positive evil."[159] This argument is more-or-less early Augustinian, in the manner of *De Libero Arbitrio*—though Augustine gives more prominence to self-loving *superbia* as the root of sin,[160] while Leibniz glides from "lack of attention" (a "cognitive" defect) to "sin" (a moral evil); the transition from the merely "privative" to the "positively" evil is not exactly explained, but it is certainly asserted. And much the same thing is true of a passage from c. 1704, treating Bayle and Jaquelot, in which Leibniz insists that "malice is not a reality, like goodness; it consists in an inclination [*tendance*] toward a good, the evil of which one does not know."[161] Here, again, a cognitive defect—evil which one "does not know"—turns into "malice" in an unspecified way. But if *le mal* simply glides or slides into *la malice* through insufficient *connaissance*, then *malevolentia* is indistinguishable from defective judgment: one has (mis)taken an apparent good, "the evil of which one does not know," for a real good. Once again, "the causes of understanding" are "lacking." (This difficulty will be examined more fully, by comparing Leibniz with Kant, in Chapter 2.)

JUSTICE, RESPONSIBILITY, AND THE CONCEPT OF SUBSTANCE

A brief, initial examination of Leibniz' concept of substance may make these difficulties more clear. And here the best course will be to examine what might be called "substance in general" first, then to move on (in Chapter 2) to Leibniz' extraordinary moral and political use of substance afterward.

When God translates a portion of essence into existence, he creates "substances" (or, as Leibniz called them after c. 1695, "monads"),[162] which are characterized by "perception" when passive and by "force" or activity when active; the Leibnizian substance is understood—to use a phrase of Hegel's—in terms of "inner activity and movement of its own active life."[163] While substances are always conjoined with bodies in existence, substances themselves are in no way material; matter can be divided and subdivided ad infinitum, but to account for perception ("intelligence" in the higher monads) and for action there must be a point of unity, a "metaphysical point" or a "formal atom" (Leibniz of course rejected material atomism) which constitutes the reality of a being. Indeed, Leibniz says flatly that "being and unity are convertible terms."[164] He believed that thought could not be conceived as a "modification" of matter, which was, for him, passive and undifferentiated; a "complete corporeal substance" (any living being having both mind and body) thus received its completeness from two sources, "that is, from the active principle and from the passive principle, of which the first is called form, soul, entelechy, primitive force [or monad], and of which the second is called primary matter, solidity, resistance."[165] Leibniz arguably never gave a wholly convincing account of why a material world—or a material element in any possible world—existed at all; sometimes matter, in his system, seems to be only the condition of the "imperfection" of all substances inferior to God, since substantial perception mediated through the senses is necessarily "confused": "if each substance taken separately were perfect, all would be alike, which is neither fitting nor possible. If they were gods, it would not have been possible to produce them. The best system of things will therefore not contain gods; it will always be a system of bodies."[166] Substances, then, are psychic beings, and the bodies with which they are associated are simply *phenomena bene fundata;* substances, as simple unities, as "subjects" of perception and change, are "true things," whereas bodies—as Leibniz urged in a letter to de Volder—are "beings by aggregation and therefore phenomena, existing, as Democritus put it, by convention and not by nature."[167] Substances can be differentiated only intensively, or qualitatively, in terms of degrees of psychic "perfection," and never extensively, or quantitatively, in terms of an "extrinsic denomination" such as position in time or space. ("I hold space to be something merely relative, as time is," Leibniz wrote in his celebrated correspondence with Samuel Clarke. "I hold it to be an order of coexistences, as time is an order of successions.")[168] "It is living substance," he insists, "which is truly a being, and matter, taken simply as mass, is only a phenomenon or well-founded appearance"—though these appearances "are not illusory, like a dream, or like a sword pointing at us out of a concave mirror, or Doctor Faustus eating up a cartful of hay . . . they are true phenomena."[169] Substances are indestructible (except by God), and can be brought into existence only by divine creation; they are translated into temporal being as parts of a system whose every element impinges on every other element; all substances are (so to speak) premodified in relation to one another, and everything that will ever happen to a substance is included in its original "concept," just as all predicates inhere logically in a subject.[170] That Pilate would condemn Christ was thus a "certainty," and had a hypothetical, though not a metaphysical necessity, since its opposite was still conceivable.[171] (This notion, the so-called *in esse* principle, will be treated with a view to its moral-political implications in Chapter 2.)

If a man takes a journey (Leibniz says), this action issues out of his concept and is, *ex hypothesi*, necessary to him; if he did not make the journey, his concept would be altered (though no universal law of metaphysical necessity would be overthrown).[172] (Sometimes, indeed, Leibniz defined freedom as the autonomous temporal unfolding of a substance or monad out of its "concept," unaffected by other substances; and he wavered between this rather Spinozistic conception and a more traditional Christian or early Augustinian conception based on free will.) In any case, all "relations" of substances are determined in advance of temporal existence and activity; substances do not affect one another in action, physically, but in advance, metaphysically, by being assigned a place in the pre-established harmony. "The intercourse of substances or monads," Leibniz says, "arises not from an influence but from a consensus originating in their preformation by God."[173] There is, for him, a continuum of substances stretching from the barely organic to God himself: bare monads have perceptions only (as in the plant's "perception" of light in the process of photosynthesis); animals have feeling and purely empirical "memory"; but spirits or minds, which are characterized by self-consciousness, memory or moral personality (on which responsibility, reward and punishment depend), and innate knowledge of the logical, mathematical and moral "eternal verities," are part of the City of God.[174] Since all substances are created as parts of a compossible whole, they all have relations; and since substance is percipient, all substances express or "represent" all other substances (as well as the whole cosmos) with varying degrees of clarity and distinctness; "this mutual connection or accommodation of all created things to each other and of each to all the rest causes each simple substance to have relations which express all the others and consequently to be a perpetual living mirror of the universe."[175] Substances are perfect to the extent that they are causes *a priori* of changes in lesser substances; thus the physical realm exists to serve the moral, and nature leads to grace.[176]

That Leibniz thought his monadology or theory of substance essential to the understanding of justice and morality is quite clear: as he said in the *New Essays* (1704), "true ethics is to metaphysics what practice is to theory, because upon the doctrine of substances in general depends the knowledge of spirits and particularly of God and the soul, which gives a proper meaning to justice and virtue."[177] And Leibniz meant that claim to have wide currency, even in the English-speaking world; only the death of Locke kept him from publishing the *New Essays*. But the difficulty with the theory of substance—apart from the possible meaning of such terms as "expression" and "representation"—is that it seems to involve a determinism which is incongruent with Leibniz' Christian-Augustinian idea of freedom and hence with the possibility of choosing to act with greater wise charity and benevolence. On the one hand, the doctrine of substance provides for moral personality (in the higher monads); for the possibility of good and evil actions, for responsibility, guilt, punishment and reward; for the autonomy of the mind from causal determination by physical factors; for a personal immortality in which actions can finally receive what they are worth. Generally, it provides for an idea of *mind* which is something more than matter and for an idea of *life* which is something more than mechanism.[179] On the other hand, however, substance comes into existence only as part of a pattern or world which is "good" as a totality; a given substance does not exist *in abstracto*, but within the constraints imposed by the principles of compossibility and of preestablished harmony—both of which involve stasis, not to say "fatalism."[180] An evil substance (for example, Judas) may be required for the (overall, general) "best," and if that substance "gets better" spontaneously, perhaps through benevolent actions, the order of the universe may be less "certain" than Leibniz usually assumes (though he sometimes indicates that the whole universe may be progressing toward "new perfections").[181] If one assumes, as he usually does, that evil is a "privative" idea which must be given reality if any world is created (and any world would be less perfect than God), then it is hard to see how all substances can attain "salvation" or act rightly. If this were not a sufficient problem, Leibniz' rather frequent definition of freedom as the unfolding of substance according to internal laws, while congruent with compossibility and preestablished harmony, cannot be reconciled with more traditional views of moral freedom; that is why Kant called Leibnizian liberty "the freedom of a turnspit."[182]

Arnauld made Leibniz aware of some of these problems in the 1680s (as will be seen in Chapter 2),[183] and he responded, ultimately, with the distinction between moral and metaphysical necessity, as well as with the argument that men's moral actions are free "because God has foreseen those actions in his ideas, just as they are, that is, free."[184] But the doctrine of the metaphysical imperfection of all men overthrew the force of these distinctions, since volition is finally dependent on possible knowledge: "We will only what appears to the intellect. The source of all errors is precisely the same in its own way as the reason for errors which is observed in arithmetical calculation . . . to will is to be brought to act through a reason perceived by the intellect."[185] And that *Protagoras*-like claim creates terrible problems for Leibniz, who usually said that goodness must be "in the will," considered as a faculty which chooses among objects of knowledge. (The problem is even clearer in the 1700 *Mantissa* to the *Codex Iuris Gentium*, in which he says that "even in our evil purposes we are moved by a certain perceived appearance of good or perfection."[186] There the crucial distinction between error and evil breaks down altogether.)

To make matters even more difficult, Leibniz sometimes admitted (a subtle form of) predestination into his system, insisting that grace and salvation were not deserved or accorded to merit—a position which is theologically orthodox (in late Augustinianism) but morally worrying.[187] If wise charity, however, is to be the foundation of a "universal" ethical-political system, one must grant an importance to "good acts" which Leibniz was hard-pressed to allow— though he was also unwilling to deny their importance, and therefore vacillated: "prayers, good intentions, good actions, all are useful and sometimes even necessary, but none of it is sufficient."[188] Good acts—such as acts of justice, charity, and benevolence—would necessarily involve alterations in the relations of rational substances, alterations presupposing a degree of moral spontaneity which important elements of "monadology" seem to disallow. "Relations have a reality dependent on the mind, like truths," Leibniz wrote in the *New Essays*, "but not the mind of men, since there is a supreme intelligence which determines them for all time."[189] For justice as charity to work, individual men would have to be individually good (and good willing); it would not be sufficient that the universe, as a totality, was "best." As Leibniz' system stands, only those beneficiaries of compossibility who find themselves nearest divinity can enjoy the possibility of acting even relatively well. Ultimately the effort to salvage God's justice by making evil a privation which might be "translated" into particular substances, including human beings, seriously weakened the possibility of men's responsibility and justice. Thus even while attempting to overthrow "Spinozism" in the *Theodicy*, Leibniz' own logic forced him to grant that

> . . . often creatures lack the means of giving themselves the will they ought to have; often they even lack the will to use those means which indirectly give a good will. . . . This fault must be admitted . . . but it is not necessary . . . for all rational creatures to have so great a perfection, and such as would bring them so close to the Divinity.[190]

If a "good will" is so hard to have, even though men "ought" to have it, it is difficult to see how Leibniz can insist on an essential link between *bona voluntas* and *caritas sapientis*—as he nonetheless does in "Agenda" (c. 1679), in which he urges that a good will or *recta intentio* is requisite if one is to fulfill his social duties.

> Next to the mind comes the will. Now a good will or a rightful intention consists in . . . the love of God and one's neighbor. For that reason one must neglect nothing which serves God's honor. . . . [One must] especially love justice, be hard on oneself and indulgent to others . . . [and] always be mindful of the general good. [It is essential] . . . to speak ill of no one . . . to be helpful to everyone . . . to suffer a small misfortune sooner than to let another suffer a great misfortune, to do nothing that one would not gladly endure himself. To give alms without ostentation; to take pity on the distressed and the unhappy, and to practice the works of charity [*Barmherzigkeit*].[191]

That is a moral agenda which any generous moralist could praise. But the point is that one must be capable of doing all these admirable things, if one "ought" to do them. Whether Leibniz leaves room for the spontaneous self-determination which would make these moral goods realizable, however, is one of the most vexed questions in his universal jurisprudence.

What would have been more in accord with wise charity as the chief moral-political virtue than Leibniz' conflation of Platonism, Thomism, and Lutheranism is pure Pelagianism; and this he sometimes approaches—quite inconsistently—in the *New Essays* ("for true goodness less knowledge suffices with more good will, such that the greatest idiot can take part in it as much as the wisest and ablest").[192] That is almost proto-Kantian in its elevating of practice over theory, and in its magnification of early Augustinian *bona voluntas*. And that is still more true of the remarkable final page of Leibniz' great essay from 1697, *Radical Origination of Things*, in which "good will," justice, charity, and the Christian religion are defined in terms of each other: "The very law of justice . . . wills that each one participate in the perfection of the universe and in a happiness of his own proportioned to his own virtue and to the good will he entertains toward the common good, by which that which we call the charity and the love of God is fulfilled, in which alone, according to the judgment of the wisest theologians, the force and power of the Christian religion itself consists."[193] There good will is equivalent to every praiseworthy thing in the cosmos.

Nonetheless the central question in Leibniz' universal jurisprudence remains: why did God create an unavoidably imperfect universe? Sometimes he suggests that God created out of goodness—an odd suggestion, unless plenitude and variety are better than the nonexistence of evil; but more usually he treats existence as a manifestation of God's glory.[194] Substances exist to "mirror" his perfections, to be "witness" to them.[195] Evidently neither of these explanations rests on "charity" traditionally understood. At most, Leibniz is able to show that the universe as a whole is best, once the decision to create *some* universe has been made. "Only the evil themselves have suffered any loss through sin," he urged in the *True Theologica Mystica*, "[but] the whole creation of God has not lost but gained through it."[196] That this doctrine is destructive of individuals Leibniz was aware without being able to do anything about it; in the *Radical Origination of Things* he said that "just as care is taken in the best-ordered commonwealth that individuals shall fare as well as possible, so the universe would not be perfect enough unless as much care is shown for individuals as is consistent with the universal harmony."[197] It is the last phrase which is crucial, and which leads to Leibniz' final statement in the *Theodicy* that "one can say that men are chosen and arranged" in the best world "not so much according to their excellence as according to the suitability which they have for the plan of God."[198] Here "the plan" (universal harmony and a defensible "world") may override individual "excellence." Presumably, however, an excellent individual would be generally benevolent and wisely charitable; how can one over-ride the very moral qualities which are praiseworthy in a God who is "sovereignly wise" rather than just sovereign?[199] Nothing less than the universal validity of "universal jurisprudence" becomes questionable.

Monadology
and Justice

Just as each monad or substance "expresses" or "represents" the universe from its point of view, so too monadology itself expresses or represents the Leibnizian moral universe: the whole universal jurisprudence of wise charity is built into Leibniz' conception of (rational) monads who see eternal moral verities and who strive to act (from benevolent motives) to realize those truths. Leibniz' "monadology"—beginning with the "Discourse on Metaphysics" (1686) and the related correspondence with Antoine Arnauld (1686–1690),[1] and culminating in the *Monadology* itself (1714)—is a theory of justice which only needs to be teased out of metaphysical and theological surroundings, much as Socrates teased "geometric" knowledge of virtue out of Meno's slave.[2] Even if Leibniz' official writings on justice vanished, one could find his ethical views "represented" in monadology. For "on the knowledge of substance, and in consequence of the soul, depends the knowledge of virtue and of justice."[3]

Leibniz always takes care to bring out the moral-political significance of his concept of "substance": he is, to be sure, concerned as a metaphysician with substance as such, but always wants to show that without (naturally immortal) substances or persons there can be no moral concepts, no "subjects" of universal justice, no "citizens" of the divine monarchy or City of God. That is one reason (among many) that Leibniz is hostile to Hobbes: if, as in *De Cive* and *Leviathan*, "all substance is body,"[4] and if mere body cannot conceive moral ideas—because "body" cannot conceive anything at all—then universal jurisprudence is ruled out by bad metaphysics, by an inadequate conception of substance.

Here, of course, Leibniz is thinking of a passage such as the one in *Leviathan*, chapter 34, in which Hobbes says that "substance and body signify the same thing," and that therefore the phrase "incorporeal substance" strives vainly to link up "words which, when they are joined together, destroy one another, as if a man should say, an Incorporeal Body."[5] Or, alternatively, Leibniz is thinking of the passage in the savagely funny chapter 46 of *Leviathan* ("Of Darkness from Vain Philosophy and Fabulous Traditions"), which follows an assault on scholastic "Aristotelity" with the insistence that the Graeco-Christian term "substantial form" is nothing but the decayed jargon of "School Divinity":

> The world (I mean not the earth only . . . but the Universe, that is, the whole mass of things that are) is corporeal, that is to say, Body: and hath the dimensions of magnitude, namely, length, breadth and depth. . . . Nor does it follow from hence, that Spirits are nothing: for they have dimensions, and are therefore really bodies.[6]

The opening chapter of *Leviathan,* which represents all "conceptions" as "movements" in the brain caused by the "pressure" of outward "objects," is for Leibniz completely inadequate; mind or *esprit* vanishes, or at least is unaccountable. Hobbes speaks, Leibniz complains, "as if it were possible to derive memory, intellect, will and consciousness from [bodily] magnitude, shape and motion alone."[7] Of course Hobbes uses moral ideas such as "ought" and "obligation"—saying in *Leviathan,* chapter 14, that once a man has "transferred" his right to a sovereign beneficiary he is "said to be obliged" not to "make void that voluntary act of his own," that he ought, and that it is his "duty," to keep covenants;[8] but in Leibniz' view Hobbes is not entitled to those terms, since the Hobbesian notion of substance makes them inconceivable within his system. Strictly speaking, for Leibniz, Hobbes views mind itself as an epiphenomenon—literally as a set of impressions made by the pressure of objects. But how (Leibniz would ask) can a pressing object "cause" the conceivability of "oughtness" or "obligation," or provide the idea of "moral necessity"? Even if so-called sense-perception (of a tree or a rock) might be accounted for in this Hobbesian way—though for Leibniz there is no "empirical" perception[9]—how would "pressure" of objects generate moral notions? For Leibniz, as for Plato and Kant, only reason can "give" ideas such as moral necessity; no empirical experience can do so, as Plato's *Phaedo* urges; it is in that moral sense that Plato, Leibniz, and Kant are all "idealists."[10] Even if Leibniz was not simply a proto-Kantian, nonetheless he would accept the argument of the *Critique of Pure Reason* that "our reason has causality" and that this "is evident from the imperatives which we impose as rules upon our active powers."[11]

Conversely, Kant would more or less accept (though only in the moral sphere) Leibniz' celebrated demi-Platonic passage in the *New Essays*: "By what means can experience and the senses give ideas? Has the soul windows? Is it like a writing-tablet? Is it like wax? It is plain that all those who think thus of the soul [Hobbes and Locke] make it at bottom corporeal. . . . Our mind is the source of necessary truths."[12] (In the *Metaphysische Anfangsgründe der Natur-wissenschaft* [1786], Kant says that Leibniz' "ill-understood monadology" or theory of substance does not "belong at all to the clarification of natural appearances," but is instead an effort of Leibniz' to offer "a strictly Platonic [*richtiger Platonischer*] conception of the world, correct in itself, insofar as the world is not an object of the senses but is regarded as a thing in itself, purely an object of the understanding."[13] And for Kant, of course, the moral "world" is indeed a thing in itself, not a mere phenomenon or "natural appearance."[14] Ernst Cassirer adds, in *Kant's Life and Thought*, that Kant correctly saw the Leibnizian monad as "that ultimate, unanalyzable unity of which we are aware as the spiritual subject in the idea of the ego. In the act of self-consciousness a unity is given to us that is not derivable from something else."[15])

Monads as Moral-Political Substances: Leibniz' Correspondence with Antoine Arnauld

The moral-political significance of Leibniz' theory of substance is nowhere brought out more clearly than in his correspondence with the great Jansenist theologian Antoine Arnauld concerning the "Discourse on Metaphysics"— and that is especially true of two of Leibniz' letters, one from 1687 summing up the first phase of this exchange, and a final one from March 1690 in which "substance" is so subordinated to justice and wise charity that it seems to be mainly the *conditio sine qua non* of morality and benevolence.

Leibniz' letter to Arnauld of October 6, 1687, begins by appealing to the authority of Plato: "regarding the [substantial] forms or the souls which I consider to be indivisible and indestructible, I am not the first to hold this opinion. Parmenides, of whom Plato speaks with respect . . . held that there was neither generation nor corruption except in appearance. Aristotle takes the same position in *De Caelo*."[16] After trying to meet a number of Arnaldian difficulties and objections in earlier letters, Leibniz goes on to stress the moral importance of rightly conceived substance:

> With regard to spirits, that is to say, substances which think and which are able to recognize God and to discover eternal truths, I hold that God governs them according to laws different from those with which he governs the rest of substances; for while all the forms of substances express the whole universe, it can be said that animal substances express the world rather than God, while spirits express God rather than the world. God governs animal substances according to the material laws of force and of the transfer of motion, but spirits according to the spiritual laws of justice, of which the others are incapable.[17]

It is for this reason, Leibniz goes on to say, that with regard to animals God operates "as a worker or a machinist," but that with respect to minds he "performs the functions of a prince or of a legislator"—a function which is "infinitely higher."[18]

If, then, for Leibniz, God is the "author" of the being (the real temporal existence) of rational substances, that is not what matters most: what matters most is the moral relations between the supreme mind and finite minds.

> [God] assumes another aspect with regard to spirits who conceive of him as endowed with will and with moral qualities: because he is, himself, a spirit and, like one among us, to the point of entering with us into a social relation, where he is the head. It is this universal society or republic of minds under this sovereign monarch which is the noblest part of the universe, composed of so many little gods under this one great God; for it can be said that created spirits differ from God only in degree, only as the finite differs from the infinite, and it can truly be said that the whole universe has been made only to contribute to the beautifying and to the happiness of this City of God.[19]

With that passing reminiscence of Augustine, Leibniz now goes on, in this 1687 letter to Arnauld, to urge that in the City of God it is "justice or love" which links finite substances with the supreme substance.

> This is why everything is so constructed that the laws of force or the purely material laws work together in the whole universe to carry out the laws of justice or of love, so that nothing will be able to injure the souls that are in the hands of God, and so that everything should result

in the greatest good of those who love him; this is why, furthermore, it must be that spirits keep their personalities and their moral qualities so that the City of God shall lose no member and they must in particular preserve some sort of memory or consciousness or the power to know what they are, upon which depends all their morality, penalties, and chastisement.[20]

It is for this moral reason, Leibniz adds, that minds must be "exempt from those transformations of the universe" which would make them "unrecognizable to themselves" and which would "morally speaking, make another person of them."[21]

That final phrase, "make another person of them," is just what the Leibnizian notion of substance rules out: each individuated rational monad knows the eternal moral verities and has memory of its own good and bad actions, so that it can be the subject of universal justice.

THE "DISCOURSE ON METAPHYSICS" (1686): THE CASE OF JULIUS CAESAR

If in the 1687 correspondence with Arnauld Leibniz brings out the general moral-political significance of substance, insisting on "justice," "love," "social relations," and the "City of God," in the celebrated (or notorious) proposition 13 of the "Discourse on Metaphysics" he does not just speak of social rapports in general: instead he follows his most famously radical statement of substance with a very striking historical example of a highly particular and vigorously political "substance," namely, Julius Caesar. What he says first, in a purely metaphysical vein, is that "the concept of an individual substance includes once and for all everything that can ever happen to it" and that "in considering this [complete] concept one will be able to see everything which can truly be said concerning the individual, just as we are able to see in the nature of a circle all the properties which can be derived from it."[22] (This is not a very fortunate comparison, since Leibniz himself wants to distinguish, in the very next paragraph of the "Discourse," between "geometrical" and "hypothetical" necessity: an "alternative" Adam, minus one or more predicates, is logically possible, and therefore Adam's action—sinning and being expelled from paradise—is not necessary in the way that "all radii of a circle are equal" is necessary.)[23]

What is revealing is that Leibniz illustrates this notion of the complete "concept of an individual substance" with the morally problematical example of Caesar. This shows that he is always centrally concerned with the practical dimension of "substance": Can there be "minds" which (being more than corporeal bundles of Hobbesian impressions) know moral truth? Can there be "spontaneity" and accountability? Are human events "certain" but not "necessary"? Did Caesar "have" to cross the Rubicon?

> Since Julius Caesar will become perpetual Dictator and master of the Republic and will overthrow the liberty of Rome, this action is contained in his concept, for we have supposed that it is the nature of such a perfect concept of a subject to involve everything, in fact so that the predicate may be included in the subject *ut possit inesse subjecto*. . . . For if anyone were capable of carrying out a complete demonstration by virtue of which he could prove this connection of the subject, which is Caesar, with the predicate, which is his successful enterprise, he would bring us to see that the future dictatorship of Caesar had its basis in his concept or nature, so that one would see there a reason why he resolved to cross the Rubicon rather than stop, and why he gained the day at Pharsalus.[24]

Leibniz does not yet say (despite his use of a Roman political-historical example to illustrate "substance") that Caesar, though despotic and finally assassinated, nonetheless contributed to the "best" world—as he would do, twenty-five years later, in the *Theodicy*, saying that the rape of Lucretia by Tarquin brought about the beginning of the Republic and the foundation of a soon-to-be universal empire as an underpinning for universal "Roman" Christianity.[25] Here, in the 1686 "Discourse on Metaphysics," he is at the fall rather than the rise of the Republic; and what worries him at this point is not so much Caesar's place and function in the "best" world, but the question whether Caesar can reasonably be held accountable for the destruction of the Republic: "it will be insisted . . . [that] since God imposes upon him this personality, he is compelled henceforth to live up to it."[26] If this insistence were right, then Caesar could not be reasonably condemned for his lack of *caritas sapientis*. But fortunately, Leibniz urges, the distinction between "metaphysical" necessity and mere divinely determined "certainty" keeps Caesar (or indeed any rational substance) from being the victim of "absolute fatality."

> But does it not seem that in this way the difference between contingent and necessary truths will be destroyed, that there will be no place for

human liberty, and that an absolute fatality will rule over all our actions as well as over the rest of the events of the world? To this I reply that a distinction must be made between that which is certain and that which is necessary. Everyone grants that future contingencies are assured, since God foresees them, but we do not say just because of that that they are necessary.[27]

And Leibniz then amplifies the distinction between the metaphysically (or geometrically) necessary and the merely certain by urging that "that which happens according to these [divine] decrees is assured, but . . . it is not therefore necessary, and if anyone did the contrary he would be doing nothing impossible in itself, although it is impossible *ex hypothesi* that that other happen."[28] Had Caesar stopped at the banks of the Rubicon, left Rome to Cicero, and returned to Cisalpine Gaul, no necessary truth would have been violated; everything Caesar did was "contingent" and could have been otherwise. But—and here lies the real problem—the mere fact that an alternative Caesar, a non-Rubicon-crossing Caesar, is logically possible, as a notion in the mind of God, does nothing to weaken the certainty (*ex hypothesi*) that Caesar would act as he did in fact. The painfully worrying part of Leibniz' argument, which alarmed even the Jansenist Arnauld (no Pelagian partisan of human freedom), is the claim that "although God assuredly chooses the best, this does not prevent that which is less perfect from being possible in itself . . . although it will never happen."[29]

If it will *never* happen that, in the historically actual world translated into real existence by God, the merely logically possible will triumph over "certainty" and divine determination, in what sense could Caesar have acted better (more charitably) than he did, or even differently? To be sure, his action flowed from his "concept," and in that sense was "his"; no external constraint shaped him, since no Leibnizian monad can suffer external constraint (by definition); but a Hobbesian notion of freedom as the mere absence of external impediments to motion (*Leviathan*, ch. 21) is not usually enough for Leibniz.[30] If even a suspected "Calvinist" such as Arnauld was worried by Leibniz' defense of the "freedom" of a rational substance, that is a strong signal of troublesome difficulty—a difficulty that will be fully brought out a little later, in comparing Leibniz' notion of freedom with that of Kant.

It is worth pointing out briefly that Leibniz never deviated very much from his 1686 doctrine of substantial freedom in later writings: in a characteristic letter to Pierre Bayle from 1702, for example, he insists

You remark, Sir, that good minds are stumped by the difficulties of the free will of man, and that they say they cannot understand how if the soul of man is a created substance it can have its own true and internal force of acting. . . . I would rather believe that without that force it would not be a substance. For the nature of substance consists, in my opinion, in that regulated tendency with which phenomena arise in an orderly fashion, a tendency which it received from the start and which is conserved in it by the author of things.[31]

At this point Leibniz, perhaps still remembering Arnauld's criticisms, allies himself with the undoubted orthodoxy of the *Summa Theologica:* "Concerning free will I am of the sentiment of the Thomists and other philosophers who believe that everything is predetermined." But that predetermination "does not prevent us from having a freedom exempt not only from constraint but even from necessity, and in that we are like God himself who is always determined in his actions since he cannot fail to choose the best."[32] (The last clause, to be sure, is a little disingenuous: for "we" are metaphysically evil and will "certainly" choose the worse.)

Leibniz' Last Letter to Arnauld: Monads and Justice

By the time he wrote his very last letter to Arnauld, from Venice in March 1690,[33] Leibniz had gotten beyond any tentativeness or defensiveness in his statement of what "substance" really is: he is no longer terribly worried about accommodating Arnauld (as in earlier letters), but is concerned to offer a terse, laconic summary of his views—in a manner which foreshadows the equally terse and laconic *Monadology*. He has arrived at a definitive position, and therefore offers a string of definitions. After presenting a very compressed proto-monadology, Leibniz makes it clear that it is "rational substances" or "intellects" or souls that matter most; and he crowns this with a foretaste of the doctrine of the *Codex Iuris Gentium* (which he had begun to prepare for 1693 publication)[34]—the doctrine that justice is *caritas sapientis,* the charity of the wise. More than any other short work, this 1690 letter to Arnauld shows that, for Leibniz, moral and political philosophy cannot be undertaken at all without an adequate idea of substance.

First Leibniz speaks of substance in a general and now-familiar way:

Each of these substances contains in its own nature the law of the continuous progression of its own workings and all that has happened to it and all that will happen to it.

Excepting the dependence upon God, all these activities come from its own nature.

Each substance expresses the whole universe, some substances, however, more distinctly than others, each one . . . according to its own point of view.[35]

But then Leibniz gives "substance" a moral and jurisprudential turn—and this "moral" part of the account is as long as the account of substance-in-general. (It must then be the case that he thought that he had sufficiently saved freedom to make it possible for him to insist on justice, charity, and benevolence as virtues that ought to be practiced.)

Intellects, or souls which are capable of reflection and of knowledge of the eternal truths and God, have many privileges which exempt them from the transformation of bodies.

In regard to them moral laws must be added to physical laws. . . .

They, taken together, constitute the Republic of the Universe, with God as the monarch.

There is perfect justice and order observed in this City of God, and there is no evil action without its chastisement, nor any good action without its proportionate reward.

The better things are understood, the more they are found beautiful and conformable to the desires which a wise man might form.[36]

We must "always be content with the ordering of the past," Leibniz goes on to say, "because it has absolutely conformed to the will of God, which can be known by the events"; but at the same time we must "try to make the future, insofar as it depends upon us, conform to the presumptive will of God or to his commandments"—above all the commandments enjoining love for God and one's neighbor. In this way we shall learn "to beautify our Sparta and to labor in well-doing, without, however, being cast down when unsuccessful, in the firm belief that God will know how to find the most fitting times for changes to the better."[37]

Those who are not content with the ordering of things cannot boast of loving God properly.

Justice is nothing else than love felt by the wise.

Charity is universal benevolence whose fulfillment the wise carry out conformably to the dictates of reason so as to obtain the greatest good.

Wisdom is the science of happiness or of the means of attaining the lasting contentment which consists in the continual achievement of greater perfection.[38]

Almost the whole of Leibniz' thought is compressed into the final page of the last letter to Arnauld, as for him the whole universe is compressed into each monad. The monadology, the theodicy, the universal jurisprudence of wise charity and *benevolentia universalis*, the moral psychology of happiness based on "perfection"—all are minutely, embryonically present in this 1690 writing.

LEIBNIZ' THEORY OF SUBSTANCE: DOUBTS ABOUT SPINOZA AND PASCAL

If the idea of substance which Leibniz wants to establish is contained in its most striking form in the "Discourse on Metaphysics" and in the closely related correspondence with Arnauld, the idea of substance which he wants to reject (in addition to Hobbes') is that of Spinoza—and that is clearest in "Doctrine of a Single Universal Spirit," from 1702. "If someone wants to maintain that there are no particular souls at all," Leibniz urges, ". . . he will be refuted by our experience, which teaches us (it seems to me) that we are something in our individuality [*en nostre particulier*], which thinks, which is aware of itself, which wills, [and] that we are distinguished from another person who thinks and who wills something else." Otherwise, he goes on, "one falls into the sentiment of Spinoza, or of several similar authors, who will have it that there is only one substance, namely God, who thinks, believes, and wills one thing in me, but who thinks, believes, and wills just the contrary in someone else"—an opinion which Pierre Bayle "has known how to make ridiculous in several sections of his *Dictionary*." And Leibniz adds that it is "more reasonable to believe that in addition to God, who is the supreme active principle, there are a number of individual actors," since there are "a number of actions and passions which are particular and opposed," and which "cannot be attributed to the same subject." These "active beings," he insists, "are nothing else than individual souls."[39] And in such souls "the mind is not a part but an image of divinity, a being which represents the universe, a citizen of the divine kingdom."[40]

Leibniz certainly never repented of his anti-Spinozism: in an important late letter to Bourguet (December 1714), he maintains that "it is just through these monads that Spinozism is destroyed, for there are as many true substances, and, so to speak, as many always-subsisting living mirrors of the universe (or concentrated universes) as there are monads—instead of which, according to Spinoza, there is one single substance only. He would be right, if there were no monads."[41] But if Spinoza were right, if all persons were not "active beings" but mere "modes" of God, then Leibnizian "universal jurisprudence" would be instantly destroyed: if there are no autonomous persons with nonillusory "wills," there cannot be "general benevolence"—for benevolence is just "good willing," and Leibniz invariably equates *benevolentia* with *caritas sapientis*. Without a certain kind of will, then, wise charity cannot serve as the heart of a justice which is more than sovereign-ordained law. (Whether Leibniz himself "saves" will, so that will can become good will, and then be equivalent to wise charity, is of course the central moral problem in his theory of substance.)

By now it is clear that for Leibniz several eminent modern thinkers (especially Hobbes and Spinoza) had drastically misconceived "substance"—and thereby, not so incidentally, deprived a wisely charitable City of God of intelligent, good-willing "citizens." And Leibniz, as is now also clear, was forced to sharpen his own notion of substance through the criticisms of Antoine Arnauld. *Le grand Arnauld* died in 1694;[42] in 1695 Leibniz published his "New System of the Nature and Communication or of Substances" in the *Journal des Savants;*[43] and soon thereafter (c. 1695–1697), he related his new theory of substance to the philosophy of yet another important modern figure, Blaise Pascal—who he thought had merely not carried the idea of a moral substance or *esprit rationel* far enough, but who had not fallen into egregious Hobbist and Spinozist errors. The Leibniz-Pascal rapport on the question of "substance" is brought out by Leibniz himself in the astonishing manuscript of c. 1695–1697, "Double Infinity in Pascal and the Monad"—a paper not even published until 1948,[44] and never before translated into English. Since the paper imaginatively amplifies Leibniz' theory of substantial forms and constitutes his most extended commentary on the greatest French religious writer and moralist of the seventeenth century, it is worth considering *in extenso* a manuscript which proves that Leibniz did not have to wait until the period of the *Monadology* (1714) to produce a "poetic" and sometimes quite fantastic version of his "New System."

Leibniz' "Double Infinity" was inspired by a celebrated passage from Pascal's *Pensées:*

> What is man in nature? A nothing in comparison with the infinite, an all in comparison with nothing, a mean between nothing and everything. . . . He is equally incapable of seeing the nothing from which he was made, and the infinite in which he is swallowed up. . . .
>
> Let man consider what he is in comparison with all existence; let him regard himself as lost in this remote corner of nature; and from the little cell in which he finds himself lodged, I mean the universe, let him estimate at their true value the earth, kingdoms, cities, and himself. What is man in the infinite?[45]

Leibniz, downplaying Pascal's implied call for fideistic humility (and ignoring his contempt for "the earth, kingdoms, cities"), seizes on *pensée* no. 72 in order to offer an extraordinarily luxuriant version of "substance":

> What M. Pascal says about the double infinity, which surrounds us while growing and while diminishing, when in his *Pensées* he speaks of the general knowledge of man, is only an entrance into my [new] system. What would he not have said, with that power of eloquence which he had, if he had come farther forward, if he had known that all matter is organic throughout, and that a portion of it (however small one compresses it) contains in a representative way, in virtue of the present diminution to infinity which it encloses, the present augmentation to infinity which is beyond it in the universe; that is to say that each small portion [of the world] contains in an infinity of ways a living mirror expressing the whole infinite universe which exists with it, so that a sufficiently great mind, armed with a sufficiently penetrating view, could see here everything that is, everywhere.[46]

But Pascal, Leibniz goes on, need not have stopped even here; and he now begins to bring up considerations which bear on the possibility of (good) willing and charitable striving. A sufficiently penetrating mind could "read" in each monad

> the entire past, and even the whole infinitely infinite future, since each moment contains an infinity of things each one of which encloses an

infinity, and since there is an infinity of moments in each hour or other part of time, and an infinity of hours, of years, of centuries, of eons, in the whole of future eternity. What an infinity of infinities infinitely replicated, what a world, what a universe, apperceptible in whatever corpuscle one cares to choose.[47]

This is extraordinary, and not just as an intimation of Kant's "starry heavens above me":[48] while half-praising Pascal for half-reaching the "new system" of substances, Leibniz asserts that infinity is so represented by (or compressed into) each monad that not only the whole past is "there" to be read (at least by an infinite mind), but the whole future. But that can be so only if all existences and all relations are fixed by a "certain" preestablished harmony. The monads in "Double Infinity" are not mere "modes" of God, à la Spinoza, or mere "effects" of God's causality, à la Hobbes—but the autonomy and spontaneity that Leibniz wants for those monads is by no means obviously saved. And if it is not, how far can Judas or Pilate or Rubicon-crossing Caesar act with wise charity? If the least monad in the cosmos encloses a certain and determined future, where is the "will" which could become *benevolentia* or *caritas sapientis*? For if (as the next passage of "Double Infinity" goes on to urge) "the whole sequence of the universe" is "placed" in "each real point which makes up a monad, or substantial unity, one of which I am myself," how far does the certainty of that universe's determined future permit "each substance" to be "truly one, unique, the original subject of life and action, always provided with perception and appetition, always including together with what it is the tendency toward what it will become?"[49] (To be sure, mere "tendency" is not morally fatal; but "certainty" and "determination" are not so innocent.)

The final paragraph of Leibniz' "Double Infinity" is both imaginative and eloquent: if, he says, a monad is "a mind, that is to say a soul capable of reflection and knowledge, it will be at once infinitely less than a God and incomparably more than the rest of the universe of creatures; feeling everything confusedly (while God knows all distinctly), knowing something distinctly (while all matter knows and feels nothing at all)." Each rational monad, he goes on to say,

> will be a small divinity and eminently a universe: God in ectype and the universe in prototype, the intelligible being always prior to the sensible in the ideas of an original intelligence, the source of things; imitating God and imitated by the universe with respect to its distinct

thoughts. Subject to God in all, and dominator of creatures, insofar as it is an imitator of God.[50]

The problem is precisely in the final clause: how far is an *imitatio dei* possible for a metaphysically evil "ectype" of God whose "confused" knowledge will lead to imperfect charity? The imaginative eloquence of "Double Infinity" does nothing to clear this up.

ANCIENTS AND MODERNS: LEIBNIZ' VIEW OF GREEK IDEAS OF SUBSTANCE IN HIS 1714 VIENNA LECTURE

If Leibniz thought that several of the most celebrated moderns had gotten "substance" wrong, and thereby left no "subjects" of universal jurisprudence—Hobbes had done this by reducing substance to body (and mind to "pressure" of objects), Spinoza by reducing substances to mere "modes" of God, without autonomy—he thought that the ancients had done much better. "I find that the philosophy of the ancients is solid, and that one should use that of the moderns to enrich it, and not to destroy it," Leibniz wrote in a 1697 letter to Joachim Bouvet. "One must consider in nature not only matter but also force, and the [substantial] forms of the ancients, or entelechies, are nothing else than forms. And by this means I believe that I have rehabilitated the philosophy of the ancients . . . without taking anything away from modern discoveries."[51]

In scattered remarks from the 1680s forward, Leibniz praises (especially) Plato for getting substance substantially right: in yet another of his letters to Arnauld (from 1687) he urges that "only individual substances and their different states are absolutely real. This Parmenides and Plato and many other ancients have indeed seen."[52] And in section 323 of the *Theodicy* one is told that "the [substantial] form or the soul has this advantage over matter, that it is the source of action, having within itself the principle of motion or change, in a word, τὸ αὐτοκίνητον, as Plato calls it."[53]

But that incidental observation in the *Theodicy* was worked up by Leibniz into a full-scale lecture, "On the Greeks as Founders of Rational Theology," which he wrote in Vienna at the same time (1714) that he produced the *Monadology* for Prince Eugene of Savoy—a lecture finally published only in 1976.[54] And in the Vienna lecture it is made very clear indeed that no moral-political philosophy can be undertaken at all unless "substance" is first correctly conceived.

Leibniz' lecture on the Greeks, which was delivered by Leibniz himself at an "Academy" in Vienna on July 1, 1714,[55] is of course interesting as evidence of the breadth of his knowledge of the history of religious ideas. But from the standpoint of political and moral philosophy its main interest lies (1) in elaborating Leibniz' debt to Platonism and (2) in showing, more particularly, that Leibniz relied on Plato (and Aristotle) in developing a monadology or concept of "substance" which would remedy the defects of "materialism" and "mechanism" and explain the immortality of the soul "naturally," without recourse to miracles or to mere "faith"—a soul which could be a subject of divine justice in Leibniz' universal jurisprudence.

It is from his first extant letter to the French Platonist Remond (January 10, 1714) that we know something of the connection between (1) and (2) in the development of Leibniz' thought: in a famous passage Leibniz says that in his youth, having learned Aristotle and having found "contentment" in Plato and Plotinus, he began to deliberate at the age of fifteen whether he would "keep the substantial forms"; that after modern "mechanism" led him to the study of mathematics, he discovered that he could not find the "final causes" *(dernières raisons)* of mechanism or the laws of motion in mathematics, that "it was necessary to return to metaphysics." It was this dissatisfaction with mechanism and materialism, Leibniz says, "which brought me to entelechies, from the material to the formal, and which finally made me understand . . . that the monads, or simple substances, are the only true substances, and that material things are only phenomena, but well-founded and well-connected ones."[56] Plato, Leibniz adds, though he had "found something" important in his notion of an immaterial *psyche* and in "looking for the source of things in final and formal causes," neglected "efficient and material" causes too much; but a more serious mistake was made by modern "materialists" who "attach themselves solely to mechanical philosophy." (Here Hobbes is plainly meant.) In his own monadology or theory of substance, Leibniz remarks, he has "brought to demonstration" truths which Plato "only advanced."[57]

Leibniz, to be sure, was no unreconstructed or perfect Platonist (as was made clear in Chapter 1). In fact Platonism, Leibniz thought, needed to be relieved of certain vestigial Pythagorean "extravagances" if its doctrine of substance was to underpin universal jurisprudence. In two separate paragraphs of the Vienna lecture, indeed, Leibniz is willing to accept only what is truly proto-Platonic in the Pythagorean theory of the natural immortality of the soul. Pythagoras, Leibniz says, diffused the doctrine, which he got "from the East," among the peoples of Greece and Italy. But to what was correct (indeed morally crucial) in the doctrine, Pythagoras added the "figment" (Leibniz speaks of *incrustamenta figmentorum*) of metempsychosis— mainly, Leibniz believes, simply out of "deference" to the "base habits" of ordinary people, who "burn less eagerly for the bare truth." Pythagoras, he says, "boasted that the transmigration of souls was divinely revealed to him, so that he was able to remember previous states." But such a doctrine, Leibniz says, is "false and no one doubts that it is mythological"; it is "vain," and even if it were true it would "reveal nothing of worth to mortals." Indeed it would be morally damaging, since souls might "migrate" away from deserved chastisements brought on by malevolence and lack of charity.[58] It was not just Pythagorean metempsychosis which was morally unacceptable to Leibniz, however: even the Platonic doctrine of "reminiscence" went too far, since "in order that knowledge, ideas, or truths be in our mind, it is not necessary that we have ever actually thought of them; they are only natural capacities." And some of Plato's followers, in Leibniz' view, abandoned "what was simpler and more solid" (though morally crucial) in Plato for "hyperbolic thoughts": Ficino, for example, "speaks everywhere only of ideas, of world-souls, of mystic numbers and of similar things, instead of following up the exact definitions of notions which Plato tried to give."[59]

That Leibniz thought the Pythagorean tradition acceptable only insofar as it was rigorously Platonic is, in any case, confirmed in published Leibnizian works: in the first of the so-called *Lettres sur Descartes et le Cartésianisme,* especially, Leibniz says of Plato that "he makes us hope for a better life with good reason, and approaches Christianity most closely. . . . It suffices to read that excellent dialogue [*Phaedo*] on the immortality of the soul or on the death of Socrates. . . . I believe that Pythagoras did the same thing and that metempsychosis was [put in] only to accommodate the vulgar."[60] And in the eleventh of his letters to the Platonist Remond (February 11, 1715) Leibniz rejects metempsychosis as incongruent with the order of the "best" world which God has justifiably chosen: "As for metempsychosis, I believe that order does not allow it at all; its rule is that everything be explicable distinctly, and that nothing happen by leaps. But the passage of the soul from one body into another would be a strange and inexplicable leap."[61]

Leibniz' consideration of the natural immortality of souls (as citizens of the divine monarchy) finally leads him, toward the end of the Vienna lecture, to a full statement of what he thinks Greek philosophy (suitably demythologized) provided in "the amplification and illustration of natural theology"—

namely, the first adequate concept of "substance." Even if, Leibniz says, some of the foundations of monadology had existed implicitly in "Eastern" ideas (above all among the Hebrews), those ideas had been "described rather obscurely" and needed to be "more distinctly expressed." The Greeks, in his view, "first brought forth a certain metaphysics (insofar as that is part of philosophy) and they recognized in an accomplished way that incorporeal substances are in God and in other minds." This is "patently clear," he goes on, "from the tradition of the Pythagoreans" and from what is reported about the philosophy of Anaxagoras, but "especially from Plato and Aristotle." For Plato, he urges, "recognized that the principle of motion could not be corporeal and that the soul is self-moved, the principle of motion, moving itself to move [*se ipsum excitans*]." Aristotle "also sought the principle, sometimes of motion, sometimes even of thought, in incorporeal substances," and he not only attributed intelligence to heavenly bodies but also recognized "that the intellect acting in man is something external to the body, and separable."[62]

Now much of this simply reinforces what is known in Leibniz' more familiar writings. In an important letter to Arnauld on substance as an "indivisible and naturally indestructible being" (1686) Leibniz praises the ancients, "and particularly Plato, who showed quite clearly that matter alone does not suffice to form a substance."[63] And in the second of the *Lettres sur Descartes* he goes so far as to say that "Plato explains divinely well incorporeal substances distinct from matter and ideas independent of the senses."[64] (In that sentence there is a double anti-Hobbism: Leibniz defends the "incorporeal substances" which Hobbes scornfully rejected as incoherent Gothic "Aristotelity," and maintains that ideas are "independent of the senses." And in the Vienna lecture he praises Plato and Aristotle for "restoring reason" to a condition of "immateriality.")[65]

Leibniz' lauding of the Greek philosophers as the founders of a "natural theology" which can be "investigated by the force of human genius" is certainly understandable if one recalls the central place which Leibniz' theory of substance or monadology occupies in his philosophy—in his moral philosophy as much as in his metaphysics. That is clear in the finest single paragraph of his *Memoir for Enlightened Persons of Good Intention*:

As for me, I put forward the great principle of metaphysics as well as of morality, that the world is governed by the most perfect intelligence which is possible, which means that one must consider it as a universal monarchy whose head is all-powerful and sovereignly wise, and whose subjects are all minds, that is, substances capable of relations or society with God; and that all the rest is only the instrument of the glory of God and of the felicity of minds, and that as a result the entire universe is made for minds.[66]

"The intellectual world (which is nothing else than the republic of the universe or the City of God)," Leibniz adds, "is so important that the whole system of bodies seems to be made only for *le monde intellectuel*."[67] Small wonder, then, that Leibniz should take so strong an interest in the first appearance of the idea of "rational substance" in Greek philosophy; for much of his own monadology echoes "the substantial form of the ancients" (to Jaquelot, 1703).[68]

The notion that persons as rational substances or minds are subjects of a "kingdom of grace" (of which God is the monarch)[69] leads back to a morally crucial earlier point in Leibniz' Vienna lecture. As was pointed out, the concept of natural immortality is a key point in Leibniz' universal jurisprudence—if rational beings are to receive what their actions are worth and if justice is not simply a legal concept confined to the "human forum" alone. As Leibniz put it in a letter to Bierling,

> I find it very bad that celebrated people, such as Pufendorf and [Christian] Thomasius, teach that one knows the immortality of the soul, as well as the pains and rewards which await us beyond this life, only through revelation. . . . All doctrines of morals, of justice, of duties which are based only on the goods of this life, can be only very imperfect. Take away the [natural] immortality of the soul, and the doctrine of providence is useless, and has no more power to obligate men than the gods of Epicurus, which are without providence.[70]

Leibniz conceived his debt to Plato, Aristotle, and Pythagoras, then, in terms of their having "more distinctly expressed" the idea of the natural immortality of substances which had existed only "obscurely" in Eastern religious thought. Leibniz' universal jurisprudence, which involves a "moral realm" within the "natural realm" in which all rational substances act justly— through the charity of the wise—requires a theory of natural immortality which (according to the Vienna lecture) received its first adequate expression at the hands of Greek philosophy. "One cannot doubt," Leibniz argues in his *Opinion on the Principles of Pufendorf*, "that the ruler of the universe, at once most wise and most powerful, has allotted rewards for the good and punishments for the wicked, and that his plan will be put into effect in a future life, since in present life many crimes remain without punishment and many good deeds without recompense."[71] (This "monarchy of minds under this great master," he adds, "must not be less lawful than a human empire: and in consequence it is necessary that virtues be rewarded and vices punished under this government—something which does not happen sufficiently in this life.")[72] But this universal jurisprudence is plausible only if "it is possible to demonstrate the immortality of the soul by natural reason."[73] And the 1714 Vienna lecture makes it clear how very much of that "demonstration" Leibniz thought could be traced to Plato and Aristotle. (At the end of the lecture Leibniz even says that while God used "the Hebrew race initially as if it were a kind of tool standing for highest providence," he finally "kindled a new light for the human race by infusing Greek minds with a love of wisdom, so that divine truths might be communicated with certain proofs against all doubts of men, progressing through the centuries to a greater subtlety of thinking."[74] With respect to philosophical adequacy, then, for Leibniz, the Greeks are even more divinely "chosen" than the Jews. And what Greek "subtlety" established was the foundations of monadology.)

Leibniz' bold claim that God "used the Hebrew race" only "initially" before kindling "new light" in the shape of Greek *philosophia*—a kind of philosophical "new testament" displacing the old—reveals again how Leibniz characteristically subordinates revelation (as something limited and "historical") to a reason which is universally available to all rational substances. Revelation, the Vienna lecture urges, was provided by God for "simpler men (who were less educated in the precepts of philosophy) through the revelations of the prophets," but Greek philosophia rests on "certain proofs" and "greater subtlety of thinking." (And so to St. Paul's contemptuous question in 1 Corinthians, "Where is the wise?,"[75] Leibniz' answer would be summary: in Athens. Leibniz' "Platonic rationalism" always outweighs mere Scripture—as will be seen more completely when Leibniz' version of "religion within the limits of reason alone" is taken up in Chapter 3.)

SUBSTANCE: PLATO AND ARISTOTLE AGAINST HOBBES AND LOCKE

Sometimes Leibniz uses a "Platonic" notion of substance not just to establish the idea of a moral subject (or citizen of the divine monarchy), but to defeat the Lockean notion that there is nothing in the understanding which has not come from the senses; that, for Leibniz, is almost as bad as "Hobbism"—and he makes that clear in his celebrated 1702 letter to the Queen of Prussia (his former pupil) which is sometimes given the title, "On What Is Independent of Sensation in Knowledge."[76] In this letter he affirms Plato and denies Locke, and relates both to his idea of substance and of moral relations.

"This thought of 'I,'" Leibniz urges, "who distinguishes himself from sensible objects, and of my own action which results from it, adds something to the objects of the senses"—such as the idea of moral necessity, which the senses will never "see." And since, he continues, "I conceive that other beings can also have the right to say 'I' (or one could say it for them), it is by this that I conceive what is called substance in general"; and it is also "the consideration of myself which furnishes me with other notions of metaphysics, such as cause, effect, action, similitude, etc., and even of logic and of morality." Thus, Leibniz insists, one can say that "there is nothing in the understanding which has not come from the senses, except the understanding itself, or he who understands."[77]

With that last sentence, which sums up the main thrust of the *New Essays Concerning Human Understanding* (written a year later),[78] Leibniz at once reaffirms an adequate notion of rational substance—as a being who has the "right" to say "I" (a moral entitlement) and who does not just passively receive "impressions" in the manner of a plant—and justifies Greek antiquity against English modernity. A great deal is packed into the opening page of the 1702 letter to the Queen of Prussia; it is a tiny *summa* of much Leibnizian doctrine. Not only that: much of it looks forward to what Kant will say in the *Critique of Pure Reason* (1781).[79]

"Being itself, and truth, are not entirely learned through the senses," Leibniz goes on to say. "For it would not be impossible that a creature have long and ordered dreams, resembling our life, such that all that one believed to perceive through the senses would only be pure appearances." It is for this reason that "we need, then, something beyond the senses, which distinguishes the true from the apparent." But here, Leibniz hopes, "the truth of the demonstrative sciences" such as mathematics, logic, and ethics may "serve to judge the truth of sensible things." For as "able philosophers both ancient and modern" have correctly remarked, even if "all that I believe that I see should be only a dream," it would nonetheless "remain always true that 'I' who think while dreaming would be something, and would think effectively in many ways, for which there must always be some reason."[80]

It is for these reasons, Leibniz continues, that "that which the ancient Platonists have remarked, is quite true and very worthy of being considered"—namely, that "the existence of intelligible things and particularly of this 'I' who thinks and which is called mind or soul is incomparably more certain than the existence of sensible things," and that, therefore, "it would not be impossible, speaking with metaphysical rigor, that there should be at bottom only these intelligible substances, and that sensible things are only appearances." But, Leibniz complains, our "lack of attention" makes us "take sensible things for the only true ones."[81] And this is exactly the demi-Platonic language of the *New Essays:* "You do not see justice as you see a horse, but you understand it no less, or rather you understand it better."[82]

Very radically, Leibniz goes on to assert that one need not even be awake to see that the "English" view of knowledge (including moral knowledge) cannot be right:

> It is also good to notice that if I found some demonstrative truth, mathematical or otherwise, while dreaming (as can indeed happen), it would be just as certain as if I were awake. Which makes it clear how much intelligible truth is independent of the truth or existence of sensible and material things outside of us.[83]

Leibniz then, having stressed the necessity of mathematics, insists that the necessity of morality is "seen" through extrasensory *lumière naturelle:* "for example, one can say that there are charitable people who are not just, which happens when charity is not sufficiently regulated . . . for in justice is comprised at the same time charity and the rule of reason. It is by *lumière naturelle* also that one recognizes the axioms of mathematics."[84] As usual, Leibniz as demi-Platonist uses, back to back, moral and mathematical examples of what rational "substances" know through "natural light," independently of sense-impressions. The Plato of *Meno* and *Phaedo* is again supported, Locke again criticized. And in the end Locke is subjected to a weaker version of the criticism which Leibniz had leveled against Hobbes: that British "empiricism," with its passive notion of a material substance which is only receptive, cannot account for (a) the conceivability of moral ideas; (b) the notion of a self with the "right to say 'I' "; (c) the self-determining activity (going beyond passive receptivity) of a self-so-conceived. ("The idea of substance, which one needs" in order to understand the notion of "the person," Leibniz complains, vanishes in English thought. "*Ces messieurs* who follow the new style of reasoning have banished substance from the reasonable world.")[85] This shows again (if further proof were needed) that for Leibniz an adequately conceived substance or monad is the substratum of all further reasoning about morality and justice. Thus the "monadology" is the *Grundlegung* of *caritas sapientis:* only a rational substance can understand the idea of what ought to be, and strive to bring it about. At least on this point, then, Leibniz would agree with Kant that "a truly philosophical jurist" will applaud the inquiry into "the ultimate principles" of philosophy which undergird "the principles of right."[86]

IS LEIBNIZ' THEORY OF SUBSTANTIAL FREEDOM "ARISTOTELIAN"?

If Leibniz' Platonic rationalism—modified by Pauline charity and Augustinian good will to the point that *caritas sapientis* is equivalent to *benevolentia universalis*—is familiar enough, the connection between Leibniz and Aristotle is stressed rather less (both by Leibniz himself and by later interpreters). It is thus a matter of some interest when René Sève says, in *Leibniz et l'école moderne du droit naturel,* that Leibniz' position on the freedom of rational substances constitutes "a reprise of the Aristotelian conception of liberty," in opposition to "the modern [Cartesian] conception of indifference."[87] Sève is arguably only half-correct: he is right about Leibniz' rejection of a Cartesian "indifferent" will which (willfully) determines itself without "sufficient reason," but he is misleading about Leibniz' alleged Aristotelianism.

To take the second matter first, Sève starts well by urging that Leibniz' conception of liberty, like Aristotle's, begins with principles which guide the diurnal practice of "legislators and jurisconsults"; but Sève takes a questionable turn when he goes on to insist that "the two elements retained by Leibniz to define free action, spontaneity and choice, are of Aristotelian inspiration."[88] (And he then cites Aristotle's *Rhetoric:* "We accomplish voluntarily all that we do in knowing it and in not being forced.")[89] But one can reasonably doubt that this passage from Aristotle wholly captures Leibniz' difficulties with will and freedom, for in Leibniz "knowing" itself is constrained by intellectual limitation or metaphysical evil which leads mere "inattention" to become (somehow) a positive moral evil—the "privative" spills over (in a never fully specified way) into *le mal moral.*[90] Moreover, while Leibnizian rational substances are not constrained or "forced" from without—by the pressure of "outward objects," as in Hobbes—nonetheless their "complete concept" eternally determines (and makes "certain") the whole of what they will do in fact.

Caesar could have refrained from crossing the Rubicon and destroying the Republic only if his "predicates" had been different.[91] (Leibnizian monads do not, à la Sartre, make their own essences[92] through anguished "existential" choices in Left Bank cafés.) Aristotle, so far as one can judge, simply did not worry about reconciling human freedom with "divine determination"— whether that determination consists in the Leibnizian notion that the idea of every monad is "imbedded" in the divine understanding from eternity, or in the Leibnizian argument that God determines the temporal existence of every monad as part of a harmonious "best" cosmos. There are, so to speak, "Christian difficulties" in Leibniz' ethics which cannot be overcome simply by appealing to what is "Aristotelian" in his practical thought. In Aristotle's *Ethics* the gods finally make a belated appearance only in Book 10 (and have no visible bearing on Aristotle's theory of human freedom and accountability in earlier books);[93] in Leibniz God is the only necessary being, and the activity of all creatures must be reconciled with divine determination.

Had Leibniz not been fully aware of this difficulty himself, he would never have made the distinction between "metaphysical necessity" and "moral necessity" central:[94] for Leibniz it is morally sufficient that Pilate's condemnation of Christ, while "certain" and "determined," was not geometrically necessary. Aristotle never drew such a distinction because he never had to; in that sense his account of human freedom is completely naturalistic. (Certainly it contains no supernatural element, such as divine grace accorded without regard to merit. Aristotle, indeed, would have regarded such an undeserved gift as unjust.)[95]

But if Sève is arguably incorrect to view Leibniz' account of substantial freedom as unproblematically Aristotelian, he is quite right to say that Leibniz always opposed the more-or-less Cartesian notion of an "indifferent" will which determines itself groundlessly, out of a kind of libertarian bravado—so that in Cartesianism *la volonté a ses raisons que la raison ne connaît point*. It is various Cartesians who are being complained of when Leibniz says that

> one will have it that the will is alone active and supreme, and one is wont to imagine it to be like a queen seated on her throne, whose minister of state is the understanding, while the passions are her courtiers or favorite ladies, who by their influence often prevail over the counsel of her ministers. . . . But it is a personification or a mythology somewhat ill-conceived. If the will is to judge, or take cognizance of

the reasons and inclinations which the understanding or the senses offer it, it will need another understanding in itself, to understand what it is offered.[96]

For Leibniz, then, Buridan's ass will never starve—because there can be no indifferent "equipoise" in the world (with no "sufficient reason" for choice).[97]

But if one spurns "Cartesian" indifferent will, as Leibniz does, that does not automatically reenthrone Aristotle in the vacant place of the irrational queen: for between Aristotle and Descartes stands the whole Christian tradition from Augustine and Aquinas to Suarez—the tradition to which Leibniz belongs in no small measure, despite his intellectual Hellenophilia. And it was that tradition which had to reconcile human freedom and divine determination. So one can accept only in a very qualified form Sève's assertion that "the moral philosophy of Leibniz constitutes a return to Aristotelo-Thomism, that is to say to an antivoluntarist doctrine of law and a naturalistic conception of liberty."[98] For while Leibniz' "antivoluntarism" is very clear indeed, and serves as the basis of his equation of Hobbes and Thrasymachus (*stat pro ratione voluntas*[99]), it is not at all obvious that this antivoluntarism is more Aristotelian than Platonic; and Thomas Aquinas was no simple "naturalist" in ethics—that would have been heretical given the post-Augustinian subordination of nature to grace,[100] and so the phrase "Aristotelo-Thomism" is in itself worrying. In any case it was Plato, not Aristotle, who was treated as a kind of honorary proto-saint by Augustinian Christianity—perhaps because the notion of a truth-loving, non-willful divinity in *Euthyphro* could be used by those who wanted to cut back the scope of sheer "Creation," who wanted to say that God creates existence but not "essence."[101] Leibniz' antivoluntarism descends more obviously from *Euthyphro,* via Augustine and Grotius, than from anything in "Aristotelo-Thomism." (This Sève himself has now acknowledged in his excellent *Leibniz: Le droit de la raison* [1994], saying that "the repeated references of Leibniz to Aristotle . . . should not disguise his global Platonism," and that "Leibniz presents himself quite particularly, if not as a neo-Platonist, then at least as the representative of a renewed Platonism.")[102]

LEIBNIZ' "CONVERSATION SUR LA LIBERTÉ" (C. 1699–1703)

Despite a frequently appearing "Platonic" tendency to view will as a mere outgrowth of *Verstand,* as correct judgment, Leibniz most of the time needs and uses "will" in a more expansive Augustinian sense. But it has already been seen that genuine freedom is problematical for him, given that everything in the "best" world is (once divinely chosen) hypothetically necessary, certain, and determined; it will "never happen" that a (logically possible) "different" Caesar will spring up once time is launched by God. This was restated with forceful economy in an important Leibnizian letter of December 1707 to Pierre Coste:

> . . . the whole universe could be made otherwise. . . . God has chosen from an infinity of possibilities that which he judged to be the most suitable [*convenable*]. But once he has chosen, one must grant that everything is included in his choice, and that nothing can be changed, since he has foreseen and regulated everything once and for all . . . such that sins and evils, which he has judged it appropriate to permit for the greatest goods, are included in some fashion in his choice. It is this necessity which one can attribute to things to come, which one calls hypothetical or consequential . . . [but] does not destroy the contingency of things and does not produce that absolute necessity which contingency cannot suffer.[103]

If the question now becomes, Does Leibniz find a freedom in rational monads which is sufficient to his own benevolent moral and political purposes? Does he make it possible, say, for Pontius Pilate to begin to act with greater "wise charity" by freeing Christ and detaining Barabbas?, the answer to that question can only be determined by looking at Leibniz' most coherent, continuous, forceful exposition of his attempted salvation of "contingency" and "spontaneity" in the remarkable "Conversation sur la liberté" (c. 1699–1703).[104] And since the "Conversation" has never been translated into English, it will be helpful to offer substantial fragments of this work while evaluating its claims. Leibniz begins with an assertion which is familiar from the "Discourse on Metaphysics" and the correspondence with Arnauld:

> Necessary is that, the opposite or the nonexistence of which is impossible or implies a contradiction; or again, necessary is that which could not not be; and contingent is that which can not be or whose nonexistence does not imply the slightest contradiction. In consequence the whole universe and all that which is found there is contingent and could be otherwise. But if a single form [*manière*] of the universe were possible, or again if everything possible happened, the universe would be neces-

sary; and that is the opinion of Hobbes, of Spinoza, of some ancients, and perhaps of M. Descartes.[105]

Leibniz then goes on to relate his notion of "compossibility" to what he has just said about necessity and contingency:

> But since it is not credible, or even possible, that all stories appear together and become true histories in some [actual] world, one must judge thereby, and for many reasons, that the world or the universe could be made in an infinity of ways, and that of these God has chosen the best. That is why, absolutely speaking, every matter of fact, the whole world and everything that happens in it, is contingent; and one can say that all the things in the world are without absolute necessity, but that they are not without all hypothetical necessity or connection. For, God having once chosen this arrangement, and foreseeing or rather regulating everything in advance, one can say that, this posed, everything is necessary hypothetically or following this supposition. . . . But, if there is no absolute necessity in passing things, one must always grant that everything there is is absolutely certain and determined.[106]

But Leibniz wants to be sure that, despite this certainty and determination, "contingency," "spontaneity," and "voluntariness" are somehow preserved; and so he goes on to say that "while we act with spontaneity insofar as an action is in us" (in our complete concept), and while "we are not without life and have no need to be pushed like marionettes" (as if we were Spinozist "modes"), and while "our spontaneity is conjoined with knowledge or deliberation or choice, which renders our action voluntary," nonetheless "one must grant that we are always predetermined, and that, besides our previous inclinations or dispositions, new impressions of objects also contribute to incline us."[107] (That last, "Hobbesian" clause cannot be taken literally, given the doctrine of the *Monadology* that "changes of the monads come from an internal principle, since an external cause can have no influence upon their inner being.")[108] Leibniz then goes on to mount a further assault on Cartesian "indifferent" will, urging that "an absolute indifference without any prevailing inclination (if it were possible)" is so far from being a privilege that it is "rather an absurdity"; for God himself, "who is the perfect being, is also the most determined to act in a way conformed to supreme reason."[109]

But if this argument saves the possibility of God's wise charity and benevolence—and it will be seen in Chapter 3 that for Leibniz "supreme reason" itself dictates the practice of those virtues—Leibniz is perfectly aware that for finite creatures suffering from "privation" and metaphysical evil, matters are not so straightforward.

> But, someone will say, if all is certain and determined, it is quite useless that I strive to do well, for whatever I do, what must happen will happen. . . . But the response is ready at hand: if it is determined that someone shall be ruined, that will happen, no doubt—but not whatever he does, for he will be the worker of his fortune, and if he neglects himself, he will himself ruin himself.[110]

Here the language is oddly equivocal: in what sense is a determined person the "worker" or maker of "his own" fortune? Perhaps because of such difficulties, Leibniz now tries to shrink the compass of "will" in a way that is briefly reminiscent of the Spinoza whom he had so often attacked—the Spinoza who urged that free will or self-determination is an illusion arising from inadequate knowledge of determining causes.[111] "We imagine ourselves," Leibniz now says, "to have a power to believe and to will what we want," but this alleged power cannot exist; for we do not "will to will, but to make, and to have." Echoing not only Spinoza but Hobbes, he asserts that "we do not at all choose our wills, because that would be by other wills, and that to infinity"—the same infinite regress of "willing to will" which Hobbes had attacked as a Scholastic "absurdity." In any choice, Leibniz continues (here reverting to Spinoza) the will "has its causes, but since we are ignorant of them and they are often-enough hidden, we believe ourselves independent—as we walk and leap without thinking that the circulation of the blood is necessary thereto."[112] This passage, astonishingly, could be set down in Spinoza's *Ethics* or Hobbes' *Leviathan,* as could the conclusion of Leibniz' paragraph: "It is this chimera of an imaginary independence which revolts us against the consideration of determination, and which brings us to believe that there are difficulties when there are none." And in the next paragraph he wavers between early Augustinian voluntariness and Spinozist "imagination": "it is true that we have spontaneity in us, and that we are the masters of our actions, that is to say, we choose what we will"; but at the same time "we will that which we find good, which depends on our taste."[113] Here again defective judgment, which may recommend what we "find good" though it is actually bad, makes "good will" a serious problem—and especially serious, again, in one who equates *caritas sapientis* with universal *benevolentia.* (Someone who knew Leibniz solely through the "Conversation sur la liberté" might easily agree with Bertrand Russell's view that Leibniz was really a closet Spinozist who used "discreditable subterfuges" to save the appearance of moral orthodoxy.)[114]

At the end of the "Conversation sur la liberté" Leibniz turns from human will and freedom back to God, and to his choice of a "best" world which is nonetheless full of evils; and he stresses once again the notion that evil is a negative "privation."

> Some people, not being able to deny these principles or fabricate another system which is sustainable, declaim against the consequences, without understanding it well: they say that in this way nothing would be praiseworthy or blameable, and that God would be unjust, cruel, the author of evil. . . . In granting that God has chosen the best [world] as his perfection demands, it is necessary that the permitting of sin be better than its exclusion, since it has come about. . . . One cannot say either that God does evil, for the good, perfection, positive reality, come from him alone—the borders or limits which are something negative (since they deny an ulterior perfection) being the fault of creatures, since they are finite, [and] alone cause ignorance, malice, and evil.[115]

The end of that passage is of course very worrying, especially in a philosopher who defines morality through charity and benevolence: finitude is a fault only in the sense that a "fault" in the earth is "faulty"; and the final clause runs ignorance, malice and evil indiscriminately together. But how can a "faulty" creature "cause" its own ignorance? (Here one sees the force of Kant's observation, in "On the Failure of All Attempted Philosophical Theodicies" [1791], that if there is "moral evil in the world" but God is held to be "innocent of it by saying that this evil is inevitable since it rests on the limitations of men as finite beings," then "we should stop calling it a moral evil" because "guilt for it cannot be attributed to me.")[116]

Having in effect foreseen the key argument of the *Theodicy* in a single phrase—"God has chosen the best [world] as his perfection demands"—Leibniz now also anticipates the later work's defense of God's justice in fashioning "the best." If someone wants to exploit the existence of evil in the best world "to overturn the divine perfections, and destroy God himself by denying his power or at least his prescience," Leibniz urges, "it is easy to show him that there is no need to go to these extremes, which are in any case absurd"—for "God has found sin and the other evils which happen enclosed in the idea of this possible universe, which he has judged the best, and which he wills because of what is good in it, beyond any other." Thus "one cannot say at all that he wills, but only that he permits, evil and misery, which could not be excluded from it without choosing another universe, but which . . . would not be the best."[117] But if God has "found" sin "enclosed" in the best world, he must have found sinners there as well (no sin without sinners); could those "determined" sinners have moved toward wise charity through increased "good will"? And if not, can one reasonably say that they ought to have done so?

KANT'S CRITIQUE OF LEIBNIZIAN FREEDOM

Leibniz' argument for the freedom which makes charity and benevolence possible—namely, that "contingency" is preserved provided there is no "metaphysical necessity" operating, so that Judas' betrayal of Christ, while certain and determined, is not geometrically necessary[118]—is unpersuasive especially from a Kantian point of view, which requires the possibility of beginning to do what one ought to do at any and every moment: it requires "absolute" spontaneity. (As Kant puts it in the *Prolegomena to Any Future Metaphysics*, freedom must be—with respect to "events" in the world—"a faculty of starting them spontaneously.")[119] By contrast in Leibniz Judas "could have" acted differently (and better) only if his "complete concept" included that different and better action, from eternity: Leibniz is clear that once the "best" world is chosen (for the sufficient reason that it is best), it has a "hypothetical" necessity and everything in it is certain and determined.

To be sure, Kant is able to posit radical freedom or perfect spontaneity because he is unconstrained by God or causality: for Kant God's real existence is indemonstrable (though atheism is also "dogmatic")[120] and therefore we cannot conceive the "complete concept" of Judas Iscariot or Francis of Assisi as "imbedded" (together with the eternal verities and logical possibilities) in the mind of God, awaiting "translation" into existence as part of a "compossible" best world; we simply cannot think that way, except dogmatically, on the Kantian view. For Kant we cannot know the complete concept of anyone or anything;[121] much less can we know that concept as determining existential "choice" in time.

As for causality, Kant's argument is that—given our finite human understanding—we cannot know causality to be anything more than a "category of understanding" which we unavoidably use in fashioning a coherent "experience" from a flood of undifferentiated sense-data: the world is causal for us (universally, intersubjectively) but no one will ever (as it were) see around the edges of human understanding to glimpse the "real world" as it may be *an sich*.[122] Since Kant excludes knowledge of God and knowledge of causality, he can posit radical freedom and absolute autonomy as inferences from known "moral necessity"—a moral necessity now unfettered by alleged "metaphysical necessity" and "metaphysical evil." For Kant we know the apodeictic certainty of "oughtness" (which enjoins respect for persons as members of the Kingdom of Ends), and we can and must take ourselves to be free, spontaneously able to accomplish what "ought" to be through the injunctions of the moral law.

> The question now is whether our knowledge of the unconditionally practical [moral] takes its inception from freedom or from the practical law. It cannot start from freedom, for this we can neither know immediately . . . nor infer from experience, since experience reveals to us only the law of appearances and consequently the mechanism of nature, the direct opposite of freedom. It is therefore the moral law . . . which first presents itself to us; and since reason exhibits it as a ground of determination which is completely independent of and not to be outweighed by any sensuous condition, it is the moral law which leads directly to the concept of freedom.[123]

Of course one can reasonably wonder where Kant "gets" the apodeictic certainty of moral law: for some (such as Karl Ameriks)[124] he just dogmatically asserts the objective reality of "oughtness." But the present point is that if one is a Kantian, one need not worry (with Hobbes) that divine "irresistible" power may make free agency or self-determination in a creature an impious "absurdity";[125] if one is a Kantian one need not worry (with Leibniz) that the eternally given complete concept of a person rules out truly spontaneous change while the world is unfolding with certainty according to God's "best" plan. But Kantian freedom is (to recall Beck's phrase) "hard doctrine"[126]—too hard for those seventeenth-century figures who would not have given up God or causality (or rather would not have reduced them to *façons de penser* whose "objective reality" remains indemonstrable).

Since, nonetheless, Kant and Leibniz share so much—above all a "Platonic" conviction that only reason can furnish moral "ideas," and an "Augustinian" conviction that "good will" is central to good morality—it is worth a little further effort to see what joins and what divides the two greatest

Enlightenment Germans to descend from a tradition of "Christian Plato-nism."

In the *Critique of Pure Reason*, Kant argues for the freedom that makes morality possible ("if our will is not free . . . moral ideas and principles lose all validity").[127] And in the "Antinomy of Pure Reason" (A533/B561), he goes on to say that freedom is "the power of beginning a state spontaneously."[128] If there is to be true spontaneity or "absolute origination," a free act will not "stand under another cause determining it in time, as required by the law of nature." Freedom as undetermined spontaneity is "a pure transcendental idea" that is "not given by any [empirical] experience."[129] Kant adds, in an important aside, that the notion of spontaneity may arise, perhaps paradoxi-cally, out of reflection on causality, spontaneity's antithesis: caused things are understood as having causes, but if one traces backward through an endless regress of causes and effects one is left unsatisfied because there is no "un-conditioned" necessity. Because of this unsatisfying conditionality of every-thing merely caused, reason, tired of "always having one foot in the air," creates for itself "the idea of a spontaneity which can begin to act of itself."[130] The only problem is that this particular "spontaneity"—God—cannot be shown really to exist. What separates Kant definitively from Leibniz (despite their Platonic and Augustinian overlappings) is God: for Leibniz God exists *ex necessitatis* (since Anselm's "ontological" proof is true), and all other beings in the cosmos are "ideas" or complete concepts in the mind of God translated into existence. Moreover (as was seen in Chapter 1) Leibniz holds that God is the "ground" though not the cause of "eternal moral verity."[131] For Kant these Leibnizian claims are simply "transcendent"—they attempt to go be-yond what can conceivably be known by us.

But if, for Kant, we cannot know the "spontaneity" of God, we must assume it in ourselves (provided no one can demonstrate its impossibility) if we do not want to suffer "the elimination of all practical freedom."

> For practical freedom presupposes that although something has not happened, it *ought* to have happened, and that its cause, [as found] in the field of appearance, is not therefore so determining that it excludes a causality of our will—a causality which, independently of those natural causes, and even contrary to their force and influence, can produce something that is determined in the time-order in accordance with empirical laws, and which can therefore begin a series of events *entirely of itself*. . . . That our reason has [such] causality . . . is evident

from the imperatives which in matters of conduct we impose as rules upon our active powers.[132]

There is, in Kant's view, only one way to save nature and freedom equally; and that way is stated in the Preface to the second edition (1787) of *Pure Reason*. The primary service which the *Critique* renders, Kant argues, is that of drawing a distinction between "appearances" and "things in themselves," between *phenomena* and *noumena*. And the point of the distinction is to make freedom possible: for if one fails to draw a distinction between *phenomena* and *noumena* then "all things in general . . . would be determined by the principle of causality, and consequently by the mechanism of nature." There is only one way in which "the doctrine of morality and the doctrine of nature may each . . . make good its position," and that is by recalling that anything in the world "is to be taken in a twofold sense, namely as appearance and as thing in itself." And given that twofold sense, "there is no contradiction in supposing" that "one and the same will is, in appearance, necessarily subject to the law of nature [causality], and so far not free, while yet, as belonging to a thing in itself, is not subject to that law, and is therefore free."[133] (Here, ironically enough, Kant uses a Platonic-Leibnizian distinction between appearance and reality to make a moral point that Leibniz would reject: for Leibniz the world of appearance is indeed only "well-founded phenomena,"[134] but any noumena would be eternally imbedded in the mind of God, and scarcely "absolutely" spontaneous.)

Kant has all of this in mind when he elaborates the formula, "phenomenally caused, noumenally free" later in the "Antinomy of Pure Reason" (A536/B564). The central question, for Kant, is whether natural causality is such that "freedom is completely excluded by this inviolable rule," or whether something (such as a human voluntary action) "may not at the same time be grounded in freedom." For if, Kant goes on, appearances are things in themselves, then "freedom cannot be upheld." But then a kind of moral bravery leads Kant to say, "Let us take our stand, and regard it as at least possible for reason to have causality with respect to appearances."[135] To be sure, reason's "causality"—our acting from a moral law given by reason—will appear as an effect in the phenomenal world: if one refrains, out of respect for a nonpathological, rational imperative, from performing a wished-for murder, if one's wish never becomes one's will, there will then be a gap in the phenomenal world (an absent corpse)—a gap that would have been filled had one permitted "pathology" to have its way.

For it may be that all that has happened in the course of nature . . . ought not to have happened. Sometimes, however, we find, or at least believe that we find, that the ideas of reason have in actual fact proved their causality in respect of the actions of men, as appearances; and that these actions have taken place, not because they were determined by empirical causes, but because they were determined by grounds of reason.[136]

If the key notion is "determined by grounds of reason"—by the moral law as a so-called fact of reason *(Faktum der Vernunft)*[137]—then it is of course not sufficient to be merely "negatively" free or not naturally determined; negative freedom must be the foundation of positive freedom, of self-determination or "will" through "grounds of reason." Practical reason, Kant insists, must "be described in positive terms, as the power of originating a series of events."

In reason itself nothing begins; as unconditioned condition of every voluntary act, it admits no conditions antecedent to itself in time. Its effect has, indeed, a beginning in the series of appearances, but never in this series an absolutely first beginning.[138]

The last claim is crucial, since the reason which can be practical (by issuing "imperatives") is "not subject to the form of time."[139] For it does not (suddenly, as it were) become the case that persons ought to be respected as "objective ends" in themselves, as the "limiting condition" of our free willing. If a particular person begins to take timeless moral truth as the motive of his will, then the outward manifestations of his newly moral activity will indeed have "a beginning in the series of appearances"; but the practical reason which serves as the ground of his will is "not itself an appearance," and is therefore not conditioned by time or causality, which bear only on (our understanding of) *phenomena*.[140] (Leibniz would of course agree with Kant that "moral necessity" is given by a reason which is "not subject to the form of time"; here they are both "Platonists." But for Leibniz such moral necessity would be co-eternal with a knowable God. And the "will" which one needs to follow moral necessity spontaneously remains problematical in Leibniz.)

Kant's theory of will and freedom is thus a kind of skepticized Pelagianism:[141] God is initially imagined by reason as "absolute originator," but only persons can be known (through morality as "fact of reason") as truly spontaneous. A single first cause is thus replaced by as many first causes as there are autonomous wills. All persons must be the "intelligible causes" of their own acts; otherwise one could not speak of those acts as "their own." If Kant is right, then the concept of a positively free will, self-determining through reason-given "objective ends" that we "ought to have," need not be "adjusted" to God or causality: for God is transcendent, and causality only a category of understanding. That is why Kant can avoid altogether the kinds of difficulties that tormented not only Leibniz but even Pascal in the wonderfully eloquent *Écrits sur la grâce:* "The question is that of knowing which of these two wills, namely, the will of God or the will of man, is the ruling one, the dominant one, the source, the principle and the cause of the other."[142] Pascal works out his own quasi-Augustinian answer with the expected subtlety; but Kant would say that the question cannot even be asked, because God and his will are transcendent for us: the only truly spontaneous causality known by us is our own "moral causality." For Kant one cannot even say, with the Molinists, that God's will "concurs" with our own, let alone that it causes it. As he argues in the *Lectures on Philosophical Theology* (1783–84), it is "not in the least conceivable how God might concur in our actions," despite our freedom, or how he "could concur as a cooperating cause of our will." For then "we would not be the author of our own actions, or at least not wholly so."[143] (In that last phrase the difference between Kant and Leibniz is patent: for Leibniz created substances cannot be "wholly" the authors of their actions, and must content themselves with the thought that their actions are "contingent" rather than "necessary." For Kant spontaneity entails absolute self-determination; for Leibniz it just means that actions unfold in time from a "complete concept," without external constraint.)

It is because of his insistence on absolute spontaneity that Kant can insist, in a celebrated passage from *Religion within the Limits of Reason Alone,* that

> In the search for the rational origin of evil actions every such action must be regarded as though the individual had fallen into it directly from a state of innocence. . . . [An evil-doer] should have refrained from that action, whatever his temporal circumstances and entanglements; for through no cause in the world can he cease to be a freely acting being. . . . It was not only his duty to have been better, it is now still his duty to better himself. To do so *must* be within his power. . . . Hence we cannot inquire into the temporal origin of his deed, but solely into its rational origin.[144]

After insisting, boldly, that inherited or transmitted "original sin" is the "most inept" and freedom-destroying way of accounting for the origin of evil[145]—Leibniz too had reservations about original sin but was cautious in questioning it—Kant finally insists that moral evil arises from neither Adam nor Satan, from neither "metaphysical evil" nor sheer "privation" (as an eternal possibility in the mind of God), but simply from the fact that a person whom we must "take" to be free "does not will to withstand" inclinations contrary to the moral law "when they tempt him to transgress."[146] The Fall, in short, is our own Creation. (Leibniz, for all of his Platonic rationalism, was not about to sweep crucial Christian "mysteries" such as Creation and the Fall away—even if he found them rather embarrassing.)

One might think—to say it only in passing—that an intuitively attractive moral doctrine might be formed using Kantian and Leibnizian fragments: that Leibniz might furnish the substance of morality (wise charity or universal benevolence) and that Kant might provide the true freedom or real self-determination which makes it possible to be benevolent. This is ruled out, however, by Leibniz' *in esse* principle, since the "complete concept" of every person is eternally given, and makes all action (good or bad) "certain." But such a *rapprochement* is ruled out even more decisively by Kant's antipathologism: after all, for Kant, love is merely a "feeling" which cannot be commanded: hence in *Religion within the Limits* he converts the Christian maxim "Love thy neighbor" into the injunction to respect fellow-men as members of the Kingdom of Ends.[147] (And then in *Practical Reason* it is urged that "respect" is a special kind of nonpathological feeling arising from an "intellectual cause.")[148] Kant, then, is a purer rationalist in ethics than Leibniz; for Kant, Leibnizian *caritas sapientis* breaks down the wall between the moral law as "fact of reason" and mere pathology. For Kant, even "sublimated" eros has no moral role at all; if any philosopher remained unbrushed by the wings of that god, it was Immanuel Kant.[149] A Leibniz-Kant synthesis, then, is not possible—at least as something that either of them would acknowledge. As usual, God is the problem; and his knowable presence or absence is decisive in shaping what Leibniz and Kant say about "substance," freedom, and morality.

Substance in Leibniz' Thought: A Few Conclusions

In the end it is harsh but not unjust to say that Leibniz seems not to manage to "save" the freedom which would make it possible for rational substances (such as human beings) to act with greater wise charity or universal benevolence—mainly because he also wants to save other things (God, "certainty," preestablished harmony) which are incongruent with full self-determination.[150] But this is a general problem in the seventeenth century, if not always for the same reasons: Hobbes, for example, says that there is "no obligation on any man, which ariseth not from some act of his own"[151]—but no human act is wholly "one's own," since Hobbesian "will" is just the "last appetite" in deliberation, and appetites are caused by perception of a world wholly determined by God.[152] Hobbes needs self-determining free agents for the coherence of his contractarian political-moral theory—since obligation arises from "covenants" of which will is "the essence"—but his theology and philosophy of science rule them out.

In the seventeenth century, indeed, only two main figures escape these difficulties: one by candor, the other by elusiveness. Spinoza can afford honestly to forego human freedom—viewed as something illusory and vain, as ignorance of determining causes—because his political-moral theory does not need that freedom: legitimate society does not come about through "voluntary agreement" (as in Locke),[153] but by "handing over" a *quantum* of power sufficient to cause sovereignty and end conflict.[154] Physics replaces metaphysics.

But the Lockean phrase, "voluntary agreement," reminds one that Locke himself "saved" free will and voluntariness ("voluntary agreement gives . . . political power to governors")[155] only through elusiveness, only by deliberately failing to link up his moral use of free will with his radical doubts about the possibility of such freedom in the *Second Reply to the Bishop of Worcester*. In the *Second Reply*, indeed, Locke says that since God "has revealed that there shall be a day of judgment," revelation must serve as "foundation enough, to conclude [that] men are free enough to be made answerable for their actions." But Locke says that this is knowable only through the "light of revelation" (not Leibnizian *lumière naturelle*), and concludes by remarking that "how man is a free agent" surpasses his "explication or comprehension."[156] But it must nonetheless be true—otherwise one falls into the "fatal necessity" of "Hobbes and Spinoza" which Locke complains of in one of his essays on Malebranche.[157] (Leibniz, of course, given his rationalist doubts about Scripture, would never have grounded something as central as freedom in revelation alone. And yet on this point it is not clear that Leibniz' rationalism is any better than Locke's fideism.)

What Leibniz ought to have, given his stress on good will and charity (or rather his fusion of these in the formula *justitia est caritas sapientis seu benevolentia universalis*),[158] is not "preestablished" but "postestablished" harmony: a social harmony brought about by the spontaneous charitable strivings of self-deter-mining agents. And sometimes he does have this, or at least tries to ("less knowledge suffices with more good will").[159] But when one asks, How is this striving possible for us?, the notorious problems of Leibniz' monadology immediately reappear. If our "predicates" do not include that charitable striving, and if all that we do is certain and determined (though admittedly not "metaphysically" necessary), then our view of "ought" does not occasion a new, spontaneous moral sequence issuing freely from us, *de novo*, in the manner of Kant. What is needed, as Stuart Hampshire urges, is the "actual" possibility of acting well in the historical world we inhabit, not just "the mere logical possibility of the alternative."[160] And Leibniz himself seems to have felt the force of such an objection, since he grants in the *Theodicy* that "there is no obligation to do that which is impossible for us in our existing state."[161]

But if Kantian freedom depends on our not being able to know divine determination, or even divine "concurrence," and if Leibniz claims to know that very determination (here standing in the impressive company of Augustine, Anselm, and Aquinas), then there is a Kant-Leibniz impasse which cannot be broken unless one of them can be demonstrated to be correct. Neither of them, however, can be conclusively demonstrated to be right; both of them just serve as fixed stars in the constellation of permanently possible world-views which have not been "swept into oblivion," in the words of Isaiah Berlin.[162] Kant's moral view combines Platonic rationalism and Augustinian voluntarism more simply and coherently than Leibniz'; but it works only if theism is "dogmatism," not the fundamental truth that Leibniz took it to be.

To be sure, Leibniz sometimes speaks as a "compatibilist" in ethics for whom a combination of factors (none "determining" *ex necessitatis*) merely "inclines" human will one way or another:

> Nothing happens without some reason. . . . It seems to me that one must not except liberty from this. . . . All those who reason about morality and politics in order to divine something about human actions tacitly use this same principle, that there is always a reason or cause which inclines the will. . . .
>
> And to explain myself more distinctly I say that Adam sinned without necessity, thought he who knew all things could know why he let himself go toward sin rather than maintain his innocence. . . . It seems that the soul never finds itself in a state of pure indifference where everything is equal, within as much as without. There is always a reason, that is to

say, a greater inclination [*penchant*] toward that which is actually chosen, which can come not only from good or bad arguments, but also from passions, customs, dispositions, bodily organs, and from the mind, external impression, more or less attention, etc. However, this tendency does not force liberty, although it inclines it. There is a great difference between a necessary cause and a concomitant which is certain.[163]

Though at the end Leibniz falls back on his usual distinction between "necessity" and mere "certainty," he earlier says that "good and bad arguments" may bear on choice—such as arguments urging (perhaps) that one ought to be "wisely charitable." But it cannot be his view that a person enjoying "Pelagian" absolute freedom weights "arguments" and then determines himself to action with perfect "Kantian" spontaneity—except insofar as that argument weighing is *already* contained in the "complete concept" of that deliberating person. A moralist needs to be able to say that "arguments" and "reasons," once weighed, can then serve as the actual motive of self-determined conduct; Kant can certainly say this, but it is not clear that Leibniz can. Indeed, his phrase, "there is always a reason or cause which inclines the will," is evasive—for while "reasons" may well "incline" the will, "causes" simply *determine* effects. Despite some hints of "compatibilism," then, Leibniz himself finally rests his case on the notion that the "certain" is not (metaphysically) "necessary." The problem of being able to do what one ought to do—act with wise charity—remains; the possibility of justice is jeopardized.

3
Theodicy as
Universal Justice

It is now clear that the idea of a "just" universal monarchy under a "wisely charitable" God (with rational, naturally immortal monads as "citizens") is the crowning element of many important Leibnizian writings: the "Discourse on Metaphysics," the correspondence with Arnauld, the "New System" (of 1695), the *Monadology* and the *Principles of Nature and Grace* (the last two from 1714), to name only a few.[1] When Leibniz speaks of "this City of God, this truly universal monarchy" (*Monadology*, prop. 86), of "this perfect government" under which "no good action would be unrewarded and no bad one go unpunished" (ibid., prop. 90),[2] of "this state with perfect government" (*Theodicy*, pt. 125), and of the moral world "of which God is the monarch through perfect government" (*New Essays* II, 27),[3] he does not use the terms "city," "monarchy," "state," and "government" lightly or inadvisedly: he wants to show, always, that "minds" or spirits stand in a moral-political relation to God. Not that this is in itself revolutionary: Platonism does this, in its true myths of eternal reward and punishment which end and crown *Gorgias* and the *Republic*;[4] and even at the end of *Timaeus* those who have been most irresponsibly mindless are converted into oysters as punishment of their "outlandish ignorance" (*Timaeus* 92c).[5] And the Bible certainly offers a moral-political account of human-divine relations: of divine monarchy and law in the Old Testament (with Saul and David anointed by Samuel), of Christian charity as "new law" in the New Testament.[6] Leibniz, for his part, as heir to these eastern-Mediterranean traditions, goes out of his way in the *Theodicy* to present God not just as "architect" of the cosmos, but as just monarch of those elements of the cosmos—minds or spirits—that know the same eternal verities which God sees.

Leibniz' largest systematic illustration of "universal" justice is nothing less than the *Theodicy*,[7] and indeed he himself says that, "I use the title theodicy because it is the justice of God which is the principal subject of that work, into which the questions of his goodness and of his holiness enter naturally."[8] What is noteworthy here is that divine "justice" is mentioned first, and has pride of place; goodness and holiness are referred to only afterward. On this point, indeed, it is revealing and important that when Leibniz began to think of writing a theodicy pleading "the cause of God" in the face of evil, in the mid-1690s, he at first used the title, "Theodicaea, or on behalf of divine justice," and then went on to amplify this title with the phrase, "Catholic demonstrations formed with mathematical certainty," drawn from "natural theology and jurisprudence."[9] This primitive title is more revealing of Leibniz' "universal" ethical purpose than is the published title *(Essays on Theodicy, or on the Goodness of God, the Freedom of Man, and the Origin of Evil).*[10] The primitive title stresses "justice" and "jurisprudence" (rather than the larger and vaguer "goodness"), and in insisting on "natural theology" and "mathematical certainty" reveals (what the text of the finished *Theodicy* later confirms) that Leibniz will exclude everything merely sectarian in favor of the "natural" and the "mathematical"—truths of reason which are "catholic" in the proper sense (universal and certain).

Leibniz' tendency to view his *Theodicy* as justice writ (very) large indeed is at its clearest, perhaps, in a remarkable letter to Placcius from 1697, in which "practical" theology virtually collapses into "universal jurisprudence."

> One must consider God . . . morally as the monarch of a perfect republic, such as is (if I can speak in this way) the city of all the minds in the universe. That posed, practical theology is nothing else than the jurisprudence of the universal republic, of which God is the sovereign director, insofar as it comprises our duties in this republic. . . . In the republic of the universe, no good work is without recompense, and no sin without chastisement.[11]

Leibniz, then, was speaking very literally when he insisted on "universal" jurisprudence: for it reveals nothing less than the duties of "all the minds in the universe." This is plainly the most ambitious notion of justice ever conceived by a serious philosopher after Plato: it must be valid for any infinite or finite spirit in any logically possible world.

Since, however, earlier thinkers—from the author of the Book of Job to Hobbes, Pascal, Malebranche, and Fénelon—had also undertaken "attempts at theodicy" *(essais de théodicée),* the distinctiveness of Leibniz' conflation of theology and justice can be brought out best by examining those earlier efforts to "justify" God which Leibniz knew well and commented on. Since Leibniz is what he is not, a comparison of "theodicies" will reveal what is authentically Leibnizian and what is just inherited from the theodicy tradition. Sometimes Leibniz was writing against a theodicist whom he found almost entirely, if brilliantly, wrong (Hobbes);[12] sometimes he was writing to correct a theodicist whom he found substantially correct but insufficiently careful (Malebranche).[13] If these matters of provenance and intellectual ancestry are first clarified, the radical distinctiveness of the *Theodicy* will stand out in higher relief.

THE JUSTICE OF GOD: LEIBNIZ CONTRA HOBBES

It seems reasonable to begin with Hobbes' theodicy efforts; for it is plain that the mature Leibniz viewed him as a kind of *summa* of dangerous moral, political, and theological errors.[14] And in fact it would be hard to imagine a theodicy more anti-Leibnizian than Hobbes': for the English philosopher's central claim is that, of the alleged "perfections" of God, we really know only omnipotence, overwhelming causal power—that we merely ascribe moral perfection (and even omniscience) to him as a mark of honor. Hence the Hobbesian universe is just an "effect" of divine causality; and we have no right to "call God before the bar" of human justice.[15] This view descends to Hobbes especially from the Book of Job, which was (for obvious reasons) Hobbes' favorite part of Scripture.

> Then answered the Lord unto Job out of the whirlwind, and said:
> . . . Wilt thou also disannul my judgment? Wilt thou condemn me, that thou mayest be righteous?
> Hast thou an arm like God? or canst thou thunder with a voice like him?
> Deck thyself now with majesty and excellency; and array thyself with glory and beauty.
> Cast abroad the rage of thy wrath: and behold every one that is proud, and abase him . . .
> Canst thou draw out Leviathan with a hook? . . . will he speak soft words unto thee? Will he make a covenant with thee?. . . .

> Where wast thou when I laid the foundations of the earth? . . .
> whatsoever is under the whole heaven is mine.[16]

And this passage (which even furnished Hobbes with the title of his most celebrated book)[17] is echoed in St. Paul's Letter to the Romans: "Hath not the potter power over the clay, of the same lump to make one vessel unto honor, and another unto dishonor?"[18]

To be slightly more precise and careful, one can say that Hobbes offers (in effect) two versions of theodicy—or rather two arguments showing why theodicy à la Leibniz cannot work; and it is hard to know which of these arguments is the more radical. Hobbes' first argument is that we cannot know the alleged "attributes" of God at all (such as his supposed "wise charity")— that "we," therefore, through a kind of universal linguistic covenant, simply ascribe attributes to him which we think admirable.[19] (By contrast Leibniz' position on this point is the quintessence of Scholastic orthodoxy: God possesses every perfection, he is omnipotent, omniscient, and perfectly good— and, since perfectly good, the creator of a fully justifiable "best" world.) In his first vein Hobbes argues that the creation and use of language is the result of agreement: it exists, he says in chapter 3 of *De Cive*, "as it were by a certain contract necessary for human society."[20] At one point, in chapter 18 of *De Cive*, Hobbes even goes so far as to insist that "to know truth, is the same thing as to remember that it was made by ourselves by the common use of words."[21] (Leibniz, with his reverence for demi-Platonic eternal verities, was especially horrified by Hobbes' radical nominalism.)[22] Hobbes' theory of language and truth as something wholly conventional is important not only as an instance of his general reliance on agreement or "covenant" in the explanation and/or defense of social phenomena, but also in relation to his theology/theodicy. Since, in Hobbes' view, language and truth are imposed by us on the world, and since we cannot truly know God, "words, and consequently the attributes of God, have their signification by agreement and constitution of men."[23] What we "know" of God is not really knowledge; we ascribe attributes to him which we think honorable—what Leibniz sarcastically calls "compliments."[24] (This, for Leibniz, is the most violently radical outgrowth of *stat pro ratione voluntas*—"let will take the place of reason.")

Given such radicalism, it is not very astonishing that Hobbes goes on, in *Liberty, Necessity, and Chance*, to redefine revelation in the light of nominalism and voluntarism—a light which Leibniz found so worrying that he devoted a large appendix to the *Theodicy* to a refutation of this late Hobbesian work.[25] Hobbes insists, boldly and sweepingly, that

> The Bible is a law. To whom? To all the world? He [Bishop Bramhall of Derry] knows it is not. How came it then to be a law to us? Did God speak it *viva voce* to us? Have we any other warrant for it than the word of the prophets? Have we seen the miracles? Have we any other assurance of their certainty than the authority of the Church? And is the authority of the Church any other than the authority of the Commonwealth, or that of the Commonwealth any other than that of the head of the Commonwealth, or hath the head of the Commonwealth any other authority than that which hath been given him by the members? . . . They that have the legislative power make nothing canon, which they make not law, nor law, which they make not canon. And because the legislative power is from the assent of the subjects, the Bible is made law by the assent of the subjects.[26]

What is striking here is not simply the assertion that the Bible is law only if made "canonical" by the sovereign, but the assertion that the general right or authority of that sovereign is derived from the "assent" of subjects—that through the sovereign considered as their authorized agent, the people *will* the Bible to be what it "is." Here Leibniz sees a multiplicity of terrible errors: to reduce religion to "the Bible," only to declare that the book has no inherent meaning and must be supplied with one by popular will and "assent," is to conflate social contract theory (a political error)[27] with radical voluntarism (an intellectual and moral error).[28] And the notion that all sovereign-made law is "canonical" is calamitous: "sovereignty" itself is bad enough, just in the legal sphere; but to say that every (English) law is "canon" or religious is to invest a Hobbesian sovereign with divine powers.[29] (And that is exactly the complaint which Leibniz will bring against Hobbesian sovereignty, as will be seen in Chapter 5.)

Hobbes does not stop, however, at redefining the attributes of God and the canonical character of Scripture in terms of covenant, consent, and "assent": he also conceives the relation of God to his chosen people, the Jews, as a consequence of consent. "By the Kingdom of God," he urges in chapter 35 of *Leviathan*, "is properly meant a Commonwealth, instituted, by the consent of those which were to be subject thereto, for their civil government."[30] Both the ancient Jews and the modern Christians, in Hobbes' view, were linked to God by consent: both recognized his authority, the Jews in an actual earthly kingdom under a kind of regency of Moses, Christians in a kingdom "to come."[31] One can even say that there are two levels of consent in God's relation to his chosen peoples: first there is a "covenant" between those who subject themselves to God as sovereign, but second, our knowledge of this covenant comes from Scripture, which is itself valid (never "true") only because we have "assented" to consider it as such, by allowing the civil sovereign to make the Bible canonical. We consent, then, to believe that God's relation to his chosen peoples is also based on consent. (For Leibniz this was simply contractarianism gone mad, extended even to heaven.) In any case, according to Hobbes, God's kingdom, whether of the old "covenant" or the new, exists "by force of our covenant, not by the right of God's power."[32]

With that last phrase, "the right of God's power," one comes to Hobbes' second argument against "theodicy" of the Leibnizian kind: for it is clear that despite his radically nominalist claim that "the attributes of God have their signification by agreement and constitution of men," he also thought (possibly inconsistently) that God can be known to have "irresistible power"—the irresistible power which causes everything in the universe (and, not so incidentally, makes human "free will" an incoherent Scholastic "absurdity").[33] Howsoever he may have insisted in his "linguistic" vein that no divine attributes are truly knowable, he often enough allowed that God has a natural "dominion" over all creatures (who cannot "resist" his power); he can be known as the omnipotent cause of the world viewed as "effect." As Hobbes puts it in *Leviathan*'s chapter 12, "there must be (as even the heathen philosophers confessed) one first mover; that is, a first and eternal cause of all things."[34] In this second vein or argument, in which one divine attribute (causal power) can indeed be known, Hobbes urges that "irresistible power" gives rise to absolute rights of dominion, and that while God in fact gave laws to the Jews as their "civil sovereign" (having been authorized by "covenant"), he could have ruled them, had he so chosen, by natural irresistible power alone. "God is king of all the earth by his power," Hobbes says, "but of his chosen people, he is king by covenant."[35] So important is "natural" dominion arising from irresistible power, from overwhelming causality, in Hobbes' view, that if any human being possessed such power *(per impossibile)* he too would enjoy universal dominion; if the natural right of any man to all things were conjoined with power that none could resist, then that person would rule the earth naturally rather than conventionally (and all other men would be required to submit on account of their weakness). As Hobbes says in chapter 31 of *Leviathan,*

> Seeing all men by nature had right to all things, they had this right every one to reign over all the rest. But because this right could not be obtained by force [owing to universal, equal weakness], it concerned the safety of every one, laying by that right, to set up men, with sovereign authority, by common consent; whereas if there had been any man of power irresistible, there had been no reason, why he should not by that power have ruled . . . according to his own discretion.[36]

In Hobbes, then, God is universal monarch solely because he alone is irresistibly powerful—simply as a matter of fact; he need be "divine" in no other way, and if a man acquired such power (though he cannot) his "right" would be equal to God's.[37]

It is precisely the irresistible power of God which Hobbes stresses—now adding that such power makes human "free will" not just absurd but impious[38]—when he defends God against charges of injustice in *Liberty, Necessity, and Chance* (against Bishop Bramhall). In Hobbes' view a bishop should not be so ignorant of Scripture as to forget St. Paul's Letter to the Romans, chapter 9, in which Paul asks whether God's exercise of irresistible power could ever be unjust. "Is there unrighteousness with God?," Paul asks. And the answer is, "God forbid."[39] If the potter has "power" over the clay, cannot God rightfully shape the actions of men in just the same way? The problem of Bishop Bramhall is that he fails to see what a reading of Paul could have told him: that "the power of God alone, without other help, is sufficient justification for any action he doth." Whatever God does, even to agents with wills, is "made just by his doing it." This is obvious to anyone who sees that "the name of justice," as used in human discourse, is "not that by which God Almighty's actions are to be measured."[40] And if Paul is not plain enough, there is always the Book of Job.

> When God afflicted Job, he did object no sin to him, but justified that afflicting him by telling him of his power. *Hast thou* (says God) *an arm like mine? Where wast thou when I laid the foundations of the earth?* and the like. . . . Power irresistible justifieth all actions really and properly, in whomsoever it be found. Less power does not. And because such power is in God only, he must needs be just in all his actions. And we, that not

comprehending his counsels, call him to the bar [to answer charges], commit injustice in it.[41]

Leibniz may have been thinking of the phrase, "in whomsoever it be found," when he insisted that if an "evil genius" seized universal dominion, he would not cease to be "wicked" and "tyrannical" simply because he "could not be resisted."[42] But to that Hobbes would reply with a passage already aimed at Bishop Bramhall: "The Bishop is nearer the calling him a tyrant than I am, making that to be tyranny, which is but the exercise of an absolute power; for he holdeth, though he see it not, by consequence, in withdrawing the will of man from God's dominion, that every man is a king of himself."[43] At least, Hobbes would say, the simple formulation which asserts only God's *causality* averts the kind of question with which Pierre Bayle tortured himself: how can a morally perfect being fail to use his perfect power to arrest evil in the universe?[44] And it was that question, of course, which provided the occasion for Leibniz' *Theodicy*—since that work is officially an answer to the *philosophe de Rotterdam*, even if "Hobbism" and "Spinozism" are the real worries.[45]

LEIBNIZ' CRITIQUE OF HOBBESIAN "THEODICY"

Leibniz' best-known version of anti-Hobbism—resting on the notion that "irresistible power" makes divinity indistinguishable from tyranny[46]—is to be found in the main body of the *Theodicy* itself, as will soon be seen; but before turning to that text it is well to remember that Leibniz (in c. 1707) wrote a manuscript called "Theodicy or Apology for the Justice of God through the Ideas of It Which He Has Given Us"—a manuscript in which Hobbes' version of the "God-justification" is specifically the central issue. (The 1707 "Theodicy or Apology" remained unpublished until 1948,[47] and has never been translated into English.)

"I use the title, *Theodicy*," Leibniz says in the 1707 manuscript, "because it is the justice of God which is the principal subject of that work, into which the questions of his goodness and of his holiness enter naturally." He then indicates that he plans "to make it clear that we have good and true notions of these attributes of God, or—what is the same thing—that we have reason to attribute justice and goodness to him, which would be groundless if those words signified nothing when one applies them to God."[48] Here the radical nominalism of *De Cive* and *Leviathan* is plainly the object under attack; Leibniz wants to insist on the moral perfection of God as something knowable. To be sure, Leibniz grants, "there are several distinguished theologians and philosophers who believe that we do not have the slightest idea of divine goodness and justice. *Sunt superis sua jura,* 'the gods above have their own laws,' the poet said." By denying that we can know the justice and goodness of God, "they respond to embarrassing difficulties about evil, about sin, about the sufferings of the good, about the prosperity of the wicked, about predestination—as if the greatness and the independence of God put him above what we call justice and reason."[49] But that, for Leibniz, simply translates the Roman maxim, *princeps legibus solutus est,* "the prince is above the law," from earth to heaven; it endows God with the least defensible aspect of "sovereignty," and makes him a cosmic Caligula.

Leibniz goes on to complain that "those who make use of what they call strict methods in matters of grace"—here hyper-Calvinists are meant—often insist on God's sovereignty in a morally harmful way. "It even seems that it would follow from this," Leibniz laments, "that one need only fear God, and that there is no way of loving him, if the perfections which can make him lovable are absolutely unknown to us; if his power and his greatness subsist, and if his goodness, his justice, and the wisdom of his government signify nothing." For how, Leibniz wonders, "can we attribute them to him with [good] grounds, if we do not even have the idea of them?"[50]

Of course, Leibniz goes on to say, one must charitably imagine that philosophers who deify *potestas* do so out of a kind of (misplaced) piety: "their purpose is no doubt to inspire in men a perfect submission to the orders of God," but it would be only "through the motive of a forced patience" which would also be valid "if one were dealing with a tyrant whom one fears and whom one does not love at all."[51] To be sure, Leibniz grants, omnipotence is one of the perfections of God, but even though he "depends only on himself," nonetheless his "will is ruled by his understanding, and his power by his wisdom"—so that God's independence does not make him "independent of the sovereign reason which is himself."[52] Here, of course, it is reason which enjoys sovereignty—again against Hobbes, for whom sovereignty is authorized *potestas.*

And in the very next paragraph it is immediately evident that Hobbes is the occasion of these 1707 reflections:

> I have since consulted the writings of many other theologians and philosophers, but particularly that of the celebrated Hobbes against

Bishop Bramhall [*Liberty, Necessity, and Chance*], which has only appeared in English . . . who have maintained an absolute necessity in all things, and who are distinguished for having exalted the right of God over creatures, to the point of saying that he has that [right] of damning the innocent. Thus it is not without knowledge, nor through the slightest prejudice or passion, that I have believed that it was necessary to take another part.[53]

It seems to him, Leibniz continues, that these "rigid dogmas" are "not always founded in reason and still less in revelation," and that—much more important—"the idea of the absolute power of a [divine] substance to whom the happiness and unhappiness of intelligent creatures is indifferent" is not the kind of idea which is able "to inspire charitable sentiments in men, who should propose to themselves the idea of God as the most perfect of all models."[54] And that is what is most worrying in "Hobbism": it cannot "inspire charitable sentiments" in men because it insists that "the passion to be reckoned upon is fear."[55] It is bad theodicy which generates bad morality.

LEIBNIZ' WORRIES ABOUT MALEBRANCHE'S VERSION OF "THEODICY"

If Leibniz found Hobbes' *potestas*-colored reading of God's justice philosophically wrong and morally dangerous, he was more nearly in accord with the theodicy speculations of Nicolas Malebranche, the late-Cartesian philosopher-theologian whom he had known (and mainly respected) since his Paris sojourn in the 1670s.[56] In a general way, indeed, Leibniz as a theodicist is philosophically least distant from Malebranche (among his main contemporaries): they are both demi-Platonists, both very mitigated Cartesians, both anti-Hobbesians. And they share difficulties over free will: Malebranche has troubles with it because of his "occasionalism" (since there is "no relation" between body and mind, God "moves our arm" on the occasion of our "willing" it);[57] Leibniz' troubles arise from "substance" and from the "certainty" of preestablished harmony. And Leibniz' own theodicy doctrines were in part occasioned by Malebranche's *Treatise on Nature and Grace* (1680)—a brilliant effort to reconcile divine justice and human evil through "Cartesian" general law.[58] Leibniz partly admired this *Treatise*—though for Malebranche the world is the best that can be achieved through general, constant, uniform law (with unfortunate "particular" effects), while for Leibniz the world is "best" *simpliciter*. The basic question is nonetheless roughly the same for Leibniz and for Malebranche: how can one reconcile God's justice and goodness with the existence of radical evil in a finite, temporal world? Both, then, worry about "universal jurisprudence"—even if Malebranche never uses that actual term.

Malebranche's argument—on which Leibniz commented for over thirty years, as Robinet has shown[59]—is that, since God governs the realms of nature and grace (equally) by general, constant, uniform laws and "general wills" *(volontés générales),* and never (or "rarely") by ad hoc "particular wills" *(volontés particulières),* the generality of his lawful operation brings about incidental particular evils which are not directly willed by him, and which therefore cannot be the basis of a (reasonable) charge that God is ignorant, capricious, malicious, or (above all) unjust.[60] The sheer, unavoidable generality of law itself incidentally throws up particular inequities—as Aristotle had pointed out in the *Nicomachean Ethics.*[61] This was an argument which interested Leibniz—a lawyer, inter alia—and which led him to say in parts 204 and 208 of the *Theodicy* that Malebranche had produced "an admirable treatise on nature and grace," and that insofar as Malebranche argues that God produces "as much perfection as is possible . . . [his] system on this point amounts to the same as mine."[62]

In the *Premier éclaircissement* of *Nature and Grace,* one sees at once that Malebranche intends to treat divine "general will" as something which is manifested in all of God's operations—as much in the realm of "grace" (morality) as in the realm of nature. Malebranche argues that "God acts by *volontés générales* when he acts as a consequence of general laws which he has established"; and nature itself, he adds, "is nothing but the general law which God has established in order to construct or to preserve his work by the simplest means, by an action which is always uniform, constant, perfectly worthy of an infinite wisdom and of a universal cause." God, on this view, "does not act at all" by *volontés particulières,* by lawless ad hoc volitions, as do "limited intelligences" whose thought is not "infinite": thus for Malebranche "to establish general laws, and to choose the simplest ones which are at the same time the most fruitful, is a way of acting worthy of him whose wisdom has no limits." At the same time, he insists, "to act by *volontés particulières* shows a limited intelligence which cannot judge the consequences or the effects of less fruitful causes."[63]

Even at this point Malebranche's argument, though officially theological, contains some points which could be read "legally," even "politically": the general will manifests itself in general laws which are "fruitful" and "worthy" of infinite wisdom, whereas particular will is "limited," "unintelligent," and "lawless." But one need not jump to premature conclusions, since Malebranche himself often "legalizes" his argument—especially in his effort to justify God's acting exclusively through "general wills." If, he says, "rain falls on certain lands, and if the sun roasts others . . . if a child comes into the world with a malformed and useless head . . . this is not at all because God wanted to produce those effects by *volontés particulières;* it is because he has established [general] laws for the communication of motion, whose effects are necessary consequences." Thus, according to Malebranche, one "cannot say that God acts through caprice or ignorance" in permitting malformed children to be born or unripe fruit to fall: "he has not established the laws of the communication of motion for the purpose of producing monsters, or of making fruits fall before their maturity"; he has willed those laws "because of their fruitfulness, and not because of their sterility."[64] Those who claim (Malebranche urges) that God ought, through special, ad hoc particular wills, to suspend natural laws if their operation will harm the virtuous (or the innocent) fail to understand that it is not "worthy" of an infinitely wise being to abandon general rules in order to find a suppositious perfect "fit" between the particular case of each finite being and a *volonté particulière* suited to that case alone.[65]

So wise, constant, and just are God's *volontés générales,* in Malebranche's view, that it is a moral wrong (on the part of man) not to accept and respect these "general wills" and to make them the measure of human conduct. In one of his numerous defenses of *Nature and Grace,* Malebranche argues that "if God did not act in consequence of general laws which he has established, no one would ever make any effort. Instead of descending a staircase step by step, one would rather throw himself out of a window, trusting himself to God."[66] But why, Malebranche asks, would it be "sin" as well as "folly" to "hurl oneself" from a window? "It would be sin," he answers, "because it would be tempting God: it would be claiming to obligate him to act in a manner unworthy of him, or through *volontés particulières*"; it would amount to telling God "that his work is going to perish, if he himself does not trouble the simplicity of his ways."[67] And in addition to sin, of course, defenestrating oneself would be "folly," for one must be "mad" to imagine that "God must regulate his action by our particular needs, and groundlessly change, out of love for us, the uniformity of his conduct."[68] For Malebranche, then, *théodicée* and *généralité* are all but equivalent.

When he was accused of "ruining" Providence—by denigrating the divine "particular wills" which are recounted in Scripture (and by adding that Scripture is a collection of "anthropologies" fit only for "weak" and "simple" minds)[69]—Malebranche struck back, arguing that it is precisely *volonté particulière*, and not *volonté générale*, which ruins Providence. And here he was writing against Arnauld, with whom Leibniz had his main correspondence concerning "substances" or monads in the period 1686–1690. In his *Réponse* to one of Arnauld's many attacks on *Nature and Grace*, Malebranche argues that if Arnauld's scripturalizing insistence on biblical miracles and constant divine "particular wills" does not overturn Providence altogether, it at least "degrades it, humanizes it, and makes it either blind or perverse."

> Is there wisdom in creating monsters by particular wills? In making crops grow by rainfall, in order to ravage them by hail? In giving to men a thousand impulses of grace which misfortunes render useless? . . . But all this is nothing. Is there wisdom and goodness in making impious princes reign, in suffering so great a number of heresies, in letting so many nations perish? Let M. Arnauld raise his head and discover all the evils which happen in the world, and let him justify Providence, on the supposition that God acts and must act through *volontés particulières.*[70]

It is Malebranche's view, in fact, that the classical "theodicy problems" most famously identified by Leibniz—reconciling a morally and physically evil world with God's power, goodness, and wisdom—can only be solved by insisting that God wills generally. These problems of universal justice Malebranche states starkly in *Nature and Grace:*

> Holy Scripture teaches us on one hand that God wills that all men be saved, and . . . that he does everything he wills; and nonetheless faith is not given to everyone, and the number that perish is much greater than that of the predestined. How can one reconcile this with his power?
>
> God foresaw from all eternity both original sin, and the infinite number of persons that this sin would sweep into Hell. Nonetheless he created the first man in a condition from which he knew that he would

fall; he even established between this man and his posterity relations which would communicate his sin to them, and render them all worthy of his aversion and his wrath. How can one reconcile this with his goodness?

God frequently diffuses graces, without having the effect for which his goodness obliges us to believe that he gives them. He increases piety in persons almost to the end of their life; and sin dominates them at death, and throws them into Hell. In a word, God undoes and redoes without cease: it seems that he wills, and no longer wills. How can one reconcile this with his wisdom?[71]

One can see why Leibniz was so struck by *Nature and Grace,* for Malebranche's anguished questions were Leibniz' as well. But for Malebranche, "generality" and "simplicity" of divine will clear up these "great difficulties," and explain how a being who loves order can permit disorder. While God truly wills to save all men, he insists, it is "order" itself—general lawfulness—which keeps God from having particular "practical wills" which would bring about universal salvation; for God "must not disturb the simplicity of his ways."[72]

In his final work, the *Réflexions sur la prémotion physique*—published in the year of his death (the year before Leibniz')—Malebranche reformulated his argument in so strong a way that Leibniz found it excessive, and harmful to universal justice:

Infinity in all sorts of perfections is an attribute of the divinity. . . . Now between the infinite and the finite the distance is infinite; the relation is nothing. The most excellent of creatures, compared with the divinity, is nothing; and God counts it as nothing in relation to himself. . . . It seems to me evident, that God conducts himself according to what he is, in remaining immobile, [even while] seeing the demon tempt, and man succumb to the temptation. . . . If God, in order to stop the Fall of Adam, had interrupted the ordinary course of his *providence générale,* that conduct would have expressed the false judgment that God had counted the worship that Adam rendered him as something, with respect to his infinite majesty.[73]

But God, Malebranche goes on to say, "must never trouble the simplicity of his ways, nor interrupt the wise, constant, and majestic course of his ordinary providence." Then perhaps fearing that he has been too harsh,

Malebranche adds that "God is infinitely wise, infinitely just, infinitely good, and he does men all the good he can—not absolutely, but according to what he is."[74]

"What he is," on this view, is precisely the problem for Leibniz. "I do not know," he wrote to Malebranche, "whether one should have recourse to the expedient [of saying] that God, by remaining immobile during the Fall of man . . . shows that the most excellent creatures are nothing in relation to him"; that way of putting the matter can be "abused," and even lead to "the despotism of the supralapsarians"[75]—those who hold that God damned the human race before the Fall. And if God were "despotic," he would of course not be wisely charitable and generally benevolent; here Leibniz seems to agree with Bayle's point that the Malebranchian God sacrifices moral goodness and justice to a "Cartesian" *recherche de la généralité*.[76] (But love matters more than mere "law" in Leibniz, as will be clear in Chapter 4.)

Despite Leibniz' fear of loveless "despotism," it is still Malebranche's last work, the *Réflexions* of 1715, which is most nearly "Leibnizian." The *Réflexions* were a response to Laurent Boursier's argument (in *De l'action de Dieu sur les créatures*) that God is a commanding "sovereign" whose will is unrestricted by any necessity to act with Malebranchian "general" lawfulness—indeed that any restriction on sovereignty causes "impotence." "What an idea of God!" Boursier jeers. "He wishes, and he does not accomplish; he does not like monsters, but he makes them; . . . his wisdom limits his power. A strange idea of God! An impotent being, an unskillful workman, a wisdom based on constraint, a sovereign who does not do what he wills, an unhappy God."[77]

In his response to Boursier's theology of sovereignty, command, and power, Malebranche minimizes the vocabulary of general and particular "will" (which had been much criticized),[78] and so *volonté générale* and general law become "eternal law," while *volonté particulière* turns into *volonté absolue et bizarre*. This is a "Leibnizian" change, since Leibniz always insisted on "eternal" moral verities, and argued for *bona voluntas*, not "absolute" or "bizarre" will. And since Leibniz had sent a copy of the *Theodicy* to Malebranche in 1711,[79] it is not extravagant to find Leibnizian influence in Malebranche's final book.

"My present design," Malebranche says in the *Réflexions*, "is to prove that God is essentially wise, just, and good . . . that his wills are not at all purely arbitrary—that is to say that they are not wise and just simply because he is all-powerful . . . but because they are regulated by the eternal law."[80] Here the argument is so close to Leibniz' paraphrase of *Euthyphro* in the "Meditation on the Common Concept of Justice" that one wonders whether Leibniz ever sent a copy of that manuscript to Malebranche. Very Leibnizian, too, is Malebranche's further argument that to say that the wills of God are "purely arbitrary," that "no reason can be given for his wills, except his wills themselves," that everything he does is just and good because he is omnipotent and has a "sovereign domain" over his creatures, is precisely "to leave the objections of the libertines in all their force."[81]

If Malebranche is Leibniz-like in using the "eternal" to defeat the "arbitrary," he also recalls the great Hanoverian in treating Hobbes as the "libertine" most to be feared. "If," Malebranche says in the *Réflexions*, "God were only omnipotent, if he were like princes who glory more in their power than in their nature," then his "sovereign domain, or his independence, would give him a right to everything."[82] That is astonishingly close to the very language of Leibniz' 1707 "Theodicy or Apology," though there is no evidence that Leibniz ever sent the manuscript to Malebranche. If God's main attribute were unrestricted omnipotence, Malebranche now complains, "Hobbes, Locke, and several others would have discovered the true foundations of morality: authority and power giving, without reason, the right to do whatever one wills, when one has nothing to fear." This legal-positivist view of either divine or human justice Malebranche calls "mad," and suggests that those who characterize God in this way "apparently prefer force, the law of brutes (that which has granted to the lion an empire over the animals) to reason."[83]

However unfair this may be to Hobbes, and still more to Locke[84]—though Hobbes does say that "irresistible power" carries with it a "right" to dominion—the point here is that in his last work Malebranche used Hobbes as the quintessential libertine advocating *volonté absolue et bizarre*, and that this demonizing of Hobbes was characteristically Leibnizian. Leibniz, indeed, with his *Euthyphro*-loving antivoluntarism, must have relished the paragraph from the *Réflexions sur la prémotion physique* in which Malebranche insists that

> If God were only all-powerful, or if he gloried only in his omnipotence, without the slightest regard for his other attributes . . . how strange his plans would be! How could we be certain that, through his omnipotence, he would not, on the first day, place all of the demons in heaven, and all the saints in hell, and a moment after annihilate all that he had done! Cannot God, *qua* omnipotent, create each day a million planets, make new worlds, each more perfect than the last, and reduce them each year to a grain of sand?[85]

If Leibniz had little use for "demons" and "saints," the notion of "new worlds" produced hourly by omnipotent "Hobbesian" divinities would have horrified him—for new worlds would displace the "best" world which God created for a sufficient reason, and which is fully justifiable in "universal jurisprudence."

It is not surprising, then, that Leibniz could send a copy of the *Theodicy* to Malebranche in the confident belief that much of it would prove congenial; and Malebranche's acknowledgment of Leibniz' present ("you prove quite well . . . that God . . . must choose the best")[86] showed Leibniz right. A shared Augustinian Platonism and love of eternal mathematical "order"[87] formed the rapport between the two philosophers; and if Malebranche was rather more "Cartesian" than his German friend, even the Oratorian father shared Leibniz' worries about the Cartesian notion that God creates mathematical, logical, and moral truth *ex nihilo*.[88] Despite these strong affinities and agreements, nonetheless, what finally stands between Leibniz and Malebranche as "theodicists" concerned with the justifiability of the universe is that the Hanoverian gives primacy to the "best" world, simply (and to universal "wise charity"), while Malebranche (for most of his philosophical career) gives prominence to "general" law which keeps the universe in a "ruined" state (since it is riddled with "particular" evils). The fact that they share Platonism, mitigated Cartesianism, and anti-Hobbism cannot altogether bridge their differences—even if, from a Hobbesian perspective, they offer mere variations on the same Platonizing error.[89]

UNIVERSAL JUSTICE IN LEIBNIZ' *THEODICY*

With the Hobbes-rejecting, Malebranche-accommodating provenance of the *Theodicy* sufficiently in place, one can now turn to this most celebrated of all Leibniz' published works—read as the "universal jurisprudence" of the City of God, valid for "all the minds in the universe."

It is true that the *Theodicy*, taken as a whole, is rather rambling and invertebrate—there is almost nothing that it is not about—and that a full commentary on every part of it would exhaust a large book. But some parts of it are concentrated and continuous—and none more so than the Preface, which is crucial to Leibniz' "universal jurisprudence" resting on "wise charity." It was surely no accident that Leibniz chose to open his only published philosophical book[90] with an account of what (precisely) Christianity had brought to religion and morality, and it is surely no accident that what Leibniz omits from Christianity is very striking. For what he says, finally, is that Christ added to the monotheism which Moses had already established (1) the idea of the natural immortality of the soul (as a rational "substance" or monad which can be the subject of divine justice), and (2) charity or love (guided by wisdom) as the core of ethics and law.[91] That is, Christ's function is purely moral in Leibniz' Preface: there is no stress on the Incarnation, the Crucifixion, the Resurrection, the Trinity, transubstantiation, grace—the problematical and even mysterious parts of Christianity which Leibniz knew to have caused infinite dissension (even schism and religious wars). Christ as incarnated by Leibniz just preaches Mosaic monotheism, natural immortality, and wise charity or universal benevolence, so that all of the worrying elements in historical Christianity yield to what can be generally accepted not just by Christian believers but by all those who think Christ morally admirable. The history of Christianity, with its endless quarrels and anathemas, gives way to a transhistorical moral core which all can ecumenically embrace.[92]

Leibniz begins the Preface with the complaint that "men in general have resorted to outward forms for the expression of their religion," that in human history "principles" have tended to be replaced by "ceremonial practices" and by mere "formularies of belief." This would not be so bad, if "religious ceremonies" and "ecclesiastical discipline" had as their aim "to accustom us to the good and to make us familiar with virtue." But before the advent of Moses and Christ this was not the case: divine light was "choked" by the "ridiculous and absurd" ceremonial of the pagans.

> Of all ancient peoples, it appears that the Hebrews alone had public dogmas for their religion. Abraham and Moses established the belief in one God, source of all good, author of all things. The Hebrews spoke of him in a manner worthy of the supreme substance.[93]

Nonetheless, Leibniz goes on to lament, "Moses had not inserted in his laws the doctrine of the immortality of souls: it was consistent with his ideas, it was taught by oral tradition." But the natural immortality of rational substances, though known by a few wise Greeks, "was not proclaimed for popular acceptance until Jesus Christ lifted the veil, and . . . taught with all the force of a lawgiver that immortal souls pass into another life, wherein they shall receive the wages of their deeds." Moses had "already expressed the beautiful conceptions of the greatness and goodness of God"; it was left for Christ to "demonstrate fully the results of these ideas, proclaiming that divine goodness and justice are shown forth to perfection in God's designs for the souls of men."[94]

At precisely this point, having stressed universal goodness and justice, Leibniz explicitly says that he "will refrain from considering here the other parts of the Christian doctrine"—trinitarianism, transubstantiation, grace, even the Incarnation.[95] The word to be made flesh is justice, and so Leibniz stresses the "natural religion" that all can embrace.

> I will show only how Jesus Christ brought about the conversion of natural religion into law, and gained for it the authority of a public dogma. He alone did that which so many philosophers had endeavored to do in vain; and Christians having at last gained the upper hand in the Roman Empire, the master of the greater part of the known earth, the religion of the wise men became that of the nations. Later also Mahomet showed no divergence from the great dogmas of natural theology; his followers spread them abroad even among the most re- mote races of Asia and Africa, whither Christianity had not been carried: and they abolished in many countries heathen superstitions which were contrary to the true doctrine of the unity of God and the immortality of souls.[96]

(Soon enough, in Leibniz' 1714 Vienna lecture on the Greeks—which was examined in Chapter 2—it turns out that what Christ did, namely to convert "natural religion into law," was precisely the conversion of "the religion of wise men" into "public dogma." For the Vienna lecture insists that the wisest Greeks and Romans already understood and embraced monotheism and natural immortality, even if their fear of being publicly executed made them circumspect in speaking too plainly.[97] Plato especially, Leibniz says in the lecture, taught the "doctrine of the unity of God" in the *Timaeus* "as if in secret," lest he suffer the same fate as Socrates. Leibniz observes, as evidence of what the wisest Greeks and Romans knew, that in Book 1 of *De Natura Deorum* Cicero has Antisthenes say that "there is one natural God, and many according to popular opinion"—a saying which recalls Plato's *Letter XIII* to Dionysius: "There are many who ask me to write whom it is not easy to put off openly, so at the beginning of the letters which are seriously intended, I put *god*; in other cases, *the gods*."[98] And Leibniz knew these letters, since he cites them in the Vienna lecture.)

Having said that Christ, "completing what Moses had begun," converted the "natural" into the "public," Leibniz goes on to urge that the remaining

great thing which Christ brought to religion and public morality was love or
charity, the wish that "the Divinity should be the object not only of our fear
and veneration, but also of our love and devotion."[99] And here Leibniz' whole
theory of wise love, especially as enriched after 1697, is compressed into a
few lines:

> [Jesus Christ] made men happy by anticipation, and gave them here
> on earth a foretaste of future felicity. For there is nothing so agreeable
> as loving that which is worthy of love. Love is that mental state which
> makes us take pleasure in the perfections of the object of our love, and
> there is nothing more perfect than God, nor any greater delight than
> in him. To love him it suffices to contemplate his perfections, a thing
> easy indeed, because we find the ideas of these within ourselves. The
> perfections of God are those of our souls, but he possesses them in
> boundless measure; he is an Ocean, whereof to us only some drops have
> been granted; there is in us some power, some knowledge, some good-
> ness, but in God they are all in their entirety. Order, proportions,
> harmony delight us; painting and music are samples of these; God is
> all order; he always keeps truth of proportions, he makes universal
> harmony; all beauty is an effusion of his rays.[100]

At the end of this remarkable paragraph, God has turned briefly into
Plato: the beautiful mathematical *kosmos* of "order," "proportion," and "universal harmony" of Book IV of the *Republic* fuses with Christian charity. (But
then *caritas sapientis*, the charity of the wise, is always both Christian and
Platonic.) The Platonic world of "delightful" harmony, however, soon reverts
to a more purely Christian version of *caritas*, in which the sign of charity is
duty toward men and advancing the common good on earth.

> It follows manifestly that true piety and even true felicity consist in the
> love of God, but a love so enlightened that its fervor is attended by
> insight. This kind of love begets that pleasure in good actions which
> gives relief to virtue, and, relating all to God as the center, transports
> the human to the divine. For in doing one's duty, in obeying reason, one
> carries out the orders of Supreme Reason. One directs all one's inten-
> tions to the common good, which is no other than the glory of God.
> Thus one finds that there is no greater individual interest than to
> espouse that of the community, and one gains satisfaction for oneself
> by taking pleasure in the acquisition of true benefits for men.[101]

"Whether one succeeds or not in this task," Leibniz argues, "one is content with what comes to pass," being "resigned to the will of God" and knowing that "what he wills is best." When we are in this benevolent "state of mind," he continues, we are not "disheartened" by failure; "we regret only our faults, and the ungrateful ways of men cause no relaxation in the exercise of our kindly disposition."

> Our charity is humble and full of moderation, it presumes not to domineer; attentive alike to our own faults and to the talents of others, we are inclined to criticize our own actions and to excuse and vindicate those of others. We must work out our own perfection and do wrong to no man.[102]

Here, characteristically, a Roman jurisprudential and moral precept (*neminem laedere*, "to harm no one"), becomes the lowest degree of charity: to be (wisely) loving, one must first refrain from injury. But here, too, charity moves away from its flirtation with Platonic eros and "harmony" in the previous paragraph, and is closer to Pauline orthodoxy: Leibniz' claim that "our charity is humble and . . . presumes not to domineer" is quite evidently a rewording of 1 Corinthians 13, in which St. Paul says that charity does not "vaunt" itself and is not "puffed up."[103] At the same time, however, the stress on reason ("in doing one's duty . . . one carries out the orders of Supreme Reason") is not misologically Pauline ("where is the wise?")—it is either quasi-Platonic or proto-Kantian, echoing *Euthyphro* and foreshadowing *Religion within the Limits of Reason Alone*.[104]

This final stress on "reason" shores up what is most characteristic of, and remarkable in, these early paragraphs of the Preface to the *Theodicy*: from other Leibnizian works one knows that (for him) reason alone can demonstrate the real existence of one perfect God (monotheism), and that reason can demonstrate the natural immortality of souls or "rational substances" or monads;[105] now reason, not mere revelation, reveals "duty" as well ("the orders of Supreme Reason"), and our duty is to be wisely charitable. So even though Christ's new law of "loving one another" is revealed in Scripture (by St. John),[106] its content is reasonable, not just something "revealed." It is reason that is revelatory. For what is merely "revealed" can be morally problematical—such as God's command to Abraham to sacrifice Isaac.[107] And Leibniz would prefer to avoid patriarchs wielding knives, together with trinitarianism, grace, and some of the *impedimenta* of Scholastic theologizing—in favor of magnifying "the common good" viewed as something equivalent to "the glory of God." For a good which is truly "common" will not be limited by sectarian doctrinal disputes; it can be the object of an overlapping consensus.[108] It is at this point—the virtual equation of duty with divine supreme reason—that Leibniz comes closest to Kant's claim in the "Canon of Pure Reason" (B847) that "so far then as practical reason has the right to serve as our guide, we shall not look upon actions as obligatory because they are the commands of God, but shall regard them as divine commands because we have an inward obligation to them."[109]

Leibniz' stress on "natural" religion (as something that Christ merely universalized) and on reason (as something revelatory of charitable duty) shows to what he gave ethical primacy. But he did so long before writing the *Theodicy;* and in a letter to Andreas Morrell (September 1698), he urges that

> Reason is the natural voice of God and it is only through her that the revealed voice of God must be justified, so that our imagination or some illusion does not deceive us. . . . If there were neither public revelation nor Scripture, men, following internal natural enlightenment, would not fail to arrive at true beatitude. But since men use their reason badly, the public revelation of the Messiah has been made necessary.[110]

This is extraordinary, and with its echoes of the scriptural criticism of both Spinoza and Malebranche,[111] it is more extreme than any statement in the *Theodicy* itself. Had not Leibniz thought that reason alone can reveal duty and that duty requires wise charity, the Christian principle of *caritas* would be lost by his minimizing of Scripture (even the New Testament)—if it is really true that one needs "the public revelation of the Messiah" only because "men use their reason badly." But if reason itself says that "the greatest of these is charity," then St. Paul merely confirms what is already true. (It is orthodox enough to say that monotheism and natural immortality are demonstrable within the limits of reason alone—that is just "Platonism"; to bring *caritas* within that perimeter is much more radical and striking.)[112]

Nor is Leibniz' 1698 letter to Morrell an exceptional, unique utterance: in "Von der Weisheit" (1694–1698), he urges that

> God already revealed true religion to men through the light of nature [*durch das Licht der Natur*], as a streaming of highest reason [*hoechsten Vernunft*] toward ours, even before the Mosaic law was given. Since, however, men seldom used their reason sufficiently, God taught men the

highest truths and rules concerning beatitude, for the fulfillment of his will, not only through wise people, but especially through Moses, and most of all through Christ.[113]

And on the next page of "Von der Weisheit," it turns out that when Christ does arrive on the scene, he only reinforces "highest reason" and "the light of nature." For "the highest rule of the Christian religion" is that "we must love God above all and other men as ourselves"—but "these are also the teachings of highest reason."[114]

> For the greatest pleasure is in the love and enjoyment of the greatest perfection and beauty . . . and God is indeed highest reason. . . . The true fruit and mark of recognition of the love of God is love of [one's] neighbors, an uncolored effort to bring about the best in general.[115]

Here charity = highest reason = God = the general good. And in a letter of 1696 to Electress Sophie of Hanover, Leibniz insists that "as for the difficulties which seem to arise from some passages of Scripture, and from our articles of faith, I daresay that if we find there something contrary to the rules of goodness and of justice, one must conclude from this that we are not using the true sense of these passages from Scripture, and of these articles of faith."[116] That is not too far from Rousseau's ringing assertion, in *La Nouvelle Héloïse,* that "I would rather believe the Bible falsified or unintelligible, than God unjust or evil-doing."[117] Not that Leibniz was always in a state of high moral indignation in subordinating "historical" to natural religion, revelation to reason, what is "written" to goodness and justice; at times, indeed, he does this in a half-joking way: "We are sending missionaries to the Indies to preach revealed religion, which is all very well. But it seems that we should have need for the Chinese to send us missionaries in their turn, to teach us the natural religion that we have lost."[118]

Sometimes, in fact (though not in published works) Leibniz allowed himself even more radical thoughts about Scripture.

> The proof of divine revelations is quite difficult, without doubt. The human race certainly would not be obliged to believe the words of a girl or of a carpenter [*d'une fille ou d'un charpentier*] who boasted of some apparitions. But the Christian religion has for itself so great a confluence of principles [*raisons*] and circumstances that one must grant that Providence has willed to make it credible to men.[119]

This is not overwhelmingly persuasive, and perhaps is not meant to be. And the language which is supposedly "supportive" is just the reverse: after all, the Virgin Mary was *une fille* and Christ was *un charpentier;* and their "apparitions" are offset only by *raisons et circonstances.* It is all very equivocal; Leibniz himself has not "willed to make it credible to men."

Despite such (unpublished) radicalism, Leibniz' usual view, most of the time, is that Christ, in preaching the new law of love and benevolence, was simply "revealing" reason's moral demands; revelation is folded into "supreme reason." What is merely historical and contingent is allowed to be present (in the Preface to the *Theodicy*) only insofar as it is congruent with "the rules of goodness and of justice." And that is very much in the spirit of Plato's *Euthyphro,* which subordinates mere stories about squabbling gods (killing and castrating each other) to the "idea" of what a truly divine being would love and revere—the eternal verities of piety, justice, and goodness.[120] (Perhaps it was Plato whom Leibniz had in mind when he urged that "a pagan philosopher can love God above all things, because reason can teach him that God is an infinitely perfect and sovereignly lovable being."[121] Here, as ever, "sovereignty" merely modifies love: Plato triumphs over Hobbism and becomes a kind of honorary pre-Christian. As will be seen in Chapter 4, on justice as wise charity, Leibniz' view is that feelings or sentiments of love should arise in proportion to the degree of "perfection" attained by the object/subject of our charity;[122] but that stress on proportion is a "Platonic" rationalist argument having nothing to do with mere revelation.)

It is worth pointing out in passing that Leibniz' derivation of *caritas sapientis* from reason (and not just from revelation) goes far back into his moral-political philosophy: as early as 1677 one finds him saying, in a letter to his original Hanoverian employer Duke Johann Friedrich, that "justice and charity are the true marks of the operation of the Holy Spirit . . . justice and charity, which natural reason dictates."[123] And it was that same natural reason which dictated the Preface to the *Theodicy* more than thirty years later.

LEIBNIZ' ETHICAL USE OF CHRIST

If Christ's "revelation" turns out to be reason—which transhistorically reveals the truth of monotheism, natural immortality, and (even) wise charity—then it is not at all surprising that Leibniz should make a very sparing, minimalist use of Christ in the *Theodicy*, and especially in the ecumenical Preface. But in part 49 of the *Causa Dei,* the Latin *summa* of the *Theodicy*—published as an appendix, together with the refutation of Hobbes' *Liberty, Necessity, and Chance*—Leibniz for once makes the Incarnation of Christ a kind of sufficient reason for the real existence of the world: "The strongest reason for the choice of the best series of events (namely our world) was Jesus Christ, God become man, who as a creature represents the highest degree of perfection."[124] Of this passage, Mark Larrimore rightly says that "nowhere in the body of the *Essais de Théodicée* does Leibniz come as close to Malebranche,"[125] especially to Malebranche's argument in the *Entretiens sur la métaphysique* (1688) that without the Incarnation God can have no motive to create a "ruined" finite world—that the *débris* of that world is redeemed by the Crucifixion, by the "blood sacrifice" of a "perfect victim."[126]

Now Leibniz, in the main body of the *Theodicy,* wants to avoid blood, crosses, and victims: he just wants Christ to reveal and establish reason, so that reason (in turn) can "give" charity, duty, and benevolence. And a slightly closer look at Malebranche's more traditional use of Christ (in what might be called a full-blooded way) will show why Leibniz confined the Incarnation to a passing paragraph in a Latin summary of his *Theodicy.* (If one usually wants to offer Christ as successful institutionalizer of the rational moral imperatives which underpin universal jurisprudence, the horrors of Golgotha do not advance that kind of "reading.") Still, part 49 of the *Causa Dei* shows that Leibniz was willing to try a "Malebranchian" justification of the world at least once.

What Malebranche urged, in the *Entretiens* and other works, is that at first sight it might seem that an *être infiniment parfait* would have no reason to create a ruined, sin-disordered world: "The world is not worthy of God: there is not even any proportion with God, for there is no relation between the infinite and the finite."[127] Malebranche realizes, in all of his efforts at theodicy, that he must show that it is in some sense "better" that a sin-stained world, now governed by "general laws" which permit monsters and grace falling uselessly on hardened hearts, should exist rather than never have been. His solution is Christian, even peculiarly Christian: the ruined world as redeemed by Christ is of greater worth than the nonexistence (or never-existence) of that world.[128] Since the Incarnation constitutes philosophical "salvation" for Malebranche, quite literally "saves" his system, and gives a perfect being a motive for creating a ruined world, a great deal—or rather everything—turns on the advent of Christ; for Malebranche, *culpa* is not simply *felix,* but philosophically essential. "The world as saved by Jesus Christ," Malebranche insists in the *Entretiens,* "is of greater worth than the same universe as at first constructed, otherwise God would not have allowed his work to become corrupted."[129]

It is in view of this that Malebranche can argue that while it is true that "everything is in disorder," this is the consequence of sin: "order itself requires disorder to punish the sinner."[130] In his *Méditations chrétiennes,* indeed, Malebranche suggests that the generally governed but ruined world expresses or symbolizes human depravity:

> The present world is a neglected work. It is the abode of sinners, and it was necessary that disorder appear in it. Man is not such as God made him: thus he has to inhabit ruins, and the earth he cultivates can be nothing more than the debris of a more perfect world. . . . It was necessary that the irregularity of the seasons shorten the life of those who no longer think of anything but evil, and that the earth be ruined and submerged by the waters, that it bear until the end of all centuries the visible marks of divine vengeance.[131]

Though divine wisdom does not appear in the ruined world "in itself," Malebranche adds, nonetheless in relation to both "simplicity" and the just punishment of sinners, the world is such that only an "infinite wisdom" could comprehend all its "beauties."[132] And the greatest of those beauties is an incarnated son of God whose bloody death repairs and restores the ruins.

But Malebranche's theodicy, in its Christocentrism, suffers from a great difficulty which Leibniz almost always managed to avoid (by containing Christ within the moral sphere). Malebranche wants to operate only with an *être parfait,* and imagine what such a perfect being would do—leaving out all scriptural "anthropology."[133] And yet the idea of a perfect being acting uniformly through "general" laws leads to deism, not to Christianity;[134] the concept of a perfect being does not yield a "son" of God who, *qua* "perfect victim," redeems a ruined and sin-disordered world. "Anthropological" Scripture does indeed yield Christ and his earthly works; but anthropology is a concession to "weak" minds. Only Christ saves Malebranche's system, and gives the Father a motive for creating a world unworthy of him; but Christ is not (and cannot be) spun out of the bare idea of "perfection." Malebranche thus needs historical Christianity, even as he claims to rely solely on the concept of *l'être parfait.* It is this need which drives him to the astonishing claim that God the Father "never had a more agreeable sight than that of his only son fastened to the cross to re-establish order in the universe."[135]

Plainly Leibniz does not want to say most of these things—why studiously avoid the Trinity only to find yourself depicting God the Father as gazing at the "agreeable" sight of the crucifixion?—and so in the body of the *Theodicy* he does not say them. Part 49 of the *Causa Dei*—written in technical Latin for Scholastic theologians, unlike the courtly French of the *Theodicy*—is more orthodox, or at least more Christ-centered, than the *Theodicy;* but what one says *en passant* to a theologian is not what one stresses in order to advance the notion that the acceptable part of revelation is just common "reason" itself, together with "the rules of goodness and of justice" as demi-Platonic eternal moral verities. The Preface to the *Theodicy* is, again, a kind of "religion within the limits of reason alone"—even if reason reveals rather more to Leibniz than it ever did to Kant.

More typically Leibnizian than the Christocentric part 49 of the *Causa Dei,* surely, is Leibniz' insistence that the love of God—what he calls "highest charity"—relates to God as such, as the perfect being, not to the "son" of the Trinity.

> The sovereign love of God above all things, taken precisely in itself, considers God only as infinitely perfect, and not at all as living [*habitant*] in the humanity of Jesus Christ—such that everything concerning Jesus Christ as man cannot enter into the mental view essential to the act of sovereign love.[136]

In this passage from c. 1687, Leibniz' Christ merely prepares us for "sovereign love" of the "infinitely perfect"—and indeed Christ as God-man is not infinitely perfect. (Given Malebranche's difficulties, Leibniz wisely leaves the derivation of a semi-perfect God-man from the *être parfait* in the veiled realm of *la mystère*.)[137]

Universal Jurisprudence in Leibniz' Theodicy

Leibniz' final object, in his universal jurisprudence, is to show that a just or wisely charitable perfect being ("God is not only charitable, but charity itself")[138] has actually chosen the "best" world from a range of logically possible ones. "It follows from the supreme perfection of God," he insists in *Principles of Nature and Grace,* "that in producing the universe he has chosen the best possible plan, in which there is . . . the most power, knowledge, happiness, and goodness in created things that the universe allowed . . . the most perfect actual world that is possible."[139] And Leibniz explicitly stresses that "one must seek the reason for the existence of the world, which is the whole assemblage of contingent things . . . in the substance which carries with it the reason for its existence, and which in consequence is necessary and eternal."[140] For even if, as Leibniz often says, finite creatures "tend" toward existence in proportion to their "degree" of perfection (*Monadology*, prop. 54), that tendency cannot amount to a self-translation into existence. Anselm's "ontological" proof is valid only for the perfect being, not for creatures who merely approach perfection. "All existences, except for the existence of God, are contingent [*Omnes existentiae excepte solius Dei Existentia sunt contingentes*]."[141]

Leibniz does not want to make matters easy for himself, however, by minimizing the objections which could be raised against God's having created a "contingent" universe through *caritas sapientis:* on the contrary, he magnifies the difficulties, and the opening sections of Book 1 of the *Theodicy* constitute a *catalogue raisonnée* of the charges that can be brought against God—by fideist skeptics such as Bayle,[142] but above all by those who use harsh Calvinist notions of unmeritable grace and salvation in a way that makes God guilty of an arbitrary "acceptation of persons."[143]

Surely Leibniz knew that he was taking a great moral risk in calling the world "best" and in ascribing "wise charity" to God; for an opponent could say that it is precisely in virtue of *caritas sapientis* that a perfect being would refrain from giving existence to "metaphysically evil" substances. If one just stresses God's power, in the manner of Job or *Leviathan,* or of St. Paul's Romans ("hath not the potter power over the clay?"), the problem disappears: then it is only a matter of what God can do—everything—not of what he "ought" to do. And at least Malebranche's "generality" of law makes God the author of the best world that can be while strictly preserving legal *généralité:* particular evils are unwilled by-products or upshots.[144] But Leibniz gives himself neither a Hobbesian nor a Malebranchian avenue of escape.

It is not just the case, Leibniz begins, that some critics allege that God is the cause of sin or moral evil (since "all creatures and their actions derive from him the reality which they have"); it is not just that some say that, "conservation being a perpetual creation . . . man is perpetually created corrupt and erring"; it is not just that "man is exposed to a temptation to which it is known that he will succumb, thereby causing an infinitude of frightful evils," so that "wickedness will hold sway and virtue will be oppressed on earth."[145] Those charges might be thought to raise doubts about the charity and perfection of God; "but it is much worse when one considers the life to come, since but a small number of men will be saved and since the rest will perish eternally"—at least on a late Augustinian or Calvinist or Jansenist view.

> Furthermore these men destined for salvation will have been withdrawn from the corrupt mass through an unreasoning election, whether it be said that God in choosing them has had regard to their future actions, to their faith or to their works. . . . One must return to the same conclusion that God is the final reason of salvation, of grace, of faith and of election in Jesus Christ . . . [and] that he gives faith or salvation to whom he pleases, without any discernible reason for his choice.[146]

So it is a "terrible judgment," Leibniz goes on to say (in *Theodicy* I, 5), that God, "giving his only son for the whole human race and being the sole author and master of the salvation of men," nonetheless "saves so few of them" and "abandons all the others to the devil his enemy," who "torments them eternally and makes them curse their creator," even though "they have all been created to diffuse and show forth his goodness, his justice and his other perfections." And this outcome "inspires all the more horror" since the "sole cause why these men are wretched to all eternity" comes from "God's having exposed their parents to a temptation that he knew they would not resist"—so that these men "are condemned to be forever rebellious against God and plunged in the most horrible miseries," even though "some of them have perchance been less guilty than some of that little number of the elect, who were saved by a grace without reason."[147]

Here, of course, Leibniz is thinking of the kind of "Augustinian" argument about God's justice which is to be found in Pascal's *Écrits sur la grâce:*

> In the condition of innocence [before the Fall], God could not with justice condemn a single man. . . .
>
> In the condition of corruption [after the Fall], God could with justice damn the entire mass. . . .
>
> Adam . . . having revolted against God . . . has infected and corrupted the entire mass of men, such that humankind has become the just object of the anger and indignation of God. [The Augustinians] understand that God has divided this mass, all equally guilty and wholly worthy of damnation; that he has willed to save a part through an

absolute will based on his pure and grace-filled pity, and that, leaving the other part in its damnation and in which he could with justice leave the entire mass . . . he willed to condemn them.[148]

Heightening rather than damping down the difficulties for a "wisely chari-table" God which are found in the Augustinian position as eloquently enun-ciated by Pascal—and even Pascal was worried enough to insist on God's justice four times in this short passage[149]—Leibniz finally says that one can see how some "theodicies" represent God "as an absolute prince employing a despotic power, unfitted to be loved and unworthy of being loved"—a despot who plunges men into an "abyss of sin" even if they have "never heard" of Jesus Christ.[150] If, despite these "horrible miseries," Leibniz can persuasively urge that the world is "best" and created in time through the justice or *caritas sapientis* of a perfect being, then his philosophical triumph is enormous.

This is why Leibniz, not just in the *Theodicy* but especially in Book IV, chapter 18, of the *New Essays*, tries to set aside quarrels over grace: he insists that we really know very little about that divine gift, and urges that our (reasonable) belief in God's justice requires us to think (*pace* Pascalian argu-ments) that even pre-Christian "pagans" may be given grace sufficient for salvation "at the hour of death," provided they have been good willing and provided they are "contrite" at that mortal hour.[151] (Leibniz dares not discard grace, but he subordinates it to justice.) "Many eminent doctors of the Roman Church," he says in the *New Essays*, "far from damning lax Protestants, have been willing to save even pagans and to maintain that the people in question may have been saved by an act of contrition, that is of penitence resting on a love of benevolence—leading to a love of God above all other things . . . It appears just that God should not withhold his grace from those who are in this state of mind."[152] But if their "state of mind" is benevolent, and if *caritas sapientis = benevolentia universalis*, then "just" pagans ought to get grace. And that is because, in Leibniz' view, one should not attribute anything to God which would be detrimental to his justice; but that, he fears, is precisely what Augustine (in his proto-Jansenist vein) sometimes does: "St. Augustine, in spite of his intelligence and insight, rushed to the other extreme and damned children who die unbaptized [pagans]."[153]

It is uncharitable of us, Leibniz thinks, to doubt the charity of God: if he is always "good and just," how can we lack faith that he will save even those *bene-volent* people who have never heard of official Christianity?

We are fortunate that God is more charitable than men . . . One can, after all, maintain that when God gives them [the pagans] grace sufficient to call forth an act of contrition, he also gives them . . . all the light of faith and all the fervor which they need for their salvation. . . . So it is not very out of the way to grant as much, at least at the point of death, to persons of good will who have not had the advantage of being instructed in Christianity, in the ordinary way. But the wisest course is to take no position regarding things of which so little is known, and to be satisfied with the general belief that God can do nothing which is not entirely good and just.[154]

This is an extraordinary paragraph: under the orthodox guise of preserving "grace," "salvation," and "faith," what really matters is a (not necessarily Christian) "good will" which a just and good divinity must respect. In these passages from the *New Essays* Leibniz reinforces the view that particular sectarian doctrines which are incongruent with universal jurisprudence must be set aside in favor of charity and goodness—the same moral principles which Leibniz used in urging Bossuet to help restore the *respublica christiana* by leaving out of account problematical theological points which cause dissension rather than concord and consensus.[155] (Though Leibniz insists that even non-Christian "persons of good will" may be saved at the last moment, he argues that his view is not "Pelagian." And in that he is right, for it is hyper-Pelagian: Pelagius had stressed the sufficiency of good willing in Christian believers,[156] but Leibniz keeps just *bona voluntas* itself, even in "pagans." Here one sees again why Leibniz could not simply be a Platonist: for it is the sight of "good will" which constrains a just God not to damn the ignorant. And nonetheless a kind of Platonism is still powerfully present, since it is the "ideas" of divine justice and goodness which come before "grace" and "faith.")

In a letter to Philippe Naudé, written only a few years after the *New Essays* (in 1707), Leibniz insists again that in order to "justify the actions of God," one must grant that "his goodness ought not to be taken into account less than his other perfections," and that "it injures his justice to believe for example that . . . men who have been living well morally, though they have never heard Jesus Christ spoken of, are eternally damned for that." Such "unreasonable dogmas" lead to a "decrying of Christianity";[157] they are not congruent with charity as something even more important than faith and grace.

LEIBNIZ' LETTER TO GRIMALDI: CHARITY BEFORE GRACE

Leibniz' effort to turn "grace" into something benign and unproblematical—a Herculean task in the grace-obsessed seventeenth century—together with his corresponding magnification of good will and charity, is at its clearest in his remarkable letter (January–February 1697) to the Jesuit father Claudio Filippo Grimaldi. Father Grimaldi, whom Leibniz had met in Rome in 1689, was president of the Mathematical Tribunal in Peking, and one of the leading figures in the Jesuit enterprise of finding an accommodation between Chinese and Western thought.[158] Leibniz' letter, little known and never translated, must first be seen as a whole, then reread for its amazing near-dissolution of grace (in favor of wise love). The letter also pulls together all of Leibniz' most characteristic social concerns: benevolence, enlightenment, and the advancement of science for both human happiness and the "glory of God."

"The goodness of God is so great," Leibniz begins, "that even those to whom revelation has never been presented are aided by another kind of grace [alio gratiae] which will never be lacking to them, provided that they are not themselves lacking in good will." For "moved by the contemplation of nature, and aided internally from on high," they can "love above all that which they take to be superior to everything in beauty and in perfection"—to the point that "finally, their souls thus prepared, God will spill the light of faith into them." One must therefore, Leibniz continues, "strive to excite in [all] hearts the love of God on which Christ insisted so much, and which reason itself recommends to us." But to see the "beauty and perfection" of God (which can generate love), one needs modern science—for "it is certain . . . that no one can be loved if his beauty remains always veiled to our sight, and that the power and the wisdom which makes the beauty of the supreme intelligence strike our eyes . . . cannot be better revealed to us than by knowledge of the marvels which constitute his workmanship."[159]

Here science, not revelation, reveals God. But Leibniz then shifts from theory to practice, from knowledge to action:

> From this it results that there are three things to be done in order to augment in us the natural light of divinity: first, to form a complete record of the marvels which have already been discovered; next, to work to discover a greater number of them; finally to relate all these discoveries, past and future, to the praise of the supreme master of the universe, and to the growth of the love of God, which cannot be sincere

in us without also including charity toward men. If we were sufficiently fortunate in having a great monarch who one day took these three points to heart, we would advance more in ten years, for the glory of God and the happiness of the human race, than would otherwise be done in several centuries.[160]

Leibniz' letter to Grimaldi is truly extraordinary for a number of reasons. In the letter Leibniz claims that revelation or Scripture is not absolutely morally essential because "another kind of grace"—namely the "contemplation of nature," leading to love for God as "superior to everything" in perfection—is sufficient provided that the contemplators of nature "are not lacking in good will" and that their contemplations are aided from "on high." To propose grace as a kind of moral alternative to revelation, then to transform grace itself into divinely aided "contemplation of nature," is to transform fundamental points of Christian doctrine into scientific enlightenment (Leibniz stresses the "natural light" of divinity). Calvin, or even Pascal, would be horrified by such a theodicy: for Pascal keeps mere science (as a manifestation of *esprit*) infinitely distanced from God and love, which is "of another order."[161]

Not that Leibniz is "heretical": the "physico-theological" proof of the existence of God, after all, infers his perfection from the observation of an intelligent world order which supposedly cannot be the product of blind chance.[162] Still, the drift of the letter to Grimaldi is steadily toward the "advancement of science," and Leibniz says explicitly that the "love" of God arising from scientific contemplation is (in effect) also "insisted on" by "our Lord" and "recommended" by reason. Evidently, for Leibniz, *caritas* is not just confined to a Gospel: science leads to it and reason suggests it, even if Christ "insists" on it. And "grace," over whose varieties—efficient, sufficient, versatile, and so on—an ocean of ink was spilled in the seventeenth century,[163] now becomes a kind of scientific *recherche* which will lead God to pour "faith" into those who (antecedently) see the beauty and perfection of nature and correctly infer God's "goodness" from it. The letter to Grimaldi is amazingly unorthodox, but equally amazingly typical of Leibniz.

To call the contemplation of nature "another kind of grace" is deliberately to weaken the distinction *between* nature and grace which had prevailed ever since Augustine wrote *De Natura et Gratia* in the fifth century. For Augustinianism, "nature" is fallen, corrupt, sinful, and needs to be redeemed by a grace which no one can acquire by his own merits or powers (that would be the

Pelagian sin of pride, the illusion of self-sufficiency).[164] But if the "contemplation of nature" is indeed in our power (as Leibniz thinks it is), and if that contemplation is "another kind of grace," then grace is in our power. From a late Augustinian perspective that would be a shocking conclusion. It is nonetheless one that Leibniz restated in various ways: "One must not imagine that all the graces of God are miraculous. When he uses the natural dispositions of our mind and the [natural] things which surround us, in order to give enlightenment to our understanding, or warmth to our heart (for well-doing), I take that to be grace."[165]

To say, then, with Leibniz, that another kind of grace is the contemplation of nature is theologically very radical—even if one goes on to say that contemplation must be shored up by good will and by aid from on high. It is (again) orthodox enough to say that the contemplation of nature leads to "love" for the perfect author of nature; but to call all of that "grace" is very unorthodox, or at least un-Augustinian, since grace for Augustine is precisely beyond our natural powers. Leibniz' stress, in the letter to Grimaldi, on "charity" and "science" is quite typical of him; but along the way something very unusual happens to *natura et gratia*. Leibniz certainly knew that some of the harsher Calvinist and Jansenist utterances about unmeritable grace (given for unfathomable reasons to an elected few) were really late Augustinian:[166] hence a partial filling in of the Augustinian chasm between nature and grace might help in religious rapprochement with alleged "Pelagians" such as the Jesuits—for example, Father Grimaldi himself. And such a filling-in would be congruent with Leibniz' theodicy project in general: to magnify reason, goodness, and justice, and to diminish the sectarian and the contested.

It is worth noting that at the very moment he was writing to Grimaldi, Leibniz had in press his treatise *Novissima Sinica* (Latest News from China), and that in this little book he amplified the connection between "the contemplation of nature" and the moral-political virtues of justice and charity. In section 8 of the Preface to the *Novissima Sinica*, Leibniz says that he remembers Father Grimaldi's "telling me in Rome how much he admired the virtue and wisdom" of the Chinese ruler, whose "love of justice" and "charity to the populace" were so meritorious; but he moves on quickly to say that "Grimaldi asserted that the [Chinese] monarch's marvelous desire for knowledge almost amounted to a faith," and that this faith-knowledge was revealed by the fact that (after years of Euclidean study) "the emperor prepared a book on geometry, that he might . . . bequeath the wisdom he had brought into his empire as an inheritance to his realm, having in view the happiness of his people even in posterity." There immediately follows a "Platonic" passage, traceable to the virtue-geometry linkage in the *Meno*, in which knowledge of geometry (as something "amounting" to a faith) displaces grace and the supernatural:

> Now geometry ought not to be regarded as the sphere of workmen but of philosophers; for, since every virtue flows from wisdom, and the spirit of wisdom is truth, those who thoroughly investigate the demonstrations of geometers have perceived the nature of eternal truth, and are able to tell the certain from the uncertain. Other mortals waver amid guesses, and, not knowing the truth, almost ask, with [Pontius] Pilate, what it is. But there is no doubt that the monarch of the Chinese saw very plainly what in our part of the world Plato formerly taught, that no one can be educated in the mysteries of the sciences except through geome-try. . . . The strength of our geometry, as soon as it was tested by the King, was so much to his liking that he easily came to believe that those who had learned thus to reason might teach correctly in other things.[167]

Here nature-contemplating, geometry-measuring scientific knowledge (as "another kind of grace") now also "amounts" to a faith: *gratia* and *fides* are swallowed up by *sapientia*, and a geometry-loving ruler who cannot have absorbed "Augustianian" grace is nonetheless both just and charitable. In this astonishing part of the *Novissima Sinica*, one almost finds *Meno*'s equation of knowledge, geometry, virtue, and justice—and this "amounts" to the (unor-thodox) faith which a Chinese ruler might have. And if that ruler knows "eternal truth" and is just and charitable, he is (in effect) a better Christian than Louis XIV, the self-styled Rex Christianissimus (whom Leibniz called Mars Christianissimus). In the preface to the *Novissima Sinica* all good things— truth, wisdom, Platonic geometry, charity, justice, virtue, popular happiness— are strongly related to one another, if not fully equated. The Chinese ruler is wise, knows the "eternal truths"; he is just and charitable. But if he is wise and charitable, is that not *caritas sapientis*—through the contemplation of nature, which is "another kind of grace"? By contrast Pontius Pilate lacks wisdom ("what is truth?") and is neither just nor charitable: he permits the judicial murder of Christ, who did the most to make charity *the* central virtue on earth. It is no accident that the wisely charitable virtues of an enlightened ruler—a Platonic geometer—are contrasted with the weak viciousness of Pilate: Leibniz could have pitched upon many bad rulers, but he singled out the one who publicly executed *caritas'* embodiment. East is East, but East is also West—when the protection of charity is at stake. As Leibniz urged in a poem (1697) for Mlle. de Scudery,

> Qu'on soit Européen, Chinois, mondain en somme,
> La magnanimité n'y regarde que l'homme.[168]

THE MAIN BODY OF THE *THEODICY:* UNIVERSAL JUSTICE

With the provenance of Leibniz' ethics-tinted religious thought sufficiently in place, and with "grace" more marginalized than in the thought of any other seventeenth-century religious thinker of the first rank, one can finally turn to Leibniz' strongest and clearest statement of the central moral and jurispru- dential thesis of the *Theodicy*—that because a morally perfect being made the world in time, freely translated "essence" or possibility into real existence, the world *must* be best, must be justifiable, despite its being riddled with horrible evils. This strong and clear statement appears in part 35 of the "Preliminary Dissertation on the Conformity of Faith with Reason," and what is interesting here is that Leibniz argues his case as a lawyer, as a "jurisconsult" *(préformation professionnelle)*—and he does this by saying that while God's conduct must be justified and justifiable, his "case" is not just like that of an ordinary criminal suspect.

Leibniz begins with Bayle's argument in the *Entretiens de Maxime et de Thémiste* (1706) that if God foreknows the fall of man—which of course he must, being omniscient and therefore knowledgeable of future contingents— he might be charged with injustice (or at least "connivance") if he fails to prevent a calamitous moral evil which his omnipotence could arrest or avert. In the same way, Bayle says, a parent who foresees that his virgin daughters will be seduced at a ball, and nonetheless lets them go, is "as guilty as the seducer"—and the plea of merely "permitting" evil, not positively causing it, will not be sufficient.[169] Here Leibniz must be careful: he does not want to say, with Hobbes, that "we" (humans) commit injustice in "calling God before the bar"[170] to answer charges; but neither does he want to say that God is to be condemned for failing to prevent all evil. He therefore, with great juris- prudential subtlety, draws a distinction between "right" and "fact": the same principles of right apply (universally) to God and man, but the facts of their "cases" are different. Bayle, Leibniz urges, "seems to demand that God be justified in such a manner as that commonly used for pleading the cause of a man accused before his judge." Bayle doubts, Leibniz goes on, "that one can justify the goodness of God in the permission of sin, because probability would be against a man that should happen to be in circumstances comparable in our eyes to this permission." In Bayle's story of a parent who permits his child to be seduced, Leibniz grants, it is quite true that "the judge would not be satisfied by the excuses of a lawyer who said that the man only permitted the evil, without doing it or willing it"; the judge would view the permissive parent as an "accessory" in the child's "sin of commission."[171]

> But it must be borne in mind that when one has foreseen the evil and has not prevented it although it seems as if one could have done so with ease, and one has even done things that have facilitated it, it does not follow on that account *necessarily* that one is accessory thereto. It is only a very strong presumption, such as commonly replaces truth in human affairs, but which would be destroyed by an exact consideration of the facts, supposing we were capable of that in relation to God. Now there is every reason to conclude unquestionably . . . that reasons most just, and stronger than those which appear contrary to them, have compelled the all-wise being to permit the evil, and even to do things which have facilitated it.[172]

It is not merely, Leibniz goes on to urge, that since God "takes care of the whole universe," all of whose parts are "connected," he must have had in mind "innumerable considerations whose result made him deem it inadvisable to prevent certain evils"; that is true, but what is really decisive is the fact that there must have been

> great or rather invincible reasons which prompted the divine wisdom to the permission of the evil that surprises us, from the mere fact that this permission has occurred: for nothing can come from God that is not altogether consistent with goodness, justice and holiness. Thus we can judge by the event, or *a posteriori*, that the permission was indispensable, although it is not possible for us to show this *a priori* by the detailed reasons that God can have had for this, since it is not necessary either that we show this to justify him.[173]

At this point Leibniz tries to meet Bayle's doubts by quoting Bayle himself: for the *philosophe de Rotterdam* had allowed in his *Reply to the Questions of a Provincial* that "sin made its way into the world; God therefore was able to permit it without detriment to his perfections; *ab actu ad potentiam valet consequentia* [one can draw a valid consequence from the act to the capacity]."

Leibniz then supplies his own paraphrase of Bayle's concession: "In God this conclusion holds good: he did this, therefore he did it well." It is not the case, then, he goes on, "that we have no notion of justice in general fit to be applied also to God's justice"; nor is it true that "God's justice has other rules than the justice known of men." Rather the facts of the divine case are "different." And he ends with a ringing reassertion of his universal jurisprudence: "universal right is the same for God and men; but the question of fact is quite different in their case and in his."[174]

God is perfect in every way, and therefore perfectly just (inter alia); if he endowed the "best" world with real existence in time—which he plainly did, since finite substances do not exist *ex necessitatis*—he must have had a morally praiseworthy "sufficient reason" for doing so. (This reason may be beyond our reason, Leibniz urges, but it cannot be contrary to it; for now we see through a glass, darkly, but then. . . .) In short, Leibniz insists, there are no conclusive "reasons at all" which can overcome "the assurance or confidence in God wherewith we can and ought to say that God has done all things well." The objections of Bayle are therefore only "prejudices and probabilities" which are "overthrown by reasons incomparably stronger."[175]

All of this is perhaps clearer in several writings leading up to the *Theodicy* than in that work itself; in a letter to Jaquelot from October 1706, for example, Leibniz insists that "on the question of the origin of evil, he who would like to bring an invincible objection against the goodness and the wisdom of God would have to prove (for example) that evil could be avoided without losing some considerably greater good." But, Leibniz says, to prove this thesis "it would not suffice to say that someone else cannot prove the contrary nor show the connection between these evils and greater goods"; for it is enough that one can say "that this connection is possible until the contrary be proved—which will not come about, inasmuch as an absurdity would follow from it, namely, that God would not have acted conformably to the most perfect wisdom."[176] Since it is true, Leibniz goes on to say, that "there is an infinitely perfect God who has permitted evil, one must say with St. Augustine that he has done it for a greater good, though it is above the power of human reason to show a priori and in detail in what this good consists." For it "suffices," he adds, "that one know in the large and a posteriori that this must be true," since "evil has come about and since God exists."[177]

And in some "Notes on Bayle" from 1706 which must have served as preliminary sketches for the *Theodicy*, Leibniz says much the same thing, and reveals his celebrated powers as a logician. "It could be true," he begins, "that we cannot explain distinctly how the physical and moral evil of man accords with the perfection of God, that is to say, in what consists the detail of the reasons which have brought God to permit these evils; but it does not at all follow from this that the objections which one makes in this regard cannot be resolved." And Leibniz finally maintains that "it is possible that God has such reasons, though we cannot grasp them." For he who wants "to put forward an objection which cannot be resolved must prove that it is impossible that God have these reasons." A successful objector would have to "bring forward an argument which infers the imperfection of God from the permission of evil," and which is such that "one cannot respond to it as is necessary." The objector's argument would have to be "in good form"—all of its propositions would have to be "agreed to" or "proved by another argument." "Now I say that such an argument does not exist," Leibniz insists. "And to say that one must admit that which reason or revelation teaches us, though there are invincible objections to it, is to suppose an impossible case."[178]

For all his doubts about Bayle, nonetheless, Leibniz thought that his Rotterdam colleague was at least seeking the justice of God, worrying about it—unlike "some" (Hobbes is plainly meant) who will not even permit God's case to come up in the court of reason. In section 37 of the *Theodicy* he comments

> One must not say either that what we call justice is nothing in relation to God, that he is the absolute master of all things even to the point of being able to condemn the innocent without violating his justice, or finally that justice is something arbitrary where he is concerned. . . . For if such were the case there would be no reason for praising his goodness and his justice; rather would it be as if the most wicked spirit, the Prince of evil genii, the evil principle of the Manicheans, were the sole master of the universe . . . What means would there be of distinguishing the true God from the false God of Zoroaster if all things depended upon the caprice of an arbitrary power and there were neither rule nor consideration for anything whatever?[179]

Leibniz had long been concerned to show that there must be sufficient "reason for praising" divine goodness and justice; he had used almost exactly the same words in the "Discourse on Metaphysics" a quarter-century earlier.[180]

But part 37 of the *Theodicy* is only an elaboration of something that Leibniz had already made clear in the Preface to that work. Those who give dispro-

portionate weight to divine omnipotence and who are "convinced that nothing comes to pass save by the will and power of God" ascribe to him
"intentions and actions so unworthy of the greatest and best of all beings"
that one would say that authors such as Hobbes have "renounced the dogma
which recognizes God's justice and goodness."[181] They imagine, indeed, that
"being supreme master of the universe, he could without any detriment to
his holiness cause sins to be committed, simply at his will and pleasure." Still
worse, they fancy that "he could take pleasure in eternally afflicting innocent
people without doing any injustice, because no one has the right to control
his actions."[182] But if Hobbes is (for Leibniz) the worst offender in this respect,
even Malebranche's assertion that there is "no relation" between the infinite
and the finite is excessive: "on the plea that we are nothing in comparison
with him, they liken us to earthworms which men crush without heeding as
they walk."[183]

Leibniz charitably grants that those who take such a view—and he is
always thinking of Hobbes' notion that God's natural "dominion" over men
comes from "irresistible power"—may imagine that they are magnifying God
by magnifying his independence of moral ideas; but they are fatally mistaken.
He makes his case in a section of the *Theodicy* which has a good claim to be
the morally central paragraph of the whole work:

> I believe that many persons otherwise of good intentions are misled by
> these ideas, because they do not have sufficient knowledge of their
> consequences. They do not see that, properly speaking, God's justice is
> thus overthrown. For what idea shall we form of such a justice as has
> only will for its rule, that is to say, where the will is not guided by the
> rules of good and even tends directly towards evil? Unless it be the idea
> contained in that tyrannical definition by Thrasymachus in Plato, which
> designated as *just* that which pleases the stronger. Such indeed is the
> position taken up, albeit unwittingly, by those who rest all obligation
> upon constraint, and in consequence take power as the gauge of right.
> But one will soon abandon maxims so strange and so unfit to make men
> good and charitable through the imitation of God.[184]

In this last paragraph, the whole of Leibnizian practical thought is present:
the more-than-vestigial Platonism, the insistence on charity as *imitatio Dei*, the
presentation of Thrasymachus as a proto-Hobbesian. In this paragraph the
ethical import of the *Theodicy* is supremely clear: that "theodicy" rightly
understood is not just a garden-variety theology but a "universal jurispru-

dence" emerges plainly. The universe must be justifiable and "best," even if it contains sin, damnation, Judas, Pontius Pilate, and Caligula.[185]

THE MIDDLE OF THE *THEODICY:* HOBBES AGAIN

For Leibniz' theodicy viewed as a "theory of justice," parts 176–178 of the *Theodicy* are especially important. Those sections reveal that the principal enemy in that work is not after all Pierre Bayle—who rarely turns out to be more than half-wrong[186]—but Hobbes, Spinoza, and their *epigone:* those who say that one cannot ascribe the common concepts of justice and goodness to God. Leibniz apparently thought Bayle to be a sincere believer who simply took refuge too quickly in a Pascalian fideism, abandoning the intensely Malebranchian rational theology of the *Pensées diverses sur la comète* under the pressure of Pyrrhonist doubts about the possibility of reconciling God's power and goodness through human reason alone.[187] The real Leibnizian worry is not about those who (at least) believe God just (through a pure act of faith): the real worry is a "supralapsarian" such as Rutherford, who (according to Leibniz) "says positively that nothing is unjust or morally bad in God's eyes before he has forbidden it, that without this prohibition it would be a matter of indifference whether one murdered or saved a man, loved God or hated him, praised or blasphemed him. Nothing is so unreasonable as that."[188] Obviously *caritas sapientis* cannot be the essence of justice, for God and men alike, if "love" and "murder" are indifferent matters. And obviously (for Leibniz) the root of the difficulty is in Descartes' claim (in the *Reply to the Six Objections*)[189] that there are no truths antecedent to God's will: Rutherford simply makes clear and distinct the dreadfulness of that doctrine, especially when it is fused with Hobbesian "sovereignty." Arguments such as Rutherford's simply "deprive God of the designation good: for what cause could one have to praise him for what he does, if in doing something quite different he would have done equally well?" (This is again, almost verbatim, the language of the "Discourse on Metaphysics.")[190]

Moving on from Rutherford in particular to more general reflections on the types of bad theodicy which wreck universal jurisprudence, Leibniz finally says

> One may teach that God established good and evil by a positive law, or one may assert that there was something good and just before his decree, but that he is not required to conform to it, and that nothing prevents

him from acting unjustly and from perhaps condemning innocence: but it all comes to the same thing, offering almost equal dishonor to God. For if justice was established arbitrarily and without any cause, if God came upon it by a kind of hazard, as when one draws lots, his goodness and his wisdom are not manifested in it, and there is nothing at all to attach him to it.[191]

If it is by "a purely arbitrary decree, without any reason," that God has established or created "what we call justice," Leibniz laments, then he can "annul" or "change" it at every moment. But if justice is "founded on reasons" which have a Platonic eternal validity, then "it is possible to say" that God will "observe" it.[192] And that must be the correct view (Leibniz urges in a 1715 letter to Greiffenkranz) because "theodicy signifies the doctrine of the justice of God."[193]

The trouble with all three of the dogmas which he has just considered, Leibniz says—"(1) that the nature of justice is arbitrary; (2) that it is fixed but it is not certain that God will observe it; (3) that the justice we know is not that which he observes"—is that, though they are "a little different," they have an identical moral effect: they equally destroy "the confidence in God that gives us tranquility, and the love of God that makes our happiness. There is nothing to prevent such a God from behaving as a tyrant and an enemy of honest people."[194] The problem comes, always, from unreasonably over-stressing omnipotence as the dominant (or perhaps only knowable) divine attribute. And this Leibniz traces, as usual, to Hobbes (who merits "much discredit") and to Spinoza (who "acknowledges no goodness in God . . . and teaches that all things exist through the necessity of the divine nature").[195]

That Leibniz was constantly thinking of Hobbes and Spinoza, not just in the *Theodicy* but as far back as the unpublished manuscript called *De Schismate* (1683), is always evident: for if Leibniz' practical thought, on its positive side, rests on a "universal" charity that should equally terminate doctrinal dispu-tation, end schism, restore the *respublica christiana*, shape the domestic policies of benevolent princes, and even animate God in choosing the "best" world, on its negative side it is colored by its unrelieved hostility to the "Hobbism" and "Spinozism" which are under attack in *De Schismate*.[196] To restore Chris-tian unity and charitable concord, Leibniz was willing to countenance merely heterodox religious and moral views: but Hobbism and Spinozism were (*De Schismate* urges) "opinions worse than any heresy"—opinions through which not just Christianity but "every religion is made to fall" ("this gangrene spreads itself more and more"). His real worry, Leibniz says, is not "libertines" who err through mere "lightness of mind," but "pseudo-philosophers" who "abuse the profession of wisdom to the destruction of mortals."[197] As a demi-Platonic believer in uncreated eternal verities, Leibniz had always been distressed by the Cartesian argument that God creates all truth in time, and in Spinoza he saw a dangerous extension of this Cartesian voluntarism: in Spinoza, Leibniz complains, everything is established by a blind "decision of will, from which it follows that the object of the divine will is not good and that the object of the divine intellect is not true [*nec objectum voluntatis divinae esse bonum, nec objectum intellectus divini esse verum*]."[198] But it is "the most serious error" to believe that "the nature of the true depends upon the divine will": here "becoming" (creation in time) must yield to Parmenidean changeless being.[199]

Turning to Hobbes, whose doctrine of unaccountable divine irresistible power he always lumped with Thrasymachus' views in the *Republic,* Leibniz grants in *De Schismate* that the sage of Malmesbury is "a man of some ingenuity and of acute eloquence" who is "not to be despised" when talking of civil matters *("in rebus civilibus non contemnendus")* but whose "crass errors in mathematics" (let no one ignorant of geometry enter here) have shown that he is "a man little capable of profound meditation"—as evidenced above all by the Hobbesian view that "all substance is body."[200] Here Leibniz' Platonism shines through variously, as in the later *Theodicy:* to be guilty of "crass errors" (such as vain circle-squaring) in mathematics is morally problematical if even Meno's slave "sees" virtue just as he sees the Pythagorean theorem,[201] and if harmony (frequently for Leibniz and usually for Plato) links eternal mathematical verity to psychology, ethics, politics, and cosmology by instantiating mathematical relationships in an available form—with harmony ever expanding, in concentric circles, from the well-tuned *psyche* to the *polis* to the *kosmos.*[202]

Here one thinks again of Leibniz' 1696 letter to Electress Sophie of Hanover urging that just as "the truth of numbers" and of "figures in geometry" are eternal verities which are "the fixed and immutable point on which everything turns," so too "order and harmony are also something mathematical and which consist in certain proportions"—and that justice itself is "nothing less than order."[203] To fit Christian *caritas* and Augustinian *bona voluntas* into this musical Greek *kosmos* admittedly taxed Leibniz' ingenuity (as was seen in Chapter 1): if charity can be viewed partly as a demi-Platonic erotic ascent from the concupiscent love of bodies to disinterested love of changeless truth, as in *Phaedrus* 256b, the "will" is both hard to incorporate into the Platonic notion that "virtue is wisdom" (*Protagoras* 349a) and difficult to reconcile with Leibniz' own belief that the eternally given "complete concept" of a person merely unfolds in time with "certainty."[204]

Hobbes, *De Schismate* allows, is "not to be despised" (a left-handed compliment) when speaking of "civil matters," but he will never uncover a universal jurisprudence as geometrically necessary as the "absolutes" of *Phaedo* 75d. And that is partly because—as was seen in Chapter 2—his notion that "all substance is body" destroys the autonomy of the mind that Plato and Aristotle had first demonstrated in their "monadologies" ("Plato explains divinely well incorporeal substances distinct from matter and ideas independent of the senses").[205] For Platonism and for Leibniz (and then later for Kant), as was clear in Chapters 1 and 2, *Leviathan*'s notion that "there is no conception in a man's mind" that has not been "begotten upon the organs of sense" by the pressure of "objects" makes moral ideas (including Hobbes' own) literally inconceivable.[206]

In a still-unpublished manuscript from the Leibniz-Archiv in Hanover, "De Bona Unitatis et Malis Schismatis" (c. 1691), which elaborates Leibniz' anti-Hobbism in *De Schismate*, the notion that the "precept" of Christian social unity is *caritas summum*, the "highest charity," is opposed to the social horrors which will come about in charity's absence: without *caritas* or "the perfection of the will" there will be "hatred and diffidence," "internecine war," "infidelity succeeded by impiety," "libertinism" [especially "in England and Holland"], and "contempt for religion everywhere." The first horrors, at least, are like those in *Leviathan*'s chapter 13—the ones which make human life "solitary, poor, nasty, brutish, and short." Characteristically, however, Leibniz in this 1691 manuscript opposes to these horrors not Hobbesian legality but "the highest charity": here too justice goes beyond harm-avoidance to arrive at love. And in the margin of "De Bono Unitatis" Leibniz appeals to the authority of Erasmus' *De Sarcienda Ecclesiae Concordia*—the late work in which the great Dutch humanist tried to overcome schismatic hatred through charity and accommodation.[207]

Leibniz' insistence on a yawning chasm between charity and "Hobbism" in this unpublished 1691 manuscript may have been prompted by his slightly earlier reading (Rome 1689) of Cudworth's *True Intellectual System of the Universe*. In his 1689 notes on the Cambridge Platonist, Leibniz recalls Cicero's words in *De Natura Deorum* I, 43–44: "Is there no natural charity [*caritas naturalis*] between the good? . . . Do you think that even human beneficence and benignity are solely due to human infirmity? . . . For what can be better or more excellent then kindness and beneficence? Represent God as devoid of either, and you make him devoid of all love, affection, or esteem for any other being, human or divine." Leibniz then notes (again) that Hobbes derives rightfulness from God's irresistible power alone *("jus Deo esse a sola potentia irresistibili"),* and complains (again) that Descartes makes "good and evil, true and false, depend upon the arbitrary will of God." Here the point is clear: even a "pagan" such as Cicero grasps universal jurisprudence (resting on *caritas naturalis* and beneficence) better than the modern trinity of Hobbes, Descartes, and Spinoza. And Leibniz must also have cherished what Cicero goes on to say in the next lines of *De Natura Deorum:* "There is something attractive in the very sound of the word 'love' [*amor*], from which the term for friendship [*amicitia*] is derived. If we base our friendship on its profit to ourselves, and not on its advantage to those whom we love, it will not be friendship at all, but a mere bartering of selfish interests. That is our standard of value for meadows and fields and herds of cattle . . . but charity [*caritas*] and friendship between men is disinterested; how much more so therefore is that of the gods, who, although in need of nothing, yet both love each other and care for the interests of men."[208] In this passage, Leibniz would say, Cicero is Roman and catholic, a kind of proto-Erasmus, if not indeed Roman Catholic.

THE END OF THE *THEODICY:* THE FALL OF THE ROMAN MONARCHY

It is noteworthy that Leibniz ends and crowns the *Theodicy* with a moral-political tale or myth, in the manner of Plato's *Gorgias* and *Republic*—and it is a Graeco-Roman tale, at that. But, not surprisingly, this moral tale does not really resolve the two capital difficulties of Leibniz' universal jurisprudence: does God act with wise charity in fashioning a world which is "best" but not good? And can human beings exhibit greater *caritas sapientis,* greater benevolence, than they actually do?

The end of the *Theodicy,* a weighty set-piece, is Leibniz' enlarged reworking of Lorenzo Valla's *Dialogue on Free Will* (written in opposition to Boethius);[209] and in this tale the Roman king Sextus Tarquin—the violator of Lucretia and destroyer of the Roman monarchy which began with Romulus and Numa[210]—consults the Oracle at Delphi (Apollo) to discover his fate. When told that he will be a rapist and an outcast, he complains of a freedom-destroying fatalism which absolves him from responsibility. Apollo replies that oracular foreknowledge of the future does not cause that future—here Apollo seems to foreknow a lot of Scholastic metaphysics—and sends Tarquin off to complain to Jupiter, who has actually translated the world into real existence.[211]

It is at this point that Leibniz' moral-political myth becomes problematical, because at first Jupiter tells Tarquin that if he will "renounce" Rome and kingship, the Fates will spin a quite different destiny for him:

> Sextus [Tarquinius], quitting Apollo and Delphi, seeks out Jupiter at Dodona. . . . Why have you condemned me, O great God, to be wicked and unhappy? Change my lot and my heart, or acknowledge your error. Jupiter answers him: If you will renounce Rome, the Fates shall spin for you different fates, you shall become wise, you shall be happy. . . . Sextus, not being able to resolve upon so great a sacrifice, went forth from the temple, and abandoned himself to his fate. . . . Theodorus, the High Priest . . . addressed these words to Jupiter: You have convinced this man of his error; he must henceforth impute his unhappiness to his evil will. But your faithful worshippers are astonished; they would fain wonder at your goodness as well as at your greatness: for it rested with you to give him a different will.[212]

Up until that last phrase ("it rested with you to give him a different will"), Tarquin seems, in sufficient measure, to be the master of his own fate: *if* he will renounce Rome—perhaps even from a motive of charity or benevolence—he will be "wise" and "happy." In this early part of the story Tarquin cannot bring himself to renounce Roman kingship; but in the sentence, "it rested with you [Jupiter] to give him a different will," one begins to see that Tarquin "could" have acted differently (and better) only if his "concept" (from eternity) had included the predicate of "not raping Lucretia," only if he had been given "a different will"—since, after all, *caritas sapientis* is universal benevolence. At first it seems that Jupiter gives a well-meaning command ("renounce Rome") that Tarquin could obey, but willfully spurns; in part 416, however, which terminates the *Theodicy*, Leibniz' strong notion (from the "Discourse on Metaphysics") that every action of a substance is "certain" and "determined" turns out to be decisive: for Tarquin was wicked "from all eternity."[213]

It is Theodorus the high priest who learns of Tarquin's eternal wickedness when he enters a vast edifice which represents the best of all possible worlds:

The halls rose in a pyramid, becoming even more beautiful as one mounted towards the apex, and representing more beautiful worlds. Finally they reached the highest one which . . . went on increasing to infinity. That is (as the Goddess explained) because amongst an endless number of possible worlds there is the best of all, else God would not have determined to create any. . . . We are in the real, true world (said the Goddess) and you are at the source of happiness. Behold what Jupiter makes ready. . . . Here is Sextus [Tarquinius] as he is, and as he will be in reality. . . . You see him going to Rome, bringing confusion everywhere, violating the wife of his friend. . . . You see that my father Jupiter did not make Sextus wicked; he was so from all eternity. My father only granted him the existence which his wisdom could refuse to the world where he is included: he made him pass from the region of the possible to that of the actual beings.[214]

"The crime of Sextus" Tarquinius, the Goddess concludes, "serves for great things: it renders Rome free; thence will arise a great empire, which will show noble examples to mankind."[215]

At the end of the *Theodicy*, then, there seems to be a tension between Leibniz' notion of rational substances as individual and autonomous—as independent "minds" which represent the universe from a unique perspective, as distinct monads that are individually morally responsible under universal jurisprudence—and the world as a harmonious whole in which the parts are sometimes sacrificed to what is best overall (so that Tarquin "serves" for great things in the universal plan).

The most striking instance of such a sacrifice of the individual to the universal is precisely in the story of Tarquin, where the Goddess explains to Theodorus that the crime of Tarquin is historically crucial: it makes Rome free. But even if the year 509 B.C. gives us the virtuous Brutus in exchange for the vicious Tarquin—which is a political and moral advance—does Leibniz really want to be a "philosopher of history" for whom the general (and generally good) outcome justifies the ruin of individuals? That is painfully close to Machiavellism; and it was Machiavelli who urged that a historically great ruler will often have to act "against charity."[216] If Tarquin is just the instrument of final universal harmony, and if he was wicked "from all eternity," in what sense could he (as an individual) have been more wisely charitable—by following Jupiter's advice and sparing Lucretia?

It is precisely at this point in the *Theodicy* that it is easy to imagine a hostile reading of Leibniz' whole "universal jurisprudence": one has only to look at the definition *justitia est caritas sapientis seu benevolentia universalis* in the light of the most celebrated Leibnizian doctrines—monadology, theodicy, preestablished harmony—and the difficulties leap out. Given Leibniz' usual equation of wise love with universal benevolence (and given his idea of a "measured" love which ought to be proportional to degrees of "perfection"),[217] the serious problem is then the relation of perfection to the "good will" that makes benevolence possible: if (again) Tarquin is insufficiently charitable because "the causes of understanding were lacking"[218] (owing to metaphysical imperfection), if he was wicked "from all eternity," then "having a good will" was not "in his power."[219] If we cannot, in the "best" world, have a better will (given our "certain" predicates), then we cannot say, with Augustine in *De Libero Arbitrio*, "What is more in the power of the will than the will itself?"[220] If this difficulty is not resolved by Leibniz' distinction between moral and metaphysical necessity—and it is not, since Tarquin's malevolence is "certain" in the best world—then it is fatal for *caritas sapientis* to be equated with universal good willing. "Our" moral perfection will not be ours except in the sense that "our" predicates are unfolding in time. And if the Augustinian component of Leibnizianism, *bona voluntas*, cannot be plausibly saved, then it matters less that one can say (rather more successfully) that measured love should be proportional to degrees of perfection. If everyone's imperfection is just "there" (though admittedly not "metaphysically" necessary), then measured love will be proportional to something uncontrollable and nonmeritorious.[221] But that would be an odd "universal jurisprudence." (Clearly Leibniz was able to imagine an "alternative" Tarquin with quite different predicates, who goes "to a city placed between two seas" where he "buys a little garden"—and yet another Tarquin who becomes King of Thrace and lives happily ever after.[222] But those are not the Tarquins whom God chose to endow with actual temporal existence as a *conditio sine qua non* of the best possible world.)

Leibniz, to be sure, was perfectly aware that such objections might reasonably be made, that someone might argue that "he who gives only to some, but not to all, the means which produce in them effectively a good will . . . has not sufficient goodness."[223] Jupiter might be charged with not giving Tarquin "a different will." But to such a charge Leibniz can only respond with his usual defense of God's justice:

It would not have been in order always to act in an extraordinary manner, and to reverse the connection of things. The reasons of this connection, by which one is placed in more favorable circumstances than another, are hidden in the depths of the wisdom of God; they depend upon the universal harmony. The best plan of the universe, which God could not fail to choose, made it so. We judge from the event itself, since God has made it, that it was not possible to do better.[224]

But then for Tarquin too it "was not possible to do better"; both he and God seem to escape the grasp of wise charity. That a somewhat different Tarquin "could have" acted better has no bearing on the conduct of the historically actual Tarquin. Universal "harmony" and "the best plan" make Tarquin "serve" by rape and treachery; once again the tension between the moral autonomy of individual monads and the general requirements of "the plan" is strongly in evidence. Small wonder that Leibniz, for all his rationalism, should need to fall back on the Pauline phrase, "hidden in the depths of the wisdom of God"—even if it is fideists who usually appeal to Pauline *O altitudo* and have their reasons for doubting reason.[225]

It remains only to wonder why Leibniz should have ended the *Theodicy* with Jupiter rather than with the Judaeo-Christian God, particularly since (as Robinet has shown) Leibniz placed his Graeco-Roman story at the end of his book only at the last moment—transferring it at the time of publication from parts 376–377, where it would have been half-buried and not very obtrusive, to the prominent and memorable place which it occupies at the end.[226] Had Leibniz not undertaken this transfer, the *Theodicy* would have ended with a wholly characteristic blast against "power" as *the* divine attribute; for at the close of part 404—the original final part, at the end of which Leibniz wrote *fin*—he offers a *reductio ad absurdum* of *potestas*-colored theodicy by criticizing the Pliny "who carps at the power of God because God cannot destroy himself."[227] If God exists *ex necessitatis*, then one cannot reasonably pull a single attribute—perfect power—out of a complex of attributes (including omniscience and perfect goodness), declare the single attribute of omnipotence the only "real" or knowable one, and then "carp" at God for not demonstrating that omnipotence with a spectacular feat of self-annihilation. Had Leibniz ended the *Theodicy* with part 404, the central theme of his theology *qua* "the jurisprudence of the universal republic"—namely, the Hobbes-subverting antivoluntarism, in which the philosopher of Malmesbury and Thrasymachus are made to embrace *stat pro ratione voluntas*—would have been brought home one last time.[228] Pliny's notion that a really omnipotent being would manifest his irresistible power by suicide is for Leibniz the ultimate refinement of willful will. Had Leibniz ended the *Theodicy* by letting Pliny (rather than God) self-destruct, there might even have been grounds for the 1737 judgment of the Jesuit-run *Journal de Trévoux* that Leibniz, by showing that a morally perfect being would use power *only* to "realize" wise charity, was tacitly engaged in the politically subversive project of undermining earthly sovereignty as *plenitudo potestatis*.[229] (Why should a king want to do what God rejects, if good conduct is an *imitatio Dei?*)

The fact remains that Leibniz did transfer Jupiter to the end of his book. Perhaps the point of *Theodicy* 416, in which the world is governed by Jupiter, is that "natural" religion has no need of Christ except as the successful "translator" of what "wise men" knew into universal practice, as the giver of a "charity" which supreme reason recommends (but fails to "institutionalize"). But to have monotheism defended by Jupiter remains bizarre, and the Father of the gods usually practiced "love" in a not very Christ-anticipating way (one thinks of the rape of Europa and the carrying off and ravishing of Ganymede).[230] When Jupiter asks Tarquin to renounce rape and Rome, he is demanding what he never strove to accomplish himself—though to complain of hypocrisy in Jupiter would not be to single out his worst fault. To be sure, all of this may be pressing too hard: perhaps Leibniz just thought that Valla's tale was a good story—mythologically intriguing and jurisprudentially serviceable enough. But to crown a huge work on "universal jurisprudence" in the "best" world with a god who is *infiniment imparfait* remains a little odd.[231]

Given the unorthodox (though entertaining) close of the *Theodicy*, in which Jupiter and Tarquin are in high relief and Christ and Moses recede into the shadows, it is best to revert (at the end) to a more characteristic summary of Leibniz' notion of theodicy as a defense of the justice of God, while drawing in his central concern for scientific enlightenment as the means to charitably advance the common good. And here the perfect text is his letter to Morrell of September 1698: "I am effectively of the opinion that God could not do better than he does, and that all the imperfections which we believe we find in the world come only from our ignorance."[232] Malebranche, then, is wrong to see "particular" evils as real, as occasioned by the sheer generality of "Cartesian" laws. "We are not yet in the true point of view to judge the beauty of things," Leibniz continues. "It is a little like astronomy, where the movement of the planets seems a pure confusion when viewed from earth; but if we were on the sun, we should find with the naked eye that beautiful disposition of the system which Copernicus discovered by force of reasoning." And then there is an echo of the remarkable manuscript "Double Infinity in Pascal," written only a year or two earlier: "As the smallest bodies are (so to speak) little worlds full of marvelous creatures, one must not imagine that there are deserts, absolutely speaking, though they are deserts for us." Despite Leibniz' Hellenophilia, he was not willing to endorse Protagoras' famous words: "One must consider that we are not the measure of all things, above all in the condition in which we presently are."[233]

Finally Leibniz reaffirms the view that the overall "best" condition of the universe justifies the outweighing of individual well-being; the doctrine of *Radical Origination of Things* (1697) is restated in a less lyrical way.

> Sins themselves are only evils for those who sin, and absolutely speaking they augment the perfection of things, as shadows are good in a painting to bring out the lights. . . . It even seems to me that these truths are so important that without comprehending them well one cannot truly esteem or love God—the indifference which some attribute to him being absolutely incompatible with a perfect wisdom and goodness.[234]

And this letter to Morrell merely anticipates what Leibniz stresses in the orthodox, Jupiter-free sections of the *Theodicy* itself:

> M. Bayle asks a little too much: he wishes for a detailed exposition of how evil is connected to the best scheme of the universe. That would be a complete explanation of the phenomena: but I do not undertake to give it; nor am I bound to do so, for there is no obligation to do that which is impossible for us in our existing state. It is sufficient for me to point out that there is nothing to prevent the connection of a certain evil with what is best on the whole. This incomplete explanation, leaving something to be discovered in the life to come, is sufficient for answering the objections, though not for a comprehension of the matter.[235]

That is unusually carefully stated, even by Leibniz' high standards. But if one compares the parts of this part (145) of the *Theodicy*, the problems of divine and human justice do not vanish: if "a certain evil" (such as the crime of Tarquin) is made acceptable by "what is best on the whole," then Tarquin will discover not ultimate enlightenment but simply eternal damnation "in the life to come." Since he was evil "from all eternity," he will be condemned for all eternity. But if justice is *caritas sapientis,* and wise charity is equivalent to *benevolentia universalis,* and "good willing" is not possible for the actual Tarquin who exists in history, then the justice of both finite and infinite beings in the Leibnizian "best" world is as problematical as ever.[236]

Justice as
Love and Benevolence

In a characteristic letter to his Florentine colleague Antonio Magliabechi (September 1697), Leibniz argues that "truly universal jurisprudence [*jurisprudentia vere universalis*]" and even the cosmic *harmonia rerum* rest on nothing other than "charity regulated by wisdom [*caritas ad normam sapientis*]"—so that he who loves wisely will make "the felicity of others [*felicitatem alterius*]" his own.[1] And this letter merely summarizes what Leibniz says at greater length in dozens of similar texts.[2]

For Leibniz there is a necessary connection between wise charity or *caritas sapientis* as the heart of universal jurisprudence and the fact that God chooses to give existence to the "best" world: our love of God flows from our knowledge of his moral perfection in choosing the best, and charity then spreads from God to his creatures (above all to those closest to him in perfection, who have the greatest "claim" to existence—namely, human beings). This is clearest in the opening of the "Discourse on Metaphysics" from 1686:

> The general knowledge of that great truth, that God always acts in the most perfect and the most wished-for way that is possible, is in my opinion the foundation of the love that we owe to God above all things, since he who loves seeks his satisfaction in the felicity or perfection of the loved object and in his actions.[3]

It is "theodicy" as understood by Leibniz which reveals that this world must be best: if rational substances or monads can be brought to see that best-ness, then they will love God wisely (with full knowledge of his moral perfection) and will love what he has produced as "best."[4] Thus Leibniz' theodicy, his monadology, and his universal jurisprudence—as was seen in the last two chapters—are mutually supporting elements of a vast structure: the "City of God" and all its "citizens."

Now that the moral and political dimensions of Leibnizian monadology and theodicy are in place, one can turn fully to the wise charity that rational monads ought to feel for the "monarch" of the best universe (and for his love-worthy creatures):

> One cannot know God as one ought without loving him above all things, and one cannot love him without willing what he wills. His perfections are infinite and cannot end. This is why the pleasure which consists in the feeling of his perfections is the greatest and most durable which can exist. That is, the greatest happiness, which causes one to love him, causes one to be happy and virtuous at the same time. . . . This knowledge should make us envisage God as the sovereign monarch of the universe whose government is the most perfect state that one can conceive . . . where all right becomes fact.[5]

Leibniz' Debt to the Gospel According to St. John

Leibniz was certainly not the first moral philosopher to try to redefine justice in terms of charity or love, not just in terms of law: while fully aware of the importance of St. Paul's "the greatest of these is charity,"[6] he always stressed especially his debt to the Gospel according to St. John, which is so hostile to viewing justice simply as ritualistic observance of the law. When John has Christ say, "a new commandment I give unto you, that ye love one another,"[7] that "new commandment" transcends law altogether: it overrides the Mosaic law in Deuteronomy which requires that adulterers be stoned to death ("let him who is without sin cast the first stone") and asserts, very radically, that "the law was given by Moses"[8] (rather than by God).

Reflecting on his moral debt to this particular gospel, Leibniz says in a letter to Andreas Morrell (from 1697) that "when one truly loves one finds his own pleasure in the felicity of the loved object, even if one should not derive the slightest utility from it. . . . Love and charity are the basis of justice . . . now charity toward one's neighbor is only a consequence of the love of God . . . St. John was right to say that there are many liars among those who say that they love God. He has also given the true sign for recognizing them. I recognize the love of God only in those who show ardor for procuring the good in general."[9]

It is noteworthy that Leibniz, in arguing for justice as "wise" charity or love, almost always cites St. John, and almost never the original commandments or even Christ's reformulation in the injunction to love one's neighbor "as oneself."[10] Why is this? It may be because Leibniz found the Mosaic ethos of the Old Testament incomplete and in some ways inadequate: if Moses had neglected to affirm the natural immortality of souls (as Leibniz thought he had),[11] he might also have neglected to make the commandment to "love others as oneself" (which for Leibniz is a universal duty of reason-provided "natural" religion) sufficiently dominant to override (say) the rule in Deuteronomy that adulterers be stoned to death.[12] The whole point of the Gospel according to St. John is to assert that dominance: the "woman taken in adultery" benefits from a love and a forgiveness that overrides legal rigorism.[13] Leibniz certainly thought that if one gives correct moral primacy to the injunction to love others, one must then modify or abolish parochial practices which are historically understandable but not finally supportable. He was, especially by the standards of his day, a philo-Semite; but he read the Old Testament with a critical eye and thought that charity was more consistently insisted on by Christ than by Moses.[14] And in that he was right.

JUSTICE AND LOVE IN SHAKESPEARE AND LUTHER

Leaping ahead in the history of "justice as love" to Shakespeare's *Merchant of Venice*, one recalls the Leibniz-like subordination of mere law to love and mercy in Portia's celebrated speech in Act IV ("the quality of mercy is not strained . . . though justice be thy plea, consider this, that in the course of justice none of us should see salvation"); and Shylock is finally destroyed by his own legalism (fleshed out by the uncharitable hatreds of some merely nominal Christians who offer nothing but "a halter, *gratis*"—that last word an ironic transmogrification of "grace").[15] And then Shakespeare rejoins the Gospel According to St. John when, in *Love's Labour's Lost*, he makes Berowne end his great speech on love (IV, iii, 364–365) with the insistence that

> . . . charity itself fulfills the law;
> And who can sever love from charity?[16]

If Leibniz is unlikely to have been familiar with Shakespeare, there is another law-diminishing text which he would surely have known well, namely, Luther's *On Temporal Authority*:

Paul says, in 1 Timothy: "The law is not made for the just, but for the unjust." Why this? Because the just does, by himself, all that all the laws require, and more; by contrast the unjust do nothing just, and that is why they need the law to instruct them, to constrain them, and to press them to act rightly. . . . It is, through the spirit and through faith, entirely in the nature of Christians to act well and justly, and better than one could teach them by all types of law.[17]

And in Leibniz' own day various minor German writers descended from Luther and Melancthon—such as the Hamburg jurisconsult Placcius, with whom Leibniz corresponded from the 1670s to the 1690s—attempted to link justice with Christian charity; Placcius himself urged in his *Sittenlehre* that "the virtue of love *(caritas)* or of rightfulness *(justitia)* is an ethical duty."[18] Despite that "charity *or* justice," however, Placcius never went beyond this sub-Lutheran assertion to develop a "universal jurisprudence" grounded in "perfection."[19]

Leibniz was thus standing in a long tradition beginning with St. Paul and St. John and continuing through Shakespeare and Luther when he insisted that justice and sovereign-ordained law are not coextensive; and in his own lifetime the most important work in which he published his argument that justice is *caritas sapientis* was to be the *Codex Iuris Gentium* (1693), in which he insists that

a good man is one who loves everybody, so far as reason permits. Justice, then, which is the virtue which regulates that affection which the Greeks call philanthropy, will be most conveniently defined . . . as the charity of the wise man, that is, charity which follows the dictates of wisdom. . . . Charity is a universal benevolence, and benevolence the habit of loving or of willing the good. Love then signifies rejoicing in the happiness of another . . . the happiness of those whose happiness pleases us turns into our own happiness, since things which please us are desired for their own sakes.[20]

LEIBNIZ ON DISINTERESTED LOVE:
THE QUARREL BETWEEN FÉNELON AND BOSSUET

Leibniz had occasion to recall his equation of justice with "wise love" during the great quarrel between Fénelon and Bossuet over pure or "disinterested" love in the late 1690s[21]—but above all in 1697. For in that year Fénelon had notoriously argued, in the *Maxims of the Saints,* that one loves God purely or disinterestedly only if one hopes for nothing (for oneself) and fears nothing— that the person who disinterestedly loves God does so even if he should somehow know *(per impossibile)* that he is to be eternally damned. And that is why Fénelon says that one must *sortir de soi* (go out of oneself), that one must even *se haïr* (hate oneself): the person who truly loves God "will have contempt for himself and hate himself, he will leave himself, he will fear himself, he will abandon himself to God, he will lose himself in him. Happy loss!"[22] (Charity is obviously problematical, on the Fénelonian view: if one loves one's neighbor "as oneself," but one's *self* evaporates, then *caritas* gives way to a kind of occidental nirvana.)

Because the Fénelon-Bossuet quarrel of 1697 occasioned Leibniz' greatest sustained burst of writing on charity, love, and benevolence—though he had defined justice as *caritas sapientis* at least as far back as 1677, a generation earlier[23]—it is worth considering a little more carefully just what Fénelon was arguing, and why he provoked such extreme reactions from everyone except Leibniz. (This will be all the more instructive inasmuch as Fénelon and Leibniz share some important overlapping affections, above all for Plato; hence their parting of the ways over "love" is a schism within the tradition of "Christian Platonism.")[24]

There is (as Leibniz was aware) a radical, almost schizophrenic split in Fénelon's thought: if he was an Archbishop and the tutor to the heir to the French throne, he was also an extreme ascetic advocating "disinterested" love to the point of self-annihilation. That split is fascinating, psychologically and biographically, but Leibniz would (and did) find it philosophically and morally distressing.

Fénelon, born in Perigord in 1651, at first had an eminently successful "worldly" career: by the 1680s he had caught the eye of Bossuet, the most powerful French ecclesiastic of the Grand Siècle, and for Bossuet he produced his *Réfutation de Malebranche,* which attacked Malebranche's idea of a "Cartesian" general providence operating through simple, constant laws, and sustained Bossuet's notion of a "particular providence" which had furnished David and Solomon to ancient Israel and Louis XIV to modern France.[25] In 1689 he was named tutor to Louis' grandson, the Duc de Bourgogne (1682–1712); and it was for his royal pupil that he was soon to write *Telemachus, Son of Ulysses*—the most-read book in eighteenth-century France (after the Bible), and one admired by Leibniz. The Archbishopric of Cambrai followed in 1695, carrying with it the titles of Duke and Prince of the Holy Roman Empire.[26]

But in the late 1680s Fénelon had also become deeply interested in the quietistic notion of a "disinterested love of God" free of hope for personal happiness—a disinterested interest fanned by the mystical pieties of his friend Mme. Guyon.[27] His insistence that one must "go out of oneself" finally yielded the *Maxims of the Saints on the Inner Life,* in which he contemptuously spurned a "purely servile love" of God resting on "the goods which depend on his power and which one hopes to obtain," and celebrated the "pure love" of the divinity which one can find only in "saints." "One can love God," Fénelon urges, "from a love which is pure charity, and without the slightest mixture of self-interested motivation." In such a love, Fénelon adds, neither the "fear of punishment" nor the "hope of reward" plays any part at all.[28] As is well known, Bossuet and others argued that Fénelon's disinterested love excluded all hope of salvation, as well as all fear of justified punishment, and thus subverted Christianity.[29] Fénelon's work was finally condemned at Rome in April 1699; in this condemnation the prime mover was Bossuet, now Fénelon's greatest enemy.[30]

One thing that may have alarmed Bossuet—who was court preacher to Louis XIV, after all[31]—was that Fénelon found an important analogy or parallel between "selfless" love of God and Graeco-Roman "disinterested" civic virtue: to magnify Spartan and Athenian "republicanism" at the expense of Versailles would not have suited Bossuet. Fénelon, a classical lover of Virgil and Plato, had insisted that "the idea of pure disinterestedness dominates the political theories of all ancient legislators." In antiquity "it was not a matter of finding happiness in conforming to that order but, *au contraire,* of devouring oneself for love of that order, perishing, depriving the self of all resources." Fénelon completes this thought with an eloquent passage which Bossuet could scarcely have relished—and which even Leibniz would have thought exaggerated: "All these [ancient] legislators and philosophers who reasoned about laws presupposed that the fundamental principle of political society was that of preferring the public to the self—not through hope of serving one's own interests, but through the simple, pure, disinterested love of political order, which is beauty, justice, and virtue itself."[32] Leibniz' view of a justice which would leave the "self" so radically out of account will soon become clear; what is already clear is that Fénelonian justice excludes everything imagined or accomplished by Louis XIV. That is most evident, perhaps, in Fénelon's "On Pure Love": .

> Nothing is so odious as this idea of a heart always occupied with itself: nothing delights us so much as certain generous actions which persuade the world (and us) that we have done the good for love of the good, without seeking ourselves therein. Self-love itself renders homage to this disinterested virtue, by the shrewdness with which it tries to take on the appearance of it.[33]

The whole of Fénelon's religious, moral, and political thought is held together by the notion of disinterested love, of going out of oneself in order to lose oneself in a greater beyond (or, in the case of God, above). The disinterested love of God, without self-interest and hope for benefits, is pure "charity" (as in Pascal's *Pensées,* in which "the self is hateful" and charity is "of another order");[34] the disinterested love of one's neighbor is "friendship" (as in Cicero's *De Amicitia,* which Fénelon so admired);[35] the disinterested love of the *polis* is an almost Rousseauean civic virtue.[36] On this view of the moral world, an austere Pascalian *charité* and a Platonic "sublimated" eros meet: small wonder that Fénelon, a brilliantly sympathetic classical scholar, loved the *Symposium* and *Phaedrus* with nonconcupiscent passion.[37]

Indeed for Fénelon the only thing "missing" in Platonism is a sufficient notion of "will" as something distinct from knowing (here Leibniz would largely agree). For it is Fénelon's Christian notion that one must will the pure love of God; and for him the most worrying thing about Jansenism is its demi-Calvinist shrinking of early Augustinian "will" to the vanishing point (to make room for triumphant grace).[38] But "will" is the spontaneous self-determination of a subject, a "self"—unless one defines "will" as fully determined "last appetite," in the manner of Hobbes' *Leviathan.*[39] Bossuet may have attacked Fénelon from an uncharitable motive, but what he says against Fénelon's notion of human motivation—that it gives a motiveless motive, a will-less will, an effacement of self-concern that is inconceivable in a finite being[40]—is not obviously wholly mistaken. From a morally suspect motive Bossuet may have shown that Fénelon's idea of "motive" is conceptually suspect. (Leibniz shared Bossuet's doubts on this point, as will be seen, but criticized Fénelon disinterestedly—and that cannot be said of Bossuet.)

The disinterestedness which Fénelon recommended is in any case a very weakened, attenuated version of "pure" love—it is what the *Maxims of the*

Saints calls "mixed" love[41] (in which the self is not yet selfless). What Fénelon really admires is withdrawal from the everyday social world, a sublimated ascent to God. For one must acknowledge "the brevity and uncertainty of life, the inconstancy of fortune, the faithlessness of friends, the illusion of great positions . . . the discontent of the great, the nothingness of all the greatest hopes, the emptiness of all the goods one possesses, the reality of all the evils that one suffers."[42] (This is at a great remove from Leibnizian "optimism"; Fénelon is too world-renouncing to declare that evils are the *conditio sine qua non* of a praiseworthy "best" world.)[43]

In a sense Fénelon ought to have been a radical ascetic, standing outside society, a Stylite on his column in the desert; instead he was Archbishop, Duke, Prince of the Holy Roman Empire, and the author of a fabulously successful moral-political novel *(Telemachus)*.[44] But it was the ascetic side which was surely the deepest one; and that emerges plainly in an astonishing paragraph from Fénelon's essay "Happiness of the Soul Which Gives Itself Entirely to God":

> It is in seeing God that one sees the nothingness of the world, which will evaporate like a mist. All forms of greatness, and their consequences, will vanish like a dream: every height will be pulled down, every power will be wiped out, every proud head will be bowed under the weight of the eternal majesty of God. On that day when he shall judge men, with one glance he will efface everything that shines in this present night, as the sun in rising effaces all the stars. One will see only God everywhere, so great will he be. . . . What has become, men will say, of those things which had enchanted our hearts? What is left of them? Alas: there remains not even the mark of the place where they stood.[45]

Leibniz, to be sure, would have recognized the magnificence of the writing: but for him the phrase, "the nothingness of the world," would be eloquently excessive—it rules out charitable striving in the world for the common good, rules out Leibniz' usual identification of "the glory of God" with *le bien général*.[46]

One often wonders, indeed: why does the Fénelonian God create a finite world full of pilgrims, most of whom will not reach their heavenly destination? Even the saints who love God purely, hoping for nothing, cannot "add" to his glory—for Christ himself added nothing, by the Incarnation, to God's lovable perfection (as Fénelon makes clear in the *Réfutation de Malebranche*).[47] Why, then, to pose Leibniz' famous question, should there be "something rather than nothing,"[48] on the Fénelonian view? All theodicies, all attempts to "plead the cause of God," are troubled by this question: it is because theodicists start with a (basically Greek) notion of an infinitely perfect being,[49] then try to ask what motive such a being can have had to create a world which is "metaphysically evil" (Leibniz) or "debris" (Malebranche)[50] or "falling into ruins" (Fénelon).[51] But no such motive is easily imaginable, given a Greek conception of perfect self-sufficiency (as in Aristotle's *Ethics* 1178b);[52] nothing finite and temporal could "satisfy" a being whose only joy would flow from self-contemplation *ad infinitum*. At least Leibniz could believe that the present world is (somehow) "best"; even that consolation seems to be denied to Fénelon.

It is hard to see why, in Fénelon, there should be any finite world (in time) at all. And this was a general problem for the thinkers of Fénelon's generation—with Malebranche saying in *Nature and Grace* (as was seen in Chapter 3) that there is no natural *rapport* between the *être infiniment parfait* and the "ruined" world, that only Christ as "perfect victim" redeems the finite.[53] It is no wonder, then, that Fénelon loved Plato so much—for it is Plato above all who in the *Republic* magnifies eternal changeless "essence," free of all Heraclitean flux, and who shrinks mere "genesis" in time to an "unsuitable" object of study.[54] But then another, biblical, Genesis becomes difficult to explain, and the Incarnation of Christ changes from "condescension" to something unintelligible.[55] It is not accidental that some very characteristic Fénelonian utterances seem more Greek, and more precisely Platonic, than "Christian": "As soon as we shall no longer have any desires or fears, with respect to the body, we shall remain freed from the law of time. The extinction of all personal will and the detachment from all that changes place us in that eternal peace for which we are made."[56] (Fénelon's natural drift is ever eastward, toward nirvana; by contrast Leibniz' deep interest in Asian thought never led him to diminish charitable will and striving, what he called *conatus* or the "inclination" to action.[57] Indeed if one equates *caritas sapientis* with universal good willing, the extinction of personal will is impossible.)

Thus one cannot imagine Leibniz' sympathizing with the version of Platonism which Fénelon insists on: "Let us love eternal beauty, which does not grow old, and which keeps from aging those who love only her; let us have contempt for this world which is already falling into ruins in all its parts."[58]

Leibniz too loved "eternal beauty," but that never led him to contempt for the world; for that world, after all, is best, is justifiable, and there is a sufficient reason for it.

LEIBNIZ' DOUBTS ABOUT FÉNELONIAN LOVE

Even if Leibniz shared with Fénelon an ardent devotion to Platonic "eternal" truth which is not caused by mere "genesis" in time, even if Leibniz and Fénelon were both (in some sense) Christian Platonists, nonetheless one cannot imagine Leibniz using the eternal and the divine against the world and the "self." One cannot imagine Leibniz indulging in the kind of radical self-abnegation which Fénelon eloquently defended in works such as "Happiness of the Soul":

> It is only those who do violence to themselves who will gain the kingdom of heaven. One must be reborn, renounce oneself, hate oneself, become a child, weep in order to be consoled, and not be of the world at all (which is cursed because of its scandals). . . . Misery to those lax and timid souls which are divided between God and the world! They will and they will not; they are lacerated at once by their passions and by their regrets; they fear the judgments of God and those of men; they are horrified by evil and ashamed of the good; they suffer the pains of virtue without tasting its consolations.[59]

Leibniz found that degree of quietistic self-abnegation not just wrong but impossible: for him true love (the basis of justice) must delight in the perfection or felicity of another, but that delight is one's own; it is a "disinterested" delight or happiness when one's joy is brought about by the perfections which are objectively there, in the person or thing loved—whether God, or one's neighbor, or a painting by Raphael.[60] (Leibniz can mention God, other persons, and Raphael in the same breath; one cannot imagine Fénelon doing so.)

Leibniz' view was that not even Fénelon himself could coherently and consistently adhere to radical self-annihilation; and as evidence he would have adduced the following (very eloquent) Fénelonian text:

> Be a true nothing in everything and everywhere; but one must add nothing to this pure nothing. It is against nothingness that there can be no siege. It can lose nothing. True nothingness never resists, and there

is no "I" with which it concerns itself. Be nothing then, and nothing beyond that; and you will be everything without dreaming of being so.[61]

For Leibniz that kind of self-losing is literally inconceivable, psychologically impossible as well as morally mistaken; and he would add that Fénelon's last clause—"you will be everything without dreaming of being so"—reveals that impossibility. For in that clause "nothing" yields not just to "something," but to "everything."

If Leibniz had grave doubts about Fénelonian "disinterested" love, he thought at the same time that "the incomparable Fénelon made a more just reputation for himself in the world by the publication of his *Telemachus* than by the manifestation of his sentiments about the love of God."[62] And on reflection it is not hard to know which parts of *Telemachus* Leibniz would especially have admired: he would not have had much use for the celebrated Fénelonian utopia of Bétique, with its Spartan, agriculture-centered, proto-Rousseauean austerity and without the arts and sciences which Leibniz' beloved Berlin Academy fostered;[63] but what he would have cherished was lasting peace grounded in charity. And such a peace is at its clearest at the end of Book ix of *Telemachus,* in which Mentor (the goddess Minerva in disguise) has just brought about concord between King Idomeneus of Salente and his onetime enemies. Mentor says, in a speech that Leibniz must have admired, that

> "Your several nations for the future will be but one, under different names and governors. Thus it is that the just gods, who formed and love the human race, would have them united in an everlasting bond of perfect amity and concord. All mankind are but one family dispersed over the face of the whole earth. All nations àre brethren, and ought to love one another as such. May shame and infamy overtake those impious wretches who seek a cruel unnatural glory, by shedding the blood of their brethren, which they ought to regard as their own. . . . Whoever gratifies his passion for glory, at the expense of humanity, is a proud monster, and not a man."[64]

The tone of that speech is rather like that of Leibniz' most famous political poem: "Whatever triumph one can obtain by war, to oblige is much greater than to conquer the earth."[65] Louis XIV was the object of those lines, as he had probably been the object of *Telemachus;* Louis' "greatness" was equally repugnant to Leibniz and to Fénelon.

All the same, Leibniz is actually closer to Bossuet than to Fénelon in the great "quietist" controversy which dominated French religious and intellectual life at the turn of the eighteenth century; for Bossuet had urged that "to detach oneself from himself to the point of no longer desiring to be happy, is an error which neither nature, nor grace, nor reason, nor faith, can suffer."[66] To be sure, Leibniz thought that Bossuet was trying to destroy Fénelon from an uncharitably "political" motive; and if one reads Bossuet's massive *Politics Drawn from the Very Words of Holy Scripture*, the only scriptural words one will not find are "the greatest of these is charity" and "a new commandment I give unto you." (For Louis XIV's court preacher, the line of Scripture which matters is Genesis 17:6, "kings will come out of you.")[67] But however uncharitable the motives of Bossuet, Leibniz thought the Bishop right in linking love with one's own happiness. And here both Leibniz and Bossuet could claim Thomist orthodoxy, for St. Thomas had insisted in the *Summa contra Gentiles* that "the final end of man, as of every intellectual substance, is called felicity or happiness."[68]

What all of this means is that, for Leibniz, massive undifferentiated Fénelonian assaults on the self (and on self-concern) are unsubtle and lead to bad moral reasoning: "Self-love brings about all the vices and all the moral virtues, depending upon whether it is well or badly understood; and while it is true to say that men never act without interest, it is also true that there are honorable and lasting interests."[69] What is needed is not the annihilation of the self but the generous expansion of the self to take in others: as Leibniz urged in a late letter to Pierre Coste (1712), "our natural affections make up our contentment: and the more one is in a natural condition [*dans le naturel*], the more one is brought to find his pleasure in the good of others, which is the foundation of universal benevolence, of charity, of justice."[70]

LEIBNIZ' LETTER TO ELECTRESS SOPHIE OF HANOVER ON JUSTICE AS CHARITY

Leibniz summarizes his argument that justice is *caritas sapientis*, or wise love, in a string of definitions in a letter from 1697 to Electress Sophie of Hanover—a letter which reveals his recent reflections on Fénelon.

> Justice is charity conformed to wisdom.
> Wisdom is the science of felicity.
> Charity is a universal benevolence.

Benevolence is a habit of loving.

To love is to find pleasure in the good, perfection, the happiness of another.

And by this definition one can resolve . . . a great difficulty which is important even in theology—how it is possible that there be a nonmercenary love, detached from hope and from fear, and from all concern for our own interest.

It is that the felicity, or the perfection of another, in giving us pleasure, enters immediately into our own felicity.

For all that pleases is desired for itself, and not through interest.

It is a good in itself, and not a useful good.

It is thus that the contemplation of beautiful things is agreeable in itself, and that a painting by Raphael moves him who looks at it with enlightened eyes, though he derives no profit from it.[71]

And in this same letter to Sophie Leibniz praises, as the main modern work which gives sufficient practical weight to charity, the *Güldenes Tugendbuch* of the German Jesuit father Friedrich Spee (1591–1635)[72]—a book now known because Leibniz not only praised it but partly translated it, interpolating his own small reservations and emendations between the lines. "From my youth I had formed these ideas" about justice as wise charity, Leibniz says. "A great prince who was at the same time a great prelate"—Johann Philipp von Schönborn, Prince-Bishop of Mainz, and Leibniz' first employer—"recommended to me the German book of Father Spee on the three Christian virtues." The preface to that book, Leibniz goes on to say, "contains a fine dialogue, in which the difference between disinterested love and love based on hope is developed in a way which is as intelligible as it is profound."[73] The key page of Leibniz' translation of Spee, with his own alterations in parentheses (set off by crosses), was apparently included[74] with his 1697 letter to Sophie:

> . . . in virtue of the love or the delectation of God we have a true benevolence for him, and we wish him (+ so to speak +) all good by a sincere inclination of our heart. . . . We do with all our heart all that we can do for the love of him, and everything we believe is conformed to his will (John 14). That is why we do gladly what he has commended, and we avoid with care what he has forbidden, in order that nothing happen that can displease him (+ to speak humanly +). . . . We want by the power of benevolence to be able to give ourselves to him entirely

and perfectly . . . (+ and to be attached to him morally, as everything is already attached to him and physically submitted +). . . .[75]

That final Leibnizian parenthetical emendation is wholly characteristic: it is not enough to be "physically submitted" to God—for that, Hobbesian "irresistible" divine power would be sufficient and efficient; men must be attached to God "morally," as the just monarch of the City of God. And a moral attachment must rest on the charity which Spee had commended. (Leibniz was also struck by the fact that Spee's *caritas* had led the government of Mainz to abolish witchcraft trials; there charity had become public policy.)[76]

But Leibniz was not content merely to link up justice and love, ethics and psychology; in another letter to Electress Sophie he fulminates against those who want to restore a Dantean *respublica christiana* by uncharitable means—by forcing Lutherans (such as Leibniz) through the gates of Rome.

> Your highness must be obliged for the good will of Mme. de Brinon [the friend and colleague of Bossuet], who opens up paradise for her, if one listens to her counsel. She supposes that one will not enter there except by the path of Rome. But one must have quite strange ideas of God, to attach his graces to the kinds of conditions which human politics has invented in order to assert itself.[77]

Unlike Mme. de Brinon and other Catholics who assert that *extra ecclesia* there is no salvation, for Leibniz, Electress Sophie "attributes nothing to God which is unworthy of him, and loves her fellow-man." It is that charitable practice, Leibniz urges, which reveals true piety and justice—"instead of which the bitter zealots who consign to the devil all those who do not agree with their caprices are truly sectarians and heretics." For instead of acting with wise charity "they hate and have contempt for their fellow-man, and make of God a tyrant or something even lower, by attributing to him plans which are equally cruel and ridiculous."[78] (The terms "tyranny" and "cruelty" are often found in Leibniz' critique of Hobbes: if one says, with chapter 31 of *Leviathan*, that God's natural "dominion" rests on "irresistible power" alone, not on love for Platonic "eternal moral verities," then the sage of Malmesbury and Thrasymachus collapse into each other.)[79]

Leibniz' concern with charitable practice as revelatory of true piety emerges most clearly in a little-known letter to Andreas Morrell from October 1697; since it synthetically draws together Leibniz' views on love, justice,

Fénelonian quietism and the centrality of benevolent action, it is worth quoting *in extenso*—not least because it has never been translated before. (It also strongly anticipates the language of the *Monadology*'s proposition 86, with its talk of the "truly universal monarchy" of a just God.)

> The world is a perfect city under God, who is its king, and the laws are governed there by the most perfect reason. . . . We shall take part in the felicity of this kingdom in proportion as we shall have had a part in it through good thoughts and good actions. . . . Thus a lazy and indifferent devotion is not solid enough, just as a simple historical faith which does not touch the heart and does not expand into good actions, or at least good efforts, is dead. . . . And according to the definition of love which I have given at other times, one loves sincerely when one attaches the felicity of others to one's own.[80]

And to make it plainer still that "others" must have equal weight with ourselves, Leibniz goes on to say, in a slightly later letter to Morrell, that "I esteem devoted people whose zeal is shown by works of charity. . . . It is practice which provides the means of appreciating minds: *ex fructibus eorum cognoscetis eos* [by their fruits you shall know them]."[81]

And if, Leibniz continues, one must express all of this in fashionably Fénelonian language, then "I believe that the total renunciation of oneself is nothing other than preferring the common good or (what is the same thing) the glory of God to one's particular interest." But this kind of renunciation, unlike quietism, "does not demand repose, but rather activity, to strive to do well as much as is possible"[82]—a doing well which embraces a *caritas sapientis* that can terminate doctrinal disputation, end "schism," restore the *respublica christiana* through agreement and concord, and even shape the domestic policies of princes.

These letters to Morrell, in fleshing out what Leibniz means by justice as "the charity of the wise," help one to appreciate the sheer historical resonance of *caritas sapientis:* if Tertullian had dug a chasm between the Graeco-Roman and the Judaeo-Christian *ethe* ("if we have Jerusalem, what need have we of Athens?"),[83] Leibniz used his synthetic moderation to pull them back together. St. Paul himself denigrates Greek *philosophia* ("where is the wise?") and preaches "Christ crucified";[84] Leibniz, moving on to 1 Corinthians 13 and to St. John, preaches Christ preaching—"a new commandment I give unto you." But Athens always colors Leibniz' Jerusalem, so that Leibniz' whole theory of wise love (to put it mathematically, as he often did) would look like this: charity = justice = proportion = eternal mathematical verity (à la *Euthyphro*); and in that formulation it is hard to know whether Christ or Plato is uppermost. But in Leibniz' thought it is always hard to know that.

JUSTICE AS WISE CHARITY:
NOT JUST *CARITAS* BUT *SAPIENTIA*

It is precisely the recollection of "Platonism," however, which should make one careful to preserve both elements of *caritas sapientis* in Leibniz' notion of justice: for it was no accident that Leibniz, possessed of an incomparable knowledge of both Christian charity and Greek wisdom, should have insisted precisely on "the charity of the wise." That Greek-Christian equilibrium is sometimes thrown off even by very good scholars—for example René Sève in his (mainly excellent) *Leibniz et l'école moderne du droit naturel:*

> When Leibniz makes "the good man" the criterion of morality and of right, he immediately defines the *vir bonus* as he who loves all others *(amans omnes)*, in other words he who is animated by charity. On this basis, and following Pauline inspiration, it becomes possible to go beyond the definition of justice through law, thought of as a norm external to the agent, in favor of an immanent movement of charity—for "love is the fulfillment of the law," and "the law is not made for the just." He who possesses—or is possessed—by charity, itself flowing from God, thus becomes his own law. Extrinsic obligation thus gives way to an internal necessity.[85]

This fine passage, with its echo of Dante's *Paradiso* ("by love possessed"),[86] certainly captures the Pauline side of Leibniz' *caritas;* what it omits, however, is *sapientis,* "of the wise"—for the Platonic dimension of Leibnizian justice, mathematics-grounded "harmony" and "proportion" (known best by the wise who "see" the eternal verities), is crucial and cannot reasonably be neglected. After all, *caritas sapientis* (not "mere" love) must be "proportional" to the degree of perfection which one recognizes in others; and "proportion" and "perfection" are not Pauline. Writing against Christian Thomasius in c. 1694, Leibniz characteristically insisted that, "I am also not in agreement with him when he makes love come before enlightenment [*la lumière*]. . . . Enlightenment is our passion, love is the pleasure which results from it, and which consists in an action upon ourselves, from which comes an effort to act thereafter on others, to contribute to the good insofar as it depends on us."[87] Here Leibniz will have his little joke: *la lumière* is our "passion," just as in Hegel's *Phenome-nology* "spirit" has a rich emotional life;[88] the point is that our passion for enlightenment *generates* love, and our love then becomes justice when wisdom reveals "degrees of perfection."

Sève is so anxious to view Leibniz as the antithesis of the "jusnaturalists" who define justice through legal obligation created by authoritative "sover-eignty" (as in Pufendorf),[89] who view obligation as something handed down "vertically," *de haut en bas,* that he overlooks Leibniz' constant "Platonic" stress on an eternal "right" which is indeed a "norm external to the agent" (though not of course a mere command given *ex plenitudo potestatis*).

So one should constantly balance Leibniz' stress on *caritas* with his equal insistence on *sapientia*. To be sure, he says in the *Opinion on the Principles of Pufendorf* (1706) that

. . . the best principles of universal jurisprudence, which collaborate also with wise theology and bring about true virtue [teach that] . . . he who acts well not out of hope or fear but by an inclination of his soul is so far from not behaving justly that, on the contrary, he acts more justly than all others, imitating, in a certain way, as a man, divine justice. Whoever, indeed, does good out of love for God and for his neighbor takes pleasure precisely in the action itself (such being the nature of love) and does not need any other incitement or the command of a superior; for that man the saying that the law is not made for the just is valid.[90]

But in the same text, and virtually on the same page, Leibniz also insists that "justice follows certain rules of equality and of proportion [which are] no less founded in the immutable nature of things and in the divine ideas, than are the principles of arithmetic and of geometry."[91] There Plato sets a limit to what St. Paul is allowed to assert about "right": charity must be proportional to perfection. (Not that this is a wholly unprecedented thought, even within Christian orthodoxy; after all, Thomas Aquinas says in the *Summa Theologica* that "our neighbors are not all equally related to God; some are nearer to him, by reason of their greater goodness, and those we ought, out of charity, to love more than those who are not so near to him."[92] Since goodness is a moral "perfection," Leibniz and Aquinas are here not so far apart.)

Leibniz' ideal society governed by "wise charity," then, is not conceived as a "community of love," still less as a love-feast, a *Liebesmahl*:[93] that is instantly clear in his common equation of wise charity with general benevolence, but also in his insistence that "wise" love must be proportional to the perfections of others—that one must stop and judge what is perfect or imperfect in them, and that love is our feeling of delight in those perfections: the self does not dissolve in a flood of undifferentiated emotion. (For that reason Leibniz would have admired not just the harmony but the very title of Bach's 1715 cantata, "Baumherziges Herze der ewigen Liebe [Charitable Heart of the Eternal Love]"[94]—for in that title Pauline charity and Platonic eternity are in equilibrium.)

Leibniz means *caritas "sapientis,"* of the wise. For "one can say that there are some charitable people who are not just at all, which happens when charity is not sufficiently rule-governed; for in justice is comprised, at once, charity and the rule of reason."[95] Or, as Leibniz puts it with more precision: "Charity is nothing else than a general friendship which extends to all, but with distinction, for it must be regulated by justice according to the degrees of perfection which can be found or introduced in objects."[96] Or again, as Leibniz says in a letter to Antoine Arnauld from 1690, charity is "a universal benevolence, whose carrying out the wise man dispenses in conformity to the measures of reason, in order to obtain the greatest good. . . . He who is just advances the good of others as much as he can without injuring wisdom."[97] But wisdom must be protected against that "injury": *neminem laedere* applies to reason and truth as well as to persons, so that "the best" does not vanish.

> General benevolence is charity itself. But the zeal of charity must be directed by knowledge so that we do not err in the estimation of what is best. Since in consequence wisdom is the knowledge of the best or of felicity, we cannot perhaps better capture the essence of justice than if we define it as the charity which resides in the wise.[98]

One would not expect the self to dissolve in an emotional flood, on the Leibnizian view of rational "substances": the monads are individual and individuated,[99] and their relations are pregiven by preestablished harmony, not by an immediate surge of eros (or even *agape*). Then on turning to Leibniz' social writings, one finds that for him *caritas sapientis* or general benevolence reveals itself sufficiently in (say) scientific endeavors aimed at advancing *le bien commun;* there "love" is a kind of well-meaning enlightenment.[100] "He who is wise will love all men, but each in proportion as the traces of divine virtue in him shine out, and in proportion as he hopes to find in him a companion ready and able to promote the common good or (what comes to the same thing) the glory of God, the giver of good things."[101] So one should not be carried away by the word "love," though Leibniz makes it ethically central; he himself was not carried away, and ecstatic transports are remote from his characteristic temperament.

LEIBNIZ' ACCOUNT OF LOVE IN "ON GENEROSITY"

Leibniz' slightly cool-to-the-touch version of love, in which *caritas* really amounts to enlightened generosity and concern for public welfare, comes out with special clarity in "Sur la générosité" (c. 1708): "We are not born for ourselves, but for the good of society, as the parts are for the whole; and we should consider ourselves only as the instruments of God—but living and free instruments, capable of concurring through our choice." But if we fail in this, "we are like monsters, and our vices are like sicknesses in nature: and no doubt we will receive punishment for it when the order of things is redressed." And Leibniz quickly relates all of this to charitable justice by going on to say that "we can judge that the principles of generosity and of justice or piety are one single thing only, instead of which interest (when it is ill-regulated) and self-love are principles of cowardice. For generosity . . . brings us close to the author of our race or being, that is to say to God, insofar as we are capable of imitating him."[102]

> We must then act in conformity to the nature of God, who is himself the good of all creatures; we must follow his intention which commands us to procure the common good insofar as it depends on us, since charity and justice consist only in that. We must have regard for the dignity of our nature, whose excellence consists in the perfection of the mind or in the highest virtue. We must take part in the happiness of those who surround us as our own, not seeking either our ease or our interest in that which is contrary to the common felicity; finally we must think of what the public hopes for from us, and what we should hope ourselves if we put ourselves in the place of others; for it is like the voice of God and the sign of a vocation.[103]

In those eloquent pages, St. Paul's first letter to the Corinthians is mainly preserved: the notion that "the greatest of these is charity" is linked up with the common good of a moral body whose "members" must subordinate themselves, charitably, to the whole (as the foot and the hand must submit to the physical body in 1 Corinthians 12).[104] But the part of 1 Corinthians which vanishes altogether is the polemic against Greek *philosophia* ("where is the wise?"); for Leibniz insists on "the perfection of the mind" so that we can "procure the common good" intelligently. (One must always remember Leibniz' insistence that "in justice is comprised, at once, charity and the rule of reason.")[105] In the discourse on generosity St. Paul is, to recall Hegel's phrase, "canceled and preserved."[106] And when Leibniz is most careful, Plato and Paul, Athens and Jerusalem, are in a state of harmonious equilibrium. (St. Paul and St. John offer charity as the first of the virtues; Plato and Aristotle offer justice as the first of the virtues.[107] How can one have both, and rank both "first"? By defining justice through charity, as *caritas sapientis;* and that is another way in which Leibniz' thought is "synthetic.")

Leibniz, then, pace René Sève, is not "possessed" by love: that verbal recollection of Dante's *Paradiso* refers after all to Justinian ("who by the primal will of love possessed / pruned from the law the unneeded and the vain"),[108] and Justinian's primal "charity" simply ordered and rationalized Roman *jurisprudentia.* "Rome" and "Law" are always central for Leibniz, as for Dante himself four centuries earlier, and for Justinian a millennium earlier;[109] love does not (or should not) make any of them "possessed" in a tortured Dostoyevskian sense. For the Leibnizian *vir bonus* must shrink from the "furious" love that undoes Shakespeare's Macbeth: "The expedition of my violent love / Outran the pauser, reason." For without that pause, as Macbeth asks, "Who can be wise?" (II, iii, 114).

Why Leibniz Is Not a "Utilitarian"

The danger inherent in Sève's magnifying of Pauline "love" and shrinking of Platonic "wisdom" is that it psychologizes Leibnizian ethics excessively, and thereby makes Leibniz seem to lead too readily to the principal school of eighteenth-century moral philosophy which built everything precisely on a "psychology" of pleasure and pain: utilitarianism.[110] And in fact Sève is not sufficiently careful when, in a chapter called "Toward Utilitarianism," he declares that "the Leibnizian critique" of modern natural-law theory (especially in Pufendorf) heralds "classical utilitarianism (Bentham, Mill . . .)."[111] But the mere fact that Leibniz insists on "pleasure" and "happiness" in shaping *caritas sapientis*—which is always defined by him as finding one's pleasure in the happiness or perfection of others, in a generous, self-expanding way[112]—does not unproblematically link Leibniz to Bentham, or even to J. S. Mill. It certainly does not link him irresistibly to Bentham, for there is no "perfectionist" strand in Benthamism: Benthamite utility *could* encompass Leibnizian love as "pleasure felt in appreciating the perfections of others" (since Benthamism must count all pleasures whatsoever[113]), but Bentham is in no position to say that we ought to love others in proportion to their degree of perfection (which is what Leibniz urges when he is careful and rigorous). One recalls again his crucial letter of 1691 to Mme. de Brinon: "Charity is nothing else than a general friendship which extends to all, but with distinction, for it must be regulated by justice according to the degrees of perfection which can be found or introduced in objects."[114]

Every pleasure counts in Bentham—even what he calls the "pleasures of malevolence," which are not ruled out but merely outweighed by the purity and intensity of the pains of the victims of malevolence.[115] Given Leibniz' constant equation of *caritas sapientis* and universal benevolence, Leibnizian wise love cannot encompass the joys of malevolence (any more than it can neglect the "perfections" of others): indeed Leibniz says flatly that malevolent pleasure is worse than crime committed with indifference ("we judge that wickedness has become greater when it passes over into pleasure").[116]

For Bentham "degrees of perfection" in others have no intrinsic moral weight *deserving* of love, and unless those perfections happen to give pleasure (by chance) they have no weight at all: it is pleasure as such (regardless of its source) which is to be "maximized" in Bentham, and that is why "pushpin is as good as poetry."[117] So John Rawls is right to call Leibniz a "perfectionist" in ethics, not a proto-utilitarian; and Albert Heinekamp is correct when he urges that for Leibniz happiness is not an "independent end" (as in "the utilitarians Bentham and Mill") but an "accompanying phenomenon" which arises from appreciating perfection.[118] This remains true even if one turns from Leibniz-Bentham to Leibniz-Mill: for while Mill was no orthodox Benthamite, and tried to urge the importance of personal self-perfection (unconstrained by the "tyranny of majority opinion"), he nonetheless "regard[ed] utility as the ultimate appeal on all ethical questions,"[119] and never succeeded in breaking decisively from Bentham's psychologism. Even Mill's "higher pleasures" in *Utilitarianism* ("better Socrates dissatisfied than a fool satisfied") are still precisely pleasures, since that which counts as "higher" is that which would give satisfaction or pleasure to a "competently acquainted" expert.[120] There is indeed a notion of perfecting oneself through the pursuit of the "higher" in J. S. Mill; but he does not seem to agree with Leibniz that our love ought to be proportioned to "degrees of perfection" in others. (Nor does he even treat charity as central in ethics—not surprisingly, given his contempt for what he took to be Christian hypocrisy, the anxious looking around to "Mr. A and Mr. B" to see "how far to go in obeying Christ").[121]

The Leibnizian stress on "proportion" and "degree," that would-be mathematical rigor in morality, descends from a Platonic tradition which turns up (for example) in Shakespeare ("take but degree away, untune that string, and hark what discord follows")[122] but which has no place in Mill. If one looks with care at Leibnizian *caritas sapientis* in the light of Leibniz' whole philosophy, then pleasure and happiness are shaped and colored by Christian and Platonic factors—by Pauline charity itself, by the wisdom which sees degrees of perfection and "eternal verities"—factors which cannot have central weight in classical utilitarianism. One can, if one likes (for all the good it does) style Leibniz a "Graeco-Christian hedonist"—but that does not make him a proto-Benthamite who "announces" the advent of *"l'utilitarisme classique."*[123] (It is worth keeping in mind Leibniz' careful choice of terms in his letter to Bossuet of 1697, in which the Hanoverian says that our love is disinterested when we find our pleasure, "not our interest or our utility," in the perfection or felicity of others.)[124]

Leibniz' Demi-Augustinianism

The whole idiom of disinterested love, of charity and generosity, limited by "degrees of perfection" which must be recognized, is anything but "utilitarian." After all, it is classically Augustinian to say that we ought to find our "delight" *(delectio)* not in concupiscence but in "higher" love (of God, truth, and our neighbor).[125] "You ought not to love yourself for your own sake, but for the sake of him [God] who is the most fitting end for your love . . . indeed when the soul flees from the unchangeable light, the ruler of all things, it does so in order that it might . . . love itself and its own body."[126] Leibniz is (roughly) within that Augustinian tradition of love governed by "light" (Platonically "unchangeable"), and therefore Sève's claim that Leibniz "announces" Bentham and Mill, while by contrast Kant is a resurrected Augustinian *("le retour à l'augustinisme opéré par Kant")*[127] fails to capture the real difference between the two great Germans. Kant is an "Augustinian" insofar as he gives primacy to "good will" as the only "unqualified" good;[128] Leibniz is an "Augustinian" insofar as he gives primacy to enlightened love.[129] Both *Aufklärer* descend from different branches of Augustinianism (though both minimize late Augustinian "grace"); but if Leibniz stressed the happiness that Kant made quite secondary in the *Critique of Practical Reason*—the Kantian *summum bonum* would be moral virtue crowned by happiness in an afterlife which we can "postulate" but never know[130]—that ties Leibniz more obviously to Augustinian "delight" than to English "utility." Sève's use of over-rigid, anachronistic categories (absolutist/consequentialist, deontologist/teleologist)[131] pushes Leibniz out of his proper "Christian-Platonist" niche and into the wrong country and the wrong tradition. At the end of his life Leibniz hoped to follow George I to England—but not to serve as the intellectual ancestor of Jeremy Bentham.

For Leibniz one does not just aim at undifferentiated happiness, howsoever desired: "The more a mind desires to know order, reason, the beauty of the things which God has produced, and the more it is brought to imitate this order in the things which God has left to its conduct, the more it will be happy."[132] And then, still more decisively: "the pleasure of the mind consists in the knowledge of perfections through their reasons."[133] This is not Bentham; it is not even J. S. Mill.

The notion that Leibniz is a proto-utilitarian who announces Bentham and Mill seizes on the word "happiness" as if that term only became morally current in modern England, and forgets that the whole Augustinian tradition insists on finding *delectio* in God, truth, and charity. Consider Leibniz' letter of July 1706 to Pierre Coste, the translator of Locke's works into French:

> Between mercenary views and the true love which one can call pure (when it has as its basis the good of the love-object) there is as much difference as between the useful and the pleasant, that is to say between that which is a good solely through the good effect which it helps to produce, and that which is a good in itself—between *uti et frui*, as St. Augustine distinguishes them well in his *City of God* Book XI, Chapter 25, and elsewhere. . . . The honorable is nothing else than what is pleasant through reason . . . [and] my definition [locates] love in the pleasure which the existence of the object gives to us, for the existing object gives it only through its perfections.[134]

When Leibniz refers to "elsewhere" in Augustine's *City of God,* he surely has in mind the celebrated passage (XV, 22) in which the Bishop of Hippo Regius insists that "we must observe due order in loving even the love itself with which we love in a good way what is worthy of love, if there is to be in us the virtue that enables us to live a good life," and that virtue is thus "a due ordering of love [*virtutus ordo est amoris*]." And Augustine adds, in a proto-Leibnizian way, that when love becomes disordered by deviating from the "eternal" (to embrace the "temporary"), such love "is as bad as when justice is abandoned." (But justice as "ordered love" is central to all of Augustine's thought, as is clear in *De Doctrine Christiana* XXVII, 28: "He lives in justice and sanctity who is an unprejudiced assessor of the intrinsic value of things. He is a man who has an ordinate love . . . he neither loves more what should be loved less, loves equally what should be loved less or more, nor loves less or more what should be loved equally." In this statement love and mathematics fuse in a Leibniz-anticipating way.)

Wise Charity: Leibniz against Hobbes, Pascal, and Locke

The distinctiveness of Leibniz' highly original insistence that justice is "the charity of the wise" can be brought out not just by comparing him with Fénelon and by separating him from British utilitarianism, but by contrasting his notion of *caritas sapientis* (or "general benevolence") with the way in which three of his celebrated contemporaries (Hobbes, Pascal, and Locke) relate, or fail to relate, justice and charity. To put it briefly, Hobbes views charity as falling beneath justice because it is really "lust" masquerading as a moral principle;[135] Pascal views charity as soaring above justice because justice is mere positive law on "one side of the Pyrenees" or the other;[136] Locke views charity as merely modifying justice in cases of extreme "want."[137] (Here Locke, as ever, is most cautious and traditional.)

And here too, as ever, Hobbes is most radical: an examination of his notion of love or charity (in *The Elements of Law*) immediately makes it clear why he could not have viewed justice as *caritas sapientis*. For while the idea of "sapience" survives in Hobbes (as knowledge of causes, not of Leibnizian "sufficient reason"),[138] love or charity is reduced not just to lust but to homosexual lust—scarcely a promising foundation for celebrating "the charity of the wise." (And then Augustinian *bona voluntas* suffers as hard a fate as *caritas:* two pillars of orthodox Christianity totter simultaneously.)

Beginning by equating good will with charity, Hobbes observes that "there can be no greater argument to a man, of his own power, than to find himself able not only to accomplish his own desires, but also to assist other men in theirs: and this is that conception wherein consisteth charity."[139] For Hobbes charity or good will is a kind of generosity *ex plenitudo potestatis:* it is what one can spare out of one's superfluous power. Hobbes goes on to discuss the most famous case of alleged charity or good will—Socrates' "assisting" of Alcibiades—in a way that turns that will into something of near-Shakespearean bawdiness, mainly by playing with the words "conception" and "conceive" in the same way that he later shaped his ribald definition of sense-perception in *Leviathan*: "There is no conception in a man's mind which hath not . . . been begotten upon the organs of sense."[140] The opinion of Plato concerning good will or "honorable love," Hobbes argues, "delivered according to his custom in the person of Socrates," is that

a man full and pregnant with wisdom and other virtues, naturally seeketh out some beautiful person, of age and capacity to conceive, in whom he may, without sensual respects, engender and produce the like. And this is the idea of the then noted love of Socrates wise and continent, to Alcibiades young and beautiful. . . . It should be therefore this charity, or desire to assist and advance others. But why then should the wise seek the ignorant, or be more charitable to the beautiful than to others? There is something in it savouring of the use of that time: in which matter though Socrates be acknowledged for continent, yet the continent have the passion they contain, as much and more than they that satiate the appetite; which maketh me suspect this Platonic love for merely sensual; but with an honourable pretence for the old to haunt the company of the young and beautiful.[141]

So much for charity or good will in this uncharitable parody of Plato's *Symposium;* in *The Elements of Law* the concept is closer to that in Lucian's *Philosophies for Sale*[142] than to that in the Gospel according to St. John. (Thus it is not surprising that Hobbes should define justice not as wise charity but as law made by an "authorized" sovereign.)[143]

If Pascal is saved for slightly later, it remains for the moment only to refer to Locke; and what he says about the relation of justice to charity is that "as justice gives every man a title to the product of his honest industry," so too "charity gives every man a title to so much out of another's plenty as will keep him from extreme want, where he has no means to subsist otherwise." Locke insists that the plentiful man is required by God "to afford to the wants of his brother," and goes on to complain of those who are "cruel and uncharitable": God has "given his needy brother a right to the surplusage of his goods, so that it cannot be justly denied him, when his pressing need calls for it."[144] In the first passage, justice defined as "a title to the product of honest industry" is merely modified by charity to relieve "extreme want"—an extreme want which may not exist at all, if everyone manages to gather sufficient plums and nuts without letting anything go to waste, and leaves "as much" which is "as good" for future appropriators.[145] Justice as an earned "title" to property is the Lockean rule, and charity modifies that rule if unfavorable circumstances so dictate. But if those circumstances never arise, if plums are universally plentiful, then charity will not even modify justice—much less become the core of justice, as in Leibniz.

Interesting as may be the comparison of Leibniz' notion of *caritas sapientis* with the love-conceptions of Hobbes and Locke, the most important comparison must be with Pascal: for Pascal in the *Pensées* gives absolute primacy to *la charité*, but absolutely denies it any place at all in mere earthly politics. He agrees with Leibniz about the central moral weight of *caritas*, but walls that supreme "order" off from contamination by *la politique*.[146] For Pascal men live in three "orders" simultaneously: the lowest order, that of the "flesh," is miserable and requires constant *divertissement* to allay reflection and despair; the middle order, that of mind or *esprit*, encompasses intellectual activities (including Pascalian geometry); the highest order is that of charity or *la volonté* and is "infinitely" separated not just from "mind" (which at least knows its finite misery) but even more decisively from the flesh (which is mindless matter).

> The infinite distance between body and mind is a symbol of the infinitely more infinite distance between mind and charity; for charity is supernatural. . . . All bodies, the firmament, the stars, the earth and its kingdoms, are not equal to the lowest mind; for mind knows all these and itself; and these bodies are nothing. All bodies together, and all minds together, and all their products, are not equal to the least feeling of charity. This is of an order infinitely more exalted. From all bodies together, we cannot obtain one little thought; this is impossible, and of another order. From all bodies and minds, we cannot produce a feeling of true charity; this is impossible, and of another and supernatural order.[147]

Now what is characteristic of Pascal is that he consigns politics wholly to the lowest, fleshly order: it is simply a matter of power, force, and useful illusions ("three degrees of latitude overturn the whole of jurisprudence"); but love is saved for the saved, a body "full of thinking members" held together by the spiritual gift of *la charité*.[148] Jurisprudence can hardly be "universal," à la Leibniz, if three degrees of latitude "overturn" it altogether. Pascal drives to brilliant extremes fleshly politics and supernatural *caritas:* they are separated by a fearful infinity ("the eternal silence of these infinite spaces terrifies me"),[149] and Christian love has no effect on a carnal sphere in which "force is Queen." Politics is part of a fallen nature, but supernatural grace is needed for the infinite ascent to charity: when Pascal called himself an "Augustinian," as did all Jansenists, he knew whereof he spoke.[150]

By contrast Leibniz strives to close up the "infinite distance" separating politics and charity: politics, "mind," and *caritas* converge in a kind of synthetic middle. No doubt this accounts for Leibniz' collapsing of everything that Pascal tried to keep infinitely distanced, as one of Leibniz' letters to Thomas Burnett (from c. 1696–97) shows clearly:

> . . . the fine accomplishments of M. Pascal in the most profound sciences [mathematics and geometry] should give some weight to the *Pensées* which he promised on the truth of Christianity . . . [But] besides the fact that his mind was full of the prejudices of the party of Rome . . . he had not studied history or jurisprudence with enough care . . . and nonetheless both are requisite to establish certain truths of the Christian religion.[151]

Evidently Leibniz either missed Pascal's point altogether, or (more likely) thought it wholly misconceived. For Leibniz universal, latitude-crossing jurisprudence and universal religion are grounded in the same rational eternal verities, while for Pascal the impotence of reason (as revealed by Montaigne in the *Essais*) drives one to fideism: "God of Abraham, God of Jacob, God of Isaac, not of the philosophers and the theologians."[152] For Pascal, St. Paul was right to ask, "where is the wise?" and to cling to "faith, hope, charity, these three." Leibniz had an equal reverence for Greek philosophy and for Pauline charity, but his synthetic moderation made him incapable of appreciating Pascal's tortured extremism. Indeed Leibniz, who maintained that "men usually hold to some middle way,"[153] would have approved Apemantus' remark to the protagonist of Shakespeare's *Timon of Athens*: "The middle of humanity thou never knewest, but the extremity of both ends."[154] The Leibnizian fusion of Greek *philosophia* and Christian *caritas*, linking Athens and Jerusalem, comes out in a characteristic paragraph which Leibniz wrote for the *Journal des Sçavans* in 1696:

> Our perfection consisting in the knowledge and in the love of God, it follows that one advances in perfection in proportion as one penetrates the eternal verities, and as one is zealous for the general good. Thus

those who are truly enlightened and well intentioned work with all their power for their own instruction and for the good of others; and if they have the means they strive to procure the increase of human enlightenment, Christian virtue, and the public happiness. This is the touchstone of true piety.[155]

The final Leibnizian fusion of "human enlightenment," "Christian virtue," and "the public happiness" would be, for Pascal, an obvious collapsing of "the three orders" into one another: for Christian virtue is isolated in the charitable sphere of *la volonté*, the "public happiness" is just gratified "flesh," and enlightenment is simply *esprit*. It is as if Leibniz were consciously knocking out the supporting walls that sustain Pascal's ascending hierarchy.

In the *Pensées* (no. 481), indeed, Pascal deliberately distances *la charité* even from "good" politics by saying that while the deaths of the "noble Lacaedemonians" (the Spartans fighting under Leonidas against the invading Persians) "scarcely touch us," the deaths of the Christian martyrs do touch us—because the martyrs are "our members" (members of the spiritual body of Christ).[156] Leibniz, by contrast, would never try to dig a gulf between social benefactors such as self-sacrificing Leonidas (saving Greek civilization from Persian "barbarism") and Christian "martyrs": on the contrary, Leibniz tries to find and encourage charity everywhere (for example in Peter the Great of Russia);[157] and there is as little room for martyrs in Leibniz' thought as there had been for Malebranchian blood, crosses, and "perfect victims." Pascal is simply too sectarian for Leibniz, as is clear in his complaint about the "prejudices of the party of Rome" in Pascalianism. For Leibniz "we" is a much broader concept than in Pascal: it is universal, and for Leibniz "our members" are all the rational substances or monads who are citizens of the divine monarchy, of the "best" world.[158] There is a sense, to be sure, in which Pascal is a more authentic "Pauline" thinker than Leibniz: for Pascal always relates charity (from 1 Corinthians 13) to the body and its members (from 1 Corinthians 12)—the spiritual body of Christ ("imagine a body full of thinking members").[159] Leibniz does not exactly secularize charity, but he makes it a universal moral-political-legal-scientific principle, and then often settles for rather attenuated forms of it. Pascal's radicalism has no room for such latitudinarian accommodativeness.

Then, too, the attitudes of Leibniz and Pascal toward the Jesuits are very revealing: Pascal views Jesuits precisely as "jesuitical," and in the *Provincial*

Letters treats them as opportunistic hypocrites who try to destroy the charitable maxim, "give to others out of your superfluity"—by showing that one cannot be absolutely certain that future poverty will never come about.[160] By contrast Leibniz corresponded with Jesuits such as Grimaldi and des Bosses, and tried to accommodate his own views to theirs (insofar as he could without actually capitulating).[161] To be sure, Pascal's personal practice of charity went well beyond Leibniz' "benevolence": Pascal gave up not just superfluity but the essential when, near the point of death, he moved out of his own house in order to help a needy family.[162] Leibniz' "general benevolence" never reaches that point—the point of true saintliness.

BOSSUET'S WEAKENING OF CHARITY: THE CRITIQUE OF LEIBNIZ

Despite Leibniz' great interest in Pascal's version of Christian *caritas*, it is certainly true that his own thoughts on the connection between charity and justice were more consistently fired by those French thinkers who were closer to his own day—above all Fénelon and Bossuet. Even if it is the case that Leibniz sided with Bossuet in thinking that Fénelonian "quietism" did too much harm to the search for personal happiness as the motive of human conduct, Leibniz would at least concede that love is at the heart of the Fénelonian ethos; and in that respect Fénelon was morally superior to the Bishop of Meaux—for Bossuet, in Leibniz' view, does the violence to *caritas* (practice) that Fénelon had done to *voluntas* (motivation).[163]

It is important and revealing, indeed, to compare Leibniz' central ethical conviction that *justitia est caritas sapientis* with the way in which Bossuet treats charity: for not only was Bossuet the leading Catholic churchman and apologist of Leibniz' day, he was also Leibniz' principal correspondent (for over a decade) in the effort to reunite the *respublica christiana* after the "schism" (the Reformation).[164] A comparison of Bossuet and Leibniz over *caritas* shows that the Bishop manages to marginalize charity, while Leibniz by contrast makes it absolutely central not just in theology but in morality and politics. Bossuet does everything in his (considerable) rhetorical power to squeeze charity out of any immediate political application. And Bossuet does not merely make Christian charity lose its place in political-social life—in favor of divine-right monarchy in the style of David and Solomon; he also opposes Leibniz' Platonic rationalism, saying that "reason can do nothing, because each calls reason the passion that transports him."[165] The twin supports of Leibnizian practical thought—Platonic rationalism and Christian charity—are under-mined simultaneously by Bossuet.

Despite Bossuet's self-representation as a traditionalist in his *Politics Drawn from the Very Words of Holy Scripture,* it is fair to note that his thought is, in its own way, as radical as "Cartesian" doubt—radical with respect to charity as the heart of Christian ethics. "Though I speak with the tongues of men and of angels, and have not charity, I am become as sounding brass, or a tinkling cymbal," St. Paul had said; "faith, hope, charity, these three: but the greatest of these is charity."[166] But Bossuet permits himself to modify what one might call the generality of charity, as something owed universally to "all men," in a way that Leibniz could never have countenanced.

In the original manuscript of the *Politics,* Book 1, article 5, Bossuet begins by saying that "to have a true idea of human society one must first think that the whole human race *en général* is a great family," indeed that "the common society and the love that all men owe one another exists always," despite the formation of particular "nations"; but he moves quickly to the notion that "the distance between places and other reasons not permitting that this love be practiced towards all, each [person] must practice it towards those who are conjoined to him by particular ties."[167] Charity, then, both begins and ends at home:

> There is the true spirit of charity, which, embracing all men, and ready to extend itself to all of them, attaches itself . . . with a more particular care to those who are presented to it by particular connections and occasions.[168]

The title of the very next section of Book 1, revealingly, is "On the love of the fatherland." Here love has become very "particular" indeed. And it is worth noticing that Bossuet's *Politics,* nearly half of whose five hundred pages are devoted to verbatim citation of Scripture, never quotes, even once, or ever refers to, 1 Corinthians 13—"but the greatest of these is charity." Indeed it is no accident that, in connection with "drawing" divine-right absolute monar-chy from "the very words of Holy Scripture," Bossuet should have found the Old Testament (with its stress on monarchy and law) much more usable than the New (with its insistence on universal charity). That becomes instantly clear in the opening pages of the *Politics:*

> God is the King of kings: it is for him to instruct them and to rule them as his ministers. Listen, then, Monseigneur, to the lessons which he gives

them in his Scripture. . . . [In ancient Israel] one sees the government of a people whose legislator was God himself . . . the finest and justest polity that ever was.

All that Sparta, all that Athens, all that Rome . . . had by way of wisdom, is nothing in comparison to the wisdom which is contained in the law of God . . .

Moses, who formed it, was instructed in all the divine and human wisdom with which a great and noble genius can be embellished . . . there was never a finer state constitution.[169]

Bossuet then recalls two monarchs whom he views not just as successors to Moses, but (in effect) as forerunners of Louis XIV:

Two great kings of this people, David and Solomon, the one a warrior, the other pacific, both excellent in the art of governing, will give you examples of it not only in their lives, but also in their precepts. . . .

Jesus Christ will teach you, by himself and by his apostles, all that can make states happy; his Gospel renders men more fit to be good citizens on earth, as it teaches them by that means to render themselves worthy of becoming citizens of heaven.[170]

Here Christianity appears rather late, and what Jesus Christ teaches is passive "good citizenship" ("render to Caesar"). But charity appears only as a kind of afterthought—as when Bossuet at first says that "[King] David . . . wanted to make an example of the Ammonites which would leave on this people an eternal impression of terror that would take away their courage for fighting, and he passed over their bodies, in all their cities, chariots armed with knives"; and then adds that "one can subtract from this severity that which the spirit of gentleness and of clemency inspires in the new law [of charity]. . . . A Christian conqueror must spare blood, and the spirit of the Gospel on this point is quite different from that of the law."[171] But why, then, as Jacques Truchet reasonably asks, "begin by elaborating so much on the severity of the law? A too-literal [biblical] exegesis is at the root of it [and] . . . yields a book whose tone is scarcely evangelical."[172] And the result is that, in Bossuet, the "new" law of love merely modifies harsh or murderous examples drawn from Judges and Kings.

Here a comparison with Leibniz will be instructive. If the German philosopher could define justice as *caritas sapientis,* and insist that wise charity "must prevail over all other considerations in the world,"[173] Bossuet was too fearful of ordinary human motivation to let justice be so defined. If, indeed, for Bossuet, charity and wisdom were fully in place, no politics would be necessary. But the chasm between charity and *l'esprit du monde* is what strikes Bossuet: "the character of the Christian is to love all men, and not to fear being hated by them; thus the spirit of fraternal charity forms the particular character of the Christians." Lamentably enough, however, "the spirit of the world, quite different from that of the Christian, encloses four spirits which are diametrically opposed to charity: the spirit of resentment, the spirit of aversion, the spirit of jealousy, the spirit of indifference. There is the progress of evil."[174] And monarchies ("Christian" as they may be) are in, and of, the world. Bossuet seems to push charity back, before the Fall; it has little present weight in politics. He cannot deny St. Paul's "the greatest of these is charity," or Christ's "a new commandment I give unto you"; but he can diminish charity by locating it principally in a prelapsarian Eden. What Bossuet never does, in the manner of Leibniz, is to suggest the "institutionalizing" of charity through the formation of academies and universities, schemes for the improvement of agriculture and commerce—plans that Leibniz drew up by the dozen.[175]

Bossuet, then, on the whole, finds the Old Testament ethos of monarchy and law more politically useful than the new law of love; and that separates him decisively from Leibniz, who viewed Mosaic law as important but incomplete (as was clear in Chapter 3). Sometimes, nonetheless, for all the fact that the *Politics* opens with the phrase, "Listen, Israël," Bossuet can be ferociously hard on the ancient Jews. In Book II of his *Histoire des variations* he says, apparently approvingly:

> St. Augustine establishes, following St. Paul, that one of the differences between Christian justice and that of the [Jewish] law, is that the justice of the law is based on the spirit of fear and terror, instead of which Christian justice is inspired by a spirit of joy and love.[176]

But more often, and more characteristically, Bossuet wants to establish continuity: to stress, in Christ's case, not his "new" insistence on love and charity, but his "royal" descent from the house of David. In this vein Bossuet wants to urge that the Church is the successor to the synagogue, that there is an unbroken line leading backward from St. Peter to Christ to David to Moses to Abraham to Adam to God—all of them (in some sense) "kings." "It is in

Jesus Christ, son of David and of Abraham, that all the nations were to be blessed."[177] Stressing continuity again, Bossuet finally says that

> It was thus that the body of Holy Scripture was formed—the Old as much as the New Testament: Scriptures which have been regarded, since their beginning, as true in everything, as given by God himself. . . .
>
> It is thus that they have come down to us, always holy, always sacred, always inviolable; some preserved by the steadfast tradition of the Jewish people, the others by the tradition of the Christian people.[178]

In this remarkable paragraph, unbroken continuity (and royal descent) matter more than the difference between the "old" and the "new" law—even if Bossuet himself has followed Augustine in drawing a line between "fear and terror" and "joy and love." This is undoubtedly why Bossuet cites chapter 13 of St. Paul's letter to the Romans—"let every soul be subject unto the higher powers"—no fewer than twenty-two times in the *Politics*,[179] but 1 Corinthians 13 not once. And his search for royal continuity between the parts of Scripture, at the expense of "new" law, sacrifices charity to monarchy in a way that is at least as radical as anything conceived by the Cartesian school of tradition-questioning doubt.[180] (By contrast Leibniz was in search of monarchs who subordinate *potestas* and *auctoritas* to *caritas*.)

Does not Bossuet, finally—a bishop, after all—subordinate charity (as the first of the Christian virtues) too much to the exigencies of *l'esprit du monde*? And when he does turn to religion, does he not cling too much to the Old Testament law that he (sometimes) describes as "harsh" and "hard," resting excessively on "fear and terror"? Does not Leibniz do better to urge that justice is the "charity of the wise"—thereby fusing 1 Corinthians 13 and a Platonic rule of the wise? Even if Victor Hugo was unjust and uncharitable in his view of Bossuet—

> Judas buvant le sang que Jesus-Christ suait,
> La ruse, Loyola, la haine, Bossuet
> L'autodafé, l'effroi, le cachot, la Bastille
> C'est nous[181]

—should not Bossuet have done better? Is not his "realism" a little too complacent and convenient—given the Christian standards that were (after all) his own? He does say, in his *Histoire universelle*, that "Jesus Christ propounded new ideas of virtue, practices that were more perfect and more purified. The end of religion, the soul of virtue, and the summary of the law, is charity. . . . On this foundation of charity, he perfected all the conditions of human life."[182] But human life includes politics and justice. To be sure, Bossuet eloquently condemns uncharitable and bad rulers: Herod, Pilate, Roboam, Saul, Antiochus;[183] but his politics does nothing to exclude or avoid them. To reconcile Hobbesian sovereignty and Pauline charity may be as hard as Leibniz thought it was.

An example will make this plainer. In Book x of the *Politics*, speaking about the regulation of marriage and of sexual practices, Bossuet cites with apparent approval (or at least without a word of criticism) the law of Deuteronomy that sexually debauched sons be turned over to magistrates by their parents and then stoned to death.[184] Sometimes Bossuet's scriptural literalism is either horrifying or thoughtless: the charitable Christ of St. John's gospel is minimized (or spends his time rendering to Caesar), but the King David driving chariots armed with knives over prostrate enemy bodies is recounted twice in detail.

What is certain is that, within the Christian tradition that was his own, Bossuet did not preserve the balance of an Augustine—acknowledging political necessity but shrinking from the deification of the profane.[185] What is equally certain is that the objections of Leibniz have a force that Bossuet could not counteract. If a Christian political philosopher must strive for the best available balance of *caritas* and *potestas*, one can say that Bossuet threw off the equilibrium in favor of power—even if one can understand his fear of the *frondeurs* and "anarchists" who frequently endangered Louis XIV.[186]

LEIBNIZ' EFFORT TO "CONVERT" BOSSUET

If Leibniz would plainly have disapproved of Bossuet's marginalizing of charity in the *Politics*, he nonetheless made a personal effort to get the Bishop of Meaux to see *caritas* in a "Leibnizian" way (and at the same time to treat Fénelon in a more charitable manner). At first Leibniz did this obliquely, through the good offices of the Abbé Nicaise, but then addressed Bossuet himself.

In 1697, in fact, Leibniz tried to get his thoughts on "disinterested" love published in France (through Nicaise), but the Abbé took refuge behind Louis XIV, who had forbidden further public disputes on this point.[187] Leibniz then, in 1698, drafted a careful letter to Bossuet himself, saying that "to love is nothing else than to find one's pleasure" (Bossuetism)—"I say pleasure and not utility or interest" (a brief nod to Fénelon)—"in the good, perfection, or happiness of another." But this letter was never sent: at the top Leibniz wrote, "à M. de Meaux, ist nicht abgegangen."[188] Whether Naert is right in saying that the new Elector of Hanover, Georg Ludwig (George I of Great Britain after 1714) "stopped the sending of the letter"[189] is not at all clear: Leibniz was certainly aware of the dangerous political dimension of the "pure love" quarrel, since he described Fénelon and Bossuet as "royal tutors."[190] But he seems to have thought that the sheer reasonability of his thoughts on pure love (or on the reunification of Christendom) would carry the day; he seems to have forgotten that it was not only (or even mainly) a question of "good arguments."

If his letter to Bossuet shows his willingness to press *caritas sapientis* on one who had great weight in French public life, it is nonetheless the slightly earlier letter to Nicaise which is philosophically fuller and more developed:

> When one sincerely loves a person, one is not seeking his own profit, nor a pleasure detached from that of the beloved person, but one seeks one's pleasure in the contentment or in the felicity of that person; and if that felicity does not please in itself, but only because of an advantage which results for us, this would no longer be a pure and sincere love. It is necessary then, that one find pleasure *immediately* in this felicity, and that one find pain in the unhappiness of the person loved; for all that which brings about pleasure immediately, by itself, is also desired for itself . . . It is clear, by the notion of love which we have just given, how we seek at once our own good for ourselves and the good of the object loved for itself, when the good of this object is immediately, finally *(ultimato)* and for-itself an end, our pleasure and our good—as happens with regard to all the things one hopes for, because they please us by themselves and are in consequence good in themselves, when one has no regard for the consequences; they are ends and not means.[191]

Plainly this argument (more "Kantian" than Benthamite) aims to steer between Scylla (Bossuet) and Charybdis (Fénelon): to M. de Cambrai it concedes "disinterestedness" (while denying that this can mean self-abnegation or *sortir de soi*); to M. de Meaux it concedes one's own pleasure (while denying that this can mean neglect of charity and benevolence). Leibniz' synthetic moderation, rolling along the *via media,* is as much in evidence as ever. And at the end of the letter to Nicaise, in a very striking paragraph, Leibniz adds that "it is thus an illusion to base union with God on inaction, since it is rather by acts and frequent practice of the divine virtues that we must maintain our union with God. . . . To will to detach oneself from himself and from his good is to play with words, or if one wants to move on to practical effects, it is to fall into an extravagant quietism, it is to will a stupid or rather affected and simulated inaction in which, on the pretext of resignation and of the destruction of the soul plunged in God, one can pass into libertinage in practice, or at least into a hidden speculative atheism, such as that of Averroës."[192]

Leibniz' Notes on William Penn

A ready and easy way to see how much weight Leibniz gives to enlightened charity in ordinary, everyday life—unlike Bossuet most of the time—is to examine his remarkable notes on William Penn from 1695.[193] In these notes Leibniz does not confine himself to "charity" in a strictly religious sense (though he certainly begins with theology), but branches out to find wise *caritas* in those beneficent scientific endeavors which advance the general good of the human race. (If, from a Pascalian perspective, this is a diluted and attenuated charity which goes beyond the "members" of a church, for Leibniz that is pure gain.)

To be sure, Leibniz begins his Penn notes with Christ himself, and with charity as recommended in the New Testament. After complaining of Penn's "far-fetched" and "mysterious" language, with its echo of "the cabal," Leibniz says that "I would not disapprove these ways of making good things valued, if I found them joined to a clear and luminous doctrine, such as was that of Jesus Christ and of the Apostles; and to the practice of a true charity such as was seen in the first Christians." For Christ teaches that "God has care of everything and that everything is numbered by him, down to our hairs; that those who love him are eternally happy . . .; that the slightest good will be recompensed, even to a glass of water given through charity to a poor person who is thirsty; and that one must rest on his providence after having satisfied one's duty." And when, Leibniz goes on, Christ "urges us to love, above all things, this great God whom he has depicted as so lovable and so good, and our neighbor as ourselves, he draws together theory and practice at once."[194]

So far the stress is on charity in a sense that would be recognized by St. Paul or St. John, or even Pascal; but then *caritas* begins to turn into *scientia* and "the general good." "Now that providence has enriched our century through so many new lights which result from the marvelous discoveries which have been made in nature, and which more and more show us its beauty, we should profit from them by applying them to the ideas which Jesus Christ gives us of God." For nothing "could better mark the divine perfections than the admirable beauties which are found in his works." Leibniz now goes on to complain that "those who pretend to a greater spirituality, and particularly the Quakers, strive to show distaste for the contemplation of natural truths." But they should "do just the opposite, if they do not want to sustain our own laziness or ignorance."[195]

Leibniz then moves on to link up rightly understood love with the science and enlightenment of his own century, saying that "the more one knows nature and the solid truths of the true sciences, which are beams [*rayons*] of divine perfection, the more one is capable of truly loving God." Since Christ has "laid the foundations of the love of God, through knowledge common to all men, it is for us to fortify those great ideas from day to day," through "new natural lights which God has given us expressly for this [purpose], and whose grace works according to the disposition of each one." And Leibniz adds that "we are ingrates if we do not profit from his benefits."[196]

Here, rather radically, as in the letter to Grimaldi examined in Chapter 3, "grace" and scientific *lumière naturelle* seem to have blended. To be sure, Leibniz instantly recalls that good practice does not require theory or advanced knowledge: "It is true that religion and piety do not depend at all on the deeper sciences, for it must be available to the simplest. But those to whom God has given the time and the means of knowing him better, and consequently of loving him with a more enlightened love, must not neglect the occasions for it, and by consequence the study of nature." Those obscurantists who "try to distance men" from such study "on the pretext of certain illuminations which they vaunt, and which consist only in the over-heated imagination, make us leave what is solid for chimeras, and flatter our negligence."[197]

In this paragraph, love is at its best when it is "enlightened": *caritas* and *la lumière* illuminate each other. And in the very next paragraph, advanced theory and good practice come back together: "The knowledge of the greatness of God and the traces of his goodness and of his wisdom consisting principally in the contemplation of the marvelous order which is revealed in all things in proportion as one penetrates to the bottom," it is clear that the love of God (and of the divine order which results therefrom) "makes it the case that we too shall strive to conform ourselves to this order, and to that which is the best." Leibniz goes on to urge that "the wise are not at all discontented with that which has come to pass, knowing well that it cannot fail to be the best," but they nonetheless "strive to make the future . . . as good as possible, knowing that if we fail in this the general order or the harmony of things will lose nothing, but it will be we who shall lose because we shall have less connection [*rapport*] to it."[198]

And in the final page of the Penn notes, all of Leibniz' concerns—theology, charitable practice, scientific advance, enlightenment, the *imitatio Dei*—come together effectively:

> The more one loves God, the more one will strive individually to take part in the divine perfections which are spread out in things, and above all in the happiness of souls, which are the best beings which we know, by contributing to our own instruction and to that of others. For all of true happiness consists only in a perpetual progression of joys coming from celestial love, or from the contemplation of the true beauties of the divine nature. It is this internal taste and this inexpressible pleasure which arises from knowledge of divine and eternal truth which makes one detach oneself easily from the vanities of the world and from all perishable things; and a person penetrated by all of this will use all of his study solely to spread this happiness to others as well, for it is thus that he takes the greatest part in the general good and in the harmony of this great order.[199]

The whole of Leibniz is present in these 1695 notes on Penn: they combine his theology (the best), his metaphysics (the perfect), and his universal jurisprudence (the wisely charitable).

LEIBNIZ ON CHARITY AND BENEVOLENCE IN HIS "DIALOGUE"

If the notes on Penn are rather late—1695, the year of the "New System"—Leibniz had long entertained roughly the same "charitable" thoughts. One of the finest earlier statements of what wise charity or universal benevolence involves is to be found in the *Dialogue sur des sujets de réligion* (1679)—which is also called "Dialogue between an Able Politician and a Churchman of Renowned Piety."[200] What is noteworthy here is that the *politique* is drawn away from the merely "politic" by a charitable churchman (who, however, acknowledges that one must indeed sometimes be politic when one is taking reasonable "precautions," even though one should finally place *caritas* uppermost).

Let us begin with those commandments which are not subject to the slightest dispute, and let us also strive, little by little, to enlighten ourselves concerning the others. Now there is no one who doubts that charity is recommended to us more than all the rest: let us then attach ourselves to it, and believe our Lord in this matter, who included in this precept both the law and the prophets. But remember that true charity includes all men, down to our enemies, not only when they are beaten, but at the height of their insults. Let us consider them as madmen for whom we have pity when they undertake all their efforts to destroy us, and whom we repulse without hatred. All the wicked are miserable, indeed, and do not deserve to be hated. They are men, they are made in the image of God, there has been some misfortune in their education or in their way of life which has made them desperate; they would all be capable of the highest perfection if we always had occasions to win them back: let us then work at this as much as we can, and let us consider that the greatest conquest is that of a soul, since there is nothing more noble in return.[201]

In the spirit of this demi-Spinozist reading of the human condition—in which bad conduct is traceable more to ignorance and maleducation than to outright malevolence[202]—Leibniz goes on to suggest that "since it is ordinarily oppression and misery which makes men quite wicked and bad-acting," and which "gives them a certain hardness of soul," enlightened people "should strive to prevent the despair of so many unhappy people who tremble." "Let us not," he recommends, "seek glory at all in those exploits which are 'great' only in the way that earthquakes are, in the ravages of countries and other public misfortunes. Let us consider that it will count as nothing to appear advantageously in history and to be unhappy in person."[203]

Following that attack on a philosophy of history which would excuse crimes if sufficient "greatness" were realized—an attack aimed at the Machiavellian notion in the *Discourses* that history will (for example) absolve Romulus of the murder of Remus because that fratricide laid the foundation of Roman greatness[204]—Leibniz goes on to offer a slightly more cautious or prudent reading of *caritas*' demands:

One must practice true charity with respect to others. Here is what that consists in, in my opinion. It is necessary not only not to hate any man, whatever defects he may have; one must even love each one in proportion to the good qualities which remain to him, for there is no man who does not have many of them. We do not know what judgment of him God makes—perhaps quite other than ourselves, who are deceived by appearances. Nonetheless it is permitted that you incline toward the side of suspicion and that you have a quite bad opinion of others, insofar as you must take precautions, above all in some matter of importance in which you can expect the worst that can be done. But, in exchange, one must have a good opinion of all men insofar as reason permits when it is a question of their good and of their well-being; there is the concord of the serpent and the dove.[205]

In any event, Leibniz has his charitable churchman say, "do not be vain enough to believe that God considers you more than some other person; do not seek your ease proudly at the expense of your neighbor; put yourself in the place of the unfortunate, and think of what you would say if you were there. Work to content everyone, and, if it is possible, act so that no one leaves you feeling sad or ill-satisfied."[206]

Last of all, in the 1679 "Dialogue," Leibniz turns to the motives which can generate "wise charity," fusing (as usual) the love of God, public service, and personal happiness.

For you should do good, through a pure pleasure in having done well, and, if you are not of this humor, you do not yet love God as you should; for the mark of the love of God is [seen] when one brings himself to the general good by a supreme ardor and by a pure move-ment of pleasure which one finds there, without other interest, as you might be pleased by a beautiful face, or in hearing a well-rehearsed concert, or in seeing a wicked and insolent person rebuffed, and a miserable innocent relieved, though you have no interest in him at all. There is the true effect of charity.[207]

Leibniz' view, then, is that love is "disinterested" in proportion to its directness and intensity: if one loves (say) a Raphael painting through an immediate pleasure and joy, without any calculation of interest—can I sell it advantageously? Will my neighbors admire my aesthetic judgment?—then one's affection is disinterested. "Disinterestedness," then, does not require self-abnegation, à la Fénelon; it does not require "losing oneself"; it just requires immediate pleasure in the "perfections" that are objectively there, in the person or thing loved. Perfection leading to unmediated joy: that is what

Leibniz insists on.[208] And here, as so often, he is in substantial agreement with Malebranche, who argues in the *Traité de l'amour de Dieu* (1697) that

> The more a perception is lively and agreeable, the more love is natural and ardent, the more the soul is filled by the object which pleases it, ... the more the pleasure is great, the less the love which it produces is interested.[209]

Malebranche adds in the same vein that "when one loves a person solely because his good qualities please us, the friendship is pure and not at all interested." And the same is true, for him, of the love of God: "if we claim to love God without his pleasing us ... we claim the impossible. We reduce the love of God or charity to a speculative judgment about the divine perfections."[210] In both Malebranche and Leibniz (who are here nearly identical), there is a very ingenious inversion of usual expectations: "disinterestedness" does not mean a dry absence of passion, and indeed the more pure, direct, and ardent the pleasure (but without the pursuit of mere "utility") the greater the disinterestedness.

Here again, for Leibniz, "Fénelonian" self-abnegation is ruled out:

> Virtuous actions are useful, but they are also agreeable in themselves to the virtuous. And it is a great benefit of Providence to have rendered virtue beautiful and good at the same time. Cicero, following the Stoics, has said some excellent things about the concurrence of the honorable and the useful, and he has well remarked that if one envisaged virtue as one ought to do, one would be charmed by its beauty.[211]

And in the same vein, in his late remarks on King's *Origin of Evil*, which he grafted onto the *Theodicy* in 1710, Leibniz insists that "the moral ideal requires that one be virtuous, grateful, and just not only through interest, through hope and fear, but still more by the pleasure that one ought to find in good actions: otherwise one has not arrived at that degree of virtue which one must strive to attain." For all of morality consists in the fact that "one cannot work better for one's own happiness than by working for the greatest good in general, which comes down to the same thing as the glory of God, that is to say, to that which regards the fundamental laws of a state."[212]

If happiness should be found by working for "the greatest good in general," by contrast finding one's happiness not in charity and benevolence but in cruelty and malevolence is the very quintessence of evil:

We judge that wickedness has become greater when it passes over into pleasure, as when a highway robber, after having killed men because they resisted him, or because he feared their revenge, becomes cruel and takes pleasure in killing them, and even in making them suffer beforehand. This degree of wickedness is judged diabolical, though the man who is tainted by it finds in this cursed pleasure a stronger reason for his homicides than he had when he killed through hope or fear.[213]

Here again proto-Benthamism is excluded: the "pleasures of malevolence" have no weight (to be counted and then overridden) because they are diabolical, and the malevolence of a devil is an inversion of benevolent wise charity.

By now it should be clear that Leibniz not only made *caritas sapientis* his central, dominant moral-political idea, but criticized others insofar as they declined to do so: Bossuet (*qua* Christian) recognized charity but nearly drove it out of the public sphere, dazzled by the *roi soleil;* Fénelon (*qua* Christian) deified love but harmed charity by preaching a quietistic nirvana in which both self and other selves evaporate; Pascal (*qua* Christian) glorified *caritas* but located it in a transcendent sphere, leaving earthly politics to be shaped by Pyrrhonist doubt, force, and *divertissement;* Locke (*qua* Christian) acknowledged charity but only let it modify property (earned by labor) in cases of "extreme want"; Hobbes (*qua* Hobbesian) mocked charity by placing it under the blanket with Socrates and Alcibiades. Everyone in the seventeenth century, for Leibniz, had got it wrong, except for Malebranche; but then Leibniz is always least distant from the great Oratorian, among his main contemporaries.[214]

LEIBNIZ' CODIFICATION OF *CARITAS SAPIENTIS* IN HIS LATE WRITINGS

It remains to consider passages from two of Leibniz' most important political writings, the *Codex Iuris Gentium* (1693) and the "Meditation on the Common Concept of Justice" (c. 1703), in which he works out and elaborates the role of "wise charity" in everyday social life and in political-legal institutions. (These are both mature works, written when Leibniz' system was more or less complete—as "systematic" as that system was ever to become.)

In the *Codex Iuris Gentium,* after saying in a now-familiar way that justice will be "most fittingly defined as the charity of the wise man [*caritas sapientis*]," that charity is "a universal benevolence or habit of loving or esteeming," and that to love or esteem is "to take pleasure in the happiness of another," Leibniz goes on to link up *caritas* with the principles of Roman jurisprudence: *neminem laedere* (to injure no one), *suum cuique tribuere* (to render to each his due), *honeste vivere* (to live honorably). That is to say, he links up the Roman Catholic (St. John's "a new commandment I give unto you") with the Roman (the "old," though not indeed Mosaicly old, law). He fuses the received jurisprudence of Europe with the received religion of Europe, and that is ingenious— pre- and post-Constantinian Rome meet not on the Milvian Bridge but in Hanover (or perhaps in Santa Sophia, since Justinian saved Roman law and built the last great Roman basilica).

In this synthetic vein Leibniz urges that while *neminem laedere* or "strict right" *(ius strictum)* requires only negative "forbearance from harm or injury," and "has its source in the need of keeping the peace," by contrast charity (or "equity") strives "after something more, to wit that while each does as much good as possible to others, each may increase his own happiness through that of others"—since our love or charity or benevolence finds its own pleasure in the felicity of others. And so, for Leibniz, *neminem laedere* or strict right merely "avoids misery"—Hobbes, in Leibniz' view, never gets beyond this— but right in the higher sense *(ius superius)* "tends to happiness, but of such a kind as falls to our mortal lot."[215]

Here, however, "our mortal lot," sheer mortality, is precisely the problem; for the notion that "we ought to subordinate life itself and whatever makes life desirable to the greater good of others," so that "it behooves us to bear patiently the greatest pains for the sake of others," is "beautifully inculcated by philosophers rather than thoroughly proved by them." However "magnificently" Cicero may have declaimed "about the beauty of virtue, the deformity of base things, about a conscience at peace with itself in the depth of a rejoicing soul," the Ciceronian notion of the soul itself must give way to the fully Christian idea of the soul (as the subject of eternal reward and punishment) before wise charity and intelligent benevolence are assured: "in order that it may be concluded by a universal demonstration that everything honorable is beneficial [*omne honestum utile*] and that everything base is hurtful, we must assume the immortality of the soul and the ruler of the universe, God."[216]

And here too, as in the now-familiar "monadology," naturally immortal "substances" or rational monads become citizens of a benevolent divine monarchy:

Thus it is that we think of all men as living in the most perfect city [*civitas*], under a monarch who on account of his wisdom cannot be deceived, and on account of his power cannot be avoided—and a monarch who is also so lovable that it is happiness to serve such a master. Therefore he who spends his soul for Him gains it, as Christ teaches [John 12:25]. By his power and providence it comes to pass that every right passes into fact [*omne ius in factum transeat*], that no one is injured except by himself, that nothing done rightly is without a reward and no sin without a punishment. . . . Thus nothing is disregarded in the Commonwealth of the universe.[217]

Since nothing is disregarded in this true cosmopolis, justice understood in this expansive sense "is called universal and comprehends all other virtues"—for "things which otherwise do not seem to concern anyone else, as for instance whether we abuse our own body or our own property, and which are beyond the range of human laws, are nonetheless forbidden by the law of nature [*ius naturale*], that is, by the eternal laws of the divine monarch." For "as it is of importance to a commonwealth, so much more is it to the universe, that no one should make a bad use of that which is his own."[218] (One must indeed "render to each his own," *suum cuique tribuere*, but that is not the final consideration.) Thus, Leibniz goes on, "learned men" have been correct to say that "natural law and the law of nations [*ius naturae et gentium*]" should be "formulated in accordance with the doctrines of Christianity, that is, according to the teaching of Christ, τὰ ἀνώτερα the sublime things, the divine things of the wise." (In insisting on τὰ ἀνώτερα Leibniz is apparently thinking of St. James [2:8], and of the saint's notion that love or charity is ἡ ἄνωθεν σοφία, "the royal law," inasmuch as it comes from the "law of the [divine] kingdom." And Leibniz would have approved of James' insistence that "faith that does nothing in practice" is "thoroughly lifeless" [2:17].)[219]

Having made justice ascend to heaven, Leibniz now brings it back to earth—or rather to the earth as he would have it. For he argues that in addition to "the eternal rights of a rational nature which flow from the divine source," Christians are linked by the "common bond" of accepted Scripture, and even—at least before the Reformation, which he calls "the schism of the last century"—by a shared idea of "a certain general commonwealth of the Christian nations, the heads of which were in sacred things the Pope [*pontifex maximus*] and in temporal things the Emperor of the Romans, who also seems to retain as much of the law of the old Roman monarchy as was needed for the common good of Christendom."[220] Here the Roman Catholic [*ius naturae*] descends to the (merely) Roman once again.

In this passage from the *Codex Iuris Gentium* there is a remarkable synthesis of pagan and Christian antiquity, law and "a new law." Everything "Roman" is preserved—down to calling the Pope by his most Roman title, that of Pontifex Maximus (a title borne by Augustus and his successors). Hobbes had called the Roman church the "ghost of the Roman Empire, sitting crowned on the grave thereof";[221] Leibniz converts that grim joke into something seriously meant. And, in advance, he heads off Voltaire's witticism that the Holy Roman Empire is "neither holy, nor Roman, nor an empire":[222] for Leibniz the "Roman" is indeed holy insofar as the highest principle of Roman *jurisprudentia*, namely, *honeste vivere*, becomes charity or piety; the moral-legal empire is still there even if *Imperium* has crumbled from Dante's time forward. (For Leibniz the "grave" of Rome is occupied by a being that is dead only in the most trivial sense.)

For Dante (*De Monarchia*, Book II) what had "moralized" Rome—despite Augustine's complaints about aggrandizing war and bloody violence[223]—was Christ's willingness to be born under Roman jurisdiction;[224] that gave Roman law (which Dante studied at Bologna), Roman *jurisdictio*, a divine warrant and coloration. And that was Leibniz' view as well: the supreme degree of Roman law, *honeste vivere*, is for him perfectly convertible into "live charitably." "Justice is nothing else than the charity of the wise . . . Universal justice is stamped with the supreme precept: *honeste [hoc est probe, pie] vivere*. . . . One can oppose it to charity, [but] then it is only the *ius strictum* [the mere prevention of harm, *neminem laedere*]."[225] Rome's afterlife was a legal one, following political death; certainly that view was shared by Dante and Leibniz. For both of them it is the *auctoritas* of the law's *jurisdictio*, not just sovereign *potestas*, that matters.

WISE CHARITY IN LEIBNIZ' "MEDITATION ON JUSTICE"

Leibniz was precisely too well trained a lawyer and too good a jurisconsult not to be well aware that charity might be viewed as "beyond" justice, as something supererogatory: as something meritorious, indeed, but not strictly "due." His answer to this charge is in the "Meditation on the Common Concept of Justice," and rests on the idea of a continuum: if you grant, as even Hobbes does, that evil ought not to be done—harming others, refusing to give what is due—you can be brought to be positively benevolent or charitable, since there is no absolute break between the negative and the positive.

Some people, Leibniz argues in the "Meditation," aim for a very restricted and negative notion of justice:

> Now I observe that some people restrict, and that others extend, the reasons for human complaints. There are those who believe that it is enough that no one does them harm, and that no one deprives them of anything they possess, and that one is not at all obliged to procure the good of another, or to arrest evil, even if this would cost us nothing and would not cause us any pain. Some who pass for great judges in this world, keep themselves within these limits; they content themselves with not harming anybody, but they are not at all of a humor to improve people's conditions; they believe, in a word, that one can be just, without being charitable.[226]

But there are (fortunately) others, he goes on, "who have larger and finer views," who would not wish that anyone complain of their lack of positive goodness.

> They would approve what I have put in my preface to the *Codex Iuris Gentium,* that justice is nothing else than the charity of the wise, that is to say goodness toward others which is conformed to wisdom. And wisdom, in my sense, is nothing else than the science of felicity. It is permitted that men vary in their use of terms, and if someone wishes to insist on limiting the term *just* to oppose it to that of *charitable,* there is no way of forcing him to change his language, since names are arbitrary. However, it is permitted that we inform ourselves of the reasons which he has for being what he calls just, in order to see whether the same reasons will not bring him also to be good, and to do good.[227]

It is fairly widely agreed, Leibniz thinks, that "those who are charged with the conduct of another, like tutors, directors of societies and certain magistrates," are "obligated not only to prevent evil but also to procure the good":

> One will perhaps wish to doubt whether a man free of commitments or a sovereign of a state has these same obligations. . . . But has one not reason to fear that men will hate us if we refuse them aid which does not inconvenience us at all, and if we fail to arrest an evil which is going to overwhelm them? Someone will say: I am content that others

do not harm me, I do not ask at all their aid or their beneficence and I do not want to do or to claim more. But can one hold to this language sincerely? Let him ask himself what he would say and hope for if he should find himself actually on the point of falling into an evil, which another could make him avoid by a turn of his hand. Would one not hold him for a bad man and even for an enemy, if he did not want to save us in this situation?[228]

Leibniz then answers his own question with a striking and picturesque "Oriental" tale: "I have read in a travelogue of the East Indies that a man being chased by an elephant was saved, because another man in a neighboring house beat on a drum, which stopped the beast; supposing that the former had cried to the other to beat [the drum], and that he had not wanted to out of pure inhumanity: would he not have had the right to complain?"[229]

But even if, Leibniz thinks, most people "will grant to me . . . that one must prevent evil for another, if one can do so conveniently," still some will not agree "that justice orders us to do positive good to others":

I then ask whether one is not obliged at least to relieve their ills? And I return again to the proof, that is to say to the rule, *quod tibi non vis fieri* [what you do not wish to have done to you]. Suppose that you were plunged into misery; would you not complain of him who did not help you at all, if he could do it easily? You have fallen into the water; he does not wish to throw you a rope to give you a means of getting out: would you not judge that he is an evil man, and even an enemy?[230]

Leibniz then imagines an even more striking case, which he thinks might inspire a reasonable person to move from *neminem laedere* to *honeste vivere:* "Let us suppose that you are suffering from violent pains, and that another person had in his house, under lock and key, a healing-fountain capable of relieving your ills: what would you not say and what would you not do, if he refused to give you some glasses of [this] water?"[231]

At this point Leibniz falls back on the notion of a continuum, with no radical breaks or leaps:

Led by degrees, one will agree not only that men should abstain from wrongdoing, but also that they should prevent evil from happening and even relieve it, when it is done; at least insofar as they can without inconveniencing themselves (and I do not examine now how far this inconvenience may go). However, some will perhaps still doubt whether one is obliged to secure the good of another, even if one can do it without difficulty. . . . But I wish to propose an intermediate case once again. A great good is going to come to you; an impediment appears; I can remove that impediment without pain: would you not believe yourself to have a right to ask it of me, and to remind me that I would ask it of you, if I were in a similar position? If you grant me this point, as you can hardly help doing, how will you refuse the only remaining request, that is, to secure a great good for me, when you can do so without inconveniencing yourself in any way, and without being able to allege any reason for not doing it, except for a simple "I do not want to"?[232]

"You could make me happy and you do not do it," Leibniz finally says; "you would complain in the same situation—thus I complain with justice."

This gradation, this moral continuum in which there is no break between negative forbearance and positive benevolence,

makes it clear that the same reasons for complaining subsist always; whether one does evil or refuses to do good is a matter of degree, but that does not change the species and the nature of things. One can also say that the absence of good is an evil and that the absence of evil is a general good. Someone makes a request of you, be it to do or to omit something. If you refuse the request, he has reason to complain, since he can judge that you would make the same request if you were in the place of him who makes it. And it is the principle of equity, or, what is the same thing, of equality or of the identity of reasons [*de la même raison*], which holds that one should grant [to others] whatever one would wish in a similar situation, without claiming to be privileged, against reason, or [without claiming] to be able to allege one's will as a reason.[233]

Here, of course, for Leibniz, one cannot use one's will as a sufficient reason for conduct, any more than God can act willfully: nonrational will is "tyranny" in a finite or infinite being.[234] Having appealed to "reason," Leibniz now makes his way back to the terminology of Roman law, urging that

perhaps one can say, then, that not to do evil to another, *neminem laedere*, is the precept of law which is called *ius strictum*, but that equity demands that one do good as well, when it is fitting, and that it is in this that the precept consists which orders that we give each his due: *suum cuique tribuere*. But this fitness, or what is due, is determined by the rule of equity or of equality: *quod tibi non vis fieri*. . . . This is the rule of reason and of our Master. Put yourself in the place of another, and you will have the true point of view for judging what is just or not.[235]

These passages make it abundantly clear that in redefining justice as *caritas sapientis*, Leibniz was not unaware of usual ideas about justice, such as "strict law" and "rendering what is due." He keeps those, as the lowest and middle degrees of received "Roman" justice; but his continuum-ism (as it were) leads him higher and higher until justice and charity are virtually indistinguishable. But charity is introduced, in the "Meditation," with great shrewdness: Leibniz relies not so much on Christian exhortation as on the notion of what reasonable people would ask for or complain of in everyday moral experience. It is not just "Rome" and "reason" that are appealed to, but garden-variety practice as well.

RECENT INTERPRETATIONS OF LEIBNIZ' *CARITAS SAPIENTIS*

All of the best scholars who have written recently and memorably on Leibniz' notion of justice as "the charity of the wise"—including Hervé Barreau, Thomas Gil, Emily Grossholz, André Robinet, J. B. Schneewind, and René Sève—are in agreement that what is most distinctive and valuable in Leibnizian justice is its insistence on an unbroken ascent from the negative *(neminem laedere)* to the positive (universal benevolence) by reasonable degrees: that Leibniz is unique and helpful insofar as he insists that the fully just man is not the one who merely brings his conduct into external conformity with "Hobbesian" negative commands, but the one who, putting himself in "the place of others," acts so well that no reasonable complaint of neglecting "the good" can be brought against him *by* others.[236] (Here one thinks of Plato's *Republic*, in which the just in Book IV gives way to the good in Books V–VII.)[237]

Hobbes, of course, had been concerned with enforceability: where there is "no law" there is "no justice," and "covenants without the sword are but words."[238] In his correspondence with Kettwig concerning Hobbes (November 1695), Leibniz is aware of this Hobbesian worry, but overrides it: "I recognize that men are constrained by reciprocal fear and by the necessity to found and to constitute a guardian power of the society; but the source of this lies in love [still] more than in fear."[239] (For Leibniz, the "passion to be reckoned upon" is love.) Still, Leibniz was no "Christian anarchist" who thought that affection could simply replace law: rather he kept (as has been seen) the "lower" degrees of law in place, and then made law ascend to embrace *caritas.*

The best Leibniz scholars have seen all of this clearly. Sève, for example, in his excellent *Leibniz: Le droit de la raison* (1994), stresses the ascent from "refraining from harm" to "doing good" by first quoting Leibniz' own text, *An jus naturae aeternum* (c. 1695): "When one is inquiring into the right and the just, it is a matter of showing how the fact of procuring the good for another [*alieni bono procuratio*], so far as this can be done without sacrificing one's own, constitutes our good: thus one inquires into the charity of the wise."[240] Sève remarks, very aptly, that "the essential point of the Leibnizian argument consists in showing that there is not a rupture but rather continuity between the action which is just in the current and narrow sense (which does not harm others) and in the proper and enlarged sense (which procures the good for others)." And Sève goes on to add, again very aptly, that the second, enlarged sense of justice as *caritas sapientis* "does not require that a supernatural quality (charity in the orthodox and theological sense) be infused into the agent, but that the latter develop his natural intellectual and practical capacities."[241]

Sève then elaborates these helpful observations by pointing out that, for Leibniz, the "others" whom we injure (or fail to help at small cost to ourselves) will reasonably reproach us "for not helping them to avoid threatened harm; for not aiding them to suppress a present evil, for not removing the obstacles to the obtaining of a good, for not directly procuring a good for them, if the person who can aid them suffers no inconvenience from it or only a very slight harm in comparison with the good procured or with the evil suppressed." And Sève, with his thorough knowledge of the history of jurisprudence, adds that "the idea corresponds to the Stoic distinction between negative benevolence and positive benevolence"—as in Cicero's claim in *De Officiis* that "the foundations of justice" involve "not harming anyone" but also "being of service to the common good";[242] what distinguishes Leibniz a little from Cicero, however, for Sève, is that the Hanoverian "blurs the frontier between these two dispositions through a continuous progression of logical degrees." For Sève, Leibniz goes beyond Hobbesian negative forbearance to insist, in *De Jure et Justitia*, that "the first principles of justice . . . must be drawn from that which is best *in toto*, so that the greatest possible perfection of the whole society will come about."[243] (That claim corresponds perfectly to an argument which Leibniz made in the 1680s, but which was first published three hundred years later: "Justice is nothing else than that which contributes to the perfection of a society.")[244]

In roughly the same spirit as that of Sève, Hervé Barreau urges in "Leibniz, précurseur de la conception universelle des droits de l'homme" (1994) that "the originality of the Leibnizian doctrine of natural right consists in its graduated character. . . . One must conceive this gradation as the call of moral consciousness in each person, who sees degrees of the good, and undertakes to realize them by beginning with the lower degrees, without ever repudiating them, since the higher degrees enclose the lower ones, which they bring to a greater perfection." For Leibniz, always ascending from "strict law" to wise charity, from fearful prudence to benevolent generosity, the object of full justice is "not only to prevent evil to us, but to procure for us what is better, thus to work for the public good, which flows back to us."[245]

And once again, in this same vein, Thomas Gil urges that "justice for Leibniz is a continuum of graduated differences (without breaks and chasms), so that there is a flowing transition [*einen fliessenden Ubergang*] between the omission of evil and the doing of good."[246] "Flowing" is just the right word: it suggests a liquid continuity with no arrests or gaps.

André Robinet, in his invaluable *G. W. Leibniz: Le meilleur des mondes par la balance de l'Europe* (1994), further elaborates the Leibnizian notion that by tiny "degrees," without breaks, we can be brought to "make people well off." And here Robinet—as in all of his Leibniz scholarship of the past forty years—keeps to Leibniz' very language:

> What would we say if another, who could help us avoid an evil "by turning his hand," will not aid us? We would take him to be an evil man, to be an enemy. In the dialectic of "the place of others," one could say that we put ourselves in the place of ourselves. . . . Degree by degree, one must end by agreeing that it is necessary "to stop the evil that is being done, and even to relieve it when it is done," at least insofar as one can without inconveniencing oneself.[247]

Robinet then cites an important passage from Leibniz' "Meditation on Justice" "One can say, then, that justice, at least among men, is the constant will to act in such a way (so far as it is possible) that no one can complain of us, when we would complain of another in a similar case. From which it is evident that, when it is not possible to act so that everyone is content, one must strive to content people as far as it is possible, and that therefore what is just is in conformity to the charity of the wise."[248]

But perhaps the most wide-ranging effort to appreciate Leibniz' notion of justice by degrees (a flowing continuum) is to be found in Emily Grossholz' "Leibniz and the Two Labyrinths" (1993), which urges that Leibniz' thought universally—in mathematics as much as in justice—is "clearer when it is understood not just in light of the principle of contradiction, but the principle of continuity as well." Grossholz goes on to show, with great care, that Leibniz' justice-continuum is "linked by infinitesimal increments." She begins by quoting a key line from the "Meditation on Justice": "You could make me happy [by a turning of the hand] and you do not do so: I complain, [and] you would complain in the same case; thus I complain with justice." Grossholz comments, very helpfully, that

> here Leibniz asks us imaginatively to run through all the permutations, as the agent who does or does not lift a hand, as the recipient who praises or complains, reminding the agent that he must also put himself in the other's place, and act and judge accordingly. . . . Leibniz explicitly invokes the principle of continuity, [and as he] sets up his *continuum*, he insists on the primacy of imagination that permits one to put oneself in another's position, to transcend one's own *point de vue*. . . . Within this *continuum*, doing harm and refusing to do good exist side by side, not severed but linked by infinitesimal increments.[249]

And that last phrase, very deliberately, reminds us that "justice by degrees," justice rising by tiny increments toward "wise charity," was conceived by the greatest mathematician of the early Enlightenment. (Here, to be sure, the "eternal verities" have moved on from the Pythagorean to the Newtonian age.)

In the notion of putting oneself in "the place of others" there is surely some idea of a sympathetic enlargement of the moral imagination; what is noteworthy, however, is that Leibniz stresses not so much a proto-Humean enlarged "sympathy"[250] as the universality of "reasons for complaint": he remains enough of a demi-Platonic rationalist to put the main moral weight on the *reasons* one might have if *quod tibi non vis fieri* is unreasonably violated in one's own case. And that is made economically clear in a small manuscript from c. 1705 (a few years after the "Meditation on Justice"), in which Leibniz epitomizes his universal jurisprudence in a half-dozen lines:

Justice is a constant will to act in such a way that no one has reason to complain of us.

To complain of someone is to blame him for causing evil to us. By evil I mean also the diminution or the stopping of our good.

To blame someone is to indicate that he acts in an unreasonable way.[251]

LEIBNIZ' DEBT TO AUGUSTINE'S *CITY OF GOD*

Leibniz' insistence that justice is a *continuum* stretching from the negative *(neminem laedere)* to the positive *(honeste vivere)*, and that such justice is bound up with a variety of Platonic notions—"higher love," quasi-mathematical harmonious order, and "eternal verity"—is unusual in a seventeenth century dominated by English contractarianism, but not absolutely unprecedented: for there is a key passage in Augustine's *City of God* which strongly foreshadows Leibnizian universal jurisprudence in its drawing together of Pauline, Platonic, and Roman jurisprudential ideas. The Bishop of Hippo Regius urges that

> Peace between human beings and God comes from ordered obedience in faith to the eternal law, which peace between human beings is ordered harmony. . . . [It is] the more ordered and harmonious society of those who enjoy God and each other in God. . . . God the teacher gives us two major precepts: the love of God and the love of our neighbor, through which we find three things to love: God, ourselves, and our neighbors. Thus when we love God we do not err in loving ourselves, and, in addition, we advise our neighbor, whom we are ordered to love as ourselves, to love God. And we would want our neighbor—be it wife, son, servant or whoever is able—to do the same for us if we are in need. In this way we will be at peace, as far as we are capable, with all people. This is the harmony whose order is, first of all, never to harm anyone, and, secondly, to aid whomever we can.[252]

If this passage were interpolated into Leibniz' "Meditation on Justice" or *Codex Iuris Gentium,* it would not greatly obtrude: for while Augustine speaks of "peace" more than does Leibniz, almost everything else in this part of the *City of God* is "proto-Leibnizian." The stress on "harmony" and "eternity" descends to both Augustine and Leibniz from Plato's *Phaedo, Republic, Philebus,* and *Timaeus;* the stress on "enjoyment" *(delectio)* is as strong in Leibniz as in the Bishop of Hippo; in both Augustine and Leibniz a measure of self-love is permitted (in contrast to the self-abnegation of Fénelonian "quietism"); the "place of others" is acknowledged by Augustine ("we would want our neighbor . . . to do the same for us") in a way that Leibniz could approve; and finally the Platonic "harmony" and "order" which Augustine and Leibniz equally cherish turns out to dictate the very maxims of Roman law ("never to harm anyone," "to aid whomever we can") which Leibniz called *la raison écrite*. Small wonder, then, that in *De Religione Magnorum Virorum* (c. 1687–1694), Leibniz could praise the *City of God* for the *"sententia S. Augustini"* that *"Deus omnia faevat optimo modo* [God does everything in the best way]."[253] (This is not to say, however, that Leibnizian optimism is congruent with the darker, proto-Jansenist side of late Augustinianism: though Leibniz himself was both a jurisconsult and a judge, he seems never to have reflected, at least in writing, on the harrowing passage in which Augustine—speaking of the well-meaning judge who tortures the innocent to death in search of the truth—finally says that "though we acquit the judge of all malice, nonetheless we must admit that human life is miserable.")[254]

To be sure, one can always ask whether Leibniz thought that "higher" justice, wise charity, and benevolence (Augustinian "aid") was legally enforceable (or even capable of being "institutionalized"). Here, however, the fact that Leibniz did not place the main stress on mere legal constraint makes this less problematical than it would be in one who (all but) equates justice with law and then views law as authoritative sovereign commands backed by sanctions—such as Hobbes.[255] (On this point Schneewind is right when he says that law is not as central for Leibniz as it is for a demi-Hobbesian such as Pufendorf.)[256] In the end, then, Leibniz finally said about justice as wise charity what he had said as early as 1670, in the *Juris et aequi elementa:*

> There are two ways of desiring the good of others, the one when we desire it on account of our own good, the other when we desire it as if it were our own good. The first is the way of him who esteems, the second of him who loves; the first is the feeling of a master to his servant, the second that of a father to his son; the first is the feeling of a man towards the tool he requires, the second that of friend to friend; in the first case the good of others is sought for the sake of something else, in the second for its own sake.[257]

Or, as Leibniz put the matter more lightly in a letter to Landgraf Ernst of Hessen-Rheinfels in the 1680s, "If I were Pope, I would want to distribute among the monks the inquiries into the truth [*les recherches de la vérité*], which serve the glory of God, and the works of charity, which serve the salvation and the good of men."²⁵⁸ The combination of science and charity—not mere *opera operata* such as masses and pilgrimages²⁵⁹—is wholly and characteristically Leibnizian.

JUSTITIA EST CARITAS SAPIENTIS: A FEW CONCLUSIONS

In the end one can say that Leibniz preserves the Christian/Pauline notion of charity as one side of justice, that he does not altogether secularize the idea of justice, but that (at the same time) the stress on "the wise" is redolent of both ancient Platonic rationalism and modern scientific Enlightenment. Here one cannot do better than to recall the words of Sève in *Leibniz: Le droit de la raison,* who urges that while Hugo Grotius had argued for a "separation" between "the domain of natural law and justice, and that of charity and divine law," Leibniz by contrast undertook "to formulate a conciliatory synthesis between the two positions [Grotian and overtly Christian]: in agreement with the religious point of view he refuses to reduce justice to the exclusive pursuit of earthly ends, but in agreement with the rationalization brought about by the moderns he no longer sees in charity the mysterious action of grace but rather a love which is conceptualizable in its means and in its end: progress, the happiness of humanity, the glory of God. Such is the sense of the Leibnizian definition of justice as 'the charity of the wise.' "²⁶⁰

For Leibniz, then, wise charity and universal benevolence, as "moral necessities," require that we (at least) not harm the world and the rational monads who are its citizens, and that we go on (by degrees) to the positive aid and help of others. In Oakeshottian language, we enter the "conversation" of the social world when our turn comes, we make our contribution, and we hope to leave that world better than we found it.²⁶¹ For Leibniz this was clear from his earliest days—for example in the *Elements of Natural Law,* which he wrote at the age of twenty-three.

> Justice is a disposition of the mind which causes no harm to anyone without necessity; but something more must be added. Certainly that person is just who must not harm another when his own need is not in question, but also he who must aid others: first of all when he can overcome the misery of others without causing his own misery.²⁶²

Leibniz never deviated from that view of a charitable continuum of infinitesimally small degrees, rising from refraining from harm to removing impediments to giving positive aid; the *Elements of Natural Law* from 1669 already foreshadow almost everything he will say later. Leibniz' "complete concept" of *caritas sapientis* was simply there, like a monad, waiting to unfold completely in time. And after that unfolding had taken place, late in life, Leibniz drew together his reflections on justice as wise charity (linking up justice, *caritas, sapientia,* and "feelings of perfection") in two crucial texts: the first, "Felicity," from c. 1694–1698, is more secular and psychological; the second, "True Piety," from c. 1710, is more conventionally Christian. But both serve to fix his final moral-political ideas.

Leibniz' most effective late effort to link up his metaphysics, psychology, and charitable ethics through the idea of "perfection" is contained in his notes on "Felicity," in which he says that

1. Virtue is the habit of acting according to wisdom. It is necessary that practice accompany knowledge.
2. Wisdom is the science of felicity, [and] is what must be studied above all other things.
3. Felicity is a lasting state of pleasure. Thus it is good to abandon or moderate pleasures which can be injurious, by causing misfortunes or by blocking better and more lasting pleasures.
4. Pleasure is a knowledge or feeling of perfection, not only in ourselves, but also in others, for in this way some further perfection is aroused in us.
5. To love is to find pleasure in the perfection of another.
6. Justice is charity or a habit of loving conformed to wisdom. Thus when one is inclined to justice, one tries to procure good for everybody, so far as one can, reasonably, but in proportion to the needs and merits of each: and even if one is obliged sometimes to punish evil persons, it is for the general good.[263]

Love of others must be an extension of one's worthiest pleasure: an expansion of oneself, a generous taking in of others, not a Fénelonian negation of self, is required. Men must scale the continuum of pleasures; near the top, just beneath the love of God, they will find love of neighbor, on which justice turns. Leibniz' most eloquent summary of this view, in his letter concerning "True Piety" (1710), urged that

Practice is the touchstone of faith. And it is not only what many people practice themselves, but what they make God practice, which betrays them.

They depict him as limited in his views, deranging and refashioning his own work at every moment, attached to trifles, formalistic, capricious, without pity with respect to some, and without justice toward others, gratifying himself groundlessly, punishing without measure, indifferent to virtue, showing his greatness through evil, impotent with respect to the good and willing it only half-heartedly, using an arbitrary power, and using it inappropriately; finally weak, unreasonable, malignant, and in a word such as they would show themselves when they have the power or when they think about having it: for they imitate only too much the idol which they adore.[264]

Idola tribus take the place of the *imitatio Dei:* perfectly unjust people fantasize a perfectly unjust God. By contrast with those people who "talk enough about the goodness of God while they destroy the idea of it," true piety shows us that "one cannot love God who is invisible when one does not love his neighbor who is visible."

Those who . . . reduce justice to [mere] rigor, and who fail altogether to understand that one cannot be just without being benevolent . . . in a word, not only those who look for their profit, pleasure, and glory in the misery of others, but also those who are not at all anxious to procure the common good and to lift out of misery those who are in their care, and generally those who show themselves to be without enlightenment and without charity, boast in vain of a piety which they do not know at all, whatever appearance they create.[265]

The sincerity of that heartfelt passage is impossible to mistake: it echoes Leibniz' defense of God's justice in the *Theodicy*, and reasserts the fundamental Leibnizian conviction that "universal right is the same for God and for men." And the notion of "lifting out of misery" recalls Leibniz' ascent from *neminem laedere* to *caritas sapientis* by a flowing continuum of infinitely small degrees. "True Piety" represents the whole of Leibnizian ethics as surely as each monad expresses the whole of the "best" world. And it also shows, not at all incidentally, that the great Leibniz scholar Jean Baruzi was correct to insist that Leibniz' notion of charity owed most to the thought of St. John: "The connection which Leibniz makes between Johannine thought and his own doctrine of the general good . . . is permanent in his mind . . . the one whom he calls 'the most sublime of the evangelists' in the *Theodicy* was always considered by him to be such."[266] For St. John had given an absolute primacy to *caritas* which is not so consistently present in St. Paul or Augustine—or, indeed, in anyone before Leibniz himself.

Practical Justice
in the Human Forum

In Leibniz' universal jurisprudence, charity exactly proportioned to degrees of perfection would produce the most nearly perfect human justice; but Leibniz was aware that this was sometimes too much to be hoped for in everyday life. He therefore attempted (as was seen in the last chapter) to fuse his definition of justice as the charity of the wise with the three great principles of Roman law, *neminem laedere, suum cuique tribuere, honeste vivere*.[1] Leibniz converted the highest degree of Roman law, "live honorably," into "live piously," or charitably, while the *ius strictum* (whose maxim is *neminem laedere*, "harm no one"), and which requires mere forbearance from violence, became for him simply the lowest form of justice—something essential but not adequate, necessary but not sufficient. The middle degree of justice, *suum cuique tribuere*, rendering to each his due, made up for Leibniz the bulk of political justice. In the *Codex Iuris Gentium* (1693), Leibniz enlarged on these distinctions. The precept of the *ius strictum* is that no one is to be injured, "lest if it be within the state, the person should have grounds for an action at law or if it be without the state, he should have the right to make war"; this lowest degree of justice, which merely averts the worst calamities, he also called "commutative" (altering the sense which Aristotle gave to that term).[2] The middle degree of justice, rendering to each his due, Leibniz sometimes called charity in a "narrow" sense, sometimes equity, sometimes "distributive" justice.[3] There are two important differences between the *ius strictum* and "equity": first, that the *ius strictum*, which is merely preservative, treats everyone equally, whereas equity or "distributive" justice looks to merit and thus treats different men differently; and second, that the *ius strictum* simply "avoids misery" and "has its source in the need of keeping peace," while equity "tends to happiness, but of such a kind as falls to our mortal lot."[4] The highest degree of justice, wise charity (or piety), is not consistently attained in everyday life, but is the guarantor of the goodness of men's actions in a wider sense: some men, without the certainty of divine justice, would not act as they should.[5]

Leibniz' Radicalism in the *Elements of Perpetual Justice*

Leibniz' conversion of Roman law into a steady ascent which finally arrives at Christian charity is at its most radical and imaginative in the *Elements of Perpetual Justice* (1695);[6] this is an astonishing work, and in many respects a very bold and innovative one. It begins by insisting that justice is not simply the "first" of the virtues, à la Aristotle or Aquinas, but that justice "contains" all of the moral virtues, and that it relates to "the public good" or "the perfection of the universe" or "the glory of God"—where those three distinct things are morally equivalent in Leibniz' usual sense (the sense that in working with wise charity for the common good of humanity one is following the "presumptive will" of God as the universe's just monarch).

> Every moral virtue, insofar as it relates to the public good, or rather, to the perfection of the universe and to the glory of God, is contained within universal justice, which is absolute. These are perfect laws, pre-scribing every duty of virtue to men.[7]

And he then defines universal "right or justice," in his now-familiar way, as *caritas sapientis.*

But the really bold and striking thing in this 1695 manuscript is that Leibniz goes on to say that "the precepts of the eternal law, which are called 'natural,' are nothing other than the laws of the perfect state. . . . The principles in question are three: *neminem laedere, suum cuique tribuere, pie vivere.* The first [to injure no one] is the precept of peace, the second [to render to each his due] is that of commodious living, the third [to live piously] is that of salvation."[8] In this paragraph, which abandons Leibniz' characteristically moderate caution, the "eternal," the "natural," and the Roman are made equivalent (as "perfect laws"), and that jurisprudential Trinity then governs not just the "human forum" but "the perfect state" of the best *kosmos:* the principles of Justinian's law code are placed on a level with eternity and nature—at least once one transforms "live honorably" *(honeste vivere)* into the "live piously" *(pie vivere)* of Christianity. No longer are *neminem laedere, suum cuique tribuere,* and *honeste vivere* just historical residues of a concrete legal and jurisprudential system; they have become the principles of "natural" (indeed of "eternal") justice. But this is not surprising in Leibniz, who could rank himself among those for whom "the Roman laws are not considered as laws, but simply as written reason [*la raison écrite*]."[9] This "written reason" of Roman jurisprudence must of course be the same reason which prescripturally revealed goodness and justice to men even before Abraham and Moses appeared on the scene.[10] (But that follows from Leibnizian jurisprudence: if charity is given by reason, and charity is the summit of "Roman" law, then Christian and Roman ethics flow from the same source: *la raison*, whether *écrite* or not.) And when Leibniz goes on to say, slightly later, that since "the love of God" or of the *summum bonum* "prevails over every other desire," the "supreme and most perfect criterion of justice consists . . . in this third precept of true piety," and that "human society itself must be ordered in such a way that it conforms as much as possible to the divine" (to "that universal society which can be called the City of God"),[11] he has finally equated the eternal, the natural, the Roman, "written reason," and the divine. And since universal justice is *caritas sapientis*, he has equated the eternal, the natural, the Roman, the reasonable, the divine, and the charitable.

Even for so very synthetic a mind as Leibniz', this is an amazing synthesis. Aquinas had kept the "eternal" and the "natural" quite distinct in the *Summa Theologica*, and had certainly viewed Roman law and jurisprudence as mere civil law *(ius civile)*. And much of (revealed) Christianity would have counted for him as "divine positive law."[12] Leibniz compresses all of these Thomistic categories into one great undifferentiated justice-lump. To be sure, after first equating all three gradations of Roman law with the natural and the eternal, even with *la raison écrite*, he then somewhat downgrades the two lowest ones, *neminem laedere* and *suum cuique tribuere*: "it is not enough to act well toward others with a view to one's own peace and commodious living, because he who does not have other motives for acting well . . . will be capable of great crimes." And therefore piety or charity must shape even the lower degrees of justice: one must want peace and commodious living not just to enhance personal "interest" but for "the procuring of the greatest good for others (without prejudicing ourselves)."[13] And that, of course, ties this 1695 work to Leibniz' more general view that justice as wise charity will encompass both the perfection (felicity, happiness) of others and our delight or joy in feeling that perfection.

If in the Preface to the *Theodicy* one had learned that the duty of wise charity is given by "supreme reason" (as Christ himself saw), in the *Elements of Perpetual Justice* charity is the heart of "living piously," and that pious living is a modified Roman *honeste vivere*—but Roman jurisprudence is now also natural, eternal, and divine: *la raison écrite*. In the end, then, Leibniz seems to want to say something like this: "Roman" justice = "Christian" *caritas sapientis* = reason = nature = eternity = divinity. The jurisprudence of the Eternal City has become eternal *strictu sensu;* the Roman has become truly "catholic," the justice of "the perfect state," the law of the "best" world. For "after the writings of the geometers there is nothing that one can compare, for force and solidity, to the writings of the Roman jurisconsults . . . never has natural law been so frequently interrogated, so faithfully understood, so punctually followed, as in the works of these great men."[14]

ROMAN LAW AND PRIVATE PROPERTY IN LEIBNIZ' THOUGHT

Leibniz treated private property in relation to the three degrees of "Roman" justice, though not always with perfect consistency. He believed that no private property at all was best, but that such austerity was usually unattainable. Society, he urged, is held together by three things—friendship, political justice, and valor. "If the first, which makes all goods common, could be observed, the second would be useless, and if men were not so far removed from justice, valor would not be needed to defend states."[15] But "human nature," he insisted, would not allow that society be founded on friendship and wise love alone; thus both private property and legal justice became necessary. As Gaston Grua puts it in his magisterial *La justice humaine selon Leibniz* (closely paraphrasing and frequently citing Leibniz' *De Tribus Iuris Praeceptis sive Gradibus*),

> Distributive justice [for Leibniz] assigns to each his own, that is to say that which it is suitable to assign to him for the public good. So far as the common good permits, one takes account here of virtue and of merits, of vices and of crimes, and this is geometric equality, proportionality in things assigned to persons. This distributive justice is exercised either by individuals over their goods, or by society in distributing common goods. . . . In the best state, with good education, everything would be distributed by the public power, and men would enjoy common goods in proportion to their virtues and merits, for the state could furnish them with all the means necessary to action.[16]

In a perfect state, Leibniz said, "all goods should be public property," and should be publicly distributed to private persons in proportion to degrees of perfection; unfortunately, neither a sufficiently enlightened public, willing to live a "convent-like" existence, nor sufficiently just and public-spirited administrators, could always be found.[17] In his *Elements of Natural Law* (1677–78), Leibniz relates these thoughts to *caritas sapientis*, saying that "if men possessed sufficient wisdom and charity," society could be regulated "in the same way as certain religious orders, such that all [property] is in the power and gift of the state," and so that jurisprudence could occupy itself with distribution alone, "encouraging" some people with rewards which lead to "the greatest utility." But, Leibniz goes on to lament, "since all of this cannot be hoped for without an enormous transformation of things," and since "men as they are today" want the property they have, "it is quite evident that to judge [property rights] in terms of the excellence of merits and of virtue is a very difficult thing." It remains true that "if the human race wanted spontaneously to establish by law a community of goods," that would be admirable—but "this is not a thing to be hoped for."[18] And therefore "geometric" distributive justice, strictly proportional to virtue and merit—as in Plato's *Laws*, Book VI, or in Aristotle's *Politics*, Book III—would require more wisdom and charity than Leibniz thought likely in modernity. (It is characteristic of Leibniz to retreat from his own radical moral-political claims: property ought to be proportional to perfection, but this is scarcely to be expected; the wisely charitable ought to rule, but little is done to guarantee that result.)

As a result of all this, men must be left to provide property for themselves (though public "benevolence" demands that no one actually suffer from want). Once this decision has been made, in Leibniz' view, private property must be considered to be protected by strict right: thus in respect to property men are to be treated equally, not in the sense that they all receive the same thing, but in the sense that they have an equal right to keep what they have (or can get without violating *neminem laedere*, "harm no one"). Redistribution of property on the basis of merits and virtues ("perfections") is too difficult and too dangerous; such a redistribution would cause an injury to private persons, in violation of the harm principle of Roman law. The principle *suum cuique tribuere*, therefore, is to apply only to goods which the state has at its disposal for distribution (or to goods which private persons wish to distribute out of benevolence).[19] The potential radicalism of Leibniz' theory of justice is thus socially defused; leveling is forbidden, and only a general expansion of the state's generosity is recommended. "It is sufficient," Leibniz wrote in his *Extensive Remarks on Jurisprudence* (1676), "that the commonwealth take care that no one becomes miserable; that men of merit can find some way to be useful; this is what is essential; for the rest, it is not very important which [citizens] possess certain things—provided that acts of violence and manifest frauds be punished and stopped."[20]

Indeed, Leibniz' more radical thoughts on property tend to be early, from the 1670s; and by the time he wrote the "Meditation on the Common Concept of Justice" (c. 1703) he had learned to accommodate property relations which have little to do with merit or virtue, perfection or charity:

> It is not permitted to deprive the rich of their goods, to accommodate the poor. . . . This is because the disorder which would be born of it would cause more general evil and inconvenience, than this particular inconvenience. Moreover, it is necessary to maintain possessions, and since the state cannot care for all of men's domestic affairs, it must preserve the ownership of goods so that each will have his own sphere which he can enhance. . . . If everything were commonly owned, it would be neglected by individuals, [unless] it were arranged [as it is] among the members of religious orders, which would be difficult in these times.[21]

Here one can feel Leibniz' reluctance: what would be "difficult in these times" is nonetheless what he would prefer.

One of the most important things about Leibniz' theory of practical justice, when joined with the gradations of the Roman law, is that he allowed no sharp breaks between duty and benevolence—as was seen in Chapter 4: in Leibniz there is none of Kant's differentiation between "perfect" and "imperfect" duties to others.[22] Justice for Leibniz is a continuum, as everything in his philosophy tends to be: there is an unbroken continuity, with no gaps, between the lowest substance and God, between life and death, between rest and motion, just as there is a continuum between abstaining from injury *(neminem laedere)* and doing good *(pie vivere)*. In the "Meditation on the Common Concept of Justice" he argues persuasively that if one grants that injury ought not to be done (as Hobbes himself will), it is hard to deny that good should be done; "whether one does evil or refuses to do good is a matter of degree." To this argument he added a psychological one—that if one wants to know what is just, one should put oneself in the place of another who might have good reason to complain of injustice.[23] Here Leibniz came to roughly the same practical conclusion as Kant: if men did not make exceptions in their own favor, they would all agree to the same rules. And this is why he urged that "the place of others" *(la place d'autrui)* was the soundest viewpoint from which to make moral and political judgments; "everything which we would find unjust if we were in the place of others, must seem to us to be suspect of injustice . . . the sense of the principle is: do not do or do not refuse lightly that which you would not like to be done to you or which another would not refuse to you."[24]

In the *Réflexions sur l'art de connaître les hommes* (1708) Leibniz put the same point in a more openly Christian way. "It is very praiseworthy to aid the unfortunate by representing to oneself what one would wish if one were in their place," he insists. "Far from this principle being bad (though we reflect on ourselves), it comes from the purest motive of charity, in conformity to the rule of our Lord, who commands that we do to others what we would have done to ourselves when the occasion arises."[25] And he makes roughly the same argument, not in a Christian but in a jurisprudential way, in his commentary (c. 1695) on Jean Domat's *Les loix civiles dans leur ordre naturel*, in which he amplifies Roman law *neminem laedere* and *suum cuique tribuere* by adding the broader idea of "putting ourselves in the place of others, and others in ours; exchange of places in thought."[26]

Leibniz' theory of practical justice (including his thoughts on property), then, is a complex amalgam of Christian charity, a metaphysics of Platonic perfectionism, Roman law, and transmogrified Aristotelian terminology; its relation to his pure philosophy is, to say the least, problematical, but taken in itself it has integrity and force. Bertrand Russell, therefore, was not justified in calling Leibniz' social thought a "mass of inconsistencies";[27] there is one central problem, namely whether, given the ideas of "substance," preestablished harmony, and compossibility, one (anyone) could act better than he does, or whether one's unavoidably limited knowledge (which then taints "the will") will bring about imperfect charity involuntarily. In essence, the question is Spinoza's—whether it is possible to distinguish between error and evil, cognitive limitations and *le mal moral*.[28] And on this point Leibniz was never perfectly consistent, though he tried heroically to maintain the distinction.

PARTICULAR STATES: CONTRA HOBBES ONCE AGAIN

Leibniz' doctrine of justice as charity regulated by wisdom was rather consistently kept in view as he worked out his theory of the state: a just political order requires both benevolence and intelligence, but not the participation of all the members of society, either in forming or in sustaining the polity—least of all by a "natural right."[29] The state, in his view, is an "unlimited unequal society"—that is, it is concerned with "the whole of life and the common good," and not simply with "certain purposes, for example, trade and commerce, navigation, warfare and travel";[30] here one is reminded of the famous passage in *Reflections on the Revolution in France* in which Burke insists that "the state ought not to be considered as nothing better than a partnership agreement in a trade of pepper and coffee, calico, or tobacco, or some other such low concern . . . it is a partnership in every virtue and in all perfection."[31] The state, moreover, for Leibniz, is founded on relations of inequality between those who rule and those who are ruled. Like Plato, Leibniz believed that it would be unjust if the best and wisest men did not rule; here he fell back on justice as a relation, as a mathematical "proportion," and took the Platonic view that social justice should be the most accurate possible transcript of "nature"[32] (including natural inequalities). In a letter to the Scottish nobleman Thomas Burnett (1699–1700), he sketched out this position, while criticizing (with infinite circumspection) the Hobbesian/Lockean theory of equal natural rights.

> I have still not had the leisure to read the entire book entitled *Two Treatises of Government*, against the principles of Mr. Filmer. I did notice, however, a great justice and solidity in the reasoning. There are, nevertheless, some passages, perhaps, which demand a more ample discussion, as among others what is said of the state of nature, and of the equality of rights of men. This equality would be certain, if all men had the same [natural] advantages; but this not being so at all, it seems that Aristotle is more correct here than Mr. Hobbes. If several men found themselves in a single ship on the open sea, it would not be in the least conformable either to reason or nature, that those who understand nothing of sea-going claim to be pilots; such that, following natural reason, government belongs to the wisest.[33]

Since equal natural rights to political participation are, for Leibniz, illusory, he made very little use—at least in his mature works—of social contract theory, which presupposes an equal right in all contractors to found legitimate states. Indeed the key idea in social contract theory is that legitimate government is the artificial creation of the "voluntary agreement" of free and equal adult moral agents:[34] but for Leibniz, as for Hume in a different way, the legitimacy of the state has nothing to do with its historical origins.[35] A "contract," therefore, is not important; but justice, welfare, benevolence, and the promotion of the common good are. Probably Leibniz denigrated the social contract precisely because Hobbes had made so much of it: in his important early work, the *Nova Methodus*, he appeared as a rather conventional contractarian;[36] but since the "state of nature" which supposedly preceded the Hobbesian contract posited a moral vacuum in which there is no justice without sovereign-ordained positive law[37]—a doctrine which Leibniz increasingly detested—he may have felt that contract theory was dangerous; if justice as wise charity is eternal and natural, then it is not artificially produced in time by a Hobbesian covenant. Contractarianism also, in Leibniz' view, introduced too great a measure of artifice into social relations; Hobbes, he complained in the *New Essays*, was not aware that "the best men, free of all malice, would unite the better to obtain their [common] end, as birds flock together to travel in company."[38] And the reason that Hobbes was not aware of this truth is clear: "His initial step was false, namely to seek the origins of justice in the fear of evil rather than in the concern for the good, as if men had to be wicked in order to be able to be just."[39]

If Hobbes was "not aware" of what the "best" men might spontaneously do, without being legally constrained, that is because, in Leibniz' view, Hobbes' dark politics is an all-too-faithful reflection of a dark psychology. One of Leibniz' most telling critiques of that tenebrous psychology is to be found in parts 219 and 220 of the *Theodicy*—not surprisingly, since the whole work can be read (reasonably) as the supreme anti-*Leviathan*.[40] Leibniz begins by insisting that "there is incomparably more moral good than moral evil in the world"—even in the merely "best" world full of physical, metaphysical, and moral evil. Here Leibniz finds an occasion to criticize "people of a malicious disposition" who "find wickedness everywhere," such as Timon of Athens (who became "somewhat misanthropic through misfortunes")—people who "poison the best actions by the interpretations which they give to them." Some people, Leibniz goes on, are true misanthropes (like Timon) who "draw evil conclusions by which their conduct is tainted"; but others "only do it to show off their own acumen." That fault of cynically showing off has been found by some in Tacitus' jaundiced histories, Leibniz says; but (more interestingly) Descartes has found such rhetorical misanthropy in Hobbes' *De Cive:*

> For although M. Descartes acknowledges that this book is by a man of talent, he observes therein some very dangerous principles and maxims, in the assumption there made that all men are wicked, or the provision of them with motives for being so.[41]

Leibniz goes on to say that Jacob Thomasius (his old philosophy teacher at Leipzig) liked to say that "the primary cause of errors in this book by Mr. Hobbes was that he took *statum legalem pro naturali* [the legal condition for the natural one], that is to say that the corrupt state served him as a gauge and rule, whereas it is the state most befitting human nature that Aristotle had in view." For according to Aristotle, Leibniz continues, "that is termed natural which conforms most closely to the perfection of the nature of the thing [*Politics* I, 1252b], but Mr. Hobbes applies the term *natural state* to that which has least art, perhaps not taking into account that human nature in its perfection carries art with it."[42] This argument is not only effective; it also anticipates Rousseau's insistence in *L'état de guerre* (c. 1756) that "Hobbes thinks that he has seen the natural man, but he has only seen a *bourgeois* of London or Paris."[43] Leibniz' view is that one "needs" Hobbesian sovereignty only if one has first misconceived nature as a "state of war" in which life is "solitary, poor, nasty, brutish, and short."[44] And it will be seen a little later what Leibniz thinks of Hobbesian sovereignty—that God alone is safely endowed with supreme power because he is supremely wise and good.[45] (Leibniz' position, as became clear in Chapter 3, is that Hobbes recognized only God's irresistible power, leaving his intellectual and moral attributes out of account as "unknowable.")

Here it is worth pointing out that even Leibniz' youthful "Hobbism" in the late 1660s and early 1670s had been very equivocal. Leibniz' own letter to Hobbes of July 1670 says that he has found "great illumination [*lucem accensam*]" in Hobbes' civil philosophy which will be useful in "undertaking a work on rational jurisprudence"; but at the same time the young German tells the elderly Englishman that "there cannot exist a state of pure nature between men, outside of all commonwealths, since God is the common monarch of all men"[46]—and that Leibnizian universalism runs counter to Hobbes' national "sovereignty," which ends at the English Channel, and which is viewed as a local salvation from the state of nature. (For Hobbes, as for John of Gaunt in Shakespeare's *Richard II*, it is "this England" that matters.)[47]

Only a year later, in June 1671, one finds Leibniz saying—in a newly discovered (1988) letter to the Dutch physician and statesman Lambert van Velthuysen of Utrecht—that Hobbes' notions of "supreme civil power," of "indivisible sovereignty," and of "absolute obedience" cannot be found on earth as we know it *(in orbe terrarum)*, that Hobbes' theories can only be true of the universe, whose governor *(rector)* God is. (Earthly life as we know it,

Leibniz declares, can involve no more than "society with security [*societatem cum securitate*]." But in any case this letter of 1671 shows Leibniz already moving away from considerations of sovereignty and absolute obedience, and towards his mature defining of right and law in terms of love or charity:

> The good man I define as he who loves everyone [*qui amat omnes*]. To love is to be pleased by the felicity of others. Right is what is possible for a good man. Obligation is what is necessary for a good man. From these definitions it is for me to demonstrate the whole of natural right theoretically.[48]

Here Hobbes is left completely behind: the negative notion of mutual forbearance from violence *(neminem laedere)* gives way to the positive procuring of good. The ripe doctrine of the 1693 *Codex Iuris Gentium* is already there, in embryo. And it is equally clearly there in a letter from the same period in which Leibniz laments Hobbes' (mis)use of brilliant talents to defend nothing more than a negative peace: "That most ingenious Hobbes could have spared us the necessity to reconsider the whole science of right, if he had not chosen as his principle the preservation of peace; this principle, which is narrower than that of justice, does not permit one to demonstrate all the theorems of natural right, but only certain ones [e.g., *neminem laedere*], while justice itself must be demonstrated by beginning with a much more universal principle."[49] And what could be more universal than a *jurisprudence universelle* resting on *caritas sapientis*?

Within a decade of the letter to Hobbes, by the early 1680s, Leibniz was combining a rejection of any Hobbesian "state of nature" with a positive insistence on justice as "the charity of the wise": in a passage published only in the 1980s, three centuries after it was written, Leibniz urges that

> By the existence of God is suspended every state of nature which is rough [*statum naturas rudis*] and bestial, of man left to himself, as well as the right of all against all; and the wise man can thus give free exercise to charity with safety, and bear witness to a good which is a refuge against evils.[50]

And in roughly the same period the centrality of a love governed by appreciation of "degrees of perfection" is already in place. "We cannot love some men" in particular, Leibniz argues, "if we do not love all men"; we "cannot love several men if we do not love all humanity"; we cannot "love the human race if we do not love God." "He who loves God," he goes on to insist, "loves all men, but each in proportion as he expresses the divine virtues in himself." For "one cannot love God without loving one's brother, one cannot have wisdom without having charity; that is the touchstone of true virtue."[51] That passage shows that by the early 1680s Leibniz' "universal jurisprudence" was substantially complete. And so what Leibniz said against any Hobbesian "state of nature" ungoverned by natural justice remained constant to the end of his life: in his 1712 observations on Hobbes in the *Remarks on Shaftesbury's Characteristics* he insisted that "our illustrious author refutes with reason those who believe that there is no obligation at all in the state of nature, and outside of government—for, obligations by pacts having to form the right of government itself, according to the author of these principles, it is manifest that the obligation is anterior to the government which it must form."[52]

That 1712 passage merely elaborates what Leibniz had said slightly earlier, in notes on Cudworth and Hobbes from 1704—notes in which Leibniz urges that if there is no natural justice before sovereign-ordained law, even "Hobbism" itself cannot work. If it is not a principle of natural law that *pacta sunt servanda*, "agreements ought to be kept," then the sovereign will have no law-making authority derived from "covenants" *(pacta)* of which human will is the "essence." "If nature," Leibniz says in the 1704 notes, "does not require that agreements be kept [*si natura non jubet pacta servari*]," the outcome will not be "sovereignty" but rather nothing: "Nothing comes from nothing; if nothing is naturally just, neither will it be artificially so."[53] But if, on the other hand, natural justice is already there—as eternal, divine, *la raison écrite*—then the Hobbesian argument that justice is sovereign-commanded positive law is wrong (or at least superfluous). Justice need not be ordained *ex plenitudo potestatis* if it is (as in *Euthyphro*) an "eternal verity." And if it is just there, quasi-Platonically, necessarily and universally, one avoids the (for Leibniz grotesque) consequence that there would be as many kinds of Hobbesian justice as there are varieties of positive law—the state of affairs famously described by Pascal in the *Pensées:* "truth on this side of the Pyrenees, error on the other."[54]

Leibniz' 1704 notes on Hobbes echo a larger and more important manuscript from 1700: indeed in his *Observations on the "Principle of Justice"* (by Samuel Coccej) there is a characteristic commentary on Hobbesian justice— Hobbes becomes Thrasymachus once again—and, tacitly, even on Lockean justice, since Coccej had adopted the more-or-less Lockean principle that God *qua* creator has the right to give "natural law" for the governance and protection of what he has created.[55] Since Leibniz does not comment directly anywhere on section 6 of the *Second Treatise*, in which Locke says that "men being the workmanship of one omnipotent and infinitely wise maker, all the servants of one sovereign master . . . they are his property, whose workmanship they are,"[56] the 1700 *Observations* count not just as a familiar assault on Hobbes but as an oblique treatment of that crucial Lockean passage in which God has a property right in us, as we have property rights in the "plums" or "nuts" which we industriously gather—provided we waste nothing and leave for future appropriators "as much" which is "as good."[57] What is striking in Leibniz' *Observations*, as will soon be clear, is that Locke finally turns into a Hobbist, however unintentionally.

Coccej, Leibniz says in section VI of the *Observations*, "affirms that the natural law is the command of the creator . . . that the will of the creator obligates the creature." But, Leibniz thinks, this will not do: "if indeed we suppose that the creature can dispose of enough power, once produced, to be no longer constrained by the creator, it will have to be considered as emancipated"—in the same way that "sons can arrive at a degree of power such that they can no longer be constrained by the parents who brought them into the world."[58] (That is a cunning objection, since a "Lockean" does not want to ground legitimate authority in perpetual paternalism, à la Filmer.)[59] Soon enough, in any case, on Leibniz' view, "Lockean" creationism collapses into purest Hobbism: "But the illustrious author [Coccej] seems to derive law from coercion alone. And thus, since generation does not give law"—sons can grow up—"neither will creation give it, but only power." But "if omnipotence is, above all, the power to do harm (in virtue of which it is said that certain people adore the devil)," one will soon have to revert to the doctrine that Plato strove so hard to overturn—one will have to "go back to the tyrannical principle enunciated by Thrasymachus in Plato: that will be just which is pleasing to the most powerful. Neither is Hobbes far from this, who bases justice on power." But since, Leibniz recalls, a Hobbesian acknowledges only God's irresistible power, not his moral and intellectual perfections, "supposing that there is a malignant God such as the Manichaeans admitted, his power would suffice to make just even the worst of things, which is repugnant to our conception of natural justice."[60]

This passage is not as charitable as it is effective: to link Hobbes to adoration of the devil and to Manichaeanism is more striking than just. All the same, in Leibniz' view, Hobbesians are wrong in overstressing God's power. In a more moderate paragraph which anticipates the *Theodicy* of ten years later, Leibniz insists that

> Justice is founded on higher and better principles—not solely on the will of God but also on his intelligence; not on his mere power but also on his wisdom. Justice is based not on the will, but on the charity of the knower. Wherefore justice has been defined by a jurisconsult as "the charity of the wise" . . . . And if we suppose, *per impossibile*, that an evil genius seized supreme power, he would not cease to be wicked and unjust and tyrannical through the fact that he could not be resisted.[61]

One cannot derive the concept of right from the mere possession of power—as Leibniz invariably says, whether he is speaking of God or man.

Fortunately, Leibniz goes on to urge in the *Observations*, the Hobbesian (and even the Cartesian) conception of God is self-destructive; here logic and St. Anselm replace devil worship and Manichaeanism. "If, for constraint, the will of the powerful is sufficient," Leibniz says, "there is no reason to require goodness in the supreme legislator." And then he suggests that "certain Cartesians say that truth itself is constructed by the will of God, and that the number four is 'even' because God commands it." But if that were true "the very existence of God would have to be arbitrary"[62]—that is, if even the ontological proof is not an eternal verity, a necessary truth. For Leibniz God cannot "create" the proof of his own existence *ex plenitudo potestatis*, any more than the "fullness" of power can fabricate justice *ex nihilo*. In the 1700 *Observations*, Hobbes, Locke, and Descartes are converted into one single three-part radical voluntarist, an unholy trinity—not very fairly, but certainly very strikingly.

Six years after the *Observations*, Leibniz brought all of his Hobbes criticism to its final perfection in his magisterial *Opinion on the Principles of Pufendorf* (1706)—a work which became celebrated owing to Barbeyrac's French translation (and hostile commentary).[63]

> [Pufendorf] defines law as "a command by which the superior obliges the subject to conform his actions to what the law itself prescribes." If we admit this, no one will do his duty spontaneously; also, there will be no duty when there is no superior to compel its observance; nor will there be any duties for those who do not have a superior. And since, according to the author, duty and acts prescribed by justice coincide

(because his whole natural jurisprudence is contained in the doctrine of duty), it follows that all law is prescribed by a superior. This paradox, brought out by Hobbes above all, who seemed to deny to the state of nature, that is [a condition] in which there are no superiors, all binding justice whatsoever (although even he is inconsistent), is a view to which I am astonished that anyone could have adhered.

"Now, then," Leibniz asks, "will he who is invested with the supreme power do nothing against justice if he proceeds tyrannically against his subjects," if he "arbitrarily despoils his subjects, torments them, and kills them under torture," if he "makes war on others without cause?"[64]

The Hobbesian doctrine of "natural" dominion through "irresistible" power, Leibniz goes on to say in the *Opinion on Pufendorf*, is a problem in both the divine and the human forum:

> It is without doubt most true, that God is by nature superior to all; all the same the doctrine itself, which makes all law derivative from the command of a superior, is not freed from scandal and error, however one justifies it. Indeed, not to mention that which Grotius justly observed, namely that there would be a natural obligation even on the hypothesis—which is impossible—that God does not exist . . . since care for one's own preservation and well-being certainly lays on men many requirements about taking care of others, as even Hobbes perceives in part . . . to pass over all this, one must pay attention to this fact: that God is praised because he is just. There must, then, be a certain justice—or rather a supreme justice—in God, even though no one is superior to him, and he, by the spontaneity of his excellent nature, accomplishes all things well, such that no one can reasonably complain of him.[65]

And then Leibniz' demi-Platonism and anti-Cartesianism are brought into play one last time, in a passage which echoes the *Euthyphro*-loving "Meditation on the Common Concept of Justice" (written two or three years earlier).

> Neither the norm of conduct itself, nor the essence of the just, depends on [God's] free decision, but rather on eternal truths, objects of the divine intellect, which constitute, so to speak, the essence of divinity itself. . . . Justice, indeed, would not be an essential attribute of God, if he himself established justice and law by his free will. And, indeed, justice follows certain rules of equality and of proportion [which are]

no less founded in the immutable nature of things, and in the divine ideas, than are the principles of arithmetic and of geometry.[66]

And therefore no reasonable person will maintain, Leibniz concludes, "that justice and goodness originate in the divine will, without at the same time maintaining that truth originates in it as well—an unheard-of paradox by which Descartes showed how great can be the errors of great men."[67] If one adds that "proportion" refers not just to Platonic geometry but to the notion that "wise" love or charity must be proportional to degrees of perfection in others, then the whole of Leibniz' universal jurisprudence is present in the *Opinion on Pufendorf*—which is really an opinion on Hobbes.

All in all, Leibniz' critique of Hobbes—pieced together from many Leibnizian writings stretching from the 1670s to the *Opinion on Pufendorf*—is complete and forceful, and includes at least the following claims: (a) Hobbes is mistaken about human nature, and therefore (b) his theory of quasi-divine "sovereignty" is equally mistaken, and (c) his idea of sovereignty rests in any case on contract or covenant, but there is no natural obligation to keep contracts in a Hobbesian "state of nature" and therefore (d) there is no escape from that "brutish" condition, but (e) Hobbes could have found "natural obligation" in nature if he had recognized quasi-Platonic "eternal moral verities,"[68] which are not the mere command of authorized sovereigns, but (f) Hobbes' notion that "all substance is body" rules out minds who could know eternal moral truths as natural obligations, and (g) Hobbes could have seen justice as more than commanded law had he not cynically defined charity as mere Socratic lust in the *Elements of Law*. Thus, for Leibniz, Hobbes is systematically wrong, architectonically erroneous: about nature, about sovereignty, about contract, about obligation, about charity. Hobbism is a brilliantly dark universal mistake.[69]

Leibniz' rejection of equal natural rights and (ultimately) of English contractarianism did not mean, however, that he dismissed the possibility of an important "popular" element in the state. This he made clear in his single most important purely political letter (to Thomas Burnett, 1701), which is also valuable for its revelation of Leibniz' devotion to a Montesquieuean (or perhaps Ciceronian) moderation and reasonability in politics.[70]

> The end of political science with regard to the doctrine of forms of commonwealths [*républiques*] must be to make the empire of reason flourish. The end of monarchy is to make a hero of eminent wisdom and virtue reign. . . . The end of aristocracy is to give the government

to the most wise and the most expert. The end of democracy, or polity, is to make the people themselves agree to what is good for them. And if one could have all three at once: a great hero, very wise senators, and very reasonable citizens, that would constitute a mixture of the three forms. Arbitrary power is what is directly opposed to the empire of reason. But one must realize that this arbitrary power is found not only in kings, but also in assemblies. . . . Thus one must think in this world of laws which can serve to restrain not only kings, but also the deputies of the people, and judges.[71]

Arbitrary power, then, was wholly rejected by Leibniz; liberty was as important to him as equality was unnatural. But this love of liberty never led him to republicanism—though he was certainly aware of republicanism's attractions, and of the fear it produced in monarchs: "all republics are odious in the eyes of kings . . . republics usually cause their neighbors to wish for comparable liberty; they tolerate all kinds of religions; the common good is the first object in their catechisms; they scarcely know corruption; they are the true seedbeds of men of genius."[72] Despite that encomium, he nonetheless insisted in the same 1701 letter to Burnett that "when one loves true liberty one is not a republican on that account, since one can find a more certain reasonable liberty when the king and the assemblies are linked by good laws, than when arbitrary power is in the king or in the multitude." If one had to choose, however, between absolutism and popular "license," Leibniz reluctantly but clearly preferred the former; "it is certain . . . that the absolute power of kings is more tolerable than the license of individuals, and that nothing is more certain to bring about tyranny than anarchy."[73]

A Crucial Early Work: The *Grundriss* of 1671

Even if Leibniz preferred absolutism over anarchy, it remains true that he did not like to concentrate on power as the main attribute of rulers. In an important (but neglected and never-translated) early work, the *Grundriss eines Bedenckens von Aufrichtung einer Societät in Deutschland* (Foundation for a Proposal for the Establishment of a Society in Germany) (1671),[74] he drew his customary sharp distinction between reason and power, and observed that a harmony of mind and power is not only the foundation not only of beauty and of justice, but of true statesmanship: "if power is greater than reason, he who possesses it is either a lamb who cannot use it at all, or a wolf and a tyrant who cannot use it well." On the other hand, the man in whom reason is greater than the power to use it is "overpowered." Accordingly, Leibniz urged, "those to whom God has given reason without power . . . have the right to be counselors," while those who have power alone "must listen patiently, and not throw good counsels to the winds." What is ideal, however, is a union of power and reason within a single person: "Those to whom God has given at once reason and power in a high degree are heroes created by God to be the promoters of his will, as principal instruments." Of the three ways of honoring God—through good words, good thoughts, and good actions—the last is best, and is accomplished (if ever) by moralists and statesmen; as "governors of the public welfare" they "strive not only to discover the brilliance of the beauty of God in nature," but to imitate it. "To praises, to thoughts, to words, and to ideas, they add good works. They do not merely contemplate what he has done well, but offer and sacrifice themselves as instruments, the better to contribute to the general good and to that of men in particular."[75]

The *Grundriss* is an exceedingly accomplished work for a twenty-five-year-old: it foreshadows much of the mature Leibniz. To be sure, the definition of love is not yet perfectly complete (as in the 1690s); and the notion of God rests on prime causality rather than on the ontological proof which Leibniz later preferred to stress. But even in 1671 the emphasis on charity, even "wise charity" or enlightened benevolence, is fully present in his praise of moralists and statesmen who attempt an *imitatio dei* through good works. The importance of science and enlightenment are fully there too, and lead to pleas for an academy of arts and sciences in Germany (though Leibniz was to wait for thirty years before the Prussian Academy was translated into existence in 1701).[76] All in all the *Grundriss* is an amazing foretaste of the later Leibniz to come: it shows that his fundamental moral, political, and scientific ideas were more or less in place by his twenty-fifth year, a quarter of a century before he used the term "monad" and nearly forty years before he made the word "theodicy" famous.

Leibniz begins the *Grundriss* with reflections on love and justice which show that only a few steps were necessary to arrive at *caritas sapientis*, but which also show that Platonic notions of "proportion" and "harmony" were always crucial to his idea of universal jurisprudence.

> Love is a joy of the heart, which considers the beauty and excellence of another heart. All beauty consists of harmony and proportion; the beauty of the heart or of the mind consists in the proportion between

mind [*Verstand*] and power [*Macht*]—which, in this world, constitutes the foundation of justice, of order, of merits, and even of the form of the state: each understands what he wants, and wants only what he understands.[77]

But unfortunately, the young Leibniz laments, a harmonious equilibrium between human capacities is not always present: if power overwhelms reason the product will be a "wolf" or a tyrant who uses power badly; if reason is powerless then it is simply overcome by *potestas.* There is only one actual being in whom knowledge [*scientia*] and power [*potentia*] are in Platonic balance—namely God, whose "sovereign mind" we should love because of the "sovereign good" which flows from it. (Even at this early date, "sovereignty" merely modifies "mind" and "good"; the Bodinian-Hobbesian understanding of sovereignty as unquestionable authority becomes recessive.)

Even in the *Grundriss* one finds Leibniz restricting what God does for particular individuals in light of what "universal harmony permits": God in 1671 can do no more for individuals than Jupiter will be able to do (four decades later) for Tarquin at the end of the *Theodicy:*

> Since God is highest wisdom [*höchste Weisheit*], it is certain that he is so just and so good that he has already loved us, we his creatures, and that he has done everything that depended on him—that is to say all that the universal harmony permits, without doing wrong to our free will—so that we will love him too; and it is on this that faith rests.[78]

Soon, as always in later writings, Leibniz begins to urge that love of God and charity towards one's neighbor are absolutely inseparable—an orthodox-enough thought, but eloquently expressed. "One must not believe and hope superficially," Leibniz argues, "but think practically, that is, act as if it were true that God loves us." To love God, he goes on, "is not to love him superficially, but to will practically, that is, to do all that is in our power" for God's most nearly perfect creatures, human beings ("the reality of love consists in doing that which is loved by the beloved").[79]

In this early work one finds Leibniz demonstrating the existence of this "lovable" God not so much through the ontological proof and the argument from design as through prime causality—in the manner of Aristotle and Hobbes. "Knowledge of the divine nature can naturally only be derived from the demonstration of his existence," Leibniz says. "This [existence] is based on the fact that, without him, it is not possible to have a primary cause."

Without showing much (if any) logical connection between God as cause and God as morally perfect—here he would later be much more careful—Leibniz nonetheless roundly asserts:

> It follows incontestably that *caritas, amor Dei super omnia*, and true contrition, on which the assurance of beatitude depends, is nothing other than *amare bonum publicum et harmoniam universalem* [to love the public good and the universal harmony] . . . for between universal harmony and the glory of God, there is the same difference as between body and shadow, person and image, *radio directo et reflexo* [a direct or reflected beam], inasmuch as one is a matter of fact, while the other is in the soul of those who know it.[80]

Leibniz now urges, in an argument which survived into his fully mature period (to be elaborated in the great *Radical Origination of Things* from 1697[81]), that "God only created rational creatures to be a mirror [*Spiegel*] wherein is reflected and multiplied, in an unending fashion, his unending harmony." Complete knowledge and love of God, he goes on, "consist in a beatific vision or celestial joy, which will bring about the concentration of endless beauty in a little point of our souls." And he elaborates this nearly mystical Platonism with prosaic scientific fact: "burning-mirrors are a natural prefiguration" of the celestial and the beatific. But the degree to which each rational creature will be able to mirror "the beauty of God and universal harmony" will be proportional to each person's "capacity for understanding."[82] (It is surely not accidental that the *Grundriss* was written in the same year that Leibniz argued that "Pilate is condemned" because the "causes of understanding" were lacking.)[83]

That doctrine of (what would become) "metaphysical evil" by the time of the "Discourse on Metaphysics" (fifteen years later) now leads Leibniz to a quasi-Platonic psychology of unequal natural "functions" and capacities which is reminiscent of the *Republic*:

> It follows that those who are of a threadbare nature, and heavy with shadows, that is to say endowed with inferior reason and power, should serve others only as mechanical instruments; and that it is sufficient if they let themselves be employed as instruments for the glory of God, or, what is the same thing, for the common good . . . and improvement of creatures.[84]

Here the equality of souls in the sight of God, always problematical for a demi-Platonist such as Leibniz, has briefly disappeared altogether. Continuing his Platonic account of the relation of social functions to psychic capacities (and incapacities), Leibniz suggests that "those to whom God has given reason without power [*Verstand ohne Macht*] have the right to give counsel," just as "those who have power ought to listen patiently" and not spurn good advice which is beyond their power. But what would be best—rare as it is—is a perfectly harmonious equilibrium of reason and power:

> Those to whom God has given at once reason and power in a high degree are heroes created by God to be the promoters of his will, as principal instruments; but misery to them if this inestimable treasure be buried. . . . It is an important point, on which the happiness and honor of the world depend, to use one's reason and one's power appropriately, for the glory of God. I believe that a conscientious man will never search for the philosopher's stone without fear and trembling, so that he will never hear, one day, these harsh words: "Be damned with your gold."[85]

With a kind of "Platonic functionalism" in place—in which, as in *Republic* 443d–e, no part of the psyche can "usurp" the functions of another part without injustice[86]—Leibniz now tilts rather more in a Christian direction: inevitably, given his effort to be a Christian Platonist. And here one already sees the primacy of charity over mere faith that will characterize the *Theodicy* forty years later.

> One can use reason and power for the honor of God in three principal ways . . . by good words, by good thoughts, and by good works, or, as people say, good deeds. When it concerns God, these things are called first *laudes et sacrificia* [praise and sacrifice], then *spes cum fide* [hope with faith], and finally *bona opera vel obedientia vel caritas efficax* [good work or obedience or efficacious charity]. *Caritas est melior fide nuda* [charity is better than bare faith]; obedience is better than sacrifice, faith is better than praise and sacrifice, from those who honor him only with their lips.[87]

After saying rather quickly that those "who honor God with praises and sacrifices are the orators and the priests" who "work to spread the glory of God and to inflame hearts with his love," Leibniz becomes more expansive in the next paragraphs of the *Grundriss*—in which he takes up the moral and political worth of philosophy and science: "As philosophers, those people adore God who discover a new harmony in nature and in art, to make his omnipotence and wisdom visible." And he laments that the "moralists and statesmen" who "neither know nor observe the marvels of nature" love God incompletely and neglect "the perfection of their soul." "Nobody can praise God with more zeal and more energy," he adds, "than he who joins knowledge of true philosophy to eloquence and poetry, and who goes beyond the limits of ordinary science."[88]

For all the importance which he accords to philosophy and science, nonetheless, Leibniz reserves the highest place in his functional hierarchy for "moralists and statesmen," who add practice *(imitatio Dei)* to theoretical knowledge and eloquence. "The third way of honoring God, that of moralists and statesmen," he says, "as governors of public things [*rectores rerum publicarum*], is the most perfect." For the men who employ this third and highest way "do not limit themselves merely to seeking the brilliance of God in nature, but strive to imitate it." They do not merely observe, and think, and speak; they produce quasi-divine "good works." They do not merely "contemplate" what God has justly done, but "sacrifice" themselves "to the general good and to that of men in particular."[89]

Leibniz then offers a *catalogue raisonnée* of human accomplishments which "imitate" divinity; and these turn out to be the same "wisely charitable" projects which he pressed on enlightened princes till the day of his death forty-five years later.

> It is these men who have discovered the marvels of nature and of art; who have invented medicines, the machines and commodities of life; who have found materials to sustain and nourish the poor, to turn men away from idleness and crime, to excite men to justice, to rewards and punishments, to the preservation of the general repose, to the good of the country, to the suppression of plague and war (so far as it is in our power and among our duties); who have spread true religion and the fear of God throughout the world; and who (finally) have sought only after the happiness of humanity, and sought to imitate what God has done on earth.[90]

And in the next passage of the *Grundriss*, enlightenment and charity come together: the Republic of Letters and the *respublica christiana* fuse. "Such felicity of the human race would be possible if there were good mutual understanding," Leibniz now argues, "and if such an accord and combination of men were not counted among the chimeras, with the *Utopia* of Thomas More, the *City of the Sun* of Campanella, and the *New Atlantis* of Bacon"—and also if (he adds caustically) "the counsels given by our most powerful gentlemen were not so removed from the search after the general good." It is nothing less than "reason, justice, and conscience" which tells us "that each man must do his duty in his sphere of activity," so that we will be "acquitted before the tribunal of God and of conscience."[91] (Up until that final Lutheran word, the rest of the sentence—with its functionalism and final judgment—is almost a paraphrase of Plato's *Gorgias.*)[92]

Leibniz ends the *Grundriss* with the earliest of his great schemes for academies of arts and sciences—plans which dominated his conversations with Czar Peter the Great, the Emperor in Vienna, and the Prussian monarchy in Berlin, forty years later.[93]

> One could, perhaps, find means which . . . could be used for the general good, for the conversation and conservation of mankind, and in honor of God.
>
> I count among these means (which can do much at little cost) the establishment, at first safe and modest, of a society or academy, as being the easiest and the most important. The Germans, excited by the example of their neighbors, would bring about a vaster combination; a stricter correspondence between learned men would be established; many fine thoughts, inventions and experiments which are so often lost would be preserved and utilized.[94]

It is, again, astonishing that all of Leibniz' central moral, political, religious, and scientific concerns are so fully and vividly present in the *Grundriss;* it is almost as if the rest of his intellectual life were simply a working out of the implications of this youthful essay.

LEIBNIZ ON THE POLITICS OF BENEVOLENCE AND ABUNDANCE

Power is essential, Leibniz always granted, to the translation of right into fact—the *Grundriss* insists, after all, that reasonable but impotent people are simply "overpowered"—but it was to the "right" that he devoted his main attention; power, though crucial, was morally neutral and undifferentiated, and helped evil men to carry out evil designs as readily as it helped wisely charitable men to be benevolent. And nothing in Leibniz is more important than benevolence. It is essential that the wise and virtuous who (ought to) rule devote all their efforts to the public welfare, not merely to prevent misery, but to promote actual improvement in both the material living conditions and the knowledge and virtue of the citizens. "The end of politics, after virtue," Leibniz wrote, "is the maintenance of abundance, so that men will be in a better position to work in common concert for those solid objects of knowledge which cause the sovereign Author to be admired and loved."[95] Leibniz' most eloquent statement in this vein—and one which brings out not his Platonizing but his modernist side—is imbedded in one of his letters (1699) to Thomas Burnett.

> You know, Sir, my principles, which are to prefer the public good to all other considerations, even to glory and money; I doubt not at all that a person of Mr. Newton's strength shares my feeling. The more staunch one is, the more one has this disposition, which is the great principle of an honorable man, and even of justice and true piety; for to contribute to the public good and to the glory of God is the same thing. It seems that the goal of the whole human race should be principally the knowledge and the development of the marvels of God, and that it is for this that God has given it the empire of this globe. And, Mr. Newton being one of those men of the world who can contribute most to this, it would be almost criminal of him to let himself be diverted by impediments which are not absolutely insurmountable.[96]

"The greater his talent, the greater his obligation," Leibniz goes on to say. "For in my opinion an Archimedes, a Galileo, a Kepler, a Descartes, a Huygens, a Newton are more important with respect to the great goal of the human race than great military men," and they are "at least on a par with those esteemed legislators whose aim has been to lead men to what is truly good and solid."[97]

If Leibniz' insistence on liberty links him to the great English liberals of his century, his emphasis on charity and welfare separated him from them; he did not stress, as did they, rights, representation, or a Benthamite "dislocability" of rulers,[98] but he was much more interested in welfare and in the general improvement of men than any English liberal. That much is apparent in a strong passage from his (otherwise somewhat sanguine) *Memoir for Enlightened Persons of Good Intention:*

The greatest and most efficacious means . . . of augmenting the general welfare of men, while enlightening them, while turning them toward the good and while freeing them from annoying inconveniences [poverty, unemployment, maleducation] insofar as this is feasible, would be to persuade great princes and their principal ministers to make extraordinary efforts to procure such great goods and to allow our times to enjoy advantages which, without this [extraordinary effort] would be reserved for a distant posterity.[99]

Leibniz assures the princes who are to make these efforts that they will be working not simply for "immortal glory" and for "their own perfection and satisfaction," but also in their own (enlightened) interest: not only will they have subjects who are "more virtuous and better-suited to serve them well," but—and here Leibniz gives more than a hint of his opinion of the general run of German aristocrats—"persons of leisure and means, instead of amusing themselves with trifles, with criminal or ruinous pleasures, and with intrigues," will find their satisfaction in becoming virtuous.[100] While English liberalism concentrated mostly on the state as a quasi-judicial authority defending natural rights (including property rights)—here it is no accident that Locke speaks of government as a "judge" rather than a sovereign[101]—Leibniz by contrast concerned himself with social well-being; in dozens of projects which he pressed on numerous princes, he advocated the setting up of economic councils which would oversee not only manufacturing and agriculture, but also public health and education (*"optima respublica intelligi non potest sine optima educatione* [the best commonwealth is not possible without the best education]"),[102] and insisted again and again that "it is much better to prevent poverty and misery, which is the mother of crimes, than to relieve it after it is born."[103] His strenuous charitable efforts to found academies of arts and sciences in a number of major capitals were successful only in Berlin; but his endeavors to interest Peter the Great of Russia, the Elector of Saxony in Dresden, and the Holy Roman Emperor in such academies shows how truly interested he was in making benevolence an important public virtue.[104]

That is clear above all in the 1712 letter to Count Golofkin (minister to Peter the Great), in which Leibniz says that "I think that his Czarist Majesty could make, very soon, some great advances" toward the end of "making letters, sciences, and arts flourish in his great empire" without "incurring great expenses." "With a few well-chosen persons, plenty of good correspondence, and several good orders," Leibniz goes on, "one will go farther in a little time (and with little expense) than one would otherwise be able to do with much time and much cost."[105]

Leibniz then indulges in some self-praise, but only to show what he could contribute to the general good of Russia:

> And because, since my youth, my great end has been to work for the glory of God through the increase of the sciences, which best mark the divine power, wisdom, and goodness (in which I have partly succeeded by divine grace, having made important new discoveries which are well-known in the Republic of Letters), and since I have preferred this end to honors and to fortune—though my research has obliged me to enter into responsibilities where I have had justice, history, and political affairs as my object—I have always been ready to turn my thoughts toward this great end, and I have only sought a great prince who has the same purpose.[106]

In this 1712 letter Leibniz goes on to say that he hopes to have found such a prince "in the person of the great Czar," and promises that Peter "will never find a person who is more zealous for this important plan and who is less concerned with his particular interest."

> Provided that I find the means and the occasions to contribute efficaciously to the common good in these matters . . . I distinguish neither nation nor party, and I should sooner see the sciences made flourishing among the Russians than to see them cultivated in a mediocre way in Germany. The country in which this shall go best will be the one which is dearest to me, since the whole human race will always profit from it, and its true treasures will be thereby augmented. For the true treasures of the human race are the arts and the sciences. This is what most distinguishes men from beasts and civilized peoples from barbarians.[107]

Leibniz thought that many rulers made the mistake of imagining that they could be glorious through their "destructions and desolations," and that it was his function to demonstrate the superiority of constructive to destructive actions. As he noted in one of his useful poems,

> Quel triomphe qu'on puisse obtenir par la guerre,
> Obliger est bien plus que conquerir la terre.[108]

THE IMPORTANCE OF EDUCATION IN LEIBNIZIAN POLITICS

Given Leibniz' insistence on *caritas sapientis*, the charity of a wise being, it is not surprising that he was centrally concerned not just with better public education, but with the better education of those who have the public in their care: most often "benevolent" princes. This is plain in the *Lettre sur l'éducation d'un prince* (1685–86)—a piece which Leibniz esteemed enough to rewrite four times (last in about 1710, the year of the *Theodicy*), but which was never fully published until the 1980s.[109] In this characteristic essay, Leibniz insists that while it is merely "useful" for the prince to know *la politique et l'art militaire* (so much for Machiavelli), it is "necessary" that a prince "be a man of good will, a courageous man, a man of judgment, and an honorable man"—for the *homme de bien* will have "great feelings of piety, of justice and charity, and will apply himself strongly to his duty." These moral qualities, for Leibniz, matter more than the "useful," and much more than the "ornamental": he would prefer a simple but pious and just ruler to "the cleverest prince in the world"—a prince who "should know to perfection all theories and practices, who should speak all languages, who should have acquired all the fine manners of foreigners, who should shine in conversation, but who, neglecting the care of public affairs and the care of those whom God has committed to him, should stop up his ears to the cries of the miserable in order not to interrupt his pleasures and, in not being moved by the disapproval of his nation and by the views of his family and of posterity, should let the state sink into decadence." Of all this, Leibniz adds, a "deplorable example" has just died (1685)—in the shape of Charles II of England.[110]

Leibniz must have known that while Charles was exiled as Prince of Wales (in the 1640s), his tutor was none other than Hobbes;[111] but Leibniz' program for the education of a prince is more like a royalist *Émile* than it is like anything in English thought.[112] While "natural goodness" is the foundation of all successful education, Leibniz argues, a tutor must understand what is psychologically suitable for a young person: "a child must be neither intimidated nor chagrined, neither deceived nor rebutted—but one must also not accustom him to being opinionated by giving him everything he wants." The way to turn him away from a "not very reasonable" desire, Leibniz goes on, "consists in the variety of pleasures." One can divert him "through pleasant actions and spectacles, which will soon begin to become instructive." At the age of four, he continues, one can begin real education, "but always under the appearance and pretext of games." Finally, however, fully adult study arrives, ushered in by a Platonic insistence on geometry reminiscent of the *Republic*, Book VII:

> Up 'til now reason has taken advantage of the imagination as an escort. But little by little one must make it go beyond this, to the things which the mind alone can know. . . . It is necessary to exercise the reason first of all in geometry and the neighboring sciences . . . [then] the prince must be led to exercise the art of reasoning in moral philosophy, in politics, and in law. . . . History will furnish cases and unusual examples, and the young prince will be a member of the Councils of ancient emperors and kings, in order to preside over his own.[113]

The moral qualities of a ruler are, of course, crucial to Leibniz, who—no democrat—thought that enlightenment and the general good must descend from the top down. In *Des Controverses* (1680) he characteristically insists that "we must work above all to achieve something considerable for the glory of God and for *le bien public*," but that the public has comparatively little to do with that good, since "it is principally for the great, to whom God has given the means to contribute effectively to the advancement of the general good," to be the main "instruments of divine glory."[114] (This strongly echoes the *Grundriss* of a decade earlier.) Leibniz hoped for little from "the common man" *(der gemeine Mann)*, lamenting in *Ermahnung an die Deutsche* (1679) that "these people are without excitement or fire, and it seems that they are made of Adamic earth, but the spirit of life has not been blown into them."[115] Again there is a tension between Leibniz' Christian egalitarianism (which he rarely gave a political dimension) and his Platonism; that is why his practical thought is sometimes a slightly unstable compound from which Christian and Platonic elements tend to precipitate out. Still, he did not confine education to "princes" entirely; in a letter to Joachim Bouvet (December 1697) he insisted that "true practical philosophy *(vera, non simulata philosophia*, as our Roman jurisconsults say) consists sooner in good arrangements for education, and for the conversation and sociability of man, than in general precepts about virtues and duties."[116] And this is true for *der gemeine Mann*, not just for future rulers.

Leibniz on Sovereignty: A Hobbesian Exaggeration

Leibniz' emphasis on charity, welfare, and reasonability led, not surprisingly, to an extreme downgrading of the concept of sovereignty, which played so important a part in much other seventeenth-century theory.[117] He did believe, with Hobbes, that the state is simply an aggregation, like a herd or an army, and that its unity is found in the unity of its rulership; the doctrine of "substance," of course, requires that only individuals be real, and thus on this point Leibniz' metaphysics and politics coincide exactly. A state, like a marble pavement made up of smaller stones, is only an *unum per accidens;* it is not a true unity, "any more than would be the water of a pond with all the fish it holds, even though all the water and the fish were frozen together."[118] But Leibniz broke with the Hobbesian view of law as the command of an "authorized" sovereign: for him it is the content of law—its promotion of the common good and the "eternal verity" of justice—which matters.

Leibniz' treatment of sovereignty was, of course, affected by his being the official apologist for a German electorate; indeed the immediate purpose of his writing his main work on sovereignty (the so-called *Caesarinus Fürstenerius* of 1677) was to show that minor German princes were as "sovereign" as the kings of France and Spain.[119] But he did not have to do violence to his own views of law and of legitimate rule to do this. Throughout his life (but especially in the 1670s) Leibniz clung to the belief that the medieval *majestas* of the Holy Roman Empire—perhaps understood only as a court of last resort for all of the Republic of Christendom—was better than the modern states system; and, this being so, he was quite willing to pull down what Bodin and Hobbes had carefully built up. "Sovereign," Leibniz said in the *Entretiens de Philarète et d'Eugène* (a French summary, in dialogue form, of the *Caesarinus Fürstenerius*), "is he who is master of a territory" and who is "powerful enough to make himself considerable in Europe in time of peace and in time of war, by treaties, arms, and alliances."[120] He removed the character of absolute supremacy from the concept of sovereignty, making it only a comparative rather than a superlative standard; and, taking the fantastic morcellization and diversity of German political forms into account, urged that it did not matter whether the sovereign "holds his lands as a fief, nor whether he recognizes the majesty of a chief, provided that he be master at home and cannot be disturbed except by arms."[121] Leibniz adhered to this merely descriptive and nonlegal conception of sovereignty long after his hopes of a revived Imperial *majestas*, together with his hopes of a reunified *respublica christiana*, began to wane.

If Leibniz had immediate practical reasons for wanting to undermine the idea of sovereignty, he had more purely philosophical ones as well; and not surprisingly, he began with an attack on Hobbes. "If we listen to Hobbes," he said in the *Caesarinus Fürstenerius*, "there will be nothing in our land [the Empire] but out and out anarchy," for "no people in civilized Europe is ruled by the laws that he has proposed." Leibniz went on to discuss, with some accuracy, Hobbes' idea of the war of every man against every man, caused by man's "natural right" to all things; his conception of the transfer of these rights (save self-defense) to the state, such that (in Leibniz' words) "each man is understood to will whatever the government or person who represents him wills." And he faithfully described Hobbes' insistence that government be unitary and centralized, because (again in Leibniz' words) "it is fruitless to divide the rights of supreme power among several persons or corporations [*collegia*]," since a division of power could cause disagreements and the state might be dissolved.[122]

Leibniz, having described Hobbes' political ideas, flatly denied their accuracy. "Hobbes' fallacy," he said, "lies in this, that he thinks that things which can entail inconvenience should not be borne at all." This insistence, according to Leibniz, is "foreign to the nature of human affairs." He admitted that "when the supreme power is divided, many dissensions can arise; even wars, if everyone holds stubbornly to his own opinion." But experience, he said, shows that "men usually hold to some middle road, so as not to commit everything to hazard by their obstinacy." He found examples of this moderation in Poland and in the United Provinces of the Netherlands: "Among the Poles, one territorial representative can dissolve the assembly by his obstinacy; in Holland, when something of great importance is being considered, such as peace, war, or treaties, the disagreement of one town upsets everything." Still, Leibniz urged, because of the "prudence and moderation of those who preside over the whole," most matters turn out well enough.[123]

Leibniz then turned to an attack on Pufendorf, whom he considered an inferior German version of Hobbes, and who had called the Empire a "political monster" in his *De Statu Imperii Germanici*.[124] "If this is true," Leibniz retorted, "I would venture to say that the same monsters are being maintained by the Dutch and the Poles and the English, and even by the Spanish and French." How unreal absolute unitary sovereignty is will be clear to those "who know what the noble orders of the kingdom of France . . . once said in public assembly concerning the fundamental laws of the kingdom and the limits of royal power." The components of the French state were not managed by "mandates given from the plenitude of power (as they say)," but by "requests, negotiations, and discussions." "Hobbesian empires," he concluded, "exist neither among civilized people nor among barbarians, and I consider them neither possible nor desirable—unless those who must have supreme power are gifted with angelic virtues." Hobbes' "demonstrations" thus "have a place only in that state whose king is God, whom alone one can trust in all things."[125] (And even in that "state," as the *Theodicy* will show, sovereign power is only the instrument of wise charity.)[126]

Taking this view of sovereignty, Leibniz could not but reject the Hobbesian doctrine of law as command (hedged round by formal requirements such as promulgation and "authentic interpretation");[127] Leibniz was a natural law theorist (though he preferred the term "universal jurisprudence" to natural law) who held that "the fault of those, who have made justice depend on power, is partly a consequence of their confounding right [*droit*] and law [*la loi*]. Right cannot be unjust, but law can be."[128] There are "fundamental maxims constituting the law itself," Leibniz observed in the *New Essays*, "which, when they are taught by pure reason, and do not arise from the arbitrary power of the state, constitute natural law."[129]

While this radical distinction between positive and natural law sometimes leads, in other theorists, to ideas of a right of revolution when the actions of rulers are "against nature," Leibniz usually treated this topic simply as a question of prudence. "I am of the sentiment of Grotius," he wrote in 1695, "and I believe that as a rule one must obey, the evil of revolt ordinarily being incomparably greater than that which causes it. I allow, however, that the prince can go to such an excess, and put the safety of the commonwealth in such danger, that the obligation to suffer ceases."[130] As Leibniz said in one of his letters to Landgraf Ernst of Hessen-Rheinfels,

> Ordinarily rebellions are more dangerous than bad government. It is true that there can be exceptions to the general rule. Grotius agrees that if a tyrant acts manifestly for the destruction of the state, one could oppose him; but it would still be necessary to act with moderation. . . . One can resist a tyrant in some circumstances, when he is a monster who seems to have vowed public ruin. . . . However, I hold that it is a greater perfection to be able to suffer without resistance, and it is this that one must advise as much as one can—men being only too much given to violence.[131]

If a ruler cannot provide security—here Leibniz agreed for once with Hobbes—"it is permitted to subjects to swear an oath of fidelity to the enemy of their master who has conquered them, their master not being able to do anything more to ensure their safety."[132] For all his differences with the author of *De Cive* and *Leviathan,* Leibniz never denied that providing security was the first obligation of the state. "My definition of the state, or of that which the Latins call *respublica,*" Leibniz wrote in 1705, "is that it is a large society whose end is the common security." It is to be "hoped," he went on, "that one can obtain for men something more than security, namely happiness, and one must apply himself to this end; but security at least is essential, and without it all well-being ceases."[133] The difference between Hobbes and Leibniz is that Leibniz concentrated on "something more than security," namely institutionalized charity and benevolence, while Hobbes, who believed that all ends other than bare existence were relative to individual "appetite," contented himself with setting up a legal context in which the collision of appetites would not be (so often) fatal.[134]

ALLEGIANCE TO SOVEREIGNS: LEIBNIZ' FULLER VIEW IN 1695

Leibniz adds a number of nuances and refinements to his usual view of allegiance and rebellion in his 1695 commentary on William Sherlock's *The Case of the Allegiance due to Sovereign Powers*—a commentary which remained unpublished until 1973.[135]

Sherlock's *The Case of the Allegiance,* published in 1691, was a defense of the rights of William and Mary to the English throne after the Glorious Revolution; and since Leibniz concerned himself with the Hanoverian succession to that throne—as will be seen more fully in Chapter 6—it was natural for him to be interested in such a work. Sherlock's was, however, a rather odd defense—perhaps because he had originally treated William and Mary as usurpers, and afterward changed his mind and his arguments—a defense which rested on a distinction between *de facto* power conferred by God, and *de jure* power authorized by "human" law. According to human law, in Sherlock's view, James II's title to the throne was still valid; but since God had seen fit to transfer power from him to William and Mary, his will conferred on them a divine right transcending any mere legal right. His whole perspective was concisely summarized in a single paragraph:

If then he who has the Legal Right may not be our King, and he who has not, may; when any such case happens, we must pay our allegiance to him who is King, though without a legal right; not to him who is not our King, though it is his [legal] right to be so. And the reason is very plain, because allegiance is due only to God's authority, not to a bare legal title without God's Authority; and therefore must be paid to him who is invested with God's Authority . . . that is, to the actual King.[136]

To those who would call this "Hobbism," Sherlock maintained, the appropriate rejoinder was that while in Hobbes (irresistible) power in itself gives a "Right to Dominion," in Sherlockism the possession of power does not constitute right but is only "a certain sign to us, that where God has placed and settled the Power, he has given the Authority" as well.[137]

Leibniz' opinion of Sherlock's work was not very high: he was an "able and eloquent" man, Leibniz allowed, but did not always "take the trouble to form distinct ideas"; as a result *The Case of the Allegiance* was "subject to a number of difficulties."[138] But those very difficulties gave Leibniz an opportunity to draw up an exposition of his own views on the distinction between *de facto* and *de jure* power, on the relation of political allegiance to the "security" provided by the state, and (above all) on "Hobbism."

As might be expected, Leibniz uses his 1695 commentary on Sherlock partly to mount a now-familiar attack on Hobbes:

> The author [Sherlock] refutes Hobbes in the eighth proposition, for having said that God has a right over all things in virtue of his omnipotence; instead of which the author believes that the sovereign right of God is based on his having created things. It seems to me that neither [argument] suffices, and that the universal right of God is based not only on the sovereign power but also on the sovereign wisdom which he possesses: which makes it such that it is madness not to obey him. Now I have noted elsewhere that justice is based on wisdom.[139]

This foreshadows the 1700 *Observations* on Coccej: neither Hobbesian irresistible power nor Lockean creation can underpin universal jurisprudence; only the Platonic "wisdom," which then becomes half of "wise charity," can do so. But what is striking in most of the 1695 commentary on Sherlock is the fact that—despite the attack on "sovereign" power—Leibniz in this work is less distant from Hobbes than in any other writing.

The very opening of the Sherlock critique, indeed, is more "Hobbesian" than is Leibniz' wont: "When an enemy makes himself master of a place, it is agreed that the inhabitants can swear the oath of fidelity to him and are bound thereby, even if the war should be unjust on the part of the conqueror."[140] This is extraordinary in one who urged elsewhere that an unjust war "is almost the greatest of crimes which can be committed."[141] It is also

extraordinary (and extraordinarily *Leviathan*-like) in one who commonly maintained that "one does not lose his rights . . . when the occasion to exercise
them does not present itself"—a strong argument against the legitimacy of
mere *de facto* power—and who argued in his defense of Hapsburg rights
during the War of the Spanish Succession that "even if it happens that *force
majeure* obliges subjects and a whole country to do homage to a conquering
usurper . . . the true lord always retains his right whole and unscathed."[142]
This is scarcely designed to show, with Sherlock, that all *de facto* power is from
God. But, although Leibniz agrees with Sherlock in the 1695 manuscript that
"even illegitimate power, when it has prevailed, is authorized by God," he
then modifies that agreement: indeed he insists that the notion that *de facto*
and *de jure* kings "are equal before God and differ only according to human
laws" is mistaken, that they differ intrinsically because "one has more right
than the other," since a mere *de facto* king is "culpable and punishable" in the
"forum" of divine justice, as are those "who have helped him to become one."
It is only in the forum of human law that *de facto* and *de jure* rulers are
"equal"[143]—and this, apparently, only because the security which any ruler
can provide is the precondition of all further goods. One must remember that
for Leibniz natural justice is not confined to human life alone, but that—as
he urged in the *Opinion on Pufendorf*—"not everything should be measured by
the goods of this life," since no one "will escape the divine vengeance, which
is deferred to a future life; and this is a solid reason by which men may
understand the duty to conduct themselves according to justice."[144] (Wise love
ought to be a sufficient motive, but it foreseeably will not always be.) In the
end, then, Leibniz does not say that all power comes equally from God, even
in the 1695 commentary taken by itself—though he comes closer to saying it
here than anywhere else. (In some earlier notes on Sherlock, from 1691, he
perhaps came closer still: recalling Augustine's observation that the main
difference between Alexander the Great and a pirate is that the former had
a larger fleet, Leibniz suggests that "between a pirate and an unjust conqueror
the difference is only one of size [*n'est que du grand au petit*]," and that having
submitted to a pirate, "I owe him a certain degree of allegiance.")[145]

More extraordinary than all of this, however, is the second paragraph of
the 1695 commentary, in which the proportion of "Hobbism" increases, even
to the point of granting the partial validity of social contract theory. "One
can say that, allegiance being relative to protection, there is a *quasi-contractus*
between the government and him who enjoys the advantages of public
safety." But Leibniz did say *"quasi" contractus,* and was quick to add that since

the obligation to obey in exchange for security was analogous to what the Roman law called *actiones in factum*—that is, to situations in which what ought to be done was derived from the particular circumstances of a case, whereas *actiones in ius* considered only established legal rights, and not peculiar facts— the duty of allegiance "would have its force, even if one had never made an oath or an agreement,"[146] simply because (apparently) one naturally owes some allegiance to those who provide the "fact" of security, whatever their legal title to rule may or may not be. In the end, then, this 1695 text does not deviate very widely from Leibnizianism in general: contract is only "quasi," and Roman law has the last word. But that is not surprising in the Leibniz who could urge that Roman "jurisprudence comprises a part of practical philosophy."[147]

It would be unjust to Leibniz to conclude without mentioning that several passages of the Sherlock commentary show what an accurate sense of political realism he possessed, as well as a fine sense of irony. The latter emerges most clearly when he speaks of men who are indecently hasty in accommodating themselves to new *de facto* powers; such men, he says, should be called "the most humble servants of events." But those who desert a prince who cannot furnish security, and not simply lightly, are not to be blamed.[148] As for Leibniz' sense of political realism, it is most apparent when he criticizes Sherlock's notion that if a subject is commanded to act against the laws by a king he is not obligated to do so: "for what shall we say," Leibniz asks, "if by this refusal you put yourself in the same danger with respect to the king, who often passes for the interpreter of the law?" A king, Leibniz says, has the "present power," while the laws in their "nakedness" are "without effect," as well as disputable in their meaning. It is safest, he seems to say, to act against the laws if one is forced to do so, because the fault will be the king's; and no one is "obliged to be a martyr for human laws."[149] This clear-eyed pragmatism is again, perhaps, closer to Hobbes than is usual in Leibniz: for him, apparently, the fact that one cannot derive the concept of right from the possession of power did not necessarily involve defending that right against such power.

THE LEIBNIZIAN STATE: A FINAL CONSIDERATION

Before passing on to Leibniz' theory of international relations, it should be noted that, while a great many seventeenth-century theorists devoted their efforts to the (theoretical) destruction of all of the medieval *collegia* existing below the level of the state, as well as the "universal" authorities existing above the level of the state,[150] Leibniz—particularly in his earlier works—tried to preserve something of the hierarchy of social forms handed down from the late Middle Ages. Thus for him the state was the "fifth degree" of natural society: above it, as the highest natural degree, was the "Church of God," comprehending both the Church *per se* and the Emperor (as head and defender of the *respublica christiana*); below it were four lesser degrees, of ascending (political) importance—husbands and wives, parents and children, masters and servants, and finally whole "households."

> If everything in the world were arranged in the most perfect way, then, first of all, parents, children, and relatives would be the best of friends, and whole families would have chosen an art of living . . . would abide in it and continue to perfect themselves in their art and direct their children to the same end. They would marry people of the same calling in order to be united through education from their parents. These clans would make up guilds or estates out of which cities would arise; these would enter into provinces, and all countries, finally, would stand under the Church of God.[151]

This hierarchy, reminiscent partly of Aristotle and partly of Althusius,[152] locked the state into a system in which it had not the (for Leibniz pernicious) freedom which the Hobbesian state enjoyed. "Natural" voluntary societies below the state level were to be "negotiated" with, made partners to consensual arrangements; while the universal authorities—albeit in a much restricted and rationalized form—were to preserve Europe against the immoderate appetites of any part of it. For "appetite"—that Hobbesian thing *par excellence*—threatened universal justice; and Leibniz would have agreed with the neo-Platonism of Shakespeare's *Troilus and Cressida* (anti-Hobbesian *avant la lettre*) in which Ulysses is made to say that

> The heavens themselves, the planets, and this centre
> Observe degree, priority, and place,
> Insisture, course, proportion, season, form,
> Office, and custom, in all line of order
> . . . . .
> O! when degree is shak'd,
> Which is the ladder to all high designs,
> The enterprise is sick
> . . . . .

Take but degree away, untune that string,
And hark! what discord follows; each thing meets
In mere oppugnancy: the bounded waters
Should lift their bosoms higher than the shores,
And make a sop of all this solid globe:
Strength should be lord of imbecility,
And the rude son should strike his father dead:
Force should be right; or rather, right and wrong—
Between whose endless jar justice resides—
Should lose their names, and so should justice too.
Then every thing includes itself in power,
Power into will, will into appetite;
And appetite, an universal wolf,
So doubly seconded with will and power,
Must make perforce an universal prey,
And last eat up himself.[153]

The antidote, for Leibniz, is a universal justice of charity and benevolence—not a sovereign state which counters appetite by crowning wolves who are "doubly seconded with will and power." For Leibniz had insisted as early as the *Grundriss* that a ruler who has more power than "reason" is "a wolf and a tyrant" who cannot use power well; but if reason reveals that wise charity is the first of the virtues, then *potestas* may be governed by *caritas*.

The Republic
of Christendom

Leibniz wanted the idea of justice as charity regulated by wisdom to have not only a philosophical plausibility, and not only an effect on the internal politics of particular states, but also an impact on (what would now be called) the international system: if charity could replace doctrinal disputation, then the greatest misfortune of Western civilization, the "schism" between Catholics and Protestants, might be overcome. "Certainly charity (which is the highest among the virtues), the love of peace, which is so recommended by Jesus Christ, and proofs of a Christian moderation," Leibniz urges, "require that one omit nothing which is in our power, and which can serve to relieve or to diminish the unhappy schism, which is so pernicious to souls and which has torn the West apart for more than a century and a half."[1]

Leibniz devoted a great deal of his life to efforts aimed at healing this split, first in laboring for years on a vast (uncompleted) work called the *Catholic Demonstrations,* which was intended to supply a Christian doctrine of sufficient imprecision and artful vagueness to be agreeable to everyone,[2] and later in a drawn-out correspondence with Bossuet[3] (who apparently had greater hopes of converting Leibniz than of compromising with Lutheran "heretics"). Leibniz ransacked the history of pre-Reformation deviationism, hoping to show that if the Catholic Church re-admitted Protestants without an excessively fine-grained examination of doctrinal differences, it would be doing no more than it had already done when it agreed to disagree on some points with the Calixtins of Bohemia and with the Greeks at the Council of Florence (1438).[4] He also urged that many of the differences between Catholicism and Protestantism were no wider than some of the differences within the Church itself—between Jansenism and Jesuitism, for example.[5] Generally, Leibniz appealed to Bossuet to bring Christendom back together on a slightly vague basis involving no apologies and no recantations; specific doctrinal disputes could be settled afterward by genuine ecumenical councils (modeled on that of Constance, 1414–1418, Leibniz' favorite).[6] "Would it not be better," he wrote in 1692, "for Rome and for the general good, to regain so many nations, though one would have to remain in a state of disagreement on some points for some time?"[7] But Leibniz and Bossuet could not agree on the status of the Council of Trent, the counter-Reformation council which was so offensive to Protestants. Leibniz tried for some time to prove calmly that the Council had never been fully recognized in France, insisting that Henri IV had omitted to endorse Trent at the time he concluded that Paris was worth a mass and ascended the French throne;[8] but Bossuet's continuing argument that the questioning of one council would lead to the questioning of all (straight back to Nicea and Chalcedon) finally provoked Leibniz into an uncharacteristic outburst:

> To say that you cannot consent to a new examination [of the Council of Trent], is only to renew the old equivocations: a new examination is necessary at least for those who have a right to doubt a pretended infallible decision; and your party is deceiving itself in trying to derive any advantage from this [council], as if it were permitted that a band of minor Italian bishops, courtesans, and hangers-on from Rome (who were believed to be little educated and little mindful of true Christianity) fabricate in a corner of the Alps, in a manner highly disapproved by the most serious men of their times, decisions which are to obligate the whole Church.[9]

Bossuet, for his part, called Leibniz "opinionated" and even a "heretic"; and when the Hanoverian succession to the British throne was assured,[10] Leibniz was no longer encouraged to seek reconciliation, in view of British hostility to the Church (which Hobbes had called the Kingdom of Darkness).[11] But his own ecumenical views never changed, and were reflected in his notion of a universal "natural" religion in the *Theodicy.* His labors in this field have sometimes been dismissed as merely politically inspired;[12] but such a view cannot explain why—to take an example—Leibniz strove so hard, in his extensive correspondence with the Jesuit father des Bosses, to reconcile his own theory of "substance" (as spirit or monad) with the Catholic doctrine of physical transubstantiation—the transformation of bread into flesh and wine into blood.[13] Whatever his motives—which were no doubt both politic and charitable—he believed that fanaticism and bloodshed could be ended throughout Europe if *caritas sapientis* replaced theological hair-splitting. On that point no passage is more eloquent than one in a letter to Mme. de Brinon (the ally and confidant of Bossuet), to whom Leibniz wrote

> The essence of Catholicism is not external communion with Rome . . . the true and essential communion, which makes us part of the body of Jesus Christ, is charity. All those who maintain the schism by their fault, by creating obstacles to reconciliation, contrary to charity, are truly schismatics; instead of which those who are ready to do everything that can be done to reestablish external communion are Catholics in effect.[14]

This passage shows just how wide-ranging Leibniz' idea of charity is: it is the foundation of political justice within particular states, the core of ethics, and the universal bond which can hold the *respublica christiana* together—provided that it is "wise" love. For it must not be forgotten that Leibniz was perhaps the last great philosopher to take the idea of "Christendom" with perfect seriousness: he was by no means a reactionary or an antiquarian, but thought that a modified and rationalized medieval system, in which largely autonomous national states devoted all their efforts to welfare and scientific achievement and lived under the protective canopy of a purified Church and morally authoritative Empire (the whole bound together by universal benevolence and tolerance), would be far superior to a system in which wholly independent absolute monarchies could pursue short-sighted gains at the expense of the universal good. In such a system charity would need to operate at every possible level of social relations from friendship and marriage to the governance of the cosmos.[15]

Leibniz' Letter to Mme. de Brinon of 1697

Leibniz, tired of being urged to convert to Roman Catholicism by Bossuet and by his crony Mme. de Brinon, finally wrote a letter to her in November 1697 in which exasperation mixes with effective (if slightly uncharitable) political satire. "I do not know why you take it as raillery," he wrote to her, "when one speaks of your conversion" to Lutheranism. "Is it that one is infallible in all things *chez vous*, or would you be the first who had known the illusions of his own party?"[16]

Without being Pierre Jurieu (the supposed author of *The Sighs of France Groaning under the Babylonian Captivity*), Leibniz continues, "I claim that all of

France will be converted one day, and that one will be ashamed of certain opinions which are current at present." He tells Mme. de Brinon that "it would be glorious for you, Madame, and even meritorious, to give a good example" by turning Lutheran—"in order to contribute to the re-placing on the path of reason and of true piety a great nation [France] which is so reasonable in everything else."

> It seems that you other people from mild climates are ashamed to listen to the remonstrances of those from the Septentrion; but it is a bad shame—the truth is from all countries. We owe to a man from Prussia [Copernicus] the reestablishment of the true system of the world; we owe to a man from Saxony [Luther] having put the human race *hors de page* [beyond having a master].[17]

Leibniz, warming to the lunacies of warmer climates, goes on to complain that "the follies of judicial astrology reign among the most spiritual nations of the Levant and of the Midi." The Italians and the Spanish, though sometimes capable of "sublime and profound thoughts," are so "opinionated and stunned by their superstitions" that they deprive themselves of the "mental advantages which nature has given them." Here the French are just far enough north to avoid the worst forms of superstitious mindlessness: "One must grant that the French are the most enlightened of the Roman [Catholic] party," and it is "this mixture of reason and pig-headedness" which has made it possible for "the finer forms of knowledge" to "flourish" in France. And Leibniz then permits himself a darkly uncharitable suspicion:

> If I were inclined to suspect people, I should believe that there is policy [*de la politique*] in the doings of the French, and that they are quite content to sustain the chimeras of others, to put themselves at the head of the party, and to profit from the credulity of the Italians, and of the Spanish, and of one part of the Germans against the other. In so thinking I would do honor to their intelligence, but not to their heart. That is why I am persuaded that there is good faith about these things among you.[18]

Leibniz then turns from the French in general back to Mme. de Brinon in particular, saying that "I have the same sentiments with respect to you, Madame; I admire the solidity of your judgment, and the niceness of your expressions, when you do not speak to me of sending to Hell everything that is not Roman." Here Leibniz is so carried away that he even forgets his own efforts to accommodate transubstantiation: "Keep, if you like, purgatory, transubstantiation, and all your seven sacraments; keep even the Pope with all his clergy, we will not oppose you in that." But what Leibniz will not countenance—and here the spirit of satire and levity vanishes—is a moral view which makes *caritas sapientis* impossible. "Keep yourself from two things only, namely, from harming the honor of God by a cult of creatures which gives a bad impression to many people; and from injuring the charity which one owes to men by a sectarian and condemning spirit . . . making [God] seem unjust and tyrannical, and, in a word, by giving him the qualities of his enemy."[19] Even in a piece which indeed begins with raillery, the doctrine of the *Theodicy* is foreshadowed.

It is not certain that Leibniz actually dispatched his rather violent letter to Mme. de Brinon:[20] the satisfaction of having written it may have been sufficient; what is clear is that on the same day he also wrote a milder, nonsatirical version which is sober and earnest in tone.

> Honoring you so much, I was extremely troubled when I thought to see you holding to sentiments which are . . . not very compatible with the love of God through Jesus Christ, which is the principal means of our future felicity. One can find himself caught up in the opinions of Rome or of Trent; but one is not thereby obliged to condemn the Protestants who are such in good faith and without being opinionated.[21]

At this point, having praised the Jesuits for their "moderation" toward the Protestants, and having condemned other Catholic "rigorists," Leibniz anticipates the *Theodicy* of thirteen years later by defending God's justice, goodness and charity. "It seemed to me, Madame, that you listened to" malevolent rigorists "a little too much not to injure charity at all, that is to say God himself"—because in attributing to him "a way of acting which is absolutely contrary to his justice and to his goodness, one destroys the true idea of it," and one "overturns what is fundamental in religion," merely in order to sustain "certain particular opinions." And once again Leibniz insists on the primacy of charitable practice: "It is not enough, Madame, to recognize the attributes of God in a theoretical and general way, when one has practical views which overturn them. . . ." For in this case "one runs the risk of only recognizing names"[22]—Hobbesian nominalism combined with nonrecognition of God's moral attributes.

And in an addendum to the second letter to Mme. de Brinon, Leibniz offers a few reflections on the relation of charity to friendship: "the late

M. [Paul] Pelisson . . . was as perfect a friend as he was an excellent man . . . I even believe that he went beyond all that and that he was beneficent in general. Friendship is particular and charity is universal; but I think that it is only charitable people who are good friends." "I pray to God that he will give us and preserve in us true charity," Leibniz finally says, "by making us place our felicity in the practical knowledge of his perfections, which brings us to imitate them by striving to do as much good as possible."[23]

Leibniz on the *Respublica Christiana:* Early Confidence and Later Doubts

Leibniz' reliance on the *respublica christiana* as chief defender of European concord (through *caritas sapientis*) was at its height during the 1670s, and appears most strongly in the *Caesarinus Fürstenerius.* In this most medieval of his political works, he spoke (almost in the manner of Dante's *De Monarchia*)[24] of the Pope and the Holy Roman Emperor as the "two heads" of Christendom, then went on to describe the kinds of supranational authority which he thought these two heads ought to have. In this vein he urged that

> the emperor is the defender or rather the chief, or if one prefers, the secular arm of the Universal Church; that all Christendom forms a species of republic, in which the Emperor has some authority, from which comes the name, Holy Empire, which should somehow extend as far as the Catholic Church; that the Emperor is . . . the born leader of Christians against the infidels; that it is mainly for him to destroy schisms, to bring about the meeting of [ecumenical] councils, to maintain good order . . . so that the Church and the Republic of Christendom suffer no damage.[25]

In this same text—which could have been written as easily in 1477 as in 1677—Leibniz recalled the great temporal authority which the Popes had had in the Middle Ages, urging that a good Pope had the right (by common consent, if not "infallibly") to "curb the tyranny and the ambition of the great, who cause so many souls to perish." And he suggested that an ecumenical council might be converted into a perpetual "general Senate of Christendom," which would replace the insecurity and bad faith of treaties, mediations, and guarantees with "the interposition of the public authority, emanating from the heads of Christendom, the Pope and the Emperor."[26] A moderate "conciliarist" of the fifteenth century might have said much the same thing.

But by the 1690s Leibniz, older and less infatuated with medieval institutions, was placing more stress on international positive law—on the treaties and guarantees which he had earlier denigrated. In the *Codex Iuris Gentium* of 1693, a collection of documents supporting the Empire's international position against French claims (and aggressions), he did not fail to mention the Emperor, the Pope, "universal jurisprudence," and Christian tradition—but mostly he insisted on the points to which France had actually agreed. In the *Codex* there was also a new emphasis on the gap between political actuality and ideality: a new realism which even led Leibniz to allow that there was something in Hobbes' view that international relations were only a perpetual war, potential or actual. This interpretation, he said, is "not so absurd as one might think if the author claims to show, not that each nation has a right to destroy the others, but that prudence obliges every nation to be perpetually on guard against the others." It could be said of many princes, Leibniz went on, that "in their palaces they play cards, and in the state with treaties." The evil designs of scheming ministers, papered over with "specious pretexts," sometimes brought about campaigns founded on hatred and vengeance alone; sometimes a prince's "bad night" led to the death of thousands; often a woman "pushed" a ruler into ill-considered and scarcely charitable actions. "History would lose some of its beauty," Leibniz concluded, "if one always knew the true causes of events, and if it were known that the most frivolous motives . . . have often caused great heroes to act."[27]

A very similar observation in a letter to Electress Sophie of Hanover (October 1691) shows how clearly such political thoughts were related to—or at least reminded him of—his central philosophical and scientific ideas. "A certain prince will not have been able to sleep tonight because of something he will have eaten this evening; this will give him troubled thoughts, and will make him take violent resolutions on matters of state. . . . There is no devil or angel which can foresee all of the small things of which great events are born, because nothing is so small as not to be created by a great variety of even smaller circumstances, and these circumstances by others, and this to infinity. Microscopes make it clear that the least things are full of variety, as much as the great."[28] Here "Double Infinity in Pascal" is foreshadowed; and while God foresees what "no devil or angel" can, he does not arrest particular evils (however horrendous) which are the *conditio sine qua non* of the "best" world.

All of these grimly realistic considerations led Leibniz to play down the (still important but) diffuse and slackening restrictive power of "Christendom" after the 1690s, and to hope that historical evidence of positive agreements might be of greater utility in restraining international violence. This does not mean that Leibniz changed his mind significantly; he only changed the emphasis. In a very late (1715) commentary on the Abbé de St. Pierre's *Project for Perpetual Peace*, Leibniz, while praising the Abbé's good intentions, urged that the medieval system, in a purified form, would be better than St. Pierre's federal scheme. That system, which had been "like a *droit des gens* among Latin Christians for several centuries," could have persisted on an even stronger footing, Leibniz suggested, had conciliarism ever been fully established; but the late medieval Popes, inferior to earlier ones, were afraid of ecumenical councils and undermined this constitutionalizing movement. This, he said, marked "the beginning of their decline," and a succession of bad Popes destroyed papal authority. "However," he added, "I believe that if there had been Popes with a great reputation for wisdom and virtue, who had wanted to follow the measures taken at [the Council of] Constance, they would have remedied the abuses, prevented the rupture, and sustained or even advanced Christian society."[29]

In a letter to Grimarest from the same year, on the same subject, Leibniz' tone was both elegiac and ironic; he had only a year to live.

> I have seen something of the project of M. de St. Pierre, for maintaining a perpetual peace in Europe. I am reminded of a device in a cemetery, with the words: *Pax perpetua;* for the dead do not fight any longer: but the living are of another humor; and the most powerful do not respect tribunals at all. It would be necessary that these gentlemen contribute a *caution bourgeoise,* or deposit in the bank of the tribunal—a king of France, for example, a hundred million *écus,* and a king of Britain in proportion, so that the sentences of the tribunal could be executed on their money, in case they proved refractory.[30]

Leibniz suggested, in half-seriousness, that a better alternative would be to "allow ecclesiastics to resume their old authority," so that interdictions and excommunications would "make kings and kingdoms tremble." "Here," he concluded, "is a plan which will succeed as easily as that of M. de St. Pierre: but since it is permitted to write romances, why should we condemn the fiction which would recall the age of gold to us?"[31] At the end, Leibniz knew that some of his ideals had become unlikely of realization—without, however, being able to give them up. Hobbes, he observed in the *New Essays,* was afraid of ghosts which he knew did not exist.[32]

Despite the lightness of his tone in this 1715 letter to Grimarest, the question whether a purified Church should intervene in political affairs was one which Leibniz always took seriously, but also one on which he never came to an absolutely firm conclusion. In some letters of the 1680s and 1690s, he urged that men owed a "passive" obedience to secular rulers, but an "active" obedience to ecclesiastics, and that the latter might at least ordain that certain things not be done, if not that anything positive be done. Finally, however, in a letter to Burnett (July 1706), Leibniz stated his definitive judgment on this matter:

> According to the law of nature, ecclesiastics in the state cannot be more than counselors, following the example of doctors whose "jurisdiction" is purely voluntary, so to speak. But the divine law has given something more to the Church, and sometimes human laws give it even more—which I do not disapprove absolutely.[33]

The last phrase is exquisitely equivocal; still it is likely that, if the Church had been purified and reuniversalized, such that general councils of all Christendom could speak with authority on Christian affairs, Leibniz would sometimes have approved of the intervention of the *respublica christiana* in temporal affairs. (After all, he clearly preferred the interposition of "Christendom" between a bad ruler and his subjects to revolution or tyrannicide.)

It is worth noticing in passing—here turning back to the 1715 letter to Grimarest—that both Leibniz and Kant begin their search for "perpetual peace" with the same grim joke: the story of a Dutch innkeeper's sign with the words *pax perpetua* painted under a graveyard scene; and both end with a kind of peace plan.[34] But between the beginning and the end they differ entirely and radically: Leibniz hopes (at least early on) for the intelligent resuscitation of a basically Dantean *respublica christiana* under universal "wise charity," while Kant hopes that even "intelligent devils" (without a trace of *caritas*), exhausted by long and devastating violence, may finally bring about a quasi-federal equilibrium of "republican" states in which consenting citizens will increasingly dissent from war.[35] (Of course, for Kant, "good will" ought to generate an automatically peaceful Kingdom of Ends; but "pathology" impedes the realization of the *Reich der Zwecke*.)[36] Leibniz' solution (especially in earlier years) is basically medieval, while Kant's is radically modern—and yet the two schemes are separated by less than a century in time. (What came between, however, was nothing less than Hume, Rousseau, and the French Revolution.)

LEIBNIZ ON INTERNATIONAL RELATIONS: THE PROBLEM OF FRENCH IMPERIALISM

The main practical problem of international relations which Leibniz had to face throughout his life was that of French expansionism. Leibniz, whose life (1646–1716) coincided almost exactly with Louis XIV's reign (1643–1715), had an ambivalent relation to France and to French culture: on the one hand, Louis' so-called *réunions*, the seizure of Strasbourg, the attack on the Empire during the Turkish siege of Vienna, the wresting of Spain away from the Hapsburgs during the War of the Spanish Succession, led Leibniz, as a German, to do what he could to shore up German defenses (and this despite his distaste for parochialism and patriotic excesses);[37] on the other hand, Leibniz' wide-ranging philosophical and scientific interests were partly produced, partly expanded, by his four-year residence in Paris, and by his continuing contact with leading French intellectuals (including Malebranche and Arnauld) whom he otherwise might not have met.[38] And his most celebrated works—the *Theodicée*, the *Monadologie*, the *Nouveaux Essais*—were all written in French. About Louis XIV himself, Leibniz seems to have had mixed feelings; Louis' aggressive wars produced savage pamphlets from Leibniz, but his patronage of culture he admired and praised to the end. His view seems to have been that Louis was a great king who nonetheless did inexcusable and even criminal things: "Ce roy pouvait faire les délices du genre humain, mais il s'est tourné à des entreprises qui sont enfin devenues le fleau de l'Europe."[39]

When viewing Louis as "the scourge of Europe," Leibniz was capable of effective and eloquent polemics:

> I find that it is the essence of French policy to weigh down its neighbors with so great a number of injuries that, reproaches not being able to increase in proportion to the injustices, she is rid all at once of the complaints which she would have drawn on herself had she done only the hundredth part of the same evils. Can an assassin who has cut the throats of a hundred passers-by with his own hand, and done other horrible things, be condemned more and punished more, in proportion, if he has already redoubled the number of his cruelties? It is only God

who forgets nothing and who finds the just measure; but, among men, the extremist evils almost efface the memory of the first ones, and one gets used to them.[40]

Leibniz then offers an inventory of French evils: "the invasion of the Spanish low-countries, in violation of an express renunciation under oath"; "war carried into Holland;" the Peace of Nijmegen "overthrown as soon as made." And Leibniz ends this telling paragraph of his 1688 *Reflections on a French Manifesto* with grim humor: "These are actions which no longer seem as black as they are, since they have been surpassed by others far more atrocious. The true secret of embellishing quite ugly things is to place them next to others still more incomparably unsightly."[41]

Leibniz' opposition to French aggression began early, with the *Consilium Aegyptiacum* (1671), which he drew up in an effort to divert an imminent French invasion of the Netherlands to a crusade against the Ottomans in Egypt. (Indeed Leibniz first went to Paris to deliver this plan to Louis XIV himself.)[42] Dutch trade, Leibniz argued, could be more effectively ruined by an attack on Egypt, sealing off Middle Eastern trade routes, than through a hazardous direct assault. Characteristically, he insisted that a Christian prince should never make war on another Christian—though Protestant—power, and that French military force should be turned on the infidel. Conjuring up visions of the glory of medieval crusades, all of which Louis would surpass, Leibniz reached even farther back into history to hint that the Egyptian conquest might be the first act of a new Alexander. But the real object of the scheme was clear: a war within Europe would be nothing but "that chimera of universal monarchy which it would be not only impious, but absurd to pursue in Europe at the cost of violence and carnage"; seizing a few Netherlandish towns would bring about "a continent in arms," fear, disaffection, and an anti-French coalition.[43]

Since the *Consilium Aegyptiacum* is celebrated but unread, and ranges in its argumentation from the effective to the bizarre, it will be worthwhile to examine a text which was once said to have inspired Napoleon's Egyptian adventures eighty years after Leibniz' death.[44] Leibniz begins the work with the claim that invading Egypt (rather than Holland) will bring Louis XIV "the sovereignty of the sea and over commerce," a "general authority over Christendom," and an "immortal glory" which will open up "a path toward the high deeds of Alexander." And if, Leibniz suggests, the ancient example of the Macedonian king is insufficient, the modern urgings of the great Bacon may have more weight: "Francis Bacon, Chancellor of England, that great man to whom we owe in great part the movement of our century toward scientific experiments, expressed himself thus, in a fragment of *De Bello Sacro:* 'Who knows, indeed, whether an avenger [of Christianity] will not rise up'?"[45]

Louis will fulfil Bacon's prophecy, Leibniz suggests, not by terrorism within Europe, but by being a good European and by saving violence for "barbarians."

> It is thanks to internal reforms that the security of the monarch and the public happiness will be confirmed. The Christian states will cultivate to perfection the arts of peace. Treaties of commerce, industry, and maritime trade—these are the only kind of rivalry which is suitable for them. Let France, I grant, raise herself above the other nations, but let her turn her arms only against the barbarians. . . . Terminate this [Dutch] war at a stroke [and] found empires where ill-success itself will cause neither fear nor dishonor. . . . There is incredible glory to be gained, and the Most Christian King will be proclaimed chief or general of Christians.[46]

In a passage probably suggested by Pericles' "Funeral Oration" in Thucydides' *Peloponnesian War*,[47] Leibniz goes on to say that "France will be proclaimed the school of Europe, the academy of illustrious minds." But he adds, more in the style of Louis' predecessor Louis IX, that such a war against Egypt will "have the character . . . of a holy war."[48]

In some rather odd pages which follow, Leibniz shows a mixture of admiration and contempt for Holland and for mercantile republicanism, but still urges Louis to turn toward the Levant:

> Every time troubles start up in Germany and in Belgium (as earlier in France), Holland—the universal refuge of sects and of exiles—sees its population and its riches grow. One can say, with reason, that this *simalcrum* of liberty is one of the basic pillars of Holland. . . . This necessity to get men for itself has been the cause that, little by little, the laws directed not only against the Arminians and the Mennonites but against the antitrinitarians themselves have lost their force. . . . They [the Dutch] see with pleasure the rigors imposed on others. . . . See by what means these [Dutch] multitudes, who live from day to day, find their satisfaction in the freedom of belief and speech. The most miserable sailor, in the tavern where he drinks his beer, believes himself a

king—which does not keep him from having to bear the heaviest burdens to earn his livelihood.[49]

This strangely grudging passage then passes on to slightly more favorable observations: perhaps Dutch freedom is not entirely a mere *simalcrum*. "This imaginary liberty," Leibniz now says, "has something real in it"; for in Holland "justice is rendered in a very praiseworthy manner, without regard for rank or riches." In Holland, indeed, "there are unknown the insolences and the demands of the opulent against the poor, of the nobles against the peasants. . . . Violence finds no place there, and no other rivalry is possible save that of ability and of work." But Leibniz cannot forbear to complain of "this mercantile spirit which the Dutch push to the point of the most sordid avarice."[50]

A more favorable view of Dutch republicanism returns when Leibniz goes on to say that Holland has flourished by taking in the world's outcasts. "From Spain came the Portuguese Jews, from Poland the Socinians banished by the latest edicts; from England those whom the Restoration [of Charles II] forced into exile." Each refugee "brought with him his knowledge: the arts, the commerce, the manufacturing industry of his country—all those things which necessity and hunger, that mistress of the arts, that excitress of the mind, obliged them to concentrate on one single point." In this way Dutch power, "weak at the beginning," has finally acquired "the stability which we admire and which it would be difficult to overturn today."[51]

By now the grudging and even patronizing tone of earlier paragraphs has disappeared, and Leibniz now avows frankly that

> what up till now has brought about the superiority of the Dutch is the patience-in-poverty and the sobriety which characterizes them, and which permits them to sell their merchandise at a better price than others. . . . This virtue, which no one can dispute in them, is in my eyes the true reason for their superiority over the French and the English, who otherwise have so many advantages over them.[52]

The Dutch, then, should be left alone; France should glorify herself elsewhere, in the East: "France has the ambition of being the first of the nations. Well, then! She will acquire the title of Queen of the East." But Leibniz then recommends Levantine violence to this future queen through some exceedingly peculiar thoughts on Machiavelli and Machiavellism. France should make an anti-Ottoman war "more useful than all of the wars undertaken for a sacred or profane purpose—a war such as Machiavelli would approve, Machiavelli who smiled at all sacred things and whose fundamental axiom says that one must hide the profane and the useful under the appearance of the sacred and the honorable."[53] Since Leibnizian "wise charity" is not very congruent with Machiavellian "realism" and historical "greatness," one must assume that Leibniz is saying in the *Consilium Aegyptiacum* that even from the lowest political viewpoint (that of the "murderous Machiavel") a war against the Ottomans is recommendable. Or perhaps his real view of Louis' future "glory" ("Queen of the East") has simply burst through the framework of this 1671 text, in a moment of barely controlled satire.

The end of the *Consilium Aegyptiacum* shows that in 1671 the youthful Leibniz could not have known that Louis XIV was much more interested in crushing Protestants than Moslems: the revocation of the Edict of Nantes fourteen years later would finally make that clear.

> It remains for me to represent to you, in a few words, the justice of this cause. It is Turkey that one invades, Palestine that one delivers, the Church whose interests one serves; in the end it is God who will compensate us for a success so much desired. . . . In the expedition which we want to undertake, the good cause and what men call the rights of war are on our side. . . . The illustrious Bacon, in a treatise on sacred war, proves very well that he who is endowed with sovereign power has the right to make war whenever it is a matter of propagating worship and religion among the barbarians.[54]

Here Leibniz suddenly remembers that wise charity is the heart of justice, and adds the caution that "war must be made with that moderation which is dictated by reason, so that . . . one does not work for the ruin or servitude of nations, but for their happiness and for their regeneration." And in his peroration he links Louis XIV with an assortment of mythical antique heroes:

> It was thus that Bacchus, Hercules, Theseus, Osiris, Sesostris, Alexander, and the other heroes acted in earlier times, who vanquished monsters and tyrants, and whose exploits are sung by fable. But such was not the conduct of Alaric, of Attila, and of Tamburlaine, who called themselves the scourges of God, and claimed to be born to make the nations submit. It was with a good moral title that a wise man said that a powerful and enlightened monarch is like the guide of the human race: that he is not only the friend of one nation, but the friend of all men,

and that he must make war not on men but on beasts, that is to say on barbarians, to defend his interests, and not for the pleasure of killing.[55]

A strange piece, the *Consilium Aegyptiacum*! It wavers between antique violence and Christian charity in a way that can be explained only by its immediate practical purpose—to flatter Louis XIV into imitating Alexander while not completely forgetting Christ. It is an oddly equivocal work, all the same: if it was once Leibniz' most famous political essay, it is very far from being his best. It is historically understandable, as a curiosity; by contrast Leibniz' doctrine that if one is wisely charitable one will not just refrain from harm but strive to do good is a living principle which stands in no need of historical support.

LEIBNIZ CONTRA LOUIS XIV:
THE *MARS CHRISTIANISSIMUS* OF 1683

If one sometimes suspects a barely veiled satirical undercurrent in the *Consilium Aegyptiacum*, there is nothing veiled about the *Mars Christianissimus* (Most Christian War-God)[56]—for this 1683 pamphlet is Leibniz' most entertaining, and also most malicious, political work: a pointed satire on Louis XIV and his imperialism which also parodies Bossuet's method of arguing from Scripture (especially the Old Testament). Taking note of a resolution made in France "to recognize no longer any judge but the sword," Leibniz observes that while treaties and moral scruples "indeed oblige ordinary men," there is "a certain law superior to all others, conforming nonetheless to sovereign justice, which releases the king from the obligation to observe them." In defense of the special right of Louis XIV to subjugate all of Christendom, Leibniz says, he will "lay the foundations of a new jurisprudence," of which the fundamental point is that "all temporal matters are [to be] submitted to the eminent right of a very great and powerful king," who, because of "destiny," should rule everybody. From this general right, he goes on, could be deduced Moses' authority over the Israelites whom he "borrowed" from the Egyptians, as well as the Israelites' authority over the Canaanites. Louis XIV, the *Mars Christianissimus* suggests, was currently the beneficiary of this right, and as such was "the true and sole vicar of the world with respect to all temporal matters." Louis' vicarate was justified, Leibniz urges, by Thrasymachus' argument, *justum est potentiori utile* (the just is that which is useful to the most powerful), "which agrees very well with what we have said about the right of a powerful monarch over the temporal affairs of men. The most powerful person in the world, always excepting the devil, is without doubt his Most Christian Majesty." He then proved that Louis was entitled, both by prophecy and by miracles which he had performed, to absolute control over the "general affairs of Christendom."[57]

> Everything which is prophesied of the Empire of Jesus Christ on earth must be understood [as applying to] the Empire of his Most Christian Majesty. . . . Jesus Christ and the prophets have always had the kings of France in mind, [since they were] destined one day to be the liberators of the Church. And, without speaking of other [scriptural] passages, can anything be more clear than this one when it says: "The lilies of the field do not spin"?[58]

Leibniz' elaborate pun on the "lilies of the field" and the *fleur de lis* of the French monarchy is a lawyer's joke about the Salic law: the lily-like female members of the French royal house should never rule, for what the French monarchy (as vicar of Christ) needs is a "temporal Schilo or hero whom the people must follow." And that hero is essential, since Schilo Louis "must do in a worldly way that which the Messiah did spiritually," and must "establish on earth, happily for the flesh, the Kingdom of Jesus Christ which millennial heretics were waiting for, quite inappropriately, in the form of Jesus Christ in person."

> Some absurd people . . . associate him with a well-known spirit; but it is not [merely] ridiculous, but impious, to attribute to the devil that which is brought about by a heavenly inspiration. In this matter those persons resemble the Jews, who said that Jesus Christ performed his miracles through the intervention of Beelzebub. . . . His Most Christian Majesty, who makes his amusement his occupation, who bothers with business only to divert himself, and whose studies go only to prove that he is sufficiently warlike, does not fail to succeed in everything he undertakes. What other inference can we draw, than that heaven has destined this King for great things? For the friends of heaven receive benefits in their sleep [Psalm 127:2]; the others can catch nothing, however they run. . . . We lack now only a Jeremiah, who could inform

all the powers of the world that those who oppose the King oppose the heavenly will at the same time.[59]

Leibniz passed on to the effects of Louis' divinely authorized mission in Germany and Italy. The minor Catholic clergy in Germany, he said, was already singing hosannas as it saw "the advance of its liberator"; Italian women, anxious to enjoy a *liberté française*, were impatiently awaiting a French garrison. France, Leibniz said, had powerful friends ready to receive it: "who would dare, henceforth, to resist priests and women conspiring at the same time?" Resistance was ultimately useless, in any case; "as rivers all converge finally at the sea, whatever their detours, in the same way it is necessary that all the powers—and particularly those of Italy and Germany—be finally engulfed." England, too, would be desolated, "as her heresy deserves." But Germans ought to be grateful, rather than resentful, since "the most expert political analysts all agree that the Republic of Germany is so monstrous and corrupt, that it needs an absolute master to re-establish good government." German liberty was, in any event, Leibniz added, only the "license of frogs, who croak and jump here and there."[60] (This passage is Leibniz' best public blast against Pufendorf's argument that the Empire was "monstrous" because it lacked "Hobbesian" sovereignty, an "absolute master.")[61]

Leibniz was not above indulging in self-parody while writing in this vein. "What is taken for misery is true felicity," he observed, and "goods are always brought about through tribulations." Germans will be happier in heaven, "when the French shall have made you miserable on earth; you will go there more willingly, leaving without regret this vale of miseries." Louis himself, Leibniz insisted, was aware that his universal vicarate brought about some (merely apparent) evils; "he himself trembles when he envisages the loss of so many thousands of souls." But he had no choice in the matter. "How can he resist the vocation from on high which obligates him? He sees that any other way of curing the ills of Christendom, except that which he undertakes by iron and fire, would be only a palliative; gangrene cannot be stopped except by means which involve cruelty."[62] Leibniz concluded the *Mars Christianissimus* with a paragraph which he (uncharitably) raised to a height of incandescent, glowing malevolence:

> There will be some who will imagine that his Most Christian Majesty would do better to begin his beautiful designs by the routing of the Turks than by the affliction of the poor Christians: but these people do not reflect at all that it is the Germans and the Flemish who live on the

frontiers of France, and not the Turks; that one must pass from one's neighbors to people far away, and move in these great matters by solid degrees, rather than by vain and perilous leaps. But, without looking for political reasons, here is one of conscience: which is that the king wishes to follow the rules of the New Testament, which commands that one begin with the Jews, and then orders that one turn *ad gentes;* and the king, in imitation of this, will create for himself, by the reduction of the Christians, a sure passage to go one day to the infidels.[63]

None of Leibniz' later anti-French writings is as powerful as the *Mars Christianissimus*, though he wrote many of them; the best, however, combine eloquence with barely contained fury and are very effective tracts. About the seizure of Strassburg—which he never forgot—Leibniz was particularly bitter: "the king needed it for the security of his kingdom; that is to say, the better to maintain what he had stolen from the Empire, he had to steal more. A beautiful reason! . . . the appetite grows while eating."[64]

When writing in this vein, Leibniz sometimes insists on the "degrees" and gradations of justice and injustice which he had treated in the "Meditation on the Common Concept of Justice"—now, however, not just in a jurisprudential but in a purely political sense. In the outraged *Reflections on a French Manifesto*, written in opposition to Louis XIV's bellicosity and expansionism, he accuses the French of moving by increasingly unjust degrees from good to evil—in a straightforward inversion of what ought to happen (the ascent from "refraining from harm" to doing positive good, from *neminem laedere* to *pie vivere*). In turning the "maxims of the Evangile" into "old stories," Christian *caritas* is the first thing to be jettisoned in France's precipitous slide toward "injustice and impiety."

From one absurdity several others are born, and one injustice ensures an infinity of others. . . . Would one believe that iniquity can mount higher? After having dashed to the ground all considerations of humanity, it was necessary to attack Heaven; and, after having violated all the laws of honorability, it remained only to break with Christianity. And that is what they are doing now. The maxims of the Evangile pass for old stories, and it is believed that the greatness of a power will not have arrived at its peak if one is obliged to fear God. That is how, by a strange gradation, one goes from virtue to virtue, from audacity to effrontery and from injustice to impiety.[65]

Here, indeed, there is an "ascent" to heaven—but only to attack it; the gods suffer the fate of Strassburg. The hierarchy of Roman law, which should rise toward "honorability" *(honeste vivere)*, is as badly treated as the charitable "maxims" of Christ; *la raison écrite* is effaced.

Leibniz was, perhaps, even more resentful of French apologists than of French military forces; power alone is brute force, but reason should know better than to rationalize. "The noise of flatterers often extinguishes feelings of conscience in those who act," he wrote in 1688, "but he who undertakes the [intellectual] defense of evil actions must be able to see them at close range, and he is miserable if he has only fantasies and far-fetched conjectures to oppose to the greatest and most real evils which a Christian and an honest man can conceive." For it is "difficult to make the world believe that white is black, that it is in order to secure public tranquillity that one takes up the arms which destroy it, and that it is for the good of Christendom that one breaks the sacred ties of Christianity."[66] The *paix éternelle* proposed by Louis XIV, Leibniz urged, is that of a "cemetery"; and he then paraphrases Tacitus' *Agricola* ("they made a desert and called it peace") by saying of the French that *Ubi servitutem stabilierint, pacem vocant* ("they brought about slavery and called it peace").[67]

As Leibniz' political connections with the Empire grew closer after 1700— he was appointed Aulic Counselor by the Emperor in 1713, and became the friend of Prince Eugene of Savoy—he wrote an increasing number of political pamphlets, and drafted several imperial responses to French claims. During the War of the Spanish Succession he wrote the *Manifesto for the Defense of the Rights of Charles III,* in which he attempted to show that France was hopelessly corrupt and that Spain would be ruined by Bourbon rule. This extraordinary piece consists of two main parts, the first a detailed refutation of the French assertion that Louis XIV's Spanish wife's renunciation of all claims to the Spanish crown on her marriage to Louis was no longer valid, the second a highly colored sketch of the disasters Spain would undergo if subjected to French "corruption." In France, Leibniz argued, "the liberties of the great and of the people have been reduced; the good pleasure of the king takes the place of everything else; even the princes of royal blood are without the slightest authority; the great are only title-holders and are ruining themselves." Centrally appointed *intendants,* "persons of little importance," he urged, "are elevated to serve as instruments for oppressing the others." Leibniz continued in a vein which, if it had been written in 1789, would have been radical indeed:

The nobility is impoverished to the last degree, vexed by quarreling and investigations, obliged to use itself up in service to the king and to sacrifice its welfare and its blood to the ambition of a conqueror. . . . Those who occupy civil positions, especially lucrative ones, having once enriched themselves at the expense of the community because they were given free rein, are now squeezed like sponges. . . . The people are trampled upon without mercy and reduced to bread and water by tithes, taxes, imposts, head-taxes, [by being required to supply] winter quarters and passage for war-makers, by monopolies, by changes in money . . . and by a thousand other inventions; and all of this is only to serve the insatiability of a Court which cares not at all about the subjects which it already has, and which seeks only to augment the number of miserable people by extending its estates.[68]

That paragraph could be invisibly woven into some of the tracts of the Abbé de Sièyes at the beginning of the French Revolution.[69] But that merely nominal ecclesiastic would have been less distressed than Leibniz over the weakening of Christianity under the Bourbon regime. "The worst thing of all," Leibniz laments in the 1703 *Manifesto*, "is that atheism walks today with its head up in France, that pretended great wits are in fashion there, and that piety is turned to ridicule." Even Spanish austerity will be powerless to arrest this "venom" which "spreads with the French spirit"; "wherever this genius puts its foot and makes itself superior, it brings it with it." To submit to French domination "is to open the door to dissoluteness and to libertinage, [and] one can be sure as well that piety cannot reign where justice is trampled under foot."[70] (For is not "live piously" or charitably the highest maxim of justice itself?)

Leibniz ends the *Manifesto* for Charles III with a rousingly rhetorical passage which is quite stirring:

Let us imagine Spain, and the provinces under her rule, under the yoke of the French, [with] morals corrupted, religion and piety scorned, honest men insulted, the people reduced to ammunition-bags, the great diminished and threadbare, foreigners masters of the power and the riches of the country, the king governing *à l'Ottomanne*, his favorites, officers, soldiers and other ministers of his power exercising harshly that which Samuel foretold for the people of Israel—dishonoring families, seizing whatever they find to their liking, and not answering complaints except by laughing or by new affronts. . . . Those who are not touched by the picture of these horrible and inevitable misfortunes are worthy of still greater evils, and do not deserve to bear the glorious name of "Spaniard."[71]

Leibniz wrote his last major anti-French pieces in 1712–13, when the Triple Alliance (Empire-Netherlands-Britain), put together to counter French power, disintegrated after the Dutch and British made separate peaces with France.[72] In his *Peace of Utrecht Inexcusable* (1713), Leibniz chided the Empire's former allies for giving up when "universal monarchy" had nearly been brought under control, and warned that "the house of Bourbon has come into a power which surpasses that of Charlemagne and equals that of the ancient Romans."[73] He put the same point even more dramatically in another tract from 1713, the *Lettre d'un patriote à la sérénissime république de Vénise*, saying that "Europe finds itself in a condition which has not been so dangerous for several centuries," since "the fatal union of the great monarchies of France and of Spain" under the house of Bourbon "raises a power which has had no parallel, at least in Europe, since the decadence of the Romans." For the family of Louis XIV, Leibniz goes on, "now possesses the better part of Europe, together with the New World and, everything being fully united, it will be incomparably more formidable than the house of Austria." And from that it follows that "the house of Bourbon is going to swallow up everything in its vicinity."[74]

In a manuscript from 1711 which remains unpublished in the Leibniz-Archiv in Hanover, Leibniz urges that if the Protestant "high allies of the North" do not hold out against France and increase their military efforts, the result will be a ruinous peace treaty (such as that of Utrecht) "which will not be too much to their satisfaction, and not very safe for the future, since it leaves a good part of the monarchy of Spain, and above all America, to the house of Bourbon, [which is] already formidable enough through France alone"—a state of affairs "which will be capable of causing the greatest revolutions in Germany, and above all in England." But if the northern Protestant allies will spend more and try harder *contre la France*, they may be able "to push this crown to the limit, and oblige it to [make] a peace such as one would hope for." Here Leibniz even allows himself a military fantasy which he must have known to be quite unlikely of realization: "One could act on the Rhine with forces much more considerable than France expects; this surprise would embarrass her; and it seems that one could penetrate through Alsace into Burgundy, and tie the hands of the Duke of Savoy, in order to enter soon after into Dauphiné and into the Lyonnais, and then stay there—which would be capable of obliging France to a prompt and secure peace."[75] Leibniz did not despair, then, of putting the Empire on a sounder military footing, and tried to forestall desperate measures by observing that "one need not cut his throat because he has lost his purse." Nor did he fail to relate his opposition to French aggression to his ideas of universal justice: condemning the "*morale à la mode*" of France, "which thinks that the utility of the state makes everything permissible," he urged that "it is necessary that powerful princes not do to lesser ones that which they would not want a more powerful one to do to them."[76] There "the place of others" and *caritas* again override "Hobbesian" *potestas*.

LEIBNIZ' OTHER FRENCH FEARS: HIS FINAL DAYS

Fear of France was also the motor force, in large measure, behind some of Leibniz' other practical political schemes, notably the gaining of the throne of Great Britain for the house of Hanover, and (earlier) the raising of that house from the status of a dukedom to that of an electorate. European liberty was safe, in his opinion, only so long as the great "northern" powers—Britain, the Netherlands, and (increasingly) Prussia—were Protestant and anti-French; and he constantly warned the English against re-admitting the Stuarts, the "creatures" of the Bourbons, to the throne.

> . . . if the wolf comes in sheep's clothing; if he pretends to accommo-date himself to your laws; if bad citizens, traitors to their country, bring the people to receive him, he will ruin your liberty by degrees: no more triennial parliament, no more ancient city-charters, no more *habeas corpus*, no more judges of integrity; everything full of false testimony, juries corrupted, tramps for bishops, courtesans for jurisconsults, satel-lites of arbitrary power.[77]

Here, in the *Peace of Utrecht Inexcusable* (as in the *Reflections on a French Manifesto*), it is by "degrees" ("a strange gradation") that liberty and justice will be subverted by courtesans and tramps; once again the infinite ascent to *caritas sapientis* is just inverted. The universal wolf of appetite, now in sheep's clothing, will destroy the English legal order which Hobbes himself had been at pains to preserve.[78]

After 1700 Leibniz wrote a number of memoranda in defense of the Hanoverian claims to the British throne, urging that everything which could be discreetly done to ensure success be done. A trustworthy and zealous person, Leibniz advised, familiar with the English language and with the "genius" of the English people, should be sent quietly to London; this envoy should make contact with "considerable" members of the House of Commons in an effort to enlist on the Hanoverian side "persons of merit, of reputation, and of authority, whose opinions will have an effect on [other] minds, and on whose friendship one can count." The Electress (Sophie), Leibniz suggested, should modestly, but with some regularity, remind the English ruler (Anne) of her claims as a Protestant granddaughter of James I; while the "republican faction" of vestigial Cromwellians and Miltonians should be convinced that a republic was too dangerous in view of the recent enlargement of French power during the War of the Spanish Succession.[79] In this effort, which he pursued for about fifteen years, Leibniz showed a great deal of tact and diplomatic subtlety, and a sharp sense of what would be psychologically effective and what offensive; he skillfully blended fears of France and of Catholicism with the justice of long-standing historical claims.

This skill and political common sense had been in evidence, too, when Leibniz, in the early 1690s, wrote a number of letters and pamphlets in an effort to raise Hanover to the dignity of an electorate. The three Rhenish electorates (Cologne, Trier, and Mainz), he argued, might soon be swallowed up by France, necessitating a new electorate more securely situated in central Germany; the balance between Catholic and Protestant forces within the Empire could be made more equitable if (Lutheran) Hanover were elevated; and it was generally a good idea, politically, that important units of a political system be given power and responsibility, so as not to create "a divorce, very prejudicial to the state, between the power of right and that of fact."[80] To avoid antagonizing the Catholics by the creation of a new Protestant electorate, Leibniz suggested, Hanover's cause should first be brought forward by Sweden (which, by the Treaty of Westphalia, was a marginal member of the Empire); Saxony and Brandenburg could then second the nomination, and Hanover would never have to appear excessively self-serving. His detailed formulation of this plan makes plain why his services as a counselor and diplomat were so highly esteemed—not just in Hanover itself, but in Berlin, Vienna, and St. Petersburg.

. . . the two Protestant electors [Brandenburg and Saxony] and, perhaps, the King of Sweden could write to the Emperor concerning the creation of a new Protestant electorate; the King of Sweden in rather positive terms, the two electors in a more reserved manner, as if pushed by the letters of the King of Sweden. . . . [Then] the Emperor would write a letter to the Electoral College as the most interested [party], communicating to them the letter of the King of Sweden and of several electors, and asking their collegial opinion. In this way the Protestant electors would give their opinions in the assembly of the Electoral College, like the others, because they would not have already taken part [openly in the process], and would not have already become demanders [of anything].[81]

If this plan were followed, Leibniz thought, success would be much more likely than if Hanover simply demanded its "rights." (It ought to be recalled, however—even as one enjoys Leibniz' constitutional ingenuity—that he preferred the re-unification of the *respublica christiana* to all of this balancing and scheming, even though he was uncommonly good at it; if France were reduced, and a purified Church restored, Hanover could be "merely" the *Kulturstaat* that he would have liked it to be.)[82]

Ironically and sadly enough, Leibniz' efforts on behalf of the house of Hanover brought him, not a final blaze of glory as chief counselor to the new ruler of Britain, but neglect and ingratitude: partly because George I wanted something more tangible than Leibniz' mere fame to compensate for the salary he and his predecessors had expended on their jurisconsult, partly because the controversy with Newton over priority in the discovery of calculus had prejudiced British opinion against him (following charges of plagiarism),[83] Leibniz was obliged to remain in Hanover to complete his history of that house. He toyed with the idea of removing to Paris, the Mars Christianissimus notwithstanding;[84] and in his last year, at the age of seventy, produced an important exchange of letters with the Newton-factotum Samuel Clarke.[85] When he died, on November 14, 1716, not a single member of the Hanoverian court attended the funeral; and it was left to Fontenelle, in the Académie des Sciences in Paris, to deliver a fitting *éloge*.[86] But Leibniz had already written a suitable epitaph for himself, one which expresses exactly his own view of his life and efforts: "Provided that something of importance is achieved, I am indifferent whether it is done in Germany or in France, for I seek the good of mankind. I am neither a phil-Hellene nor a philo-Roman, but a *philanthropos*."[87] And he had, long since, summarized the whole sense of his social philosophy in a single sentence. "Justice is . . . that which is useful to the community, and the public good is the supreme law—a community, however, let it be recalled, not of a few, not of a particular nation, but of all those who are part of the City of God and, so to speak, of the state of the universe."[88]

Conclusion

Obviously a social world fully and completely governed by the Leibnizian principle of justice as "wise charity" would be a good one, and certainly better than our present social world: if wise charity *(caritas sapientis)* or "universal benevolence" actually shaped private social relations, the domestic policies of states, and international conduct between states, that would constitute not just getting beyond chaos and violence, but also the transcendence of the merely legalistic justice that Hume deplored but thought inescapable. ("If every man had a tender regard for another," Hume says in the *Treatise of Human Nature,* "[then] the jealousy of interest, which justice supposes, could no longer have place. . . . Increase to a sufficient degree the benevolence of men . . . and you render justice useless."[1] Leibniz' "solution," famously, is to *equate* justice and benevolence.)

But one can say of several political-moral theories that their "realization" would be (somehow) advantageous: if Platonism were realized the wise few who know the eternal moral verities would be at the helm;[2] if Aristotelianism were realized each citizen would be rewarded and honored in proportion to the value of his contribution to the common good of the city;[3] if Kantianism were realized one would get (ideally) the Kingdom of Ends and universal respect for morally equal "persons," or at least universal republicanism and movement (by "infinite approximation") "towards eternal peace."[4] Even problematical and worrying theories, such as those of Machiavelli and Hobbes, have their attractive sides: if one realized what is best in Machiavelli, there would be an intelligently resuscitated Rome, a golden age of Antonine civic virtue worthy of imitation when *fortuna* presents the opportunity;[5] and if one realized what is acceptable in Hobbes one would get general legal security and the absence of fear of violent death.[6]

Since most great political theories have at least one attractive side or aspect, and a few theories have more than a mere "side" which is praiseworthy, the hard question is whether Leibnizian "wise charity" or universal benevolence is an especially estimable social doctrine—in principle and in general, and forgetting (or bracketing) the fact that Leibniz does not invariably live up to what is best in his own views. If one provisionally sets aside theological and metaphysical worries—does God act with "wise charity" in fashioning a "best" world? Can human beings spontaneously act *(now)* with greater charity and benevolence?—and if one suppresses Leibniz' suggestion that wisdom is the province of a few only, then a chastened, purified version of *caritas sapientis* is the most attractive and persuasive residue of a tradition of "Christian Platonism" stretching over two millennia. And that is no small encomium: if correct it would mean that Leibnizian ethics, on balance, is more acceptable than the achievements of Augustine, Aquinas, and Suarez.[7]

The advantage of a "realized" Leibnizian *caritas sapientis* over a "realized" Kantian Kingdom of Ends—to mention two intuitively attractive moral views which try to draw together reason-given "Platonic" moral ideas and "Augustinian" good will—is that Leibniz "cancels and preserves" eros—though some would say that Leibnizian love *qua* universal benevolence cancels the erotic more than it preserves it. And some will even say that Kant himself, in insisting on respect for persons as "objective ends"—where "respect" is a special, nonpathological feeling generated by an "intellectual cause" (the idea of what "ought" to be)[8]—manages to cling to attenuated moral feeling, if not to "erotic" feeling (even "sublimated" erotic feeling, in the manner of Plato's *Phaedrus*).[9] But if one sets aside Kant's account of respect as a "subjective" feeling which follows on "objective" knowledge of the moral law (as "fact of reason") in the *Critique of Practical Reason*,[10] then the general drift of Kantianism is toward the erecting of a high wall between "ought" and mere "pathology": "those who cannot think imagine that feeling will help them out."[11] In this respect Kant is the purest rationalist in ethics who ever lived; it is not the wings of eros which carry him to the Kingdom of Ends.

Here Leibniz is more traditional: like Plato, like Augustine, he preserves a version of eros—admittedly a version rather cool to the touch—while also insisting on the Platonic rationalism which so affected Kant (though in the practical sphere only, as the *Critique of Pure Reason* reveals).[12] It is really a matter of whether one thinks that love (including self-love) is an integral and necessary part of any adequate morality—so that, in Leibniz' words, "the good man is he who loves everyone"[13]—or whether such "feeling" is morally irrelevant (even harmful): that one simply "ought" to act well, and that "oughtness" or moral necessity is given by practical reason alone.[14]

It is because it is so hard to pronounce on this question—perhaps impossible, since it involves deciding what counts as a moral view—that the tension between Leibniz and Kant looks like an eternal one. What one can surely say is that Plato and Leibniz (though they are certainly not coextensive) strive to preserve, in some transformed form, the most powerful "affective" aspect of human existence, love, while Kant ("respect" apart) thinks that the "pathological" has no place at all in morality. And that is why Kant reconstructs the injunction to "love your neighbor as yourself" to read, respect your fellow-man as an end-in-himself, once you know him to be such an end.[15] For Leibniz the wise love of others—which steadily ascends from refraining from harm *(neminem laedere)* to *caritas sapientis*—generates present happiness and promises eternal felicity; for Kant, happiness (as a part of the *summum bonum*) may possibly come to the virtuous (who have acted from good will) in an afterlife which one can postulate but never demonstrate.[16] (The *summum bonum* ought to be, but nothing can guarantee its reality.) Happiness is central in Leibnizian ethics, in the here and now (though it is a special kind of happiness which should be generated by "perfection," and is not just undifferentiated Benthamite pleasure); happiness is marginal (though not dispensable) in Kantian ethics and is postponed to a nonguaranteed future in which God (if he turns out to exist) will crown virtue with happiness.[17] (From a Leibnizian point of view, Kantian "moral" theology is simply too attenuated—God and immortality are merely possible, merely nonrefutable—and happiness is too marginalized. And in response to that Kant would have accused Leibniz of uncritical dogmatism and of celebrating "heteronomous" motivation.)[18]

Leibniz and Kant are the modern heirs of both Platonic rationalism and Augustinian voluntarism in the Newtonian age: for both Germans (as for *Phaedo*), absolute moral ideas must be given by trans-temporal reason, and cannot be derived from mere phenomena;[19] for both Germans (as for early Augustine) *bona voluntas*—being "good willing" or bene-volent—is morally crucial.[20] But Kant is arguably more successful than Leibniz in fusing a Platonic idealist and Augustinian voluntarist inheritance, and then in giving it an egalitarian-republican "turn," for at least three reasons: (1) Kant does not "mathematize" ethics by saying (as Leibniz often still does) that justice is "harmony" or "proportion";[21] (2) Kant does not have to reconcile good will (and "absolute spontaneity") with divine omnipotence and omniscience—which perhaps cannot be done at all;[22] (3) Kant's radical egalitarianism (which

Nietzsche called "underhanded Christianity")[23] leads to a politics not just of "benevolence" but of "universal republicanism" of consenting equal citizens (and then to an "eternal peace" which flows from dissent to war and violence); the political institutions proposed by Kant as suitable for free and equal moral persons—republicanism, consenting citizenship, final peace through "sad experience"—do not have to rest on the hoped-for benevolence of enlightened rulers. (Indeed for Kant even "intelligent devils," male- rather than bene-volent, can embrace republicanism and peace from enlightened self-love—though a not-merely-political Kingdom of Ends produced by good will always remains Kant's ideal.)[24] Leibniz always hoped for "wisely charitable" statesmen but saw no method of ensuring their presence; for Kant one can reasonably hope (without irresponsible utopianism) that acceptable institutions may come about through infinite approximation in time, even if *motiva moralia* never improve at all.[25]

Kant, then, gives moral primacy to good will ("the only unqualifiedly good thing on earth") and urges respect for persons as ends-in-themselves *from* good will; but in his politics and philosophy of history he is prepared to let an "objective end" such as peace be approximated through "devilish" but enlightened self-love;[26] Leibniz wants "good will" to operate equally in the moral and political spheres—after all, *caritas sapientis* is universal good willing, universal benevolence—but lets "good will" mean an expansion of self-love to take in the good of others (in whose perfection one finds happiness). So Kant confines a very pure and austere form of *bona voluntas* to the moral sphere alone, but hopes for an approximation to decent politics through mere legal motivation; Leibniz insists on benevolence universally, in ethics and politics, but systematically breached Kant's strict distinction between moral good will and "heteronomous" legal incentives. In Leibniz *bona voluntas* is (for a Kantian) "eudaemonistic" and heteronomous, but valid throughout the whole practical sphere (moral-political-legal); in Kant good will just means striving to actualize the Kingdom of Ends, but has no political dimension at all—indeed for Kant good will's absence (or weakness) necessitates legality's presence.

But Kant's "solution" to the problems that vexed Leibniz—ruling out human knowledge of God and causality, so that the former becomes a "postulate" and the latter a "category of understanding"—would not have impressed Leibniz (or Malebranche or Fénelon, or even Hobbes). Kant takes refuge in the limits of our knowledge;[27] he builds on what we "cannot" know. Leibniz, however, thought that we could know God, as did most seventeenth-century philosophers; and if one starts with God impossible problems may unavoidably arise in moral philosophy. Either an infinitely perfect being will have no sufficient reason to create a finite world in time which can be (at best) "best"—as in Leibniz, Malebranche, and Fénelon; or there will be no creation at all which can be called "good," as in Spinoza; or divine "irresistible power" alone is knowable and the justice of the universe is only a compliment or mark of "honor," as in Hobbes.[28] All of these views are morally problematical, and some would say morally ruinous.

But that does not make wise charity any less intuitively attractive: a social world fully shaped by Leibnizian universal benevolence would plainly be a good one, and perhaps even the "best" (in a nontheological sense). If one abstracts God from Leibnizianism one is left with this morally attractive residue; but how can one abstract the "necessary" being who is the ground of all truth (including universal jurisprudence) and the cause of all existence? What is morally attractive in Leibniz—charity, benevolence, generosity—may struggle against what he took to be necessarily true. That, indeed, is the problem in Leibniz.

For all of Leibniz' most serious problems flow from God: God's conduct in translating a merely "best" world into real existence has to be justified in the face of appalling evils *(Theodicy);* his perfect foreknowledge of future contingencies does not lead him to arrest terrible consequences (such as the Fall, and later the "schism") through "wise charity"; he is the ground (though not the cause) of the "complete concepts" of all substances or monads—whose freedom to act (spontaneously), with greater charity and benevolence, is constricted by the "certainty" of God's determined cosmos ("Discourse on Metaphysics" and *Monadology*).[29] It might at first seem more promising, then, to "bracket" God, to keep *caritas sapientis* as a purely moral idea not resting (necessarily) on theology or Scripture (here Christ would become simply Rousseau's *homme de bonne société*),[30] and to seek "post-established" harmony, brought about by a concatenation of the spontaneous charitable strivings of finite beings—as against the pre-established harmony of divine determination. But this is just what one cannot do: for Leibniz there is one necessary being whose essence entails existence. The "Anselmian" strand in Leibniz cannot be lifted out—except as a provisional thought-experiment. One can only make this version of Leibniz work by doing unacceptable violence to him.

It may well be the case that Leibniz could not have done better in the construction of his "universal jurisprudence," given the components of Christian orthodoxy which he felt constrained to retain (though his version of "natural" religion in the *Theodicy* jettisons an enormous amount of historical baggage). After all, Christian morality tries to reconcile extremes that would have defeated an Aristotle: it tries to keep a God who is perfectly powerful, knowledgeable, and good (but who at a minimum must "permit" evil) and tries also to keep created individuals who are absolutely responsible for good actions ("charity") and still more for their own salvation. There is a terrific tension in Christianity between absolute determination and absolute responsibility.[31] Small wonder that the effort to reconcile God and man, to justify both as a pair without severing them, should have led even Augustine to swerve from proto-Pelagian human freedom in *De Libero Arbitrio* (c. 395 A.D.) to proto-Calvinist inscrutable "election" through unmeritable divine grace (in the 420s);[32] small wonder that Hobbes should have magnified God (more particularly his "irresistible power") and declared human self-determination an incoherent and impious Scholastic "absurdity" (though he did not go to the point of making men mere "modes" of God's substance, à la Spinoza); small wonder that Kant, being more apodeictically certain of "the moral law" than of God's demonstrable existence, should have judged divine attributes unknowable and celebrated human "absolute spontaneity."

But if one does not want to vibrate between Pelagianism and Calvinism to the point of writing *Retractions* (Augustine),[33] or diminish man (Hobbes), or diminish God (Kant); if one wants to keep a demonstrably extant divinity who produces a justifiable "best" world in which everything is "certain" and "determined," and if one wants to keep sufficient human freedom to be able to say that charity is "morally necessary" and ought to be realized on earth, then the Leibnizian solution—certainty without "necessity," freedom only insofar as it is reconcilable with "substance," compossibility, and preestablished harmony—recommends itself. It is the best of all possible salvations of Christian ethics. That does not make Leibnizianism as a whole any more credible, but it helps to show why a man of supreme gifts should have tried to fuse elements which seem antithetical and even bent on mutual destruction.[34]

In the end it is quite clear what Leibniz opposes and what he favors in the moral-political sphere: he is against tyranny, despotism, and willfulness, and he is for charity, benevolence, and generosity. That is why he constantly argues against the "dangerous opinion" that "all justice, all morality comes not from the nature of things but from the despotic will of God [*non rerum natura sed despotico quodam Dei arbitrio constet*]."[35] If one historicizes and personalizes these dislikes and likes, he is hostile to Descartes, Hobbes and Spinoza (as radical voluntarists who deny or destroy Platonic eternal verities), and he is favorable to Plato, St. Paul, and (much of) Augustine—indeed unless one recalls Leibniz' prominent place in modern mathematics and science he will look briefly (in the moral sphere) like an ancient chastising modernity. Robert Mulvaney, in his excellent "Divine Justice in Leibniz' 'Discourse on Metaphysics' " (1975), captures Leibniz' philosophical likes and dislikes, hopes and fears, perfectly when he says that "Leibniz' life-long opposition to Cartesian voluntarism and to the Hobbesian-Thrasymachean identification of justice and power" led him to insist that there is "a standard of goodness [which is] objective, so to speak, even for God." And Mulvaney goes on to say, more clearly than any recent Leibniz interpreter, that this "standard" consists in "the principles of justice contained in the Roman law"—especially when *honeste vivere* rises from "live honorably" to "live piously," and piety in turn becomes "wise charity"— and that "this makes of the Roman law a considerably more *a priori* body of legal and moral prescriptions than has typically been realized."[36] (This correct view would be readily supported by Leibniz' remarkable equating of Roman jurisprudence with nature, eternity, divinity, charity, and "written reason" in the *Elements of Perpetual Justice* [1695]; that text, which comes from the same year as the "New System" of substances, makes it even more clear that for the mature Leibniz the jurisprudence of the Eternal City is truly eternal, indeed *la raison écrite.*)[37]

But it is easier for Leibniz to establish and maintain his moral-political aversions than his preferences: the whole of what he opposes can be summed up in *stat pro ratione voluntas,* "let will take the place of reason." He detests radical voluntarism in God or men, in heavenly or earthly politics: his description of a willful, norm-creating Cartesian-Hobbesian God in the *Theodicy* is an account of a monarch who fails to be wisely charitable on a cosmic scale.[38] (After all, Hans-Peter Schneider is right when he says, in *Justitia Universalis* [1967], that Leibniz' *Theodicy* is "his masterpiece in the philosophy of right," and that when Leibniz translated the word "theodicy" into German the equivalent he chose was *Gottrechtslehre*—"the doctrine of God's justice.")[39]

If it is a grateful task to oppose radical voluntarism—which in its purest form would overthrow logic itself, by denying all necessary truth—it is precisely the "wise charity" that Leibniz sets against *stat pro ratione voluntas* which is as problematical as it is intuitively attractive. If wise charity and universal benevolence are equivalent for all rational substances, but if Leibniz has as much trouble finding a place (or a possibility) for "good will" in his certain and determined kosmos as he seems to have—if Tarquin was wicked "from all eternity" and could not actually (historically) have acted more benevolently, sparing Lucretia and Rome—and if the "wisdom" which makes up half of "wise" charity is unavailable to those in whom "the causes of understanding" are lacking,[40] then Leibniz' effort to draw together Plato and Paul, Athens and Jerusalem (both soon under Roman jurisdiction), may not produce a coherent synthesis which is stable enough to oppose *stat pro ratione voluntas* as successfully as Leibniz hoped. The moral attractiveness of wise charity is never in doubt; but its availability to Caesar or Tarquin or Judas or Pilate is certainly in doubt. It is Leibniz himself, after all, who concedes in the *Theodicy* that "there is no obligation to do that which is impossible for us in our existing state."[41] Whether God would not have been more wisely charitable to keep those four historical personalities as mere "ideas" eternally "imbedded" in the divine understanding, without temporal existence—so that the four would not have been obligated to strive for a *caritas* and benevolence which was "certainly" beyond them ("from all eternity")—remains a perpetual problem in Leibnizian "universal jurisprudence."

But if one provisionally sets aside Leibniz' equation of "wise charity" and "universal benevolence" (on the grounds that "having a good will" is what is most problematical for him), and if one concentrates just on *caritas sapientis* as a balance between Pauline charity and Platonic wisdom, one finds that Leibniz sometimes draws together Christian love and Platonic "mathematizing" of ethics in an effective way. And this does not happen only in mature works; indeed one of Leibniz' most persuasive Paul-Plato syntheses is to be found in his letter of November 1671 to Antoine Arnauld—written when Leibniz was only twenty-five, fifteen years before the great Arnauld-Leibniz correspondence over "substance" and freedom.[42]

In the early parts of this letter, the more recognizably Christian parts, Leibniz insists on both "love" and "wisdom" in his definition of justice—even if he has not yet arrived at the form of words, *justitia est caritas sapientis*, which he used from 1677 until his death in 1716.

> I define the good or just man as one who loves everyone; love, as pleasure taken in the happiness of another, sorrow in the unhappiness of another. . . . From this I deduce all the theorems of the right and the equitable. . . . Thence it appears that the just man, the man who loves everyone, strives to aid all men, even when he is unable, just as necessarily as the rock tends to fall, even when it is hanging. I show that

all obligation is vindicated in the highest striving [*conatus*]; that it is the same thing to love all men and to love God, the seat of universal harmony: indeed that it is the same thing to love truly, or to be wise, and to love God, above all things, that is, to be just.[43]

One might think that this 1671 linking of *caritas* and *sapientia*, which stops just short of welding charity and wisdom into the post-1677 phrase, *caritas sapientis*, would use precisely "wisdom" as a bridge to a Platonism in which the wise few know the eternal verities—or, alternatively, that the phrase "universal harmony" could echo the harmony of the spheres in the last book of the *Republic*.[44] But instead Leibniz comes up with a very ingenious reading of "aid to all men" which insists that such aid has mathematically measurable "multiplying" effects. It is the Plato who deplored ignorance of geometry, and who made Socrates rescue Meno's slave from such ignorance, who dominates here; but when one recalls that changeless geometry is meant to illuminate changeless "virtue" in *Meno*, and that justice is a harmony which participates in mathematics in the *Republic*, then the connection of all these "absolutes" through consonance, through avoiding a dissonant *psyche, polis,* or *kosmos,* is manifest. Stressing the bearing of numbers on "aid" to men, Leibniz now says, in his 1671 letter to Arnauld, that

> To aid [others] proceeds not from the principle of addition but from that of multiplication. . . . Indeed all which is given [to someone] will be multiplied by its reflection on many others, and in consequence in aiding one one aids several. . . . This difference between addition and multiplication has a great usefulness even in the doctrine of justice. To aid is to multiply and to harm is to divide. The reason for this is that the one who is aided is a mind, and that a mind can apply all things to all other things while using them—which in itself is to augment or multiply them. If it be the case that one [person] is wise to the value of three and powerful to the value of four, the total value of this person will be twelve and not seven; for wisdom can utilize power of any degree whatever.[45]

This is an amazing tour de force of "applied" mathematics, resting on "Platonic" foundations. But when, by the time of the *Codex Iuris Gentium* (1693), Leibniz had come to view the "wisdom" which makes up half of "wise charity" as knowledge of "degrees of perfection" in rational monads—knowledge which reveals how much each rational substance deserves to be loved—

those "degrees" no longer have much to do with either "multiplication" or "addition." And when talk of "degrees" of human perfection (leading to reasonably "measured" love) reminds one of permanent Leibnizian problems—can a given monad "perfect" itself morally, given the "certainty" of its predicates in the general divine plan?—one sees why, in 1671, Leibniz tried to confine Platonic measuring of "degrees" to the question of "aid" alone. It is plausible enough to say that aid "multiplies" itself by reflection on others; when one is concerned with a more worrying "mathematical" idea, namely, "degrees of perfection" in finite monads, one cannot help asking how far Leibnizian substances can control their own self-perfection by "willing" it. Leibniz always strives to preserve a Platonic strand in his thought, early and late: in his mature writings "wise" love should be proportional to merit and desert—but how far "merit" and "desert" survive in Leibnizian ethics is a real question. The later efforts to link charity and wisdom are deeper than the tour de force of 1671, but also much more problematical.

It should be acknowledged that one can minimize or even eliminate the difficulty of having a "good will" in Leibniz' ethics—a free will which becomes *bona voluntas* through wise charity—by saying that Leibniz does not really need "early Augustinian" will (free and then good) because his ethics are descriptive and "naturalistic." One can say, with the Leibniz scholar Ursula Goldenbaum, that Leibniz is merely claiming that a person will (in fact) be happier if he rejoices in the felicity of others, if he loves others wisely. On this view Leibniz is simply a moral psychologist, revealing what will tend to make us happy given that we are surrounded by others who are also concerned with their happiness—he becomes a theorist of intelligent accommodativeness.[46] It is obvious that this kind of reading can work for some Leibnizian passages, such as the already-cited lines of Leibniz' 1712 letter to Coste: "Our natural affections make up our contentment, and the more one is in a natural condition, the more one is brought to find his pleasure in the good of others, which is the foundation of universal benevolence, of charity, of justice." Even in this passage, however, and despite the repetition of "natural," Leibniz is not merely describing an other-accommodating psychology: he is, as usual, linking up justice with charity and benevolence, and his constant view is that we *ought* to be good willing (as in the *Theodicy*, where Leibniz admits that men find it hard to "give themselves the will they ought to have"). If justice = *caritas sapientis* = universal good willing, and if good will *ought* to prevail, then Leibniz does indeed need "early Augustinian" will (first free and then good); his "naturalistic" utterances are much more complicated than a merely descriptive moral psychology. And so the central problem in Leibniz' practical thought remains: does he furnish the (finite) beings who could be wisely charitable or just? Can the "citizens" posited in his "universal jurisprudence" actually do what he himself calls "morally necessary"?

To be sure, if one isolates some particular moral-political strand in Leibniz' thought, and severs that strand from problematical or compromising foundations or relations, one can inflate that single strand into a whole social doctrine which will be "Leibnizian"—if not necessarily something that Leibniz himself would embrace. And one can do this on the right or on the left of the political spectrum.

Michael Oakeshott, for example, who is widely thought to have been the most important and eloquent conservative political theorist to have written in English in the twentieth century ("conservative" despite a fathomless skepticism traceable to Montaigne and Hume[47]) isolates Leibniz' notion of the monad as a "living mirror" of the world, and transforms that metaphysical metaphor into "Oakeshottian" conservatism—into the notion that education is an initiation into a long-ongoing "conversation" with deep historical roots. Education, he insists,

> is the transaction between the generations in which newcomers to the scene are initiated into the world which they are to inhabit. This is a world of understandings, imaginings, meanings, moral and religious beliefs, relationships, practices, states of mind. . . . To be initiated into this world is learning to become human; and to move within it freely is being human, which is an 'historic,' not a 'natural' condition.[48]

It is in understanding education as "a human condition in which newcomers are initiated into an inheritance of human achievements of understanding and belief" that Oakeshott presses into service Leibniz' "living mirror" imagery from the *Principles of Nature and Grace:*

> Education . . . is learning to look, to listen, to think, to feel, to imagine, to believe, to understand, to choose and to wish. It is a postulant to a human condition learning to recognize himself as a human being in the only way in which this is possible: namely, by seeing himself in the mirror of an inheritance of human understandings and activities and thus himself acquiring (in the words of Leibniz) the character of *un miroir vivant, doué d'action interne,* acquiring the ability to throw back upon

the world his own version of a human being in conduct which is both a self-disclosure and a self-enactment.[49]

This is a brilliant "historicizing" of Leibniz' notion of "substance." Since, however, Oakeshott was a fine historian of philosophy, he would have immediately acknowledged that "self-enactment" and "choosing" are problematical if one keeps the whole of Leibniz intact, not just the striking image of *un miroir vivant:* a mirror does indeed do more than just passively "reflect," it also "throws back"—but how far a Leibnizian monad throws back something that is fully its own, by "choice" and "self-enactment," is a real question. Oakeshott retains the strand of Leibniz which can be readily historicized and (as it were) "conservatized"; but if one had asked Oakeshott whether he believed in some other key facet of Leibniz' practical philosophy—for example, in demi-Platonic "eternal moral verities" enjoying universal geometrical necessity—one would have received a look of mingled pity and amusement.[50] Since, however, Oakeshott drew a line between Platonic-Kantian rationalism and Hegelian idealism, viewing the first as ruinously false and the second as largely true,[51] one sometimes finds him echoing the most nearly "idealist" parts of Leibniz' *New Essays;* when Oakeshott urges that "a learner is not a passive recipient of impressions" and that therefore "analogies of clay and wax, of receptacles to be filled and empty rooms to be furnished, have nothing to do with learning and learners,"[52] he is rejecting the Hobbesian notion of mind as a collection of brain-motions caused by the "pressure" of outward "objects" (though he was the finest Hobbes interpreter of modern times) in favor of that part of Leibnizianism which Hegel could favor in the *Phenomenology of Mind.*[53]

But at the left end of the social-political spectrum, Leibniz has been viewed—thanks to his stress on charity, benevolence, and welfare (relieving the poverty which is "the mother of crimes")—as a proto-socialist who was only contingently and incidentally a courtier and a servant of princes (owing to seventeenth century circumstances). More than a century ago Paul Janet insisted in his authoritative *Histoire de la science politique* that "state socialism would not have frightened Leibniz very much."[54] But one need not locate Leibniz on the left solely through charitable "welfare"; one can politicize a Leibnizian metaphysical doctrine—as does Gareth Stedman-Jones in his history of socialism when he suggests that Leibniz' notion of "force" and forces *(Kräfte)* may be the remote ancestor of Marx' "forces of production."[55] (The

English, Hobbesian-Lockean tradition of mechanistic materialism, for Stedman-Jones, contains no dynamic notion of self-moving force, but that is just what is needed for the transition from unintelligent to "dialectical" materialism.) Marxism could only have arisen, for Stedman-Jones, within a philosophical tradition in which dynamics transformed Cartesian and Hobbesian physics—in short, the German tradition inaugurated by Leibniz.

> It is not usually asked why German socialism differed so markedly from that of England or France. . . . Any historical sense of Marx's rooted-ness in a tradition of discourse larger than himself is generally lost. . . . The Leibnizian view was that force or energy was the essence of matter, that everything had form as well as matter and therefore possessed a vital principle which was the source of its spontaneous activity and motion. In England, on the other hand, force was external and matter was divorced from motion.[56]

Though Stedman-Jones goes on to acknowledge that there were "substantial difficulties in adapting Leibniz to a historical and social perspective" of the Marxian sort,[57] he still believes that Leibnizian "force" and *Kräfte*, suitably "socialized" (in both senses), are what make Marx so much more persuasive than Owen or Fourier.

Still, the more natural reading of Leibniz as a proto-socialist flows from *caritas* sooner than "force." Just as one can tilt Kant's Kingdom of Ends leftward, so that no one is used as a means to an arbitrary end (capitalist profits and the extraction of "surplus value" from proletarians),[58] one can tilt *caritas sapientis* leftward into a kind of benevolent protectionism—though that would scarcely be "democratic socialism." But if one stressed the autonomy of rational monads—what Oakeshott called "self-enactment"—one could even imagine democratic socialism as an "outgrowth" of Leibnizian ethics which has finally transcended seventeenth-century limitations. Bits of Leibniz can be pulled rightward, or pushed leftward—even if Leibniz took himself to be a tolerant moderate traveling on a broad *via media*.[59]

A final concluding word: Leibniz' insistence that justice is *caritas sapientis*, and that wise charity is coextensive with "universal benevolence," would not have astonished ancient and early Christian writers who linked justice with friend-ship, love, and affection—Plato, Aristotle, Cicero, St. Paul, St. John, Augustine. (Much of Book VIII of Aristotle's *Nicomachean Ethics*, for example, treats the close relationship of justice and friendship; and his *Politics* insists that "community depends on friendship."[60]

But in modernity all of this has become unfamiliar at best, and alien at worst: Machiavelli urges that in politics it is more important to be feared than loved, and says that a new prince must be ready to act "against charity" in the pursuit of historical greatness;[61] Hobbes treats charity as thinly veiled lust masquerading as principle, and argues that "the passion to be reckoned upon is fear";[62] Rousseau views Christian ethics of universal love as worthy but as inimical to Spartan-Roman civic virtue ("Christianity creates men rather than citizens");[63] Kant sees love as a mere "pathological" feeling with no intrinsic moral worth, and insists on "respect" for persons rather than on "charity" for neighbors; Hegel views "ethical" love as confined to marriage and the family, and defines the public sphere of the state through law and the "struggle for recognition";[64] Nietzsche interprets Christian ethics (and even Socratic morality as attacked by Callicles in *Gorgias*) as weakness and plebeian resentment, "rationalized" into charity and humility;[65] Freud views love as a "libidinal" tie which cannot be stretched beyond a small community, and which in any case is just "aim-inhibited" sexuality (whose repression leads to neurosis and violence).[66] Even a supreme early modern Christian such as Pascal, who gives absolute primacy to charity in the *Pensées*, views that love as transcendent and supernatural ("of another order"), with no bearing whatever on an earthly politics which is only "fleshly" and force-governed—the realm of illusion and *divertissement*.[67] (For Leibniz, by contrast, true politics cannot be distinguished from the charity which rejoices in the felicity of others: "True politics consists in justice and in charity, and a great prince cannot be better served than when the happiness of the people makes up his own.")[68] In many ways Leibnizian "wise charity" is the last flowering (or last gasp) of a long and distinguished Graeco-Roman-Christian tradition which was to be definitively overturned by Hume, Rousseau, and Kant no more than a half-century after Leibniz' death. (Voltaire's *Candide* shows that by the 1750s it was wise and witty to say that only an *idiot savant* such as Dr. Pangloss could possibly imagine that this is the "best" possible world and that a justice of charity and benevolence regulates it.)[69] Leibniz epitomized a world view which was on the edge of extinction; Hegel might have been thinking of Leibniz' effort to reanimate Christian Platonism when he said that "the owl of Minerva takes flight only with the falling of dusk."[70]

And yet who can doubt that the world would be better if Leibnizian universal jurisprudence were in place—if every rational substance in the universe not only refrained from harm but rejoiced in the "perfection" of others? Who can doubt that the world would be best if wise charity and universal benevolence actually prevailed?[71] Only an ungenerous heart would fail to be moved by so generous a moral vision.

Notes

Abbreviations

ACAD. ED.—G. W. Leibniz, *Sämtliche Schriften und Briefe,* edition of the Berlin-Branden-burg (formerly Prussian) Academy of Sciences (Berlin, Darmstadt, Leipzig, etc., 1923–). Cited by Reihe (Series), Band (Volume), and page number—for example, Acad. Ed. IV, 3, 111, refers to the fourth series *(Politische Schriften),* vol. 3 (1987), p. 111.

BARUZI—Jean Baruzi, *Leibniz et l'organisation réligieuse de la la terre* (Paris, 1907).

DUNCAN—G. M. Duncan, trans., *The Philosophical Works of Leibniz,* 2nd ed. (New Haven, 1908).

DUTENS—Louis Dutens, *God. Guil. Leibnitii . . . Opera Omnia* (Geneva, 1768).

F DE C—A. Foucher de Careil, *Oeuvres de Leibniz* (Paris, 1859–1875).

GER.—C. I. Gerhardt, *Die Philosophischen Schriften von G. W. Leibniz* (Berlin, 1875–1890).

KLOPP—Onno Klopp, *Die Werke von Leibniz* (Hanover, 1864–1884).

LATTA—Robert Latta, ed., *The Monadology and Other Philosophical Writings* (Oxford, 1898).

LOEMKER—Leroy Loemker, trans. and ed., *Leibniz: Philosophical Papers and Letters,* 2 vols. (Chicago, 1956); 2nd ed., Dordrecht, 1969 (cited as Loemker, 2nd ed.).

MOLLAT—G. Mollat, *Rechtsphilosophisches aus Leibnizens Ungedruckten Schriften* (Leipzig, 1885).

NE—Leibniz, *New Essays Concerning Human Understanding* (cited by book, chapter, and part, for example, *NE* IV, iii, pt. 1; further references also given to page numbers in the Langley and Bennett-Remnant translations).

RILEY—Patrick Riley, trans. and ed., *Leibniz: Political Writings,* 2nd ed. (Cambridge, 1988).

ROMMEL—C. von Rommel, *Leibniz und Landgraf Ernst von Hessen-Rheinfels* (Frankfurt, 1847).

RUCK—E. Ruck, *Die Leibniz'sche Staatsidee* (Tübingen, 1909).

TEXTES INÉDITS—Leibniz, *Textes inédits,* ed. G. Grua (Paris, 1948).

THEODICY—Leibniz, *Theodicy: Essays on the Goodness of God, the Freedom of Man, and the Origin of Evil,* ed. A. Farrer, trans. E. M. Huggard (New Haven, 1952), cited by book and part, for example, *Theodicy* III, 337, usually followed by the page of the Huggard translation.

VORAUS EDITION—*Voraus Edition zur Reihe VI (Philosophischen Schriften)* [supplement to Series VI of the Academy Edition], ed. H. Schepers (Leibniz-Forschungsstelle der Universität Münster, 1982–1991).

Introduction

1. See B. Fontenelle, *Éloge de Leibniz,* in *Pensées de Leibniz sur la religion et la morale,* 2nd ed., 2 vols. (Paris, 1803), I, 1–70. (This is still the most eloquently appreciative life of Leibniz after more than 250 years.) See also Roger Ariew, "G. W. Leibniz, Life and Works," in *The Cambridge Companion to Leibniz,* ed. Nicolas Jolley (Cambridge, 1995), pp. 18–42; and above all Latta's splendid brief biography in *Leibniz: The Monadology and Other Philosophical Writings* (Oxford, 1898). (Robert Latta was one of the first Leibniz scholars to give full weight to Leibniz' political and moral thought, and provided the first translated fragments of the *Codex Iuris Gentium* for the English-speaking world). The standard life of Leibniz is still that of G. E. Guhrauer, *Leibniz: Eine Biographie,* 2 vols. (Breslau, 1842).

2. Leibniz, "Meditation on the Common Concept of Justice," in Mollat, pp. 66–72.

3. Leibniz, letter to Thomas Hobbes (July 1670), in Ger. I, 82–83. For a fine commentary on Leibniz' early "Hobbism," see André Robinet, *G. W. Leibniz: Le meilleur des mondes par la balance de l'Europe* (Paris, 1994), pp. 12ff.

4. Robert Latta, "Introduction," in Latta, pp. 5–10; Ariew, "Life and Works," pp. 20–22.

5. Patrick Riley, "Introduction" to *Leibniz: Political Writings,* 2nd ed. (Cambridge, 1988), pp. 33–34; Paul Ritter, *Leibniz's Aegyptischer Plan* (Darmstadt, 1930), passim; Robinet, *Leibniz: Le meilleur des mondes,* pp. 251ff.

6. Guhrauer, *Leibniz: Eine Biographie,* I, 22ff.

7. Latta, "Introduction," pp. 6–8; Ariew, "Life and Works," pp. 24ff.

8. Patrick Riley, *The General Will before Rousseau* (Princeton, 1986), pp. 26ff., 251–253; Ferdinand Alquié, *Le cartésianisme de Malebranche* (Paris, 1974), pp. 10ff.; Geneviève Rodis-Lewis, *Malebranche* (Paris, 1965), pp. 73ff.

9. Philippe Sellier, *Pascal et S. Augustin* (Paris, 1970), passim.

10. Latta, "Introduction," pp. 8ff.; Fontenelle, *Éloge de Leibniz,* pp. 3ff. See also Kurt Müller and Gisela Krönert, *Leben und Werk von Leibniz: Eine Chronik* (Frankfurt, 1969), pp. 48ff.

11. Latta, "Introduction," pp. 7ff.; Ariew, "Life and Works," pp. 27ff.

12. André Robinet, *G. W. Leibniz: Iter Italicum* (Florence, 1988), pp. 13ff. Also cited in W. Totok, "Fulgurationen von Prof. Dr. André Robinet, Paris," in *25 Jahre Gottfried Wilhelm Leibniz-Gesellschaft* (Hanover, 1992), p. 37.

13. Gaston Grua, *Jurisprudence universelle et théodicée selon Leibniz* (Paris, 1953), pp. 165ff.

14. Benson Mates, "Leibniz and the Phaedo [and Theaetetus]," in *Studia Leibnitiana, Supplementa XII* (Wiesbaden, 1975), pp. 135–148; Latta, "Introduction," p. 9.

15. Fontenelle, *Éloge de Leibniz*, p. 18: "M. Leibniz étoit grand jurisconsulte."

16. On the Leibniz-Grotius *rapport*, see the judicious remarks of René Sève, *Leibniz: Le droit de la raison* (Paris, 1994), pp. 83ff., and of J. B. Schneewind, "Kant and Natural Law Ethics," *Ethics*, 104 (October 1993): 54ff.

17. Robinet, *Iter Italicum*, pp. 41ff.

18. See Dante, *De Monarchia*, III; Fontenelle, *Éloge de Leibniz*, pp. 8ff.; Riley, "Introduction," pp. 30ff.

19. Leibniz, *Caesarinus Fürstenerius (De Suprematu Principum Germaniae)* (Frankfurt, 1677), chs. 9–11; English translation in Riley, pp. 111–120.

20. The "Meditation" and the *Opinion* are both translated (in full) in Riley, pp. 45–75. For an excellent treatment of the "Meditation," see Emily Grossholz, "Leibniz and the Two Labyrinths," in *Leibniz and Adam*, ed. M. Dascal and E. Yahira (Tel Aviv, 1993), pp. 65ff.

21. See the superb essay by Robert J. Mulvaney, "Divine Justice in Leibniz's 'Discourse on Metaphysics,'" in *Studia Leibnitiana, Supplementa XIV* (Wiesbaden, 1975), pp. 61–82.

22. Leibniz, "Introduction" to the *New Essays Concerning Human Understanding*, in Latta, pp. 358–359: "Our systems differ greatly. His [Locke's] has more relation to Aristotle and mine to Plato, although in many things both of us have departed from the doctrine of those two ancient writers."

23. Leibniz, *Theodicy*, II, 175–183, pp. 236ff. For the fullest treatment of the *Theodicy* as a "theory of justice," see Hans-Peter Schneider, *Justitia Universalis: Quellenstudien zur Geschichte des 'Christlichen Naturrechts' bei Gottfried Wilhelm Leibniz* (Frankfurt, 1967), esp. pp. 476ff.

24. Leibniz, *Monadology*, in Latta, props. 85ff., pp. 267–271. For a reading of the *Monadology* as a "theory of ethics," see Catherine Wilson, "Aspects of Leibniz' Monadology," in *The Leibniz Renaissance* (Florence, 1989), pp. 302–303.

25. Leibniz, *Codex Iuris Gentium* (Praefatio) (Hanover, 1693), pts. xi–xiii; English translation in Riley, pp. 170–174.

26. See especially Grua, *Jurisprudence universelle*, pp. 167ff., and E. Naert, *Leibniz et la querelle du pur amour* (Paris, 1959), passim. See also Patrick Riley, "Introduction" to Fénelon, *Telemachus, Son of Ulysses* (Cambridge, 1994), pp. vii ff.

27. See, for example, Leibniz, *Considerations on the Question of the English Succession*, in Klopp VIII, 250ff. See also the valuable remarks of Vittorio Mathieu in the "Introduzione" to his *Scritti politici e di diritto naturale di Gottfried Wilhelm Leibniz* (Turin, 1951), pp. 30ff.

28. Mathieu, "Introduzione," pp. 48–49; A. Foucher de Careil, *Leibniz et Pierre le Grand* (Paris, 1874), passim. See also Gerda Utermöhlen, "Leibniz im brieflichen

Gespräch über Russland," in *Leibniz and Europa: VI Internationaler Leibniz-Kongress*, Vorträge II Teil (Hanover, 1995), pp. 304ff.

29. L. Couturat, *La logique de Leibniz* (Paris, 1901), pp. 501–528; Hans S. Brather, *Leibniz und seine Akademie* (Berlin, 1993), passim; Sève, *Leibniz: Le droit de la raison*, pp. 221ff.

30. For Leibniz' correspondence with Remond, see Ger. III, 599ff. On Leibniz' letters to Clarke, see Daniel Garber, "Leibniz' Physics and Philosophy," in *Cambridge Companion to Leibniz*, ed. Jolley, pp. 303–305.

31. See above all letter no. 2 to Grimarest (1712), in Riley, pp. 183–184.

32. Diderot, *Encyclopédie*, ed. Assézat (Paris, 1875), XV, 440.

33. The "official" statement of this doctrine is to be found in the *Codex Iuris Gentium* (Praefatio), pt. xi. See also Robinet, *Leibniz: Le meilleur des mondes*, pp. 94ff. ("Le sorite mur de la psychojurisprudence de l'amour"), and Gaston Grua, *La justice humaine selon Leibniz* (Paris, 1956), pp. 168–180.

34. Leibniz, "Meditation on the Common Concept of Justice," in Riley, pp. 45ff. See also Leibniz, *Observationes de Principio Juris*, sec. ix, in Dutens IV, iii, 370ff.

35. Plato, *Republic*, bk. IV, in *Collected Dialogues*, ed. E. Hamilton and H. Cairns (New York, 1961), p. 686.

36. 1 Corinthians 13 (KJV).

37. The Platonism is clearest in Book I (c. 395 A.D.) of this early work.

38. Hume, *Treatise of Human Nature*, in *Hume: Theory of Politics*, ed. F. Watkins (Edinburgh, 1951), bk. III, pt. I, ch. 2, "Moral Distinctions Not Derived from Reason," pp. 12ff.

39. Rousseau, *Émile*, trans. B. Foxley (London, 1910), p. 7 (for the "Spartan mother"; see also Patrick Riley, *The General Will before Rousseau*, pp. 181ff. For "the general will" in Rousseau, see Judith N. Shklar, *Men and Citizens: A Study of Rousseau's Social Theory* (Cambridge, 1969, 1985), pp. 165–169, 189–194.

40. Kant, *Fundamental Principles [Groundwork] of the Metaphysic of Morals*, trans. T. K. Abbott (Indianapolis, 1949), p. 54: "[A] rational nature . . . must be conceived, not as an end to be effected, but as an independently existing end." For the phrase, "pure moral teleology," see Kant, *Über den Gebrauch Teleologischer Prinzipien in der Philosophie*, in *Immanuel Kants Werke*, ed. Ernst Cassirer (Berlin, 1922), IV, 514. See also Patrick Riley, "The Elements of Kant's Political Philosophy," in *Kant and Political Philosophy*, ed. R. Beiner and W. J. Booth (New Haven, 1993), esp. pp. 19ff.

41. On this crucial point, see Chapter 2.

42. John 13:34 (KJV).

43. This would seem to be the natural conclusion of Aristotle's *Ethics* 1178b, in which "contemplation" is the sole activity left to a divinity.

44. Leibniz, *Monadology*, in Latta, props. 85ff., pp. 267–271.

45. Leibniz, *Theodicy*, trans. Huggard, II, 181ff. See also Hans Poser, "Die Beste der möglichen Welten?" in *Leibniz: Le meilleur des mondes*, ed. A. Heinekamp and A. Robinet, *Studia Leibnitiana*, Sonderheft 21 (Stuttgart, 1992), pp. 24–27.

46. Leibniz, letter to Joachim Bouvet (December 1697), in Acad. Ed. 1, 14, 831 (Berlin, 1993).

47. Especially Bertrand Russell in the "Leibniz" chapter of his *History of Western Philosophy* (New York, 1944). For Leibniz' statement of what is "most important," see his letter to Thomas Burnett (February 1697), in Acad. Ed. 1, 13, 555.

48. Leibniz, *Principles of Nature and Grace*, prop. 7, in Latta, p. 415.

49. Ibid., props. 8–10, pp. 415–417. For a full treatment of "the best" as a political-moral idea, see Chapter 3.

50. Kant, *Critique of Pure Reason*, trans. Norman Kemp Smith (London, 1929), A840/B868, pp. 658ff.: "The ancients in their use of the term 'philosopher' always meant, more especially, the moralist."

51. Kant, *Über eine Entdeckung, nach der alle neue Kritik der Reinen Vernunft durch eine ältere entbehrlich gemacht werden soll*, in *Werke*, ed. Cassirer, VI, 68ff. The passage on Leibniz is translated in Latta, pp. 208–211. Kant's entire text, in English translation, is given as an appendix in H. Allison, *The Kant-Eberhard Controversy* (Baltimore, 1973).

52. Kant, *Über eine Entdeckung*, in *Werke*, ed. Cassirer, VI, 68ff. Trans. in Latta, pp. 208–211.

53. Ibid.

54. Leibniz, letter to Electress Sophie of Hanover (1696), in *Textes inédits*, I, 379.

55. Luc Ferry, *Homo Aestheticus: The Invention of Taste in the Democratic Age*, trans. Robert de Loaiza (Chicago, 1993), pp. 156–157.

56. Nietzsche, *Twilight of the Idols*, in *The Portable Nietzsche*, trans. and ed. Walter Kaufmann (New York, 1954), pp. 484–485.

57. Nietzsche, "Arrows and Maxims," in *The Portable Nietzsche*, trans. and ed. Kaufmann, p. 379.

58. Schneewind, "Kant and Natural Law Ethics," pp. 57–58.

59. See, for example, Leibniz, *De Schismate* (1683), in Acad. Ed. IV, 3, 256–257. For a full treatment of this important text, see Chapter 3.

60. See, for example, Leibniz, *Discours de métaphysique*, in Ger. IV, 427; see also Leibniz' letter to Electress Sophie (1696), in Ger. IV, 293–294.

61. Leibniz, *Theodicy*, trans. Huggard, passim.

62. Leibniz, *Monadology*, in Latta, prop. 54, p. 247.

63. See, for example, Leibniz, *Codex Iuris Gentium* (Praefatio), pts. xi–xiii—as well as the numerous Leibniz texts cited in Chapter 4.

64. Leibniz, "Meditation on the Common Concept of Justice," in Riley, p. 50.

65. See Sève, *Leibniz: Le droit de la raison*, pp. 221ff.; see also Leibniz, *De Tribus Juris Naturae*, in Mollat, p. 14.

66. For a different view of the theory-practice connection in Kant, see Onora O'Neill, "Reason and Politics in the Kantian Enterprise," in *Kant's Political Philosophy*, ed. H. Williams (Chicago, 1992), pp. 50ff.

67. Kant, *Critique of Pure Reason*, trans. Kemp Smith, A592/B620ff., pp. 500ff.

68. This is particularly true of Leibniz' celebrated 1671 letter to Wedderkopf (Loemker I, 226–227).

69. Spinoza, *Ethics*, pt. II, prop. 48.

70. Leibniz, *Memoir for Enlightened Persons of Good Intention*, in Klopp X, 10; English translation in Riley, p. 105.

71. Dutens IV, iii, 274.

72. Latta, pp. 8off.; Fontenelle, *Éloge de Leibniz*, pp. 45ff.

73. See, for example, Leibniz, "Meditation on the Common Concept of Justice," in Riley, p. 52, in which Christian-Platonic moral and political principles are immediately followed by an extended treatment of microscopes. For Leibniz' relation to van Helmont, see Allison P. Coudert, *Leibniz and the Kabbalah* (Dordrecht, 1995), pp. 25ff.

74. See Ernst Cassirer, *The Individual and the Cosmos in Renaissance Philosophy*, trans. Mario Domandi (New York, 1963), ch. 3.

75. Leibniz, *NE* I, Acad. Ed. VI, 6, 70–71 (ed. A. Robinet and H. Schepers). A few words—such as "substance" and "monadology"—have been interpolated (in brackets) to connect this passage to the present interpretation.

76. Leibniz, letter to Basnage de Beauval (1698), in Ger. v, 64.

77. Ibid.

78. Of these writings the most important by far is the *Manifesto for the Defense of the Rights of Charles III* (1703), translated in Riley, pp. 146ff. (original French text in F de C III, 368ff.). For an excellent account of the circumstances which occasioned the *Manifesto*, see Francisco José Diez Ausin and Lorenzo Pena, "Leibniz on the Allegiance Due to a De Facto Power," in *Leibniz und Europa: VI Internationaler Leibniz-Kongress*, Vorträge I Teil (Hanover, 1994), pp. 173–175.

79. Cited in Mulvaney, "Divine Justice in Leibniz' 'Discourse on Metaphysics,' " p. 61.

80. Ibid., pp. 61–62. But Mulvaney pushes a good argument too far when he urges that Leibniz "rejected the solipsism of Descartes, the monism of Spinoza, the political atomism of Hobbes . . . precisely because of his own rigorous commitment to public welfare and good order." (*Studia Leibnitiana, Supplementa XIX*, [Stuttgart, 1980], p. 224.) Leibniz' motivation was never so exclusively political.

81. Robert Merrihew Adams, *Leibniz: Determinist, Theist, Idealist* (Oxford, 1994), pp. 194–195.

82. Leibniz, letter to Thomas Burnett (1696), in Acad. Ed. I, 13, 557 (Berlin, 1987).

83. Richard Rorty, "Pragmatism, Relativism, Irrationalism," in Rorty, *Consequences of Pragmatism* (Minneapolis, 1982), pp. 16off.

84. John Rawls, *A Theory of Justice* (Cambridge, Mass., 1971), pp. 15ff., 39ff.

1. Foundations

1. See particularly Leibniz' letter to Remond (1714), in Ger. III, 606–607 (also in Loemker II, 1064); *NE* I, i (trans. A. G. Langley [London, 1896], pp. 66–67).

2. In the "New System of the Nature of Substances" (1695), for example, Leibniz held that Malebranchian "occasionalism"—according to which God "moves our arm" on the occasion of our "willing" it—posits a *Deus ex machina* who operates by miracles (pts. 12–14); in Latta, pp. 311–313.

3. Leibniz, letter to Thomas Burnett (May 1706), in Ger. III, 307; in the same letter Locke's theory of substance is heavily criticized: "*M. Lock* [sic] *a raisonné un peu à la legère.*"

4. Ibid. For Kant's comparable argument, see *Fundamental Principles,* trans. Abbott, pp. 29ff.

5. Leibniz, *Theodicy,* trans. Huggard, "Preliminary Dissertation," pt. 35, p. 94.

6. Acad. Ed. II, 1, 79. Well treated by Robinet in *Leibniz: Le meilleur des mondes,* p. 67.

7. Leibniz, *Monadology,* in Latta, props. 85–86, pp. 267–268. See Werner Schneiders, "Respublica Optima," *Studia Leibnitiana,* IX, no. 1 (1977): 1ff.

8. Leibniz, letter to Landgraf Ernst of Hessen-Rheinfels, in Rommel, p. 232.

9. Leibniz, letter to Landgraf Ernst of Hessen-Rheinfels (c. 1690), in *Textes inédits,* I, 238–239. The object of this criticism is Antoine Arnauld.

10. Ibid.

11. Leibniz, letter to Electress Sophie (1696), in *Textes inédits,* I, 379.

12. Duns Scotus, *Philosophical Writings,* trans. R. Wolter (Indianapolis, 1964), pp. 28–29.

13. Cited by Ernst Cassirer in *Individual and Cosmos in Renaissance Philosophy,* pp. 162–163.

14. Leibniz, *Reflections on . . . Hobbes' "Liberty, Necessity, and Chance,"* in Leibniz, *Theodicy,* trans. Huggard, p. 403. See Yves-Charles Zarka, "Leibniz lecteur de Hobbes," in *Le meilleur des mondes, Studia Leibnitiana,* Sonderheft 21, ed. A. Heinekamp (Stuttgart, 1992), esp. pp. 124–127.

15. Leibniz, *NE* III, v, pt. 12.

16. See Leibniz, *Observationes de Principio Juris,* sec. ix, in Dutens IV, iii, 270ff.

17. Leibniz, "Meditation on the Common Concept of Justice," in Riley, p. 50.

18. Leibniz, *Opinion on the Principles of Pufendorf (Monita quaedam ad Samuelis Pufendorfi Principia),* in Dutens IV, iii, 275. (English translation in Riley, p. 66ff.) For Leibniz' harsh critique of Pufendorf, see René Sève, *Leibniz et l'école moderne du droit naturel* (Paris, 1989), pp. 101ff., and Schneewind, "Kant and Natural Law Ethics," pp. 54ff.

19. Leibniz, letter to Kortholt (November 1713), in Dutens IV, iii, 267.

20. Leibniz, "Selection from Paris Notes" (1672–1676), in Loemker I, 246; also in *De*

Summa Rerum: Metaphysical Papers, 1675–1676, trans. G. H. R. Parkinson (New Haven, 1992), p. 27. Cf. Leibniz, *Dialogue sur des sujets de religion*, in F de C II, 53.

21. Leibniz, letter to Andreas Morrell (September 1698), in *Textes inédits*, I, 139.

22. Leibniz, *Monadology*, in Latta, prop. 48, p. 244. (In the *Theodicy*, II, 150, Leibniz relates divine power-knowledge-will to the three "persons" of the Trinity.)

23. Leibniz, "Meditation on the Common Concept of Justice," in Riley, p. 50.

24. Beginning in 1677; see above all Grua, *La justice humaine selon Leibniz*, pp. 168ff. See also Patrick Riley, " 'New' Political Writings of Leibniz," in *Leibniz und Europa: VI Internationaler Leibniz-Kongress*, Vorträge I Teil, pp. 621ff.

25. Leibniz, *Elementa Iuris Naturalis*, Acad. Ed. VI, 1, 481. For an exhaustive treatment of this work, see Werner Schneiders, "Naturrecht und Gerechtigkeit bei Leibniz," in *Zeitschrift für Philosophische Forschung*, 20 (1966): 607ff. For a fine commentary on justice as *caritas sapientis*, see Thomas Gil, "Einheit und Vielfalt in Leibnizens Gerechtigkeitstheorie und Wissenschaftskonzeption," in *Leibniz und Europa: VI Internationaler Leibniz-Kongress*, Vorträge I Teil, pp. 253ff.

26. Leibniz, letter to Arnauld (1690), in Loemker II, 360.

27. Leibniz, "Meditation on the Common Concept of Justice," in Riley, p. 57: "One cannot envisage in God any other motive than that of [his own] perfection . . . he has nothing to consider outside himself."

28. Ibid., p. 47: "Hobbes, who is noted for his paradoxes, has wished to uphold almost the same thing as Thrasymachus: for he wants God to have the right to do everything, because he is all-powerful. This is a failure to distinguish between right and fact." (Rousseau makes the same argument in *Du contrat social*, bk. I, ch. 3 [Vaughan II, 26–27].)

29. Leibniz, letter to Mme. de Brinon (1691), in Klopp VII, 296.

30. Leibniz, letter to Electress Sophie (1696), in *Textes inédits*, I, 379.

31. Leibniz, letter to Remond (1714), in Loemker II, 654: cf. Leibniz, *On the General Characteristic*, in Loemker I, 339ff. See also Donald Rutherford, "Philosophy and Language in Leibniz," in *Cambridge Companion to Leibniz*, pp. 224ff., esp. pp. 226ff. ("the universal characteristic").

32. Leibniz, *Opinion on the Principles of Pufendorf*, in Riley, p. 71 (original in Dutens IV, iii, 280).

33. Aquinas, *Summa Theologica* II, ii, Q58, Art. 4.

34. Aristotle, *Nicomachean Ethics*, 1105b, 1136a ff. (in *The Works of Aristotle*, ed. W. D. Ross [Oxford, 1925], vol. IX).

35. Leibniz, *Grundriss eines Bedenckens von Aufrichtung einer Societät in Deutschland* (1671), F de C VII, 29. For a full treatment of this extraordinary early work, see Chapter 5.

36. Leibniz, letter to the Duchess of Orléans (1706), in Klopp IX, 164.

37. On the difficulties involved in integrating Christian *bona voluntas* into Greek philosophy, see Hannah Arendt, *The Life of the Mind: Willing* (New York, 1978),

pp. 3–7, 84–110. See also Patrick Riley, *Will and Political Legitimacy* (Cambridge, Mass., 1982), pp. 2ff.

38. On this point see John Rawls, "Kantian Constructivism in Moral Theory," *Journal of Philosophy*, 77, 9 (September 1980): 554–572 (esp. part III).

39. Leibniz, "Meditation on the Common Concept of Justice," in Riley, pp. 46–50.

40. Leibniz, "Discourse on Metaphysics," prop. 2, in Loemker 1, 466. Virtually the same language recurs in the *Theodicy* a quarter-century later—as will be shown in Chapter 3.

41. Leibniz, *Dialogue sur . . . religion*, in F de C II, 532.

42. Leibniz, revision note for the *Nova Methodus*, Loemker 1, 556. For the importance of these revision notes, see Robinet, *Leibniz: Le meilleur des mondes*, pp. 121ff.

43. Leibniz, *Elements of Natural Law*, Loemker 1, 210 (original Latin of the *Elementa Iuris Naturalis* in Acad. Ed. 1, 1, 430ff.). For a helpful commentary, see Robert J. Mulvaney, "The Early Development of Leibniz's Concept of Justice," *Journal of the History of Ideas*, 29, no. 1 (January 1968): 58ff., esp. 60ff.

44. Leibniz, *Codex Iuris Gentium* (Praefatio), pt. xi, in Riley, p. 171: "Charity is a universal benevolence, and benevolence the habit of loving or of willing the good." In the same vein, see Leibniz' 1699 letter to Malebranche, in Ger. II, 358, and his 1706 letter to Pierre Coste, in Ger. III., 383–385.

45. Leibniz, *Theodicy*, trans. Huggard, "Preliminary Dissertation," pt. 43, and bk. 1, pts. 3–5.

46. Ibid., title page.

47. Leibniz, *Elements of Natural Law*, in Loemker 1, 210 (*Elementa Iuris Naturalis*, Acad. Ed. VI, 1, 459). But this is a very early statement from c. 1671.

48. See above all Machiavelli, *The Prince*, ch. 18, in which charity is overridden when historical success is at stake. ("Faith" is also overridden in the same passage; it is as if Machiavelli were deliberately inverting 1 Corinthians 13.) Leibniz' letter (1669) to Thomasius is in *Leibniz-Thomasius Correspondance*, ed. R. Bodéüs (Paris, 1993), p. 108.

49. See, for example, Leibniz' letter to Pierre Coste (December 1707), in Ger. III, 400: "Sins and evils, which he [God] has judged it fitting to permit for [the attainment of] greater goods, are included in some way in his choice."

50. Leibniz, "Observations on King's 'The Origin of Evil,' " in *Theodicy*, trans. Huggard, p. 428.

51. Leibniz, letter to Bierling (1696), in Dutens v, 386; Leibniz, *Refutation of Spinoza*, in Duncan, p. 264.

52. Leibniz, letter to Arnauld (1687), in Loemker 1, 516.

53. Leibniz, *Theodicy*, trans. Huggard, II, 183, p. 242.

54. Descartes, *Reply to the Six Objections*, in *The Philosophy of Descartes*, trans. R. M. Eaton (New York, 1927), pp. 264–266.

55. Leibniz, letter to Eckhard (1677), in Loemker, 2nd ed., p. 181.

56. Plato, *Republic*, esp. bk. VII (in *Collected Dialogues*).

57. Leibniz, letter to Remond (1715), in Ger. III, 637.

58. Leibniz, letter to Thomas Burnett (1699), in Ger. III, 264; English translation in Riley, p. 192.

59. Leibniz, *Theodicy*, trans. Huggard, II, 182, pp. 240–241.

60. Ernst Cassirer, *Leibniz' System in seinen Wissenschaftlichen Grundlagen* (Marburg, 1902), pp. 428ff.

61. Leibniz, "Meditation on the Common Concept of Justice," in Riley, p. 45.

62. Leibniz, "Unvorgreiffliches Bedencken über eine Schrift Genand *Kurtze Vorstellung*," in *Textes inédits*, I, 432ff. Leibniz wrote this work with his colleague Molanus—for whom he was to write the *Opinion on the Principles of Pufendorf* in 1706; only the parts written by Leibniz himself are cited here.

63. Ibid., p. 433.

64. For Leibniz' anti-Cartesianism on this point, see Werner Schneiders, "Leibniz und die Frage dem Grund des Guten und Gerechten," in *Studia Leibnitiana, Supplementa IV* (Wiesbaden, 1969), pp. 85–111.

65. Leibniz, "Unvorgreiffliches Bedencken," in *Textes inédits*, I, 440–441.

66. Of St. Paul's trinity—"faith, hope, charity, these three"—Leibniz retains the only virtue which is other-regarding: *caritas*.

67. Leibniz, "Unvorgreiffliches Bedencken," in *Textes inédits*, I, 441.

68. Ibid., p. 433.

69. Leibniz' "global Platonism" is brought out especially well by Sève in *Leibniz: Le droit de la raison*, pp. 6–9—even if Sève later exaggerates a little when he likens Leibniz' proposed academies of arts and sciences to Plato's "nocturnal council" in the *Laws*.

70. *Phaedo* 74b–75d, in *Collected Dialogues*, pp. 57–58.

71. Ibid. (75d).

72. Plato, *Meno* 85b–d, in *Collected Dialogues*, p. 370.

73. A. E. Taylor, *Plato: The Man and His Work* (London, 1929), pp. 289ff.

74. Plato, *Meno*, in *Collected Dialogues*, passim; Plato, *Euthyphro* 9e–10e.

75. Plato, *Republic* IV (443d–e), in *Collected Dialogues*, p. 686.

76. Leibniz, *Elements of Law and Equity* (1669–70), in Leibniz, *Selections*, ed. P. Wiener (New York, 1951), p. 1.

77. Ibid.

78. Leibniz, "Discourse on Metaphysics," in Loemker, 2nd ed., sec. 26, p. 320. (Leibniz' references make it clear that *Meno* is the work being discussed.)

79. Ibid.

80. Leibniz, "Observations on King's 'The Origin of Evil,' " in *Theodicy*, trans. Huggard, pp. 428–429.

81. Leibniz, *The Art of Discovery*, in *Selections*, ed. Wiener, pp. 50–51; original in Couturat, *La logique de Leibniz*, pp. 175–182.

82. Ibid. (Wiener ed.), p. 51.

83. See above all Leibniz' letter to Mme. de Brinon (May 1691), F de C I, 216: "Charity . . . must be regulated by justice according to the degree of perfection which can be found or introduced in objects." Well treated by Grua in *Jurisprudence universelle*, p. 214.

84. Leibniz, *True Method in Philosophy and Theology*, in *Selections*, ed. Wiener, p. 59.

85. Alfred North Whitehead, *Process and Reality* (corrected ed., New York, 1978), p. 39.

86. Plato, *Phaedrus* 256b, in *Collected Dialogues*, p. 501.

87. For example in the *Codex Iuris Gentium* (Praefatio), pt. xi.

88. Plato, *Protagoras* 352b–353a, in *Collected Dialogues*, p. 344.

89. Ibid.

90. Arendt, *The Life of the Mind: Willing*, pp. 3–7, 84–111.

91. Leibniz, *Code Iuris Gentium* (Praefatio), pt. xi; English translation in Riley, p. 171.

92. Leibniz, "De Abstractis," in *Textes inédits*, II, 576.

93. Leibniz, "De Bono Unitatis et Malis Schismatis," unpublished manuscript (LH I, 7, 1 Bl.1–2) in Leibniz-Archiv, Hanover.

94. Augustine, *De Libero Arbitrio* I, 12; cf. also Augustine, *De Trinitate* XIII, vi, 9: "Unless something is done by the will, it can be neither a sin nor a good deed . . . punishments and rewards would be unjust if man did not possess free will." One cannot imagine Plato saying anything like this. For Kant, see *Fundamental Principles* [*Grundlegung*], trans. Abbott, pp. 18ff.

95. Leibniz, *Causa Dei*, pt. 98, cited in Naert, *Leibniz et la querelle du pur amour*, p. 164; full text of *Causa Dei* in Ger. VI, 439ff.

96. Leibniz, *Thoughts on the Principles of Descartes*, in Loemker II, 639.

97. Ovid, *Metamorphoses* VII, 20–21: "Video meliora proboque, Deteriora sequor."

98. Leibniz, *Codex Iuris Gentium* (Praefatio), pt. xi.

99. Ibid.; English translation in Riley, p. 171.

100. See especially Leibniz, *Judgment of the Works of the Earl of Shaftesbury* (1712), in Ger. III, 407ff.; English translation in Riley, p. 196: "Individual friendship is little-recommended by our religion, which directs us toward charity, that is to say, toward a general benevolence."

101. Particularly in bks. VIII and x.

102. Leibniz, letter to Huet (1679), in Dutens V, 458ff.

103. Grotius, *De Jure Belli ac Pacis*, I, i, x. For a helpful commentary on Grotius' political and moral thought, see Richard Tuck, *Natural Rights Theories* (Cambridge and New York, 1979), pp. 74ff.

104. Kant, *Critique of Pure Reason*, trans. Kemp Smith, A819/B847, p. 644.

105. Leibniz, *Theodicy*, trans. Huggard, II, 184, p. 243.

106. Leibniz, *Notes on Spinoza's Ethics*, in Duncan, pp. 21–22.

107. Leibniz, on Burnet's *Necessity of Faith*, in *Textes inédits*, I, 252. For a fuller account of seventeenth-century neo-Platonic opposition to Cartesian radical voluntarism, see Patrick Riley, *The General Will before Rousseau*, pp. 56–63.

108. Cited in Sève, *Leibniz et l'école moderne du droit naturel*, pp. 107–108.

109. Leibniz, "Unvorgreiffliches Bedencken," in *Textes inédits*, I, 433.

110. Leibniz, cited in John Hostler, *Leibniz's Moral Philosophy* (London, 1975), p. 59 (an excellent study).

111. Leibniz, *NE* I, ii, pts. 12–13 (Acad. Ed. VI, 6, 96).

112. See above all Leibniz, *Opinion on the Principles of Pufendorf*, in Riley, pp. 67–68.

113. Bertrand Russell, *A Critical Exposition of the Philosophy of Leibniz* (Cambridge, 1937), pp. 172–175.

114. Leibniz, *Meditationes de Cognitione, Veritate, et Ideis*, in Ger. IV, p. 424 (English translation in Latta, p. 275).

115. Leibniz, *Monadology*, in Latta, prop. 45, p. 242.

116. Patrick Riley, "Leibniz' Unpublished Remarks on the Abbé Bucquoi's Proof of the Existence of God" (includes publication of Leibniz' manuscript from 1711), *Studia Leibnitiana*, XV, no. 2 (1983): 215–220.

117. Ibid. (Leibniz' 1711 ms., ¶3).

118. Ibid.

119. Leibniz, "Discours de Métaphysique," in Ger. IV, 427.

120. Ibid.

121. Hobbes, *Leviathan*, ed. M. Oakeshott (Oxford, 1946), ch. 31, p. 234.

122. Leibniz, "Meditation on the Common Concept of Justice," in Riley, p. 48.

123. Plato, *Phaedo* 75d.

124. Leibniz, *Memoir for Enlightened Persons of Good Intention*, in Klopp X, 10; English translation in Riley, p. 105.

125. See above all Leibniz, "New System," in Latta, p. 312ff.

126. Leibniz, "Radical Origination of Things," in Loemker II, p. 791 (original Latin in Ger. VII, pp. 302ff.).

127. Ibid., passim. On this same point see also Leibniz, *Monadology*, in Latta, props. 53–54, p. 247.

128. Here the key text is Leibniz, fourth letter to Clarke (1715), pts. 4 and 6, in Ger. VII, p. 372: "There are no two indiscernible individuals."

129. Leibniz, *Theodicy*, trans. Huggard, I, 31, p. 142.

130. Ibid., III, 367, p. 345.

131. Leibniz, "Discourse on Metaphysics," prop. 13, in Loemker I, 478.

132. Leibniz, *Principles of Nature and Grace*, prop. 10, in Latta, p. 417.

133. Leibniz, letter to Bourguet (1714), in Ger. III, p. 573: "All the possibles are not at all compossible. Thus the universe is only a collection of a certain selection of compossibles." Cf. *NE* III, vi, pt. 12.

134. Leibniz, *Radical Origination of Things*, in Loemker II, p. 791.

135. Leibniz, *Theodicy*, trans. Huggard, I, 21, p. 136.

136. Ibid., III, 335, pp. 326–327.

137. Leibniz, *De Libertate Creaturae et Electione Divina*, in *Textes inédits*, I, 381: "Quia Deus

est justus, hinc non est causa mali." Leibniz is particularly concerned to be able to make this claim, since the rest of his text must justify the existence of Judas and of Pontius Pilate.

138. See especially Grua, *Jurisprudence universelle*, pp. 118ff.

139. Leibniz, *Theodicy*, trans. Haggard, I, 23, p. 137.

140. Hegel, *Lectures on the History of Philosophy*, trans. E. S. Haldane and F. H. Simson (London, 1896), III, 341.

141. Leibniz, *Theodicy*, trans. Huggard, I, 43, 47, 84, pp. 147, 149, 168. It is this aspect of Leibniz' *Theodicy* which is styled "monstrous" in Lewis White Beck's *Early German Philosophy* (Cambridge, Mass., 1969), p. 238. But Beck seems to be on questionable ground when he asserts (ibid., p. 235) that "eighteenth century optimism was an optimism of hope and work, his [Leibniz'] an optimism of faith and, he claimed, of reason." But Leibniz was a rationalist, not a fideist (à la Pascal or Bayle), and his insistence on charity precisely privileges "work" (good works) above hope and/or faith.

142. Leibniz, *Monadology*, ed. Latta, prop. 42, p. 240.

143. Leibniz, *Theodicy*, trans. Huggard, I, 31, p. 142.

144. Ibid., "Preliminary Dissertation," pt. 35, p. 94. Here Leibniz is citing (with approval) an argument of Bayle's.

145. Leibniz to Andreas Morrell (September 1698), in *Textes inédits*, I, 137: "I am effectively of the opinion that God could not do better than he does, and that all the imperfections which we believe we find in the world come only from our ignorance. We are not yet in the true point of view to judge the beauty of things."

146. Above all in Augustine, *De Libero Arbitrio*, bk. I.

147. Leibniz, *Theodicy*, trans. Huggard, I, 11, p. 130.

148. Leibniz, letter to Bourguet (1713), in Ger. III, p. 558.

149. Malebranche, *Dialogues on Metaphysics*, no. 9, pt. V (original in *Oeuvres complètes de Malebranche*, ed. A. Robinet et al. [Paris, 1958], vol. x).

150. Ibid., pt. VI.

151. Leibniz, *Theodicy*, trans. Huggard, "Preface," p. 57.

152. Ibid., III, 350, p. 335.

153. Ibid., "Summary of the Controversy reduced to Formal Arguments," answer to objection II, p. 379.

154. Ibid., III, 288, pp. 302–303.

155. Russell, *Critical Exposition of the Philosophy of Leibniz*, 2nd ed. (1937), p. 202.

156. Leibniz, letter to Magnus Wedderkopf (1671), in Loemker I, 226–227. It is true that Leibniz later had reservations about the strength of the claims in this letter.

157. Leibniz, "Discourse on Metaphysics," prop. 30, Loemker I, 496–497. Cf. *Theodicy* III, 416, in which Tarquin is evil "from all eternity."

158. Leibniz "Dialogue on Liberty," in *Textes inédits*, I, 365.

159. Ibid.

160. Augustine, *De Libero Arbitrio*, bk. I.

161. Leibniz on Jaquelot, c. 1704, in *Textes inédits*, II, 489.

162. Latta, "Introduction," in Latta, pp. 33–34. The term "monad" had been used by Giordano Bruno, but Leibniz attributes it to Pythagoras.

163. Hegel, *Phenomenology of Mind*, trans. J. Baillie (London, 1910), p. 108.

164. Leibniz, "New System," in Loemker II, 741–745; Leibniz, letter to des Bosses, in Ger. II, 304.

165. Leibniz, letter to Thomas Burnett (1698), in Ger. III, p. 227—part of a long commentary on Stillingfleet's attempted refutation of Locke's *Essay*.

166. Leibniz, *Theodicy*, trans. Huggard, II, 200, pp. 251–252. See also Ger. VI, p. 172.

167. Leibniz, letter to de Volder (1703), in Loemker II, 864.

168. Leibniz, third letter to Clarke (1715), pt. 4, in Ger. VII, 363.

169. Leibniz, letters to des Bosses, in Loemker II, 978 and 1001.

170. Leibniz, "Discourse on Metaphysics," props. 8 and 13, in Loemker I, 471ff.

171. Ibid., prop. 30, pp. 496–497.

172. Leibniz, letter to Arnauld (1686), in Ger. II, 52.

173. Leibniz, *On Nature Itself*, in Loemker II, 817. See also Massimo Mugnai, "Leibniz' Theory of Relations," in *Studia Leibnitiana, Supplementa XXVIII* (Stuttgart, 1992), pp. 111ff.

174. Leibniz, letter to Queen Sophie Charlotte (c. 1702–1703), in Klopp X, 193; letter to Bourguet (1714), in Loemker II, 1079; *NE* II, xxvii, pt. 9; letter to Gabriel Wagner (1710), in Duncan p. 281. See above all *Monadology*, in Latta, props. 85ff., pp. 267ff.

175. Leibniz, *Monadology*, in Latta, prop. 56, p. 248.

176. Leibniz, *On Vital and Plastic Natures*, in Loemker I, 956ff.; *Specimen Dynamicum*, in Loemker II, 723; *Monadology*, in Latta, props. 85ff., pp. 267ff.; *Principles of Nature and Grace*, in Latta, props. 15ff., p. 421ff.

177. Leibniz, *NE* IV, viii, pt. 9.

178. Nicholas Jolley, *Leibniz and Locke: A Study of the New Essays on Human Understanding* (Oxford, 1984), pp. 37ff.

179. On this last point anticipating Kant's *Critique of Judgment*, Part II ("Teleological Judgment").

180. Leibniz' main discussion of "fatalism" is in the *Theodicy*, trans. Huggard, "Preface," pp. 54ff. But here he is a little elusive: while Stoic and "Turkish" fatalism are criticized, he upholds a *Fatum christianum* on the grounds that Christians "have to do with a good master" who wills the universal "best."

181. Leibniz, *Radical Origination of Things*, in Loemker II, 798.

182. Kant, *Critique of Practical Reason*, trans. L. W. Beck (Indianapolis, 1956), pp. 100–101.

183. Robert C. Sleigh, Jr., *Leibniz and Arnauld: A Commentary on Their Correspondence* (New Haven, 1990), pp. 48ff. (ch. 4).

184. Leibniz, *Theodicy*, trans. Huggard, III, 365, pp. 343–344. But even here he urges that "the actions of the [human] will are determined in two ways, by the foreknowledge or providence of God, and also by the dispositions of the particular intermediate cause, which lie in the inclinations of the soul."

185. Leibniz, *Thoughts on the Principles of Descartes*, in Loemker II, 637–639.

186. Leibniz, *Mantissa* to the *Codex Iuris Gentium* (1700), in Loemker, 2nd ed., pp. 424–425.

187. For the late Augustinian view, see *De Natura et Gratia*, secs. 58–59: "Why did Pelagius want to defend nature alone [while neglecting grace]? . . . If justice derives from our nature [alone], Christ died in vain." See also Augustine, *De Correptione et Gratia*, passim.

188. Leibniz, letter to Malebranche, in Ger. I, p. 300.

189. Leibniz, *NE* II, xxx, pt. 4 (Acad. Ed. VI, 6, 265).

190. Leibniz, *Theodicy*, trans. Huggard, II, 120, pp. 192–193.

191. Leibniz, "Agenda," in Acad. Ed. IV, 3, 900. For a fuller treatment of this essay, see Riley, " 'New' Political Writings of Leibniz," in *Leibniz und Europa: VI Internationaler Leibniz-Kongress*, Vorträge I Teil, pp. 622–623.

192. Leibniz, *NE* II, xxi, pt. 67 (Acad. Ed. VI, 6, 206–207).

193. Leibniz, *Radical Origination of Things*, in Latta, p. 349.

194. Leibniz, *Monadology*, in Latta, prop. 86, p. 267: "He would have no glory were not his greatness and his goodness known and admired by spirits [*esprits*]."

195. Loemker I, 563–564. Cf. Nicholas of Cusa, *Cribratio Alchoran*, 16: "God created all things for the manifestation of his glory."

196. Leibniz, *On the True Theologica Mystica*, in Loemker II, 610.

197. Leibniz, *Radical Origination of Things*, in Loemker II, 796.

198. Leibniz, *Theodicy*, I, 105, cited in Grua, *Jurisprudence universelle*, p. 494. Leibniz goes on to add, with disconcerting complacency, that "in the same way it may occur that a stone of lesser quality is made use of in a building or in a group because it proves to be the particular one [needed] for filling a certain gap." The analogy is probably borrowed from Malebranche's *Traité de la nature et de la grâce* (1680), discourse II, xvii, which asserts that Christ sometimes makes use of "great sinners" in the edifice of his Church, "just as the mind of an architect thinks in general of squared stones . . . when these sorts of stones are necessary to his building." (Malebranche, *Treatise of Nature and Grace*, ed. and trans. Patrick Riley [Oxford, 1992], p. 144.) For the Leibniz-Malebranche *rapport* more generally, see André Robinet, *Malebranche et Leibniz: Relations personnelles* (Paris, 1955)—a splendid edition of all the correspondence between the two philosophers, with valuable commentary.

199. Leibniz, *Memoir for Enlightened Persons of Good Intention*, in Klopp X, 10; English translation in Riley, p. 105. For Leibniz' subversion of "sovereignty" as conceived by Bodin and Hobbes, see Robinet, *Leibniz: Le meilleur des mondes*, pp. 183ff.

2. Monadology and Justice

1. See the "Introduction" to H. T. Mason, ed. and trans., *The Leibniz-Arnauld Correspondence* (Manchester, 1967), pp. xv ff.; see also André Robinet, "La signification du Discours de Métaphysique de Leibniz," *Revue de métaphysique et de morale*, 76 (1960): 195ff.

2. Plato, *Meno*, 85bff., and esp. 89a.

3. Leibniz, letter to Pierre Coste (1712), in Ger. III, 428. The phrase appears in Leibniz' comments on Shaftesbury's *Characteristics*—a copy of which had been sent to Leibniz by Coste.

4. This is Leibniz' formulation, but it corresponds well enough to Hobbes' own language—for example, the claim in *Leviathan*, ch. 34, that "substance and body signify the same thing" (Oakeshott ed., p. 256).

5. *Leviathan*, ch. 34.

6. Ibid., ch. 46, Oakeshott ed., pp. 439–440.

7. Ibid., ch. 1, Oakeshott ed., p. 7. Leibniz' complaint is to be found in *De Schismate* (1683), in Acad. Ed. IV, 3, 258.

8. *Leviathan*, ch. 14, Oakeshott ed., p. 86. Whether Hobbes' notion that "will" is equivalent to "the last appetite" in deliberation (*Leviathan*, ch. 6) is adequate to his own moral purposes is questionable: if "wills . . . make the essence of all covenants" (*Leviathan*, ch. 40), but will is "last appetite," then "the last appetite makes the essence of all covenants." But if the covenants which generate authorized sovereigns are mere converging appetites, what becomes of Hobbes' moral theory? See Riley, *Will and Political Legitimacy*, ch. 2.

9. Leibniz, *Principles of Nature and Grace*, prop. 2, in Latta, p. 407.

10. Plato, *Phaedo*, 75d; Kant, *Critique of Pure Reason*, trans. Kemp Smith, A313/B370ff., pp. 310ff.: "Plato found the chief instances of his ideas in the field of the practical. . . . It is . . . in regard to the principles of morality, legislation and religion . . . that Plato's teaching exhibits its quite peculiar merits." See also Hector-Neri Castaneda, "Leibniz and Plato's *Phaedo*," in *Leibniz: Critical and Interpretive Essays*, ed. Michael Hooker (Minneapolis, 1982), pp. 124ff.

11. Kant, *Critique of Pure Reason*, trans. Kemp Smith, A547/B575, p. 472.

12. Leibniz, *NE* II, i, 2 and I, i, 5.

13. Kant, *Metaphysische Anfangsgründe der Naturwissenschaft*, in *Werke*, ed. Cassirer, IV, 413.

14. Kant, *Critique of Pure Reason*, trans. Kemp Smith, A553/B581ff., pp. 476ff. "Reason is not itself an appearance."

15. Ernst Cassirer, *Kant's Life and Thought*, trans. J. Hayden (New Haven, 1981), p. 99.

16. Leibniz, letter to Arnauld (9 October 1687), in Ger. II, pp. 111ff.; English trans. in Mason, *The Leibniz-Arnauld Correspondence*, pp. 143ff., and in Loemker, 2nd ed., pp. 342ff. (passage on Parmenides at p. 342).

17. Ibid. (Loemker, 2nd ed.), pp. 346–347.

18. Ibid.

19. Ibid.

20. Ibid. As early as his 1671 letter to Arnauld, Leibniz had linked justice and love (Ger. I, pp. 73–74); well treated by Sève in *Leibniz: Le droit de la raison,* pp. 205ff.

21. Ibid. (Leibniz' 1687 letter to Arnauld), pp. 346–347.

22. Leibniz, "Discourse on Metaphysics," in Loemker, 2nd ed., prop. 13, pp. 310–311. On Leibniz' use of Julius Caesar, see Ursula Goldenbaum, "From Adam to Alexander and Caesar: Leibniz' Shift from Logic and Metaphysics to a Theory of History," in *Leibniz and Adam,* pp. 365ff.

23. Leibniz, "Discourse on Metaphysics," in Loemker, 2nd ed., pp. 310–311.

24. Ibid.

25. Leibniz, *Theodicy,* trans. Huggard, III, 416, p. 372.

26. Leibniz, "Discourse on Metaphysics," in Loemker, 2nd ed., pp. 310–311.

27. Ibid.

28. Ibid.

29. Ibid. It is especially striking that Arnauld should have been distressed by this claim, since in his edition of Augustine's *De Correptione et Gratia* (Paris, 1644) he had warned Christians not to fall into the "criminal pride" of the "Pelagians" who, through "unhappy presumption," treat man as free and not in need of redemptive grace (Introduction, pp. 4–7).

30. Hobbes, *Leviathan,* ch. 21, Oakeshott ed., pp. 137–138.

31. Leibniz, letter to Pierre Bayle (1702), in *Selections,* ed. Wiener, pp. 181–182.

32. Ibid.

33. Leibniz, letter to Arnauld (March 1690), in Ger. II, pp. 134–138; English trans. in Mason, *The Leibniz-Arnauld Correspondence,* pp. 169ff., and in Loemker, 2nd ed., p. 360.

34. The director of the Imperial Library in Vienna gave Leibniz the idea for the *Codex* in 1690; see Müller and Krönert, *Leben und Werk von Leibniz: Eine Chronik,* p. 122.

35. Leibniz, letter to Arnauld (1690), in Loemker, 2nd ed., p. 360.

36. Ibid.

37. Ibid. The "Spartan" reference comes from a fragment of Euripides' *Telephus* quoted in Cicero's *Letters to Atticus* (4.6.2.) and in Plutarch's *Moralia* (472e, 602b). For Leibniz (unlike Rousseau in the *First Discourse*), Sparta would need to be "beautified"—mainly by academies of arts and sciences.

38. Leibniz, letter to Arnauld (1690), in Loemker, 2nd ed., p. 360.

39. Leibniz, "Doctrine of a Single Universal Spirit" (1702), in Ger. VI, pp. 536–537. Leibniz makes much the same point in a 1702 letter to Bayle himself, in Ger. III, pp. 66ff.: "If one takes action away from [created substances], and therefore the consequences of action, or passing on to other actions, I do not see what remains to them." See also Daniel Fouke, "Divine Causation and the Autonomy of Nature in Leibniz," *Archiv für Geschichte der Philosophie,* 76, no. 2 (1994): 188–189.

40. Leibniz, letter to Hansch (July 1707), in Dutens II, 225 (English trans. in Loemker, 2nd ed., p. 595).

41. Leibniz, letter to Bourguet (1714), in Ger. III, p. 575.

42. On *le grand Arnauld,* see Sleigh, *Leibniz and Arnauld,* pp. 26–47.

43. Leibniz, *Monadology,* in Latta, pp. 297ff.

44. First published by Grua in *Textes inédits,* II, 553–555.

45. Pascal, *Pensées,* no. 72 (Brunschvicg numbering), trans. W. Trotter, in *The Great Books: Pascal* (Chicago, 1952), pp. 181–184. To be sure, Leibniz would only have known the defective Port-Royal edition of the *Pensées;* but in that edition no. 72 is reasonably intact. See also Mara Vamos' valuable "Pascal's *Pensées* and the Enlightenment," in *Studies on Voltaire and the Eighteenth Century,* vol. 97 (Banbury, 1972), pp. 5ff.

46. Leibniz, "Double Infinity in Pascal and the Monad," in *Textes inédits,* II, 553.

47. Ibid.

48. Kant, *Critique of Practical Reason,* trans. Beck, pp. 166–167.

49. Leibniz, "Double Infinity," in *Textes inédits,* II, 554.

50. Ibid., p. 555.

51. Leibniz, letter to Joachim Bouvet (1697), Acad. Ed. I, 14, 833.

52. Leibniz, letter to Arnauld (October 1687), in Loemker, 2nd ed., p. 342.

53. Leibniz, *Theodicy,* trans. Huggard, III, 323, p. 321.

54. "On the Greeks as Founders of Rational Philosophy," first published by Patrick Riley in *Journal of the History of Philosophy,* 13, no. 4 (1976): 205ff., with the permission of the Leibniz-Archiv at the Niedersächsische Landesbibliothek (Hanover).

55. Ibid., p. 205; Müller and Krönert, *Leben und Werk von Leibniz,* p. 245.

56. Leibniz, letter to Remond (January 1714), in Ger. III, pp. 605–607.

57. Ibid.

58. Leibniz, "On the Greeks," p. 216 (Leibniz' text). This is even clearer in the *New Essays:* "In case such a transmigration [of souls] were true . . ., there would not be sufficient moral identity to say that it would be one and the same person." Cited in Samuel Scheffler, "Leibniz on Personal Identity and Moral Personality," *Studia Leibnitiana,* 8, no. 2 (1976}: 228.

59. Leibniz, letter to Abbé Foucher (1686), in Ger. I, 380.

60. In A. Foucher de Careil, ed., *Nouvelles lettres et opuscules inédits de Leibniz* (Paris, 1857), p. 4.

61. Leibniz, letter to Remond (February 1715), in Ger. III, 635.

62. Leibniz, "On the Greeks," p. 216 (Leibniz' text). Cf. Leibniz' letter to Abbé Foucher, in Ger. I, 392, where Plato and Aristotle appear in a less flattering light. In this letter Leibniz says that while Plato recognized something of a correct doctrine of substance, he "could not get away from his doubts," and that while Aristotle recognized the necessity of "putting something other than extension in

bodies," he fell short of adequacy by not understanding "the mystery of the duration of substances."

63. Foucher de Careil, *Nouvelles lettres et opuscules,* p. 240.
64. Ibid., p. 14.
65. Leibniz, "On the Greeks," p. 216 (Leibniz' text).
66. Leibniz, *Memoir for Enlightened Persons of Good Intention,* in Klopp x, 10; English translation in Riley, p. 105.
67. Leibniz, letter to Jaquelot (1704), in Ger. III, 475.
68. Leibniz, letter to Jaquelot (1703), in Ger. III, 458.
69. Leibniz, *Monadology,* props. 85–87, in Latta, pp. 267–268.
70. Leibniz, letter to Bierling (1713), Dutens v, 390.
71. Leibniz, *Opinion on the Principles of Pufendorf,* in Riley, 67 (original Latin in Dutens IV, iii, 276–277).
72. Leibniz, *Lettre de M. G. G. Leibniz sur la philosophie chinoise,* in Dutens IV, i, 206.
73. Leibniz, *Opinion on . . . Pufendorf,* in Riley, p. 67.
74. Leibniz, "On the Greeks," p. 216 (Leibniz' text).
75. 1 Corinthians 1:20.
76. In Ger. VI, 502–503; English translation in Loemker, 2nd ed., pp. 547ff.
77. Ibid. (Ger. VI, 502.)
78. Jolley, *Leibniz and Locke,* p. 49ff.
79. Cf. Kant, *Critique of Pure Reason,* trans. Kemp Smith, A553/B581ff., pp. 476ff.
80. Leibniz, "On What Is Independent of Sensation in Knowledge," in Ger. VI, 503.
81. Ibid.
82. Leibniz, *NE* III, v, pt. 12. "The qualities of mind are not less real than those of body."
83. Leibniz, "On What Is Independent of Sensation in Knowledge," in Ger. VI, 503.
84. Ibid. It is common enough in the late seventeenth century to draw morality from *lumière naturelle*—Pierre Bayle, for example, uses the notion in his *Commentaire philosophique* (1686) to defeat obscurantists who would use Scripture to justify cruelty and persecution (in *Oeuvres diverses* [The Hague, 1737], II, 105–107).
85. Leibniz, "Compte rendu de la Vindication de Stillingfleet et de la lettre de Locke" (1698), in Acad. Ed. VI, 6, 17.
86. Kant, *Rechtslehre,* trans. B. Hastie (Edinburgh, 1887), p. 116. (This crucial passage is omitted in the Ladd and Reiss translations of this work.)
87. René Sève, *Leibniz et l'école moderne du droit naturel* (Paris, 1989), p. 88. Any criticism of this remarkable book should begin by recognizing it as the finest contribution to the study of Leibniz' practical thought since Gaston Grua's magisterial volumes in the 1950s. Sève is always intelligent and well informed, and even his questionable judgments are never groundless. (To be sure, Leibniz constantly uses the Aristotelian language of "distributive" and "commutative" justice in his

jurisprudential writings; but he alters the sense which Aristotle had attached to the terms.)

88. Ibid., pp. 88–89.

89. Aristotle, *Rhetoric* 1368b 10, in *Works*, ed. Ross, vol. XI.

90. Leibniz, *"Dialogue on Liberty,"* in *Textes inédits*, I, 365.

91. Leibniz, "Discourse on Metaphysics," prop. 13, in Loemker, 2nd ed., pp. 310–311.

92. Jean-Paul Sartre, *Existentialism Is a Humanism*, trans. P. Mairet (London, 1948), pp. 28–49.

93. Aristotle, *Nicomachean Ethics* 1178b ff., in *Works*, ed. Ross, vol. IX.

94. See Leibniz, *Theodicy*, trans. Huggard, III, 367, p. 345.

95. Aristotle, *Politics*, bk. III, 1283a ff., in *Works*, ed. Ross, vol. X.

96. Leibniz, "Observations on King's 'The Origin of Evil,'" in *Theodicy*, trans. Huggard, p. 421.

97. See, inter alia, Leibniz' letter to Pierre Coste (December 1707), in Ger. III, 402–403: "While we have a liberty of indifference which saves us from necessity, we never have an indifference of equilibrium, which exempts us from determining reasons. . . . The universe is not like an ellipse or other such oval, which a straight line drawn through its center can cut into two congruent parts."

98. Sève, *Leibniz et l'école moderne du droit naturel*, p. 69.

99. Leibniz, "Meditation on the Common Concept of Justice," in Riley, p. 46. The phrase "stat pro ratione voluntas" is adapted from Juvenal, *Satirae* VI, 223.

100. Especially in late works such as *De Natura et Gratia* and *De Correptione et Gratia*.

101. Here the most prominent figure would be Leibniz himself; but Grotius would also be important.

102. Sève, *Leibniz: Le droit de la raison*, p. 8, n. 1.

103. Leibniz, letter to Pierre Coste (1707), in Ger. III, 400–401.

104. Leibniz, "Conversation sur la liberté," in *Textes inédits*, II, 478ff.

105. Ibid., p. 478.

106. Ibid.

107. Ibid., p. 480.

108. Leibniz, *Monadology*, in Latta, prop. 11, p. 223.

109. Leibniz, "Conversation sur la liberté," in *Textes inédits*, II, 480.

110. Ibid., p. 481.

111. Spinoza, *The Improvement of the Understanding*, in The *Philosophy of Spinoza*, ed. J. Ratner (New York, 1927), pp. 175ff.: "Men are deceived because they think themselves free . . . the infant believes that it is by free will that it seeks the breast."

112. Leibniz, "Conversation sur la liberté," in *Textes inédits*, II, 482.

113. Ibid.

114. Russell, *Critical Exposition of the Philosophy of Leibniz*, 2nd ed. (1937), pp. 191ff., esp. p. 197.

115. Leibniz, "Conversation sur la liberté," in *Textes inédits,* ii, 485.

116. Kant, "On the Failure of All Attempted Philosophical Theodicies," in M. Despland, *Kant on History and Religion* (Montréal, 1973), p. 286.

117. Leibniz, "Conversation sur la liberté," in *Textes inédits,* ii, 485.

118. Ibid., pp. 478–479; Leibniz, "Discourse on Metaphysics," in Loemker, 2nd ed., prop. 13, pp. 310–311.

119. Kant, *Prolegomena to Any Future Metaphysics,* in *Kant Selections,* ed. L. W. Beck (New York, 1988), p. 214.

120. Kant, *Critique of Pure Reason,* trans. Kemp Smith, A584/B612, pp. 495ff.

121. Ibid., A381ff., pp. 354ff.: "The whole of rational psychology, as a science surpassing all powers of human reason, proves abortive."

122. Ibid., A445/B473ff., pp. 409ff.

123. Kant, *Critique of Practical Reason,* trans. Beck, p. 29.

124. Karl Ameriks, "Kant's Deduction of Freedom and Morality," *Journal of the History of Philosophy,* 19, no. 1 (January 1981): 70ff.

125. Hobbes, *Leviathan,* ed. Oakeshott, ch. 46, p. 446.

126. Lewis White Beck, *A Commentary to Kant's Critique of Practical Reason* (Chicago, 1960), p. 191.

127. Kant, *Critique of Pure Reason,* trans. Kemp Smith, A468/B496, p. 425.

128. Ibid., A533/B561, p. 464.

129. Ibid.

130. Ibid., A534/B562, p. 465.

131. Leibniz, *Notes on Spinoza's Ethics,* in Duncan, pp. 21–22.

132. Kant, *Critique of Pure Reason,* trans. Kemp Smith, A534/B562, p. 465.

133. Ibid., Bxxvi–xxviii, pp. 27–28.

134. Leibniz, letter to Burnett (1699 or 1700), in Ger. iii, 260.

135. Kant, *Critique of Pure Reason,* trans. Kemp Smith, A536/B564, A549/B577, pp. 466, 473.

136. Ibid., A550/B578, pp. 474–475.

137. Kant, *Critique of Practical Reason,* trans. Beck, pp. 46–49.

138. Kant, *Critique of Pure Reason,* trans. Kemp Smith, A554/B582, p. 476.

139. Ibid., A551/B579, p. 475.

140. Ibid., A554/B582, p. 476.

141. See George Armstrong Kelly, *Idealism, Politics, and History: Sources of Hegelian Thought* (Cambridge, 1969), pp. 98ff. This is the most imaginative treatment in English of the whole of Kant's "practical" thought.

142. Pascal, *Écrits sur la grace,* in *Oeuvres de Blaise Pascal,* ed. L. Brunschvicg (Paris, 1914), xi, 129.

143. Kant, *Lectures on Philosophical Theology,* trans. A. Wood and C. Clark (Ithaca, 1978), p. 148.

144. Kant, *Religion within the Limits of Reason Alone,* in *The Philosophy of Kant,* trans. C. J. Friedrich (New York, 1949), pp. 388–389.

145. Ibid., p. 389.
146. Ibid., pp. 393–394.
147. Ibid., bks. II and III.
148. Kant, *Critique of Practical Reason*, trans. Beck, pp. 76ff.
149. Kant, *Critique of Judgment*, trans. J. C. Meredith (Oxford, 1952), pp. 126–129.
150. This difficulty is captured dramatically by Martine de Gaudemar in *Leibniz: De la puissance au sujet* (Paris, 1994), p. 252: "How is a Leibnizian ethics possible, if the Kingdom of God arrives without us? When the created being has no other task than that of contributing to the best of all possible worlds and of celebrating it, does he not work toward a realization which is already present through the fact of divine creation?" For a very different view of Leibniz on freedom, see G. H. R. Parkinson, "Leibniz on Human Freedom," in *Studia Leibnitiana*, Sonderheft 2 (Wiesbaden, 1970). But Parkinson declines to discuss the very things which make Leibnizian freedom problematical: "nothing will be said here about the problem whether there can be any human freedom in 'the best of all possible worlds,' or about the question . . . whether a man can be free even though there is a 'complete concept' of that man." But this excludes, by sheer *fiat*, the most worrying difficulties.
151. Hobbes, *Leviathan*, ed. Oakeshott, ch. 21, p. 141.
152. Ibid., chs. 1–6; see also Riley, *Will and Political Legitimacy*, ch. 2.
153. Locke, *Two Treatises of Government*, ed. P. Laslett (Cambridge, 1970), p. 401.
154. Spinoza, *Theologico-Political Treatise*, ch. 16, in *Works of Spinoza*, trans. R. H. M. Elwes (New York, 1951), I, 199ff.
155. Locke, *Two Treatises*, p. 401.
156. Locke, *Second Reply to the Bishop of Worcester*, in *The Works of John Locke* (London, 1812), IV, 492. See the comparable passage in Locke's letter to Molyneux (1693) in *The Correspondence of John Locke* (Oxford, 1979), IV, 625–626: "I cannot have a clearer perception of anything than that I am free, yet I cannot make freedom in man consistent with omnipotence and omniscience in God."
157. Locke, "Remarks on Some of Mr. Norris's Books," in *Works*, x, 255–256; here Locke complains that "Hobbes and Spinoza" resolve "all, even the thoughts and will of men, into an irresistible fatal necessity."
158. Leibniz, *Codex Iuris Gentium* (Praefatio), pt. xi.
159. Leibniz, *NE* II, xxi, pt. 67.
160. Stuart Hampshire, *The Age of Reason* (New York, 1956), p. 167. See also Gilles Deleuze, *The Fold: Leibniz and the Baroque*, trans. T. Conley (Minneapolis, 1993), p. 69: "Human liberty is not safeguarded [by Leibniz] inasmuch as it has to be practiced in this existing world. In human eyes it does not suffice that Adam may not sin in another world, if he is certainly sinning in this world."
161. Leibniz, *Theodicy*, trans. Huggard, II, 145, p. 214.
162. Isaiah Berlin, "Does Political Theory Still Exist?" *Philosophy, Politics, and Society*, 2nd ser. (Oxford, 1964): 14–15.

163. Leibniz, letter to Antonio Alberti (1689), cited in Robinet, *Inter Italicum*, pp. 150ff.

3. Theodicy as Universal Justice

1. The two most striking versions are to be found in Leibniz' last letter to Arnauld (March 1690) and in propositions 84ff. of the *Monadology*—both discussed in Chapter 2.

2. Leibniz, *Monadology*, in Latta, props. 86–90, pp. 267ff.

3. Leibniz, *Theodicy*, trans. Huggard, II, 125, p. 199; *NE* II, 27, 14 (Acad. Ed. VI, 6, 240).

4. Plato, *Gorgias* 523a ff. and *Republic* 614b ff., in *Collected Dialogues*, pp. 303ff. and 838ff. It is possible (to say no more) that Leibniz ends the *Theodicy* with Jupiter because Plato ends *Gorgias* with Zeus; in both cases the god serves as defender of cosmic justice.

5. Plato, *Timaeus* 92c, in *Collected Dialogues*, pp. 1210–1211.

6. Samuel and 1 Kings; John 13:34 (KJV).

7. On this point the unsurpassed classic study is that of Gaston Grua, *Jurisprudence universelle et théodicée selon Leibniz*, passim; see also Schneider, *Justitia Universalis*, passim. For a more critical view of Leibnizian universal jurisprudence, see Robert Merrihew Adams, "Leibniz' Theories of Contingency," in Hooker, ed., *Leibniz: Critical and Interpretive Essays*, p. 279: "[In the *Theodicy*] the frequent and unelucidated use that the book makes of the terms 'moral necessity,' 'hypothetical necessity,' and 'incline without necessitating' leaves the reader with a less necessitarian impression of Leibniz' thought than those terms would leave if they were accompanied by the explanations of their meanings that are presented or suggested by his less public writings." Adams concludes that the *Theodicy* is a less than candid presentation of Leibniz' views.

8. Leibniz "Théodicée ou Apologie de la justice de Dieu," in *Textes inédits*, II, 495.

9. Leibniz, "Theodicaea," in *Textes inédits*, I, 370.

10. Leibniz, *Theodicy*, trans. Huggard, title page.

11. Leibniz, letter to V. Placcius (1697), in Dutens VI, 84ff.; discussed in Adams, *Leibniz: Determinist, Theist, Idealist*, pp. 89ff.

12. See especially Leibniz, "Théodicée ou Apologie de la justice de Dieu," in *Textes inédits*, II, 495ff.

13. Leibniz, *Theodicy*, trans. Huggard, II, 203ff., pp. 254ff. See also Patrick Riley, "Introduction" to Malebranche, *Treatise on Nature and Grace* (Oxford, 1992), pp. 43ff.

14. Leibniz, letter to Pierre Coste, in Ger. III, 419: "Hobbes est plein de bonnes pensées, mais il a coutume de les outrer."

15. Hobbes, *Liberty, Necessity, and Chance*, in *English Works*, ed. W. Molesworth (London, 1841), V, 115–116. Hereafter *EW*.

16. Job 40–41, 38 (KJV).
17. On the title page of *Leviathan* is to be found Hobbes' Latin paraphrase of Job: "Non est potestas super terram qui comparetur ei [there is no power on earth who compares with Him]." As applied to an earthly sovereign, this is a bold reading of Scripture: the attributes of God are brought down to earth.
18. Romans 9:21 (KJV).
19. Hobbes, *Leviathan*, ed. Oakeshott, ch. 11, pp. 69ff.
20. Hobbes, *De Cive*, ed. S. Lamprecht (New York, 1949), pp. 46ff., 198.
21. Ibid., p. 198.
22. Leibniz, "Théodicée ou Apologie de la justice de Dieu," in *Textes inédits*, II, 495–496: "We have good and true ideas of the attributes of God, or, what is the same thing, we have reason to attribute justice and goodness to him—which would be groundless if these words signified nothing."
23. Hobbes, *Leviathan*, ed. Oakeshott, ch. 31, pp. 238–241.
24. Ibid.
25. Leibniz, *Reflections on the Work That Mr. Hobbes Published in English on Freedom, Necessity, and Chance*, appended to *Theodicy*, trans. Huggard, pp. 393ff.
26. Hobbes, *Liberty, Necessity, and Chance*, in *EW*, V, 179.
27. Leibniz, On Shaftesbury's *Characteristics*, in Ger. III, 424–425; English translation in Riley, p. 196.
28. On this point see Werner Schneiders, "Leibniz und die Frage dem Grund des Guten und Gerechten," in *Studia Leibnitiana, Supplementa IV* (Wiesbaden, 1969), pp. 85–111.
29. Leibniz, *Caesarinus Fürstenerius*, chs. 9–11; English translation in Riley, pp. 113–120.
30. Hobbes, *Leviathan*, ed. Oakeshott, ch. 35, p. 268.
31. Ibid., pp. 268–270.
32. Ibid.
33. Ibid., chs. 6 and 46, pp. 38, 445–446.
34. Ibid., ch. 12, p. 71.
35. Ibid., p. 77.
36. Ibid., ch. 31, pp. 269–270.
37. Ibid.
38. On this point see Willis Glover, "God and Thomas Hobbes," in *Hobbes Studies*, ed. K. Brown (Oxford, 1965), pp. 141–168.
39. Romans 9:14, see also 3:5–6.
40. Hobbes, *Liberty, Necessity, and Chance*, in *EW*, V, 114–116.
41. Ibid.
42. Leibniz, *Observationes de Principio Juris*, in Dutens IV, iii, 370ff.
43. Hobbes, *Liberty, Necessity, and Chance*, in *EW*, V, 215–216.
44. Bayle, *Entretiens de Maxime et de Thémiste*, in *Oeuvres diverses*, IV, 57ff.
45. Leibniz, *Theodicy*, trans. Huggard, "Preface," pp. 63ff.

46. Leibniz, "Discourse on Metaphysics," prop. 2, in Loemker 1, 466. See also Leibniz, "Théodicée ou Apologie de la justice de Dieu," in *Textes inédits*, II, 496, which urges that Hobbes and others who stress divine omnipotence alone supply only "the motive of a forced patience, which would have effect even if one had to do with a tyrant, whom one fears and does not love at all."

47. Leibniz, "Théodicée ou Apologie de la justice de Dieu," in *Textes inédits*, II, 495ff.

48. Ibid., p. 495.

49. Ibid., p. 496; Ovid, *Metamorphoses* IX, 500.

50. Leibniz, "Théodicée ou Apologie de la justice de Dieu," in *Textes inédits*, II, 496.

51. Ibid.

52. Ibid., pp. 496–497.

53. Ibid., p. 497.

54. Ibid., p. 498.

55. Hobbes, *Leviathan*, ed. Oakeshott, ch. 14, p. 92.

56. See especially André Robinet, *Malebranche et Leibniz: Relations personnelles*, passim.

57. "Introduction" to Malebranche, *Treatise on Nature and Grace*, ed. and trans. Riley, p. 54 (the passage concerning God's "moving our arm" is from *Recherche de la vérité*, VI, ii, 3).

58. Malebranche, *Treatise on Nature and Grace*, ed. and trans. Riley, discourse 1, 112ff.

59. Robinet, *Malebranche et Leibniz*, passim.

60. Malebranche, *Treatise on Nature and Grace*, ed. and trans. Riley, discourse 1, pt. xviii, p. 118.

61. Aristotle, *Nicomachean Ethics*, 1137b, Ross ed.

62. Leibniz, *Theodicy*, trans. Huggard, II, 204 and 208, pp. 254–255, 257.

63. Malebranche, *Treatise on Nature and Grace*, ed. and trans. Riley, "First Illustration," sec. xv, pp. 210–211.

64. Ibid., discourse 1, sec. xviii.

65. Ibid., sec. lvii.

66. Malebranche, *Réponse au livre de Mr Arnau[l]d, Des vrais et des fausses idées*, in *Oeuvres complètes de Malebranche*, ed. A. Robinet (Paris, 1958), VI–VII 43.

67. Ibid.

68. Ibid.

69. Malebranche, *Treatise on Nature and Grace*, ed. and trans. Riley, discourse 1, sec. lvii, p. 20.

70. Malebranche, *Réponse au livre de Mr. Arnau[l]d*, in *Oeuvres complètes*, VI–VII, 592.

71. Malebranche, *Treatise on Nature and Grace*, ed. and trans. Riley, discourse 1, secs. xxxix–xli, pp. 127–128.

72. Cited in Ginette Dreyfus, *La volonté selon Malebranche* (Paris, 1958), p. 114.

73. Malebranche, *Réflexions sur la prémotion physique*, in *Oeuvres complètes*, XVI, 118.

74. Ibid.

75. Leibniz, letter to Malebranche (December 1711), cited in Malebranche, *Oeuvres complètes*, XIX, 815.

76. Bayle, *Entretiens de Maxime et de Thémiste*, in *Oeuvres diverses*, IV, 57–62.

77. Laurent Boursier, *De l'action de Dieu sur les créatures* (Paris, 1713), pp. 47, 79.

78. Especially by Arnauld, Bossuet, and Fénelon—see Riley, *The General Will before Rousseau*, pp. 48–50 (Arnauld), 64ff. (Bossuet and Fénelon).

79. See Robinet, *Malebranche et Leibniz*, pp. 416ff.

80. Malebranche, *Réflexions sur la prémotion physique*, p. 101.

81. Ibid., p. 104.

82. Ibid., p. 98.

83. Ibid., p. 93.

84. Unfair in the sense that Locke reserves "sovereign" power for God alone, and treats "governors" as mere "judges" who are exercising a delegated "trust."

85. Malebranche, *Réflexions sur la prémotion physique*, p. 100.

86. Cited in Robinet, *Malebranche et Leibniz*, p. 417.

87. For the centrality of "order" in Malebranche, see above all his *Traité de morale* (1684), in *Oeuvres complètes*, X, 41–42.

88. On this point see Alquié, *Le cartésianisme de Malebranche*, pp. 226ff.

89. "The same" in the sense that both postulate a Platonic realm of "eternal moral verities," and shrink mere divine "omnipotence" (à la *Euthyphro*).

90. Leibniz, *Monadology*, in Latta, p. 14.

91. Leibniz, *Theodicy*, trans. Huggard, "Preface," pp. 49ff.

92. See, for example, Leibniz' letter to Andreas Morrell (December 1696), in *Textes inédits*, I, 103–105: "I have ordinarily found that those persons who wanted to pass for the most pious were all ice when it was a question of truly doing good. . . . Those who are of a sectarian or schismatic humor . . . can have neither charity nor enlightenment in its true purity."

93. Leibniz, *Theodicy*, trans. Huggard, "Preface," p. 50.

94. Ibid., pp. 50–51.

95. Ibid., p. 51.

96. Ibid.

97. Leibniz, "On the Greeks," pp. 214ff. (Leibniz' text).

98. Plato, letter XIII, in *Collected Dialogues*, 363b, p. 1563. Whether this letter is by Plato or merely "Platonic" is not a central issue here.

99. Leibniz, *Theodicy*, trans. Huggard, "Preface," p. 51.

100. Ibid.

101. Ibid., pp. 51–52.

102. Ibid., p. 52. The last sentence is remarkably "Kantian": after all, Kant frequently argues that we must perfect ourselves (morally) and advance the happiness of others (see *Critique of Practical Reason*, trans. Beck, pp. 34ff.).

103. 1 Corinthians 13:4.

104. Especially the passage near the beginning of *Religion* in which Kant urges that reason proposes "objective ends" that we "ought to have"; see *Religion within the*

Limits of Reason Alone, trans. T. M. Greene and H. Hudson (New York, 1960), p. 6n.

105. Leibniz, "On the Greeks," pp. 213ff. (Leibniz' text).

106. John 13:34.

107. Genesis 22. Leibniz must have been distressed by the argument of Genesis 22:1 that God "tempted" Abraham by ordaining the sacrifice of Isaac—for no "wisely charitable" perfect being would issue such a decree, least of all as a "test."

108. The phrase is John Rawls', from *Political Liberalism* (New York, 1993), p. 78 (inter alia).

109. Kant, *Critique of Pure Reason,* trans. Kemp Smith, B847, p. 644.

110. Leibniz, letter to Morrell (1698), in *Textes inédits,* I, 139. To be sure, Leibniz is here using "reason" partly to counter the mysticism of Boehme which Morrell apparently found attractive.

111. See, for example, Malebranche, *Treatise on Nature and Grace,* ed. and trans. Riley, discourse I, sec. lvii, p. 136): "Scripture is . . . full of anthropologies."

112. At least in the sense that the proofs of the existence of one single God have always been "rational" proofs (for example, perfection entails necessary existence), while deriving any particular moral content from "reason" is much more problematical. Even Kant must (as it were) flesh out "reason" by saying that rational beings necessarily regard themselves as "ends"—and that then permits him to posit a Kingdom of Ends. (Since charity is "affective," it is even more problematical as a dictate of "reason.")

113. Leibniz, "Von der Weisheit" (c. 1694–1698), in *Textes inédits,* II, 585ff.

114. Ibid.

115. Ibid. Here love is made less simply "affective" by being generated by "the greatest perfection."

116. Leibniz, letter to Electress Sophie (1696), in *Textes inédits,* I, 380.

117. Rousseau, *La Nouvelle Héloïse,* ed. R. Pommier (Paris, 1960), pp. 671–672.

118. Cited in Naert, *Leibniz et la querelle du pur amour,* p. 103.

119. Leibniz, letter to Landgraf Ernst of Hessen-Rheinfels (1685), in *Textes inédits,* I, 196.

120. Plato, *Euthyphro,* 5c ff., in *Collected Dialogues,* pp. 173ff.

121. Leibniz, "Dialogue de Poliandre et Théophile," cited in Grua, *La justice humaine selon Leibniz,* p. 150 n. 1.

122. Leibniz, "Von der Weisheit," in *Textes inédits,* II, 585ff. (Many more texts in this vein cited in Chapter 4.)

123. Leibniz, letter to Johann Friedrich (1677), in Acad. Ed. II, 1, 301; treated in Grua, *Jurisprudence universelle,* p. 442.

124. Leibniz, *Causa Dei,* pt. 49, in Ger. VI, 446.

125. Mark Larrimore, "Leibniz' Religious and Moral Philosophy in the *Theodicy*"

(Ph.D. dissertation, Department of Religion, Princeton University, Spring 1994).

126. Malebranche, *Entretiens sur la métaphysique*, in *Oeuvres complètes*, XII–XIII, 97.

127. Malebranche, *Traité de la nature et de la grâce*, in *Oeuvres complètes*, V, "Troisième Eclaircissement," pt. 11.

128. On this point see Henri Gouhier, *La Philosophie de Malebranche et son expérience réligieuse* (Paris, 1926), pp. 97–103.

129. Malebranche, *Entretiens sur la métaphysique*, in *Oeuvres complètes*, XII–XIII, 207.

130. Malebranche, *Méditations chrétiennes et métaphysiques*, in *Oeuvres complètes*, X, 39.

131. Ibid., p. 73.

132. Ibid.

133. Malebranche, *Treatise on Nature and Grace*, ed. and trans. Riley, discourse I, sec. lvii, p. 136.

134. On this point see Alquié, *Le cartésianisme de Malebranche*, pp. 453ff.

135. Malebranche, *Traité de morale*, in *Oeuvres complètes*, XI, 41.

136. Leibniz, c. 1687, in *Textes inédits*, I, 80. Cf. Leibniz on Spinoza, March/April 1677, *Textes inédits*, I, 161: "The love of God above all things is . . . the principle of true religion. This love is greater in proportion as it is more enlightened."

137. Leibniz, remarks on Toland's *Christianity Not Mysterious*, in Dutens V, 142ff.: "Nothing keeps God from revealing dogmas to us which we can never understand. . . . The divine things present impenetrable abysses to all human intellegence."

138. Leibniz, "Unvorgreiffliches Bedencken," in *Textes inédits*, I, 430.

139. Leibniz, *Principles of Nature and Grace*, in Latta, prop. 10, p. 417.

140. Leibniz, *Theodicy*, trans. Huggard, I, 7, p. 127.

141. Leibniz, *De Libertate* (c. 1680), in *Textes inédits*, I, 288. Cf. Leibniz, "Dialogue entre Théophile et Polidore," 1679, in *Textes inédits*, I, 286: "Possible things, having no existence, have no power to make themselves exist, and in consequence one must seek out the choice and the cause of their existence in a being whose existence is already fixed and consequently necessary in itself."

142. Leibniz, *Theodicy*, trans. Huggard, "Preface," pp. 62ff.

143. Ibid., pp. 58–59.

144. Malebranche, *Treatise on Nature and Grace*, ed. and trans. Riley, discourse I (entire), pp. 112ff.

145. Leibniz, *Theodicy*, trans. Huggard, I, 3–4, pp. 124–125.

146. Ibid., I, 4–5, pp. 125–126.

147. Ibid., I, 5, p. 126.

148. Pascal, *Écrits sur la grace*, in *Oeuvres*, XI, 135–137. For an excellent commentary see Jan Miel, *Pascal and Theology* (Baltimore, 1969), pp. 65ff.

149. See Riley, *The General Will before Rousseau*, pp. 14–25.

150. Leibniz, *Theodicy*, trans. Huggard, I, 5, p. 126.

151. Leibniz, *NE* IV, xviii, ed. Remnant and Bennett, p. 502.

152. Ibid., p. 500.

153. Ibid., p. 501.

154. Ibid., p. 502.

155. Leibniz, letter to Bossuet (1699), F de C II, pp. 264–265. "The third means [of reunifying Christendom] is that of abstraction or suspension, or leaving out of account certain points on which one cannot agree . . . by setting them aside until the decision of a future ecumenical Council." (English translation in Riley, p. 190.)

156. See Étienne Gilson, *Introduction à l'étude de St. Augustin* (Paris, 1929), pp. 177ff. ("la liberté chrétienne").

157. Leibniz, letter to Naudé (1707), in *Textes inédits*, II, 501.

158. Robinet, *Iter Italicum*, pp. 121ff.

159. Leibniz, letter to Father Claudio Filippo Grimaldi, S.J., in Dutens V, 75ff. (also Acad. Ed. I, 13, 515ff.).

160. Ibid.

161. Pascal, *Pensées*, no. 792 (Brunschvicg numbering), trans. Trotter. For a fine commentary, see Nannerl Keohane, *Philosophy and the State in France* (Princeton, 1980), pp. 270ff.

162. Kant, *Critique of Pure Reason*, trans. Kemp Smith, A621/B649ff., pp. 518ff.

163. See Voltaire, *Dictionnaire philosophique*, article "grace," cited in F. Alquié, *Malebranche* (Paris, 1977), pp. 82–84. A jaundiced but very funny account of "grace" in seventeenth-century theological controversies.

164. Meagher, *Augustine: An Introduction*, pp. 263ff.

165. Leibniz, letter to Electress Sophie of Hanover (October 1691), Acad. Ed. I, 7, 34–35. For fears about "Pelagianism," see Antoine Arnauld, "Introduction" to Augustine's *De Correptione et Gratia*, pp. 4ff.: "There are no mysteries which God hides so well from proud sages, as the mysteries of grace."

166. Ibid. See also Cornelius Jansen[ius], *Augustinus* (Louvain, 1640), bk. 3, ch. 20. To be sure, when Leibniz was not trying to conciliate latitudinarian Jesuits, but was rather striving to draw Lutherans and Calvinists closer together, he could cling to the orthodox late Augustinianism that both Protestant sects espoused: "I find with St. Augustine, Thomas Aquinas, and Luther [in] *De Servo Arbitrio* that God is the final reason of things, and that those who speak of [divinely] foreseen good qualities, be it faith or works of charity, as causes of the favorable decrees of God, say the truth, but that they do not say enough, because these same good qualities, being also gifts of God, depend on other decrees, whose final motive can finally only be the good pleasure of God, which is not tyrannical, nor without reason, but which has as its object that abyss and that depth of riches of which St. Paul speaks, that is to say, the harmony and the perfection of the universe" (1695; Acad. Ed. I, 12, 168–169). And in the same vein a few months later, Leibniz added that "since the will to receive that which God offers us"—such as the *bene-volent* will to be charitable—"is a gift of God," it follows

that "everything finally comes down to pure grace, as St. Augustine so well understood" (p. 534). On this late Augustinian (even proto-Calvinist) view, our very capacity for *caritas sapientis seu beneviolentia universalis* is not "in our power"; small wonder that Leibniz more often (though never consistently) tried to minimize unmeritable grace(s) in favor of benevolent charity. But whether he was "a Catholic *in foro interno*" (his own self-description) or a late Augustinian Lutheran (another self-description) is impossible to determine definitively. (It may be that he remained unable to swallow the Pelagian human autonomy which is needed to underpin his own notion of justice as good-willing "wise charity.")

167. Leibniz, "Preface to *Novissima Sinica*," secs. 8–9, in *Leibniz: Writings on China*, ed. Daniel Cook and Henry Rosemont (Chicago, 1994), pp. 49–50.

168. "Whether one is a European, a Chinese, in short a world citizen, Magnanimity is concerned only with man [as such]." Leibniz, poem for Mlle. de Scudery (1697), Acad. Ed. I, 14, 752.

169. Bayle, *Entretiens de Maxime et de Thémiste*, in *Oeuvres diverses*, IV, 67.

170. Hobbes, *Liberty, Necessity, and Chance*, in *EW*, V, 115–116.

171. Leibniz, *Theodicy*, trans. Huggard, "Prelim. Diss.," secs. 32–33, pp. 92–93.

172. Ibid., sec. 33, p. 93.

173. Ibid., sec. 35, p. 94.

174. Ibid.

175. Ibid., sec. 37, p. 95.

176. Leibniz, letter to Jaquelot (October 1706), in *Textes inédits*, I, 64ff.

177. Ibid.

178. Leibniz, "Notes sur Bayle" (1706), in *Textes inédits*, I, 63.

179. Leibniz, *Theodicy*, trans. Huggard, "Prelim. Diss.," pt. 37, p. 95.

180. Leibniz, "Discourse on Metaphysics," prop. 2, in Loemker I, 466. The close connection between the "Discourse" and the *Theodicy* is brought out best by Mulvaney, "Divine Justice in Leibniz's 'Discourse on Metaphysics,' " p. 63.

181. Leibniz, *Theodicy*, trans. Huggard, "Preface," pp. 58–59.

182. Ibid.

183. Ibid.

184. Ibid., p. 59. Most of Leibniz' moral-political purposes in the *Theodicy* are present in the "Preface" alone.

185. For Leibniz no inventory of monsters and criminals can weaken the certainty that the actual world must be "best"—that simply follows from the moral perfection of God.

186. In many cases, indeed, Leibniz quotes Bayle with substantial approval—or cites Bayle's better passages against his worse ones.

187. See Elisabeth Labrousse, *Pierre Bayle* (The Hague, 1964), II, 187ff. A splendid book, especially on the Malebranche-Bayle *rapport*.

188. Leibniz, *Theodicy*, trans. Huggard, II, 176, pp. 236–237.

189. Descartes, *Reply to the Six Objections,* in *The Philosophy of Descartes,* trans. Eaton, pp. 264–266.

190. Leibniz, "Discourse on Metaphysics," prop. 2, in Loemker 1, 466.

191. Leibniz, *Theodicy,* trans. Huggard, II, 176, p. 237.

192. Ibid.

193. Leibniz, letter to Greiffenkranz (1715), in Ger. VI, 12n.

194. Leibniz, *Theodicy,* trans. Huggard, II, 177, p. 237.

195. Ibid., II, 172–174, pp. 234ff.

196. Leibniz, *De Schismate,* in Acad. Ed. VI, 3, 256–257.

197. Ibid., p. 257.

198. Ibid.

199. Plato, *Parmenides* 130b ff., in *Collected Dialogues,* pp. 924ff.

200. Leibniz, *De Schismate,* p. 257.

201. Plato, *Meno* 82b ff., in *Collected Dialogues,* pp. 365ff. Cf. Leibniz, "Discourse on Metaphysics," prop. 26, in Loemker, 2nd ed., p. 320.

202. Plato, *Republic* 443c–444a, 614b ff., in *Collected Dialogues,* pp. 686, 838ff.

203. Leibniz, letter to Electress Sophie (1696), in *Textes inédits,* 1, 379.

204. Again see Arendt, *The Life of the Mind: Willing,* pp. 3–7, 84–110.

205. Leibniz, *Lettres sur Descartes et le cartésianisme,* ed. A. Foucher de Careil (Paris, 1857), p. 14.

206. Hobbes, *Leviathan,* ed. Oakeshott, ch. 1, p. 7.

207. Leibniz, "De Bono Unitatis," Leibniz-Archiv, LH 1, 7, 1, Bl. 1^r–2^1.

208. Leibniz, notes on Cudworth's *True Intellectual System of the Universe,* in *Textes inédits,* 1, 328.

209. In Latta, pp. 13–14; Austin Farrer, "Introduction" to *Theodicy,* trans. Huggard, pp. 7ff.

210. Livy, *History of Rome,* bk. 1.

211. Leibniz, *Theodicy,* trans. Huggard, III, 413, pp. 369–370.

212. Ibid.

213. "Wicked from all eternity" is unusually strong for the *Theodicy;* more usually in this work Leibniz speaks of motives which "incline without necessitating," and so on. But in the present passage his chief concern is to acquit God of the charge of causing Tarquin's moral badness (III, 416). Cf. Leibniz' refutation of Stegman, c. 1710: "God . . . decreed at once about the totality of things from eternity, as if they were separated by no intervals of time"; cited in Nicholas Jolley, "An Unpublished Leibniz MS on Metaphysics," *Studia Leibnitiana,* 7 (1975): 170.

214. Leibniz, *Theodicy,* trans. Huggard, III, 416, p. 372.

215. Ibid. On this point see Herbert Breger, "Schwierigkeiten mit der Optimalität," in *Leibniz: Le meilleur des mondes,* ed. A. Heinekamp and A. Robinet, *Studia Leibnitiana,* Sonderheft 21 (Stuttgart, 1992), pp. 99ff.

216. Machiavelli, *The Prince*, ch. 18.
217. Leibniz, letter to Nicaise (1699), in Ger. II, 587: "Truly pure love, as opposed to interested love . . . always exists when the good, happiness or perfection of another makes up our pleasure and happiness." (One could multiply instances in which Leibniz says the same thing, almost verbatim.)
218. Leibniz, letter to Wedderkopf (1671), in Loemker I, 226–227.
219. The notion that having a good will is "in our power" is to be found in Epictetus and (above all) in Augustine; see Neal W. Gilbert, "The Concept of the Will in Early Latin Philosophy," *Journal of the History of Philosophy*, 1 (October 1963): 17–35.
220. Augustine, *De Libero Arbitrio* III, 1, trans. R. P. Russell as *The Free Choice of the Will*, in *The Fathers of the Church*, vol. 59 (Washington, D.C., 1968), p. 167.
221. Leibniz, letter to Morrell (September 1698), in *Textes inédits*, I, 139: "Love . . . chooses among the possibles that which is best."
222. Leibniz, *Theodicy*, trans. Huggard, III, 415, p. 371.
223. Ibid., "Summary of the Controversy Reduced to Formal Arguments," Objection VII, p. 385.
224. Ibid., "Answer to Objection VII," p. 386. See also J. Bouveresse, "Leibniz et le problème de la 'science moyenne,'" *Revue internationale de Philosophie*, 48, no. 188 (1994): 115.
225. For example, Pascal in the *Pensées*, who uses Montaigne's skepticism against Descartes' rationalism: "I cannot forgive Descartes."
226. See André Robinet, "Leibniz: La Renaissance et l'age classique," in *Leibniz et la Renaissance, Studia Leibnitiana, Supplementa XXIII*, ed. A. Heinekamp (Wiesbaden, 1983), pp. 12ff.
227. Leibniz, *Theodicy*, trans. Huggard, III, 404, p. 365.
228. Then section 404 would have reinforced sections 175–178, in which Hobbesianism, Spinozism, and Cartesianism are found morally objectionable. See Robinet, "Leibniz: La Renaissance et l'age classique," pp. 26–27, 36.
229. See Catherine Wilson, *Leibniz' Metaphysics: A Comparative and Historical Study* (Princeton, 1989), pp. 296ff.
230. It was Plato who insisted that unworthy tales about the gods are morally ruinous and are used by mortals to excuse wrongdoing; see *Laws* I, 636d, in *Collected Dialogues*, p. 1237.
231. A Platonic objection—which Leibniz as demi-Platonist might have heeded. For a different view of Leibniz' use of Valla, see Nancy S. Streuver, *Theory as Practice: Ethical Inquiry in the Renaissance* (Chicago, 1992), pp. 132–133.
232. Leibniz, letter to Morrell (1698), in *Textes inédits*, I, 137–138.
233. Ibid., p. 138.
234. Ibid.
235. Leibniz, *Theodicy*, trans. Huggard, II, 145, p. 214.
236. It is not obvious, however, that Leibniz' difficulties arise from aestheticism—

despite Loemker's claim that "the aesthetic character of Leibniz' ethics" is revealed by "his principles of the best possible and his ideal harmony." ("The Ethical Import of the Leibnizian System," in *The Philosophy of Leibniz and the Modern World*, ed. Ivor le Clerc [Nashville, 1973], pp. 207ff.) While this objection may be valid with respect to "harmony," it is not obvious that it has much bearing on "the best."

4. *Justice as Love and Benevolence*

1. Leibniz, letter to Magliabechi (1697), in Acad. Ed. 1, 14, 520.
2. Most of these are catalogued in Grua, *La justice humaine selon Leibniz*, pp. 168–180.
3. Leibniz, "Discourse on Metaphysics," prop. 1, in Loemker, 2nd ed., p. 305.
4. Leibniz, *Principles of Nature and Grace*, in Latta, prop. 17, p. 422 (inter alia).
5. Leibniz, "Meditation on the Common Concept of Justice," in Riley, pp. 58–59.
6. 1 Corinthians 13:13 (KJV).
7. John 13:34 (KJV).
8. John 13:34, 8:7, 1:17; for Deuteronomy, see 22:22–24.
9. Leibniz, letter to Andreas Morrell (1697), in Acad. Ed. 1, 14, 254–255.
10. It is only in Christ's reformulation of the Commandments that the injunction to "love thy neighbor as thyself" appears (Matthew 22:39); the version of the Commandments in Exodus and Deuteronomy is not explicit on this point.
11. Leibniz, *Theodicy*, trans. Huggard, "Preface," pp. 50–51.
12. Deuteronomy 22:22–24 (KJV).
13. John 13.
14. Leibniz, *Theodicy*, trans. Huggard, "Preface," pp. 50ff.
15. Shakespeare, *The Merchant of Venice*, Act IV, sc. 1, 184ff., 379.
16. Shakespeare, *Love's Labour's Lost*, Act IV, sc. iii, 364–365.
17. Cited in Sève, *Leibniz et l'école moderne du droit naturel*, p. 107 n. 176.
18. Placcius, *Sittenlehre*, cited in Schneider, *Justitia Universalis*, pp. 316–317.
19. Ibid.
20. Leibniz, *Codex Iuris Gentium* (Praefatio), pt. xi; English translation in Riley, p. 171.
21. See especially Louis Cognet, *Le crépuscule des mystiques: le conflit Fénelon-Bossuet* (Paris, 1958), passim.
22. Fénelon, *Explication des maximes des saints*, ed. Albert Cherel (Paris, 1911), pp. 118–130. The "happy loss" passage is from Fénelon's "Bonheur de l'ame," in *Oeuvres de Fénelon* (Paris, 1835), I, 330.
23. Grua, *Jurisprudence universelle*, pp. 26ff. Not altogether convincing is the claim of Gregory Brown in "Leibniz's moral philosophy" that the notion of *caritas sapientis* is an effort to mediate between the "egoistic psychology of Hobbes" and the "altruism" of Grotius' "natural sociability" (Cambridge Companion to Leibniz, ed. Jolley, p. 426). Even if this was Leibniz' object at the time of the

Nova Methodus (1667), he was hardly attempting to save Hobbism in his mature writings.

24. As rethought by Augustine and Plotinus.

25. See above all Jeanne-Lydie Goré, *L'iteneraire de Fénelon* (Paris, 1957), pp. 33ff.

26. Ibid., pp. 454ff.

27. Cognet, *Le crépuscule des mystiques*, passim.

28. Fénelon, *Maximes des saints*, ed. Cherel, pp. 118–130.

29. Bossuet, "Avertissement" to *Quatre écrits sur les maximes des saints*, in Michel Ter-estchenko, "La volonté deracinée dans la doctrine de Fénelon du pur amour," *Les études philosophiques* (Paris, 1992), no. 2, p. 170.

30. Henri Gouhier, *Fénelon philosophe* (Paris, 1977), pp. 79ff. (a magisterial study of Fénelon as philosopher).

31. See Patrick Riley, "Introduction" to Bossuet, *Politics Drawn from the Very Words of Holy Scripture* (Cambridge, 1990), pp. vii ff.

32. Fénelon, "Sur le pur amour," in *Oeuvres* (1835 ed.), I, 307–309.

33. Ibid., p. 309.

34. Pascal, *Pensées*, no. 792 (Brunschvicg numbering), trans. Trotter, pp. 326–327.

35. Cicero, *De Amicitia*, v: "We believe then that one must seek after friendship not through hope for the advantages which one will draw from it, but because the fruit of friendship is in friendship itself" (Fénelon's version in "Sur le pur amour," in *Oeuvres*, 1835 ed., I, 307).

36. See above all Rousseau's tale of the Spartan mother with a civic *volonté générale* at the beginning of *Émile* (Foxley ed., p. 7).

37. Fénelon "Sur le pur amour," in *Oeuvres* (1835 ed.), I, 308 (on Plato's *Symposium*).

38. See Hink Hilenaar, *Fénelon and the Jesuits* (The Hague, 1967), pp. 40–51.

39. Hobbes, *Leviathan*, ed. Oakeshott, ch. 6, p. 38.

40. Bossuet, "Avertissement" to *Quatre écrits*, in Terestchenko, "La volonté deracinée," p. 170.

41. Fénelon, *Maximes des saints*, ed. Cherel, pp. 118–130.

42. Fénelon, "Bonheur de l'âme," in *Oeuvres* (1835 ed.), I, 330.

43. Leibniz, *Theodicy*, trans. Huggard, "Preface," p. 23.

44. Fénelon, *Télémaque, fils d'Ulysse* (Paris, 1922), "Introduction" by Albert Cahen (passim).

45. Fénelon "Bonheur de l'âme," in *Oeuvres* (1835 ed.), I, 331.

46. For example, in Leibniz, "Felicity" (c. 1694–1698), in Riley, pp. 82–84.

47. Fénelon, *Réfutation du systeme du Père Malebranche*, in *Oeuvres* (1835 ed.), II, 284.

48. Leibniz, *Principles of Nature and Grace*, prop. 7, in Latta, p. 415.

49. Cf. Aristotle, *Nicomachean Ethics*, 1178b ff.

50. Malebranche, *Méditations chrétiennes et métaphysiques*, in *Oeuvres complètes*, ed. Robinet, XI, 73.

51. Fénelon, "Bonheur de l'âme," in *Oeuvres* (1835 ed.), I, 321.

52. Aristotle, *Nicomachean Ethics*, 1178b.

53. Malebranche, *Treatise on Nature and Grace,* ed. and trans. Riley, discourse I, pt. I, sec. iii, pp. 112–113.
54. Plato, *Republic,* bk. VII, 526b, in *Collected Dialogues,* pp. 758–759. The word "unsuitable" is at 526e.
55. Perhaps this is why Fénelon speaks so much of God and so little of Christ.
56. Fénelon, letter to Mme. de Maintenon, in *Correspondance de Fénelon,* ed. J. Orcibal (Geneva, 1975–), II, 254–255.
57. See Donald Rutherford, "Metaphysics: The Late Period," in *Cambridge Companion to Leibniz,* ed. Jolley, pp. 138ff.
58. Fénelon, "Bonheur de l'âme," in *Oeuvres* (1835 ed.), I, 331.
59. Ibid., p. 329.
60. Leibniz, letter to Electress Sophie (1697), in Acad. Ed. I, 14, 53–60.
61. Fénelon, cited in Goré, *L'itenéraire de Fénelon,* II, 178.
62. Leibniz, cited in Naert, *Leibniz et la querelle du pur amour,* p. 98.
63. On Fénelon's utopia of Bétique, see *Telemachus,* ed. Riley, bk. VII, pp. 108–114.
64. Ibid., bk. IX, p. 147.
65. Leibniz, poem to Mlle. de Scudery, in Klopp VI, 177.
66. Bossuet, "Avertissement" to *Quatre écrits,* in Terestchenko, "La volonté deracinée," p. 170.
67. See Bossuet, *Politics from Scripture,* ed. Riley, pp. xxv ff.
68. Thomas Aquinas, *Summa contra Gentiles,* III, 25.
69. Leibniz, "Aux maximes et pensées diverses von Marquise de Sable und Abbé D'Ailly," in *Voraus Edition zur Reihe VI* of Leibniz' *Philosophischen Schriften,* ed. H. Schepers et al., Faszikel 9 (Münster, 1990), p. 2191. Also in Grua, *Textes inédits,* II, 575.
70. Leibniz, letter to Coste (1712), in Ger. III, 428.
71. Leibniz, letter to Electress Sophie (1697), Acad. Ed. I, 14, 56ff.
72. Cf. Leibniz' letter to Andreas Morrell (December 1696), in *Textes inédits,* I, 104: "I do not know whether you have read the books of Father Spee, S.J., who was an excellent man. . . . There are such fine and profound thoughts which are at the same time so well formulated to touch even the popular mind (caught up in the world) that I was charmed by it [the *Güldenes Tugendbuch*]. Above all he recognized and recommended this great secret of the true love of God."
73. Leibniz, letter to Electress Sophie (1697), in Acad. Ed., I, 14, 59–60.
74. Leibniz, translation of Spee's *Güldenes Tugendbuch,* in Acad. Ed. I, 14, 891ff.
75. Ibid.
76. See Leibniz' letter to Morrell (December 1696), in *Textes inédits,* I, 104–105: "The Elector [of Mainz] was still a canon in Würzburg when Father Spee told him these things [about witchcraft trials], but he was so touched by them that as soon as he became Bishop [of Mainz] he caused these proceedings to be terminated."
77. Leibniz, letter to Electress Sophie (1697), in Acad. Ed. I, 14, 70ff.
78. Ibid.

79. Leibniz, notes on Cudworth (1704), in *Textes inédits*, I, 239: "Plato Hobbesianam doctrinam eleganter exhibet, de. rep. lib. 2 [Plato offers an elegant exposition of 'Hobbesian' doctrine (in) *The Republic*, Book 2]."

80. Leibniz, letter to Andreas Morrell (October 1697), in Acad. Ed. I, 14, 254–255 (also in *Textes inédits*, I, 114–115). For the primacy of charity over "dead" faith, see also Leibniz' letter (1695) to Herzogin Benedikte, Acad. Ed. I, 11, 350: "We are in the state of salvation when we have living faith accompanied by charity."

81. Leibniz, letter to Andreas Morrell (September 1698), in *Textes inédits*, I, 137.

82. Ibid.

83. Tertullian, *De praescriptiones heraeticorum*, ch. VII, cited in *Alexander to Constantine*, ed. Ernest Barker (Oxford, 1955), pp. 448–449.

84. 1 Corinthians 1 (KJV).

85. Sève, *Leibniz et l'école moderne du droit naturel*, pp. 106–107.

86. Dante, *Paradiso*, canto VI, cited by A. P. d'Entrèves in *Natural Law* (London, 1951), ch. 1.

87. Leibniz, to the Abbot of Loccum (c. 1694), in *Textes inédits*, I, 87. According to Grua (ibid., p. 85), Thomasius had urged that "the essence of man (as of God) is not thought but love."

88. On this point see Judith N. Shklar's remarkable *Freedom and Independence: The Political Ideas of Hegel's Phenomenology of Mind* (Cambridge, 1979), "Topography of the *Phenomenology*."

89. Sève, *Leibniz et l'école moderne du droit naturel*, pp. 105ff.

90. Leibniz, *Opinion on Pufendorf*, in Riley, p. 72.

91. Ibid., p. 71.

92. Thomas Aquinas, *Summa Theologica*, II-II, Q26, art. 6, reply to Objection 2.

93. To be sure, for Leibniz Christ was "wisely charitable"; but he never uses the Last Supper as an instance of wise love.

94. J. S. Bach, text of the cantata, "Baumherziges Herze der ewigen Liebe," BWV 185 (Weimar, 1714).

95. Leibniz, letter to Queen Sophie-Charlotte (1702), cited in Grua, *Jurisprudence universelle*, p. 212 (see also Ger. VI, 489, 495, 503).

96. Leibniz, letter to Mme. de Brinon (May 1691), F de C I, 216 (also in Acad. Ed. I, 6, 198).

97. Leibniz, letter to Arnauld (1690), cited in Grua, *Jurisprudence universelle*, pp. 214–215. See also Yvon Belaval, *Études leibniziennes* (Paris, 1976), pp. 44–45: "The originality of Leibniz consists in this conciliatory inventiveness. . . . In defining justice as *caritas sapientis* he unites, in a new way, through love, the justice of the understanding and the justice of the will."

98. Leibniz, *De Justitia et Novo Codice*, in *Textes inédits*, II, 621–622.

99. Leibniz, *Monadology*, in Latta, props. 1ff., pp. 217ff.

100. Leibniz, *Memoir for Enlightened Persons of Good Intention*, in Riley, pp. 105–106.

101. Leibniz, *De Tribus Juris Naturae et Gentium Gradibus*, in Mollat, p. 13.

102. Leibniz, "Sur la générosité," in *Lettres et opuscules inédits de Leibniz,* ed. A. Foucher de Careil (Paris, 1859), pp. 170–172.

103. Ibid., p. 171.

104. 1 Corinthians 12:14–24 (KJV).

105. Leibniz, letter to Queen Sophie-Charlotte (1702), cited in Grua, *Jurisprudence universelle,* p. 212 (see also Ger VI, 489, 495, 503).

106. On the notion of "canceling and preserving" in Hegel, see George A. Kelly's brilliant *Idealism, Politics, and History: Sources of Hegelian Thought* (Cambridge, 1969), p. 311.

107. Aristotle, *Politics,* bk. III (Ross ed.).

108. Dante, cited in d'Entrèves, *Natural Law,* ch. 1.

109. A. P. d'Entrèves, *Dante politico e altri saggi* (Turin, 1955), pp. 18ff.

110. Bentham, *Principles of Morals and Legislation* (London, 1970), ch. 1, p. 11: "Nature has placed mankind under the governance of two sovereign masters, pain and pleasure." Bentham adds that pain and pleasure govern "all we do."

111. Sève, *Leibniz et l'école moderne du droit naturel,* pp. 223–224.

112. Leibniz, "Sur la générosité," in *Lettres et opuscules inédits* de Leibniz, ed. Foucher de Careil, pp. 170–172 (inter alia).

113. Bentham, *Principles of Morals and Legislation,* ch. 4, pp. 38ff.

114. Leibniz, letter to Mme. de Brinon (1696), F de C I, 216.

115. Bentham, *Principles of Morals and Legislation,* ch. 5, pp. 42ff.

116. Leibniz, "Observations on King's 'The Origin of Evil,'" in *Theodicy,* trans. Huggard, sec. 17, p. 422.

117. Rawls, *A Theory of Justice,* pp. 29ff.

118. Ibid., p. 310, n. 38; Albert Heinekamp, "Das Glück als Höchstes Gut in Leibniz' Philosophie," in *The Leibniz Renaissance* (Florence, 1989), pp. 99ff., esp. pp. 119–120.

119. J. S. Mill, *On Liberty,* in *The Philosophy of John Stuart Mill,* ed. M. Cohen (New York, 1961), p. 198.

120. J. S. Mill, *Utilitarianism,* in *The Philosophy Of Mill,* ed. Cohen, ch. 2, pp. 332–333.

121. Mill, *On Liberty,* ed. Cohen, p. 233.

122. Shakespeare, *Troilus and Cressida,* Act I, sc. iii, 109–110.

123. Sève, *Leibniz et l'école moderne du droit naturel,* p. 223. In trying to keep love and wisdom in equilibrium, Leibniz is reminiscent of Shakespeare's *Measure for Measure,* Act *III,* sc. ii, 163–164: "Love talks with better knowledge, and knowledge with dearer love." The Duke of Vienna says this precisely when accused of unjust rule.

124. Leibniz, letter to Bossuet (1698), F de C II, 252.

125. Augustine, *De Libero Arbitrio* II, 19, 50–II, 20, 54, cited in R. Meagher, *Augustine: An Introduction* (New York, 1978), pp. 175–177.

126. Augustine, *De Doctrina Christiana* I, 22, 20–23 (also cited in Meagher, *Augustine: An Introduction,* p. 187).

127. Sève, *Leibniz et l'école moderne du droit naturel,* p. 224ff.
128. See Patrick Riley, *Kant's Political Philosophy* (Totowa, 1983), pp. 18–20.
129. Augustine, *De Doctrina Christiana,* I, 22, 20–23.
130. Kant, *Critique of Practical Reason,* trans. Beck, pp. 126ff.
131. Sève, *Leibniz et l'école moderne du droit naturel,* passim.
132. Leibniz, cited in Grua, *La justice humaine selon Leibniz,* p. 53.
133. Ibid.
134. Leibniz, letter to Coste (1706), in Ger. III, 384. In view of the conclusive reasons for *not* viewing Leibniz as a utilitarian, it is difficult to accept "Leibniz's utilitarianism" as advocated by Joachim Hruschka in "The Greatest Happiness Principle and Other Early German Anticipations of Utilitarian Theory," *Utilitas,* 3, no. 2 (November 1991): 165ff. Hruschka urges that "Bentham's adherent, the Glasgow advocate James Reddie," published "various formulations" of the "greatest happiness principle" worked out before Bentham, and that Reddie cited (as anticipating Bentham) Leibniz' *Observationes de Principio Juris,* in which there is talk of the "greatest good." But the mere fact that a Benthamite *claimed* Leibniz' authority settles nothing.

   To be sure, Leibniz says in the *Observationes* that "to act in accordance with supreme reason is to act in such a manner that the greatest quantity of good available is obtained for the greatest multitude possible and that as much felicity is diffused as the reason of things permits." But even if Leibniz' *Observationes* were "available in Britain" (as Hruschka claims), Leibniz does not thereby become a proto-Benthamite: for Leibniz our happiness or felicity is a "feeling of perfection" which comes from appreciating degrees of perfection in "others" (God, one's neighbor, and so on). That "feeling of perfection" is love, and justice is "wise love" *(caritas sapientis)* which gives rise to happiness. This is Christianized Platonism, or neo-Augustianism, not incipient Benthamism. Love as a "feeling of perfection" which draws us to God and to fellow-men has no relation to Bentham: if "pushpin is as good as poetry," then nothing (not even God) has any *intrinsic* weight. "The reason of things"—Leibniz' concluding phrase, which Hruschka overlooks—can only "bear" felicity which flows from love of perfection; Benthamism by contrast can "bear" any pleasure whatever that is not outweighed by a more considerable pain.

   Even in the *Observationes* Leibniz says flatly that the principle of right or justice is *caritas sapientis,* and therefore Hruschka's notion that Leibniz equates natural rights/law with the "greatest happiness" *simpliciter* is simply wrong. (In fact, Leibniz' few lines about "happiness" and "felicity"—perfectly Augustinian notions, or even Aristotelian—are imbedded in a surrounding text which argues much more fully for Roman law, Cicero, God's perfection, Christian charity, and "eternal verity": *not* a collection of Benthamite ideas, in short.
135. Hobbes, *The Elements of Law,* ed. F. Tönnies (Cambridge, 1928), p. 34.
136. Pascal, *Pensées,* trans. Trotter, p. 83: "We see neither justice nor injustice which

does not change its nature with change of climate. . . . A strange justice that is bounded by a river! Truth on this side of the Pyrenees, error on the other."

137. Locke, *Two Treatises of Government*, ed. P. Laslett (Cambridge, 1970), "First Treatise," pts. 41–42, pp. 187–188. The celebrated "Second Treatise" is silent on this point.

138. Hobbes, *Leviathan*, ed. Oakeshott, ch. 5, p. 30.

139. Hobbes, *Elements of Law*, ed. F. Tönnies, p. 34.

140. Ibid.

141. Ibid.

142. Lucian, *Philosophies for Sale*, in *Selected Satires of Lucian*, ed. L. Casson (Chicago, 1962), pp. 322–323, in which Socrates is made to say, "I'm the best person in the world to leave with handsome young boys. I don't love their bodies—it's the soul I consider beautiful."

143. Hobbes, *Leviathan*, ed. Oakeshott, ch. 13, p. 83.

144. Locke, *Two Treatises*, ed. Laslett, pp. 187–188.

145. Ibid., "Second Treatise," pts. 28ff., p. 306ff.

146. Pascal, *Pensées*, no. 792 (Brunschvicg numbering), trans. Trotter, pp. 326–327.

147. Ibid.

148. Ibid., *Pensées*, nos. 483ff. (Brunschvicg numbering), trans. Trotter, pp. 258ff. For an interpretation see Riley, *The General Will before Rousseau*, pp. 14–24.

149. Pascal, *Pensées*, no. 206 (Brunschvicg numbering), trans. Trotter, p. 211.

150. See especially Sellier, *Pascal et S. Augustin*, passim. See also Jean LaPorte, *La doctrine de Port-Royal: Les vérités sur la grâce* (Paris, 1923), pp. 248ff.

151. Leibniz, letter to Thomas Burnett (1696–97), in Ger. III, 196.

152. Cited in Sellier, *Pascal et S. Augustin*, p. 217.

153. Leibniz, *Caesarinus Fürstenerius*, ch. XI, in Acad. Ed. IV, 2, pp. 58f.; in Riley, p. 119.

154. Shakespeare, *Timon of Athens*, Act IV, sc. iii, 300–301.

155. Leibniz, for the *Journal des Sçavans* (1696), in Acad. Ed. I, 13, 232 (sent to Étienne de Chauvin).

156. Pascal, *Pensées*, no. 481 (Brunschvicg numbering), trans. Trotter, p. 257.

157. See particularly Utermöhlen, "Leibniz im brieflichen Gespräch über Russland," passim.

158. Leibniz, *Monadology*, in Latta, props. 85ff., p. 267ff. (inter alia).

159. Pascal, *Pensées*, nos. 481ff. (Brunschvicg numbering), trans. Trotter, pp. 257ff.

160. Pascal, *Provincial Letters*, trans. T. McCrie, in *Great Books: Pascal*, letter XI, pp. 86ff.

161. Leibniz, letter to Des Bosses, in Ger. II, 435–437, 450–452.

162. Sellier, *Pascal et S. Augustin*, passim.

163. This is probably why Leibniz stresses charity so much in his letters to Bossuet's colleague, Mme. de Brinon—for example, the one of May 1691, F de C I, 216.

164. For this correspondence see F de C II, passim (which includes Bossuet's letters to Leibniz).

165. Bossuet, *Cinquième avertissement aux protestants*, in *Oeuvres* (Paris, 1841), IV, 403. Bossuet usually traces his antirationalism to St. Paul: "What have the philosophers gained . . . with their reasonings so artfully arranged? . . . Is it not with reason that St. Paul cries, 'Where is the wise?' " (*Histoire universelle*, in *Oeuvres*, I, 239).

166. 1 Corinthians 13 (KJV).

167. Bossuet, *Politique tirée des propres paroles de l'Écriture Sainte*, ed. J. le Brun (Geneva, 1967), excerpts from Bossuet's 1679 manuscript, p. 455. (English translation by Patrick Riley: Bossuet, *Politics Drawn from the Very Words of Holy Scripture* [Cambridge, 1990], passim.)

168. Ibid. *(Politique)*, 1679 ms., p. 455.

169. Ibid., pp. 1–2.

170. Ibid., p. 2.

171. Cited in J. Truchet, *La Politique de Bossuet* (Paris, 1966), pp. 29–30.

172. Ibid., p. 30.

173. Leibniz, letter to Mme. de Brinon (1696–97), in Klopp VII, 296.

174. Bossuet, "La charité fraternelle," in *Pensées chrétiennes et morales*, in *Oeuvres* (1841 ed.), IV, 769.

175. Riley, "Introduction" to *Leibniz: Political Writings*, pp. 24–26.

176. Bossuet, *Histoire des variations des églises protestantes*, in *Oeuvres* (1841 ed.), IV, 47. This is often viewed as Bossuet's finest single work.

177. Bossuet, *Histoire universelle*, p. 238.

178. Ibid., pp. 248–249.

179. Le Brun's table of scriptural citations, appended to his edition of Bossuet's *Politique*, shows no reference whatever to 1 Corinthians 13, but shows twenty-two references to Romans 13.

180. On Cartesian doubt, see Étienne Gilson, *Descartes, Discours de la méthode, texte et commentaire* (Paris, 1925), pp. 79ff.

181. "Judas drinking the blood that Jesus Christ exhaled; the ruses of Loyola, the hatred of Bossuet; the *autodafé*, the terror, the dungeon, the Bastille: that's us." Victor Hugo, *La Légende des siècles: Voix basses dans les ténèbres*, cited in Truchet, *Politique de Bossuet*, p. 9.

182. Bossuet, *Histoire universelle*, cited in Thérèse Goyet, *L'Humanisme de Bossuet* (Paris, 1965), II, 300–301. (But Goyet exaggerates Bossuet's concern for Christian charity as well as his devotion to Plato and Aristotle.)

183. See, for example, Bossuet, *Politique*, bk. X, art. VI, prop. 8 (on Antiochus); Riley trans., *Politics*, pp. 402–403.

184. Bossuet, *Politique*, ed. Le Brun, p. 392.

185. To recall the language of Michael Oakeshott, who also called Augustine and Montaigne "the two greatest men who have ever lived" (letter to the author, 1986).

186. Bossuet, *Oraison funèbre de Michel Le Tellier* (1686), in Truchet, *Politique de Bossuet,* pp. 183–184.

187. See Naert, *Leibniz et la querelle du pur amour,* p. 40.

188. Ibid., p. 41.

189. Ibid., p. 40ff.

190. Leibniz, letter to Gilbert Burnet [?], March 1697, in *Textes inédits,* I, 106. (At this point Leibniz was incompletely informed about the Bossuet-Fénelon struggle.)

191. Leibniz, letter to Nicaise (August 1697), cited in Naert, *Leibniz et la querelle du pur amour,* pp. 64–65.

192. Ibid.

193. Leibniz, notes on "Extrait d'un journal écrit en anglais en voyage, que William Penn, auteur du livre, a fait en Allemagne et en Hollande en compagnie de Robert Barclay et de quelques autres Trembleurs, l'an 1677," in *Textes inédits,* I, 88ff.

194. Ibid., pp. 90–91.

195. Ibid., p. 91.

196. Ibid.

197. Ibid., pp. 91–92.

198. Ibid., p. 92.

199. Ibid.

200. Leibniz, *Dialogue sur des sujets de réligion* (1679), in F de C II, 534ff.

201. Ibid., p. 537.

202. For a full treatment of this point see Chapter 2.

203. Leibniz, *Dialogue sur religion,* in F de C II, 538ff.

204. Machiavelli, *Discourses,* bk. I, ch. ix.; here Machiavelli is trying to overcome Augustine's argument (*De Civitate Dei* XIX) that Romulus rose to "bad greatness" through murder, and that Romulus and Remus are morally parallel to Cain and Abel ("the city's walls stained with a brother's blood"). A copy of the *Discourses* was in Leibniz' personal library; see Gerda Utermöhlen, "Die Literatur der Renaissance und des Humanismus in Leibniz' privater Büchersammlung," in *Leibniz et la Renaissance, Studia Leibnitiana, Supplementa XXIII* (Wiesbaden, 1983), p. 225.

205. Leibniz, *Dialogue sur réligion,* in F de C II, p. 541.

206. Ibid.

207. Ibid., p. 542.

208. See, inter alia, Leibniz' letter to Pierre Coste (May 1712), in Ger. III, 428.

209. Malebranche, *Traité de l'amour de Dieu,* ed. E. Roustan (Paris, 1923), pp. 86, 89.

210. Ibid., p. 103; see also the passages from Malebranche's *Première lettre au P. Lamy,* in Roustan's edition of *Traité de l'amour de Dieu,* p. 149. For a fuller treatment of love and charity in Malebranche, see Riley's "Introduction" to *Treatise on Nature and Grace,* pp. 44ff.

211. Leibniz, "Sur l'art de connaître les hommes," in *Lettres et opuscules inédits de Leibniz,* ed. Foucher de Careil, p. 139.

212. Leibniz, letter to Thomas Burnett (December 1705), in Ger. III, 302. Leibniz adds that morality that "demands more practice than precepts."

213. Leibniz, "Observations on King's 'The Origin of Evil,'" in *Theodicy,* trans. Huggard, sec. 17, p. 422.

214. See Robinet, *Malebranche et Leibniz,* passim.

215. Leibniz, *Codex Iuris Gentium* (Praefatio), pts. xii–xiii, in Riley, pp. 171ff.

216. Ibid., pt. xiii, in Riley, p. 173.

217. Ibid., pp. 173–174.

218. Ibid., p. 174.

219. Ibid. For the possible reference to St. James, see Latta, p. 295, n. 54.

220. Leibniz, *Codex Iuris Gentium* (Praefatio), pt. xv, in Riley, pp. 174–175.

221. Hobbes, *Leviathan,* ed. Oakeshott, ch. 47, p. 457.

222. See, inter alia, J. Morley, *Voltaire* (London, 1919), pp. 320ff. (for Voltaire's treatment of Rome).

223. Augustine, *De Civitate Dei,* bks. XIV–XV, XIX.

224. Dante, *De Monarchia,* bk. II, 22–24.

225. Leibniz, "Meditation on the Common Concept of Justice," in Riley, pp. 54, 60.

226. Ibid., in Riley, pp. 53–54.

227. Ibid., p. 54.

228. Ibid.

229. Ibid.

230. Ibid., p. 55.

231. Ibid.

232. Ibid.

233. Ibid., pp. 55–56.

234. See especially Leibniz, *Theodicy,* trans. Huggard, II, 175–178, pp. 236ff.

235. Leibniz, "Meditation on the Common Concept of Justice," in Riley, p. 56.

236. See, inter alia, Leibniz, "Définitions" (c. 1701–1705), in *Textes inédits,* II, 666: "Justice is a constant will to act in such a way that no one has any reason to complain of us." Cf. Leibniz, "La place d'autrui," ibid., II, 699ff.

237. Plato, *Republic,* bks. IV–VII, in *Collected Dialogues,* pp. 661ff.

238. Hobbes, *Leviathan,* ed. Oakeshott, ch. 15, p. 94.

239. Leibniz, letter to Kettwig (November 1695), in *Textes inédits,* II, 653. Leibniz cites his own *Codex Iuris Gentium,* published two years earlier, and repeats the claim that justice "*(mia definitione) sit caritas sapientis.*"

240. Sève, *Leibniz: Le droit de la raison,* pp. 85ff. (Original Latin text of *An jus naturae aeternum* in *Textes inédits,* II, 637–639.)

241. Sève, *Leibniz: Le droit de la raison,* pp. 85ff.

242. Ibid., pp. 85–86. See also Cicero, *De Officiis* I, 10.

243. Sève, *Leibniz: Le droit de la raison,* p. 88. Here Sève gives the wrong Leibniz title:

he says that he is citing Leibniz' *De Tribus Juris Praeceptis sive Gradibus,* but actually quotes Leibniz' *De Jure et Justitia* (from *Textes inédits,* II, 618).

244. Leibniz, cited in *Voraus Edition,* p. 42; also cited in Robinet, *Leibniz: Le meilleur des mondes par la balance de l'Europe,* p. 150.

245. Hervé Barreau, "Leibniz, précurseur de la conception universelle des droits de l'homme," in *Leibniz und Europa: VI Internationaler Leibniz-Kongress,* Vorträge I Teil, p. 45.

246. Thomas Gil, "Einheit und Vielfalt in Leibnizens Gerechtigkeitstheorie und Wissenschaftskonzeption," in *Leibniz und Europa,* p. 257.

247. Robinet, *Leibniz: Le meilleur des mondes,* pp. 118–119.

248. Ibid.

249. Emily Grossholz, "Leibniz and the Two Labyrinths," in *Leibniz and Adam,* p. 76. See also François Duchesneau, *Leibniz et la méthode de la science* (Paris, 1993), pp. 336ff. Cf. Leibniz' letter (1691) to Thévenot, Acad. Ed. I, 7, 354: "When one has come *ad series,* one has guarantees of the truth, and the case is won."

250. Hume, *Treatise of Human Nature, Hume: Theory of Politics,* ed. F. Watkins (Edinburgh, 1951), bk. III, i ("Moral Distinctions Not Derived from Reason").

251. Leibniz, "Définitions," in *Textes inédits,* II, 666–667.

252. Augustine, *De Civitate Dei,* bk. XIX, 13–15 (also cited in Meagher, *Augustine: An Introduction,* p. 170).

253. Leibniz, *De Religione Magnorum Virorum,* in *Textes inédits,* I, 39.

254. Augustine, *De Civitate Dei,* bk. XV.

255. Hobbes, *Leviathan,* ed. Oakeshott, chs. 13–15, 26–28, pp. 172ff.

256. Schneewind, "Kant and Natural Law Ethics," pp. 54ff.

257. Leibniz, *Juris et aequi elementa,* cited in Latta, pp. 284–285 (from Mollat p. 30).

258. Leibniz, letter to Landgraf Ernst von Hessen-Rheinfels (1686), in Rommel II, p. 207; treated in Grua, *La justice humaine selon Leibniz,* p. 216.

259. Hegel, *Philosophy of History,* trans. J. Sibree (New York, 1956), p. 379 (for the contemptuous phrase, *opera operata*).

260. Sève, *Leibniz: Le droit de la raison,* p. 85.

261. Michael Oakeshott, "The Voice of Poetry in the Conversation of Mankind," in his *Rationalism in Politics* (London, 1962), pp. 197ff.

262. Leibniz, in Acad. Ed. VI, 1, 433–435.

263. Leibniz, "Felicity," in Riley, pp. 82–84 (original French text in *Textes inédits,* II, 579ff.).

264. Leibniz, "La véritable piété," in *Textes inédits,* II, 499–500.

265. Ibid., p. 500.

266. Jean Baruzi, "Du 'Discours de Métaphysique' à la Théodicée," *Révue philosophique de la France et de l'étranger,* 10, no. 12 (1946): 390–409. Baruzi's views are well treated by Agustin Andreu Rodrigo in *Leibniz, das europäische Christentum und die Theodizee,* in *Leibniz und Europa: VI Internationaler Leibniz-Kongress,* Vorträge I Teil, pp. 633ff.

5. Practical Justice in the Human Forum

1. See, inter alia, Leibniz, *Tria Praecepta* (c. 1677–78), in *Textes inédits*, II, 616–617. See also Leibniz, *Juris Naturalis Principia* (after 1695), in ibid., II, 639–641.
2. Leibniz, *Codex Iuris Gentium* (Praefatio), pt. xii, in Riley, p. 172.
3. Ibid.
4. Ibid., pts. xii–xiii, pp. 172–174.
5. Leibniz, *NE* IV, viii, pt. 9.
6. Leibniz, *Elementa Juris Perpetui* (1695–1697), in *Scritti politici e di diritto naturale*, ed. Vittorio Mathieu, 2nd enl. ed. (Turin, 1965), pp. 192ff.
7. Ibid. Cf. Leibniz' letter to Christian Wolff (February 1705): "Our good, the general good *(bonum publicum)*, and the glory of God are not to be distinguished as means and ends, but as parts and whole, and it is the same thing to seek our true good, or to serve the general good and God" (cited in Klaus Jacobi, "Zur Konzeption der praktischen Philosophie der Leibniz," *Studia Leibnitiana, Supplementa XIV* [Wiesbaden, 1975], pp. 152–153).
8. Ibid., p. 196.
9. Leibniz, "Suite des réflexions sur le livre intitulé *Loix civiles dans leur ordre naturel*" (by Jean Domat), in *Textes inédits*, II, 652.
10. Leibniz, *Theodicy*, trans. Huggard, "Preface," pp. 49ff.
11. Leibniz, *Elementa Juris Perpetui*, in *Scritti*, ed. Mathieu, p. 197.
12. Thomas Aquinas, *Summa Theologica*, II-II, Q90–97.
13. Leibniz, *Elementa Juris Perpetui*, in *Scritti*, ed. Mathieu, pp. 195–197.
14. Leibniz, "Suite des réflexions," in *Textes inédits*, II, 649–652. For the encomium of Roman law, see Leibniz' letter to Kestner, in Dutens IV, pt. 3, pp. 267ff. (written in July 1716).
15. Leibniz, *Portrait of the Prince*, in Riley, p. 98. (Leibniz' authorship of this work has recently been questioned—but he says the same thing in many other writings.)
16. Grua, *La justice humaine selon Leibniz*, p. 121.
17. Leibniz, *De Tribus Juris Naturae*, in Mollat, p. 14.
18. Leibniz, *Elements of Natural Law*, in Leibniz, *Scritti politici e di diritto naturale*, ed. Mathieu, p. 127.
19. Leibniz, *Codex Iuris Gentium* (Praefatio), pts. xi–xii, in Riley, pp. 171ff.
20. Leibniz, *Extensive Remarks on Jurisprudence*, in Acad. Ed. IV, 1, 572.
21. Leibniz, "Meditation on the Common Concept of Justice," in Riley, p. 64.
22. Kant, *The Metaphysical Elements of Justice [Rechtslehre]*, Introduction, "Division of the Metaphysics of Morals in General," pt. II (in *Political Writings*, ed. H. Reiss [Cambridge, 1970]).
23. Leibniz, "Meditation on the Common Concept of Justice," p. 70.
24. Leibniz, *Notes on Social Life*, "The Place of Others," in *Textes inédits*, II, 699–701.
25. Leibniz, "Réflexions sur l'art de connaître les hommes," in *Lettres et opuscules inédits de Leibniz*, ed. Foucher de Careil, pp. 149–150.

26. Leibniz, "Analyse de Jean Domat, *Les Loix Civiles dans leur Ordre Naturel*," in *Textes inédits*, II, 648.

27. Russell, *Critical Exposition of the Philosophy of Leibniz*, 2nd ed. (1937), pp. 191ff.

28. On this point, see Chapter 2.

29. Leibniz, letter to Thomas Burnett (1699–1700), in Ger. III, 264.

30. Leibniz, *On Natural Law*, in Loemker II, 705.

31. Burke, *Reflections on the Revolution in France*, VII, 2(a), in *Burke's Politics*, ed. R. Hoffman and P. Levack (New York, 1959), p. 318.

32. Plato, *Republic*, bk. IV, 443d–e, in *Collected Dialogues*, p. 686.

33. Leibniz, letter to Burnett (1699–1700), in Ger. III, 264.

34. See Riley, *Will and Political Legitimacy*, ch. 1, "How Coherent Is the Social Contract Tradition?"

35. Hume, "Of the Original Contract," in *Hume: Theory of Politics*, ed. Watkins, pp. 193–209.

36. Leibniz, *Nova Methodus*, in Dutens IV, iii.

37. Hobbes, *Leviathan*, ed. Oakeshott, ch. 15, p. 94: "Before the names of just and unjust can have place, there must be some coercive power . . . and such power there is none before the erection of a commonwealth . . . where there is no commonwealth, there nothing is unjust."

38. Leibniz, *NE* III, ch. l.

39. Leibniz, letter to Thomas Smith (1695), in Acad. Ed. I, 12, 259. This is certainly one of Leibniz' most insightful comments on the psychological basis of "Hobbism."

40. Not just in sections 219 and 220, but in sections 175–178 and (above all) 404; for the work would have ended with 404 had not Leibniz moved his story of Tarquin and Jupiter to the end of the book.

41. Leibniz, *Theodicy*, trans. Huggard, II, 219–220, pp. 264–265.

42. Ibid.

43. Rousseau, *L'état de guerre*, in *Political Writings*, ed. C. Vaughan (Cambridge, 1915), I, 305–306.

44. Hobbes, *Leviathan*, ed. Oakeshott, ch. 13, p. 82.

45. Leibniz, *Caesarinus Fürstenerius*, ch. XI, in Acad. Ed. IV, 2, pp. 58f.; in Riley, p. 120.

46. Leibniz, letter to Hobbes (July 1670), in Loemker, 2nd ed., p. 106.

47. Shakespeare, *Richard II*, Act II, sc. 1, 50–51.

48. Leibniz, letter to Lambert van Velthuysen (June 1671), in *Studia Leibnitiana*, 22, no. 2 (1990): 151ff. (intro. Albert Heinekamp); quotation at 161.

49. Leibniz, letter from 1670, in Acad. Ed. II, 1, 54.

50. Leibniz, cited in *Voraus Edition*, p. 1385; also cited in Robinet, *Leibniz: le meilleur des mondes*, p. 93.

51. Leibniz, in *Voraus Edition*, p. 1145.

52. Leibniz, *Remarks on Shaftesbury's Characteristics*, in Riley, p. 196.

53. "Ex nihilo nihil fit; si nulla est naturalis justitia, nec erit artificialis." Leibniz, notes on Cudworth, in *Textes inédits*, I, 329.

54. Pascal, *Pensées*, no. 294 (Brunschvicg numbering), trans. Trotter, p. 83. For Pascal as skeptic and Pyrrhonist, see, for example, S. M. Mason, *Montesquieu's Idea of Justice* (The Hague, 1975), p. xii ff.

55. Leibniz, *Observations on the Principle of Justice* (1700), in Dutens IV, iii, 370ff.

56. Locke, *Two Treatises*, ed. Laslett, "Second Treatise," sec. 6.

57. Ibid., secs. 25–34.

58. Leibniz, *Observations* (1700), sec. VI, in Dutens IV, iii, 370ff.

59. Locke, *Two Treatises*, ed. Laslett, "Second Treatise," secs. 73, 118.

60. Leibniz, *Observations* (1700), sec. VII, in Dutens IV, iii, 370ff.

61. Ibid., sec. IX, pp. 370ff.

62. Ibid., sec. XIII, pp. 370ff.

63. Leibniz, *Opinion on the Principles of Pufendorf* (1706), in Riley, sec. IV, p. 70.

64. Ibid.

65. Ibid., p. 71.

66. Ibid.

67. Ibid.

68. Ibid., pp. 71–72; see also Leibniz, "Unvorgreiffliches Bedencken," in *Textes inédits*, I, 432–434. For Leibniz' "global Platonism," see Sève, *Leibniz: Le droit de la raison*, p. 8, n. 1.

69. Leibniz, letter to Coste (July 1711), in Ger. III, 419: "Hobbes est plein de bonnes pensées, mais il a coutume de les outrer." For an interpretation which sees Hobbes as central to Leibniz' thought, see Ursula Goldenbaum, "*Vorwart*" to *Leibniz: Philosophische Schriften und Briefe, 1683–1687* (Berlin, 1992), ix–xxxix. (Goldenbaum is especially good at bringing out Leibniz' early attachment to Hobbes and Spinoza; whether she gives sufficient weight to his hostility to "Hobbism" and "Spinozism" after the 1670s is another matter.)

70. Here one thinks, for example, of Cicero's "constitutionalism" in *De Republica*, bk. II, 39: "A form of government which is an equal mixture of the three good forms is superior to any of them by itself."

71. Leibniz, letter to Burnett (1701), in Ger. III, 277.

72. Leibniz, *Securitas Publica Interna et Externa* (1670–71), II, no. 53, in F de C VI, 225–226.

73. Leibniz, letter to Burnett (1701), in Ger. III, 278.

74. Leibniz, *Grundriss eines Bedenckens von Aufrichtung einer societät in Deutschland* (1671), in Acad. Ed. IV, 1, 530 ff.

75. Ibid., p. 531.

76. Brather, *Leibniz und seine Akademie*, pp. 83ff.

77. Leibniz, *Grundriss*, in Acad. Ed. IV, 1, 531.

78. Ibid., pp. 531–532.

79. Ibid., p. 531. Cf. Leibniz' letter to Antoine Arnauld (November 1671), in Ger. I, 73–74 (written at the same time as the *Grundriss*).

80. Leibniz, *Grundriss*, in Acad. Ed. IV, 1, 532.

81. Leibniz, *Radical Origination of Things*, in Latta, pp. 337ff.

82. Leibniz, *Grundriss*, in Acad. Ed. IV, 1, 532.

83. Leibniz, letter to Wedderkopf (1671), in Loemker I, 226–227.

84. Leibniz, *Grundriss*, in Acad. Ed. IV, 1, 532.

85. Ibid., p. 533.

86. Plato, *Republic*, bk. IV, 443d–e, in *Collected Dialogues*, p. 686.

87. Leibniz, *Grundriss*, in Acad. Ed. IV, 1, 533.

88. Ibid., p. 534.

89. Ibid., p. 535.

90. Ibid., p. 536.

91. Ibid.

92. Plato, *Gorgias*, esp. 523a ff., in *Collected Dialogues*, pp. 303ff.

93. Latta, "Life and Works of Leibniz," in Latta, pp. 14–15.

94. Leibniz, *Grundriss*, in Acad. Ed. IV, 1, 536.

95. Leibniz, letter to Thomas Burnett (1699–1700), in Ger. III, 261.

96. Ibid.

97. Ibid.

98. Bentham, *A Fragment on Government*, ed. F. C. Montague (Oxford, 1891), pp. 131ff.

99. Leibniz, *Memoir for Enlightened Persons of Good Intention*, in Riley, p. 107.

100. Ibid., p. 108.

101. Locke, *Two Treatises*, ed. Laslett, "Second Treatise," sec. 13, pp. 293–294.

102. Leibniz, *De Tribus Juris Naturae*, in Mollat p. 18.

103. Leibniz, in Klopp X, 14.

104. Ibid., pp. 23–26.

105. Leibniz, letter to Count Golofkin (1712), F de C VII, 502ff.

106. Ibid.

107. Ibid.

108. "Whatever triumph one can gain by war, it is much better to oblige than to conquer the earth." Leibniz, poem for Mlle. de Scudery, in Klopp VI, 177.

109. Leibniz, *Lettre sur l'éducation d'un prince*, in Acad. Ed. IV, 3, 542–557.

110. Ibid.

111. M. Oakeshott, "Introduction" to *Leviathan*, p. viii.

112. In the sense that each stage of education must correspond to the appropriate level of psychological development.

113. Leibniz, *Lettre sur l'éducation d'un prince*, in Acad. Ed. IV, 3, 549, 553–554.

114. Leibniz, *Des Controverses*, in Acad. Ed. IV, 3, 211.

115. Leibniz, *Ermahnung an die Deutsche*, in Acad. Ed. IV, 3, 805.

116. Leibniz, letter to Joachim Bouvet (December 1697), in Acad. Ed. I, 14, 830.

117. See especially all F. H. Hinsley, *Sovereignty* (Cambridge, 1963), passim.

118. Leibniz, letter to Arnauld, in Ger. II, 76. Thus Gierke's objection in *Natural Law and the Theory of Society* (Oxford, 1934), p. 137, that Leibniz attained to a conception of the state as a "mere" *persona ficta* (rather than as a corporate "personality") is misconceived: Leibniz' metaphysics and theory of substance could not permit him to view the state as a so-called real personality.

119. See particularly Robinet, *Leibniz: Le meilleur des mondes par la balance de l'Europe*, pp. 251ff.

120. Leibniz, *Entretiens de Philarète et d'Eugene*, in F de C VI, 347.

121. Ibid.

122. Leibniz, *Caesarinus Fürstenerius*, in Acad. Ed. IV, 2, 58; in Riley, p. 118.

123. Ibid.

124. Pufendorf, *De Statu Imperii Germanici* (as treated by Leibniz), discussed in Hans-Peter Schneider, "Leibniz' Gedancken zur Ordnung vom Kirche und Staat," *Studia Leibnitiana, Supplementa IV* (Wiesbaden, 1969), pp. 234–248.

125. Leibniz, *Caesarinus Fürstenerius*, in Acad. Ed. IV, 2, 60; in Riley, p. 119.

126. Leibniz, *Theodicy*, trans. Huggard, II, 175–178, pp. 236–238.

127. Hobbes, *Leviathan*, ed. Oakeshott, ch. 26, pp. 172ff.

128. Leibniz, "Meditation on the Common Concept of Justice," in Riley, p. 50.

129. Leibniz, *NE* IV, vii, pt. 19.

130. Cited in E. Ruck, *Die Leibniz'sche Staatsidee* (Tübingen, 1909), p. 94. (I am grateful to the late Professor Carl Joachim Friedrich of Harvard University for the gift of this rare work in 1969.)

131. Leibniz, letter to Landgraf Ernst of Hessen-Rheinfels (1683), in Riley, pp. 185–186 (original text in Rommel II, 138).

132. Leibniz, letter to Falaideau, in Klopp IX, 143.

133. Ibid.

134. Hobbes, *Leviathan*, ed. Oakeshott, chs. 13–15, pp. 80–105.

135. Patrick Riley, ed. and trans., "Leibniz' 1695 commentary on William Sherlock's *The Case of the Allegiance Due to Sovereign Powers*," *Journal of the History of Philosophy* (July 1973): 319ff.

136. William Sherlock, *The Case of the Allegiance Due to Sovereign Powers* (London, 1691), p. 15.

137. Ibid.

138. Leibniz, letters to Thomas Burnett, in Ger. III, 176, 180.

139. Leibniz, on Sherlock, ed. Riley, in *Journal of the History of Philosophy*, p. 324 (Leibniz' text, p. 335).

140. Ibid., p. 322.

141. Leibniz, letter to Landgraf Ernst von Hessen-Rheinfels, in Rommel, p. 370.

142. Leibniz, *Observations sur le Projet d'une paix perpétuelle*, in F de C IV, 332.

143. Leibniz, on Sherlock, ed. Riley, p. 323.

144. Leibniz, *Opinion on the Principles of Pufendorf*, in Riley, pp. 67–68.

145. Leibniz, notes on Sherlock (1691), in *Textes inédits,* II, 888.
146. Justinian, *Institutes,* bk. IV, sec. vi, 4.
147. Leibniz, "Suite des réflexions sur le livre intitulé *Loix civiles dans leur ordre naturel,*" in *Textes inédits,* II, 649ff.
148. Leibniz, on Sherlock, ed. Riley, p. 332.
149. Ibid., pp. 332–333.
150. Otto von Gierke, *The Development of Political Theory,* trans. B. Freyd (London, 1939), pp. 259ff.
151. Leibniz, "Divisio Societatum," *On Natural Law,* in Riley, p. 80.
152. J. Althusius, *Digest of Political Method,* ed. C. J. Friedrich (Cambridge, Mass., 1932), passim.
153. Shakespeare, *Troilus and Cressida,* Act I, sc. iii, 85–124. For an extraordinary reading of this speech as "Tory" conservatism, see Samuel H. Beer, *British Politics in the Collectivist Age* (New York, 1969), pp. 3–5 (in any event the speech reflects the Renaissance Platonism of the *Timaeus*).

6. The Republic of Christendom

1. *Projet de Leibniz,* in F de C II, 169.
2. Leibniz, *Catholic Demonstrations* (excerpts), in Loemker I, 86–90.
3. Cf. Klopp IX, 182.
4. Leibniz, letters to Bossuet, F de C II, 264–271.
5. Ibid. Leibniz appears to be correct on this point, since (even within the Church) Jansenists were accused of being closet Calvinists and Jesuits of being secret Pelagians (for example by Pascal in the *Provincial Letters*).
6. Leibniz, *Observations on the Abbé de St. Pierre's "Project for Perpetual Peace"* (1715), in Riley, p. 180: "I believe that if there had been Popes [such as Gregory VII] with a great reputation for wisdom and virtue, who had wanted to follow the measures taken at Constance, they could have remedied the abuses [within the Church], prevented the rupture, and sustained or even advanced Christian society."
7. Leibniz, letter to Bossuet, in F de C I, 273.
8. Leibniz, letter to Dutteron (1699), in F de C II, 250ff.
9. Leibniz, letter to Bossuet, in F de C II, 258–259.
10. For Bossuet's charge of "heresy," see his letter to Paul Péllisson (27 December 1692), cited in Jacques le Brun, "Le concept d'hérésie à la fin du XVII siècle: la controverse Leibniz-Bossuet," in *Studia Leibnitiana, Supplementa XIV* (Wiesbaden, 1975), pp. 91ff., esp. p. 99.
11. Hobbes, *Leviathan,* ed. Oakeshott, bk. IV (passim).
12. Leibniz, letters to des Bosses, in Loemker II, 969ff.
13. On this point see D. Rutherford, "Metaphysics: The Late Period," in *Cambridge Companion to Leibniz,* ed. Jolley, pp. 158ff.

14. Leibniz, letter to Mme. de Brinon, F de C I, 163, (also in Acad. Ed. I, 6, 235). In a letter to Landgraf Ernst of Hessen-Rheinfels (November 1687) Leibniz goes still further: speaking of himself he urges that "he who is Catholic *in foro interno* is like a man unjustly excommunicated *clave errante*. But it is necessary that he desire external communion with all his power, and that it is not in his power to enjoy it. This has nothing in common with those who are truly schismatics, and who do not have this disposition which is so necessary to union and so conformed to charity" (in Acad. Ed. I, 5, 9).

15. Leibniz, *Institutionem Iuris Perpetui* (1695), in Mollat, p. 1.

16. Leibniz, letter to Mme. de Brinon (1697), in Acad. Ed. I, 14, 741–743.

17. Ibid.

18. Ibid., p. 742.

19. Ibid., p. 743.

20. Ibid., p. 741 ("Introductory Note").

21. Leibniz, letter to Mme. de Brinon (second letter, 1697), in Acad. Ed. I, 14, 744–745.

22. Ibid., pp. 745–746.

23. Ibid. See also Leibniz, *Judgment of the Works of the Earl of Shaftesbury* (1712), in Riley, p. 196: "The remark [of Shaftesbury] is also good . . . that individual friendship is little-recommended by our religion, which directs us towards charity, that is to say, towards a general benevolence."

24. Dante, *De Monarchia*, esp. bk. III.

25. Leibniz, *Caesarinus Fürstenerius*, "Preface to the Reader," in Acad. Ed. IV, 2, 15–16; in Riley, pp. 111–112.

26. Ibid., pp. 16–17.

27. Leibniz, *Codex Iuris Gentium* (Praefatio), pts. i–ii, in Riley, pp. 165–169.

28. Leibniz, letter to Electress Sophie (October 1691), in Klopp VII, 147.

29. Leibniz, *Observations on the Abbé de St. Pierre's "Project for Perpetual Peace,"* in Riley, p. 180.

30. Leibniz, letter to Grimarest, in Riley, p. 183.

31. Ibid., p. 184.

32. Leibniz, *NE* II, xxxiii, pt. 18.

33. Leibniz, letter to Thomas Burnett (1706), in Ger. III, 310–311.

34. For a comparison of Leibniz and Kant on this point, see Riley, *Kant's Political Philosophy*, ch. 6. See also Pierre Laberge, "Leibniz, Rousseau, Kant, et l'abbé de St. Pierre," in *Leibniz und Europa: VI Leibniz-Kongress*, Vorträge I Teil, pp. 429–435.

35. Kant, *Towards Eternal Peace*, "First Appendix," in *Political Writings*, ed. Reiss, pp. 117–118.

36. Ibid., pp. 116–120. On this point see Patrick Riley, "Politics' Homage to Morality: Kant's Eternal Peace after 200 Years," in *Proceedings of the VIII International Kant-Congress* (1995), ed. H. Robinson, vol. 3 (Milwaukee, 1996), pp. 231ff.

37. Leibniz, *Institutionem Iuris Perpetui*, in Mollat p. 1. For a reading of Leibniz as a

"German patriot," see E. Pfleiderer, *G. W. Leibniz als Patriot, Staatsmann und Bildungsträger* (Leipzig, 1870); written at the moment of the Franco-Prussian War, the book makes Leibniz into a proto-Bismarck (through heroic transmogrification).

38. See Loemker I, 12ff.; Latta, "Life and Works of Leibniz," in Latta, pp. 5–10.

39. "This king could bring about the joys of the human race, but he turned toward undertakings which finally became the scourge of Europe." Leibniz, in Klopp x, 28.

40. Leibniz, *Remarks on a French Manifesto*, F de C III, 86.

41. Ibid.

42. Latta, "Life and Works of Leibniz," in Latta, pp. 5–6. See also Ritter, *Leibniz's Aegyptischer Plan*, passim.

43. Leibniz, *Consilium Aegyptiacum*, Acad. Ed. IV, 1, 267–268.

44. Ritter, *Leibniz's Aegyptischer Plan*, ch. 1.

45. Leibniz, *Consilium Aegyptiacum*, pp. 267ff.

46. Ibid., pp. 273–274.

47. Thucydides, *The Peloponnesian War*, trans. F. Crawley (New York, 1951), pp. 105–106. See Werner Jaeger, *Paideia*, 1, 420ff.

48. Leibniz, *Consilium Aegyptiacum*, p. 284.

49. Ibid., pp. 356ff.

50. Ibid.

51. Ibid., p. 358.

52. Ibid., pp. 359–360.

53. Ibid., p. 376.

54. Ibid., pp. 378–379.

55. Ibid., p. 379.

56. Written originally in Latin, and translated into French by Leibniz himself; plainly he meant this work to have an impact.

57. Leibniz, *Mars Christianissimus*, in Riley, pp. 125–126 (original text in Acad. Ed. IV, 2, 470ff. [Leibniz' French translation]).

58. Ibid. (Riley ed.), p. 127.

59. Ibid., p. 128.

60. Ibid., pp. 129–130.

61. See ibid. (Riley ed.), note to *Caesarinus Fürstenerius*, pp. 117–118n. See also Patrick Riley, "Three Seventeenth-Century German Theorists of Federalism," *Polity*, 6, 3 (1976): 7ff.

62. Leibniz, *Mars Christianissimus*, in Riley, p. 144.

63. Ibid., p. 145.

64. Leibniz, *Remarks on a French Manifesto*, in F de C III, 88 (also in Acad. Ed. IV, 3, 77ff.).

65. Ibid.

66. Ibid., p. 84 (F de C).

67. Leibniz, *Réflexions sur la déclaration de la guerre*, (1688–89), Acad. Ed. IV, 3, 131.

68. Leibniz, *Manifesto for the Defense of the Rights of Charles III*, in Riley, pp. 159–160 (original French text in F de C III).

69. See, for example, Abbé de Siéyès, *What Is the Third Estate?* trans M. Blondel (London, 1963), passim.

70. Leibniz, *Manifesto for Charles III*, in Riley p. 158.

71. Ibid., p. 163.

72. Leibniz, *Peace of Utrecht Inexcusable*, in F de C IV, passim.

73. Ibid., p. 131.

74. Leibniz, *Lettre d'un patriote a la sérénissime république de Venise* (1713), in F de C IV, 175ff.; for a commentary see Robinet, *Leibniz: Le meilleur des mondes*, pp. 236–237.

75. Leibniz, 1711 manuscript (LH XI, 5, B1.61), in Leibniz-Archiv, Niedersächsische Landesbibliothek, Hanover (cited with permission).

76. Leibniz, *Considerations Relating to Peace and War*, in F de C IV, 193; see also F de C III, 117 and 282.

77. Leibniz, *Peace of Utrecht Inexcusable*, in F de C IV, p. 134.

78. Hobbes, *Leviathan*, ed. Oakeshott, chs. 26–28, pp. 172–209.

79. Leibniz, *Reflections on an English Treatise Which Contains the Means Which Mme. the Electress of Brunswick [Hanover] Should Use to Assure the Effective Right of the English Succession for Herself and Her Posterity*, in F de C IV, 222.

80. Leibniz, *Treatise . . . Touching the Creation of a Ninth Electorate in Favor of the Protestants*, in Klopp VI, 262.

81. Ibid., pp. 268ff.

82. Leibniz, *Lettre sur l'education d'un prince*, pp. 546ff. (which gives a clear indication of what Leibniz prized in state activity).

83. Latta, "Life and Works of Leibniz," in Latta, pp. 9–10; Fontenelle, *Éloge de Leibniz*, pp. 60–61.

84. Ibid.

85. Ibid.

86. Latta, pp. 15–16.

87. Leibniz, letter to des Billettes, in Loemker II, 775.

88. Leibniz, *Institutionem Iuris Perpetui*, in Mollat p. 1. Leibniz had said almost the same thing in his early *Nova Methodus*, pt. 14 (Acad. Ed. VI, 1, 300–301): "Just or unjust is that which is useful or harmful to the public. 'Public' means first the world, whose rector God is, then the human race, and finally [particular] commonwealths [*Reipublicae*]."

Conclusion

1. Hume, *Treatise of Human Nature*, bk. III, ii, 44.

2. Plato, *Republic* 428e–429a, in *Collected Dialogues*, p. 670: "It is by virtue of its smallest class and minutest part of itself, and the wisdom that resides therein, in

the part which takes the lead and rules, that a city established on principles of nature would be wise as a whole."

3. Aristotle, *Politics*, trans. E. Barker (Oxford, 1946), bk. III.

4. Kant, *Towards Eternal Peace*, in *Political Writings*, ed. Reiss, pp. 117–118.

5. Machiavelli, *Discourses*, bk. I, ch. X.

6. Hobbes, *Leviathan*, ed. Oakeshott, chs. 13–15, pp. 80ff.

7. Suarez is certainly the most subtle and fully developed of the late Scholastic moralists; see above all his *Treatise on Laws and God the Lawgiver* (1612), passim.

8. Kant, *Critique of Practical Reason*, trans. Beck, pp. 76ff.

9. Plato, *Phaedrus* 254a–256b, in *Collected Dialogues*, pp. 500–501.

10. Kant, *Critique of Practical Reason*, trans. Beck, p. 46.

11. Kant, *Groundwork of the Metaphysic of Morals*, trans. T. K. Abbott (Indianapolis, 1949), pp. 28ff.

12. Kant, *Critique of Pure Reason*, trans. Kemp Smith, A313/B370ff., pp. 310–313.

13. Leibniz, *De Tribus Juris Praeceptis sive Gradibus*, 1677–78(?), in *Textes inédits*, II, 608: "Vir bonus est qui amat omnes." But Leibniz immediately adds that "reason" should "regulate" that love (ibid.).

14. Kant, *Critique of Pure Reason*, trans. Kemp Smith, A547/B575, pp. 472–473. For a defense of Leibniz *contra* Kant on this point, see Kurt Hildebrandt, *Leibniz und das Reich der Gnade* (The Hague, 1953), pp. 373–375.

15. Kant, *Religion within the Limits*, trans. Greene and Hudson, bks. II and III.

16. Kant, *Critique of Practical Reason*, trans. Beck, pp. 126ff.

17. Ibid.

18. Kant, *Über eine Entdeckung*, in *Werke*, ed. Cassirer, VI, 65ff.

19. Kant, *Groundwork*, trans. Abbott, pp. 26–29.

20. Ibid., pp. 11ff.

21. Kant, *An Enquiry into the Distinctness of the Fundamental Principles of Natural Theology and Morals* (the Prize Essay), in Kant, *Selections*, ed. L. W. Beck (New York, 1988), p. 35: "Nothing has been more harmful to philosophy than . . . the idea of imitating mathematics as a method of thinking where it cannot possibly be used."

22. Kant, *Critique of Pure Reason*, trans. Kemp Smith, A584/B612ff., pp. 495ff.

23. Nietzsche, *Twilight of the Idols*, in *The Portable Nietzsche*, ed. Kaufmann, pp. 490ff.

24. Kant, *Groundwork*, trans. Abbott, pp. 44ff.

25. Kant, *The Conflict of the Faculties* (1798), in *Political Writings*, ed. Reiss, pp. 187–188: "The profit which will accrue to the human race as it works its way forward will not be an ever increasing quantity of morality in its attitudes." Here Kant departs from his more sanguine view of moral progress in *Idea for a Universal History* (1784).

26. Kant, *Towards Eternal Peace*, in *Political Writings*, ed. Reiss, pp. 117–118.

27. Kant, *Critique of Pure Reason*, 1787 Preface ("B"), trans. Kemp Smith, Bxxv, p. 26.

28. Hobbes, *Leviathan*, ed. Oakeshott, ch. 31, pp. 248–251.

29. Leibniz, "Discourse on Metaphysics," prop. 13, in Loemker, 2nd ed., pp. 310–311.

30. See Rousseau, *Lettres écrites de la montagne* (Amsterdam, 1764), pp. 131–132; see Riley, *The General Will before Rousseau*, pp. 194–195.

31. It was this collision between divine determination and human self-determination which led Kant to say, understandably, that "it is not in the least conceivable how God might concur in our actions" (*Lectures on Philosophical Theology*, trans. A. Wood and G. Clark [Ithaca, 1978], p. 148).

32. See, for example, Augustine, *De Correptione et Gratia*, passim.

33. Augustine, *Retractiones* (c. 427–430), passim.

34. Pierre Bayle, viewing (roughly) the same antithetical elements and antinomies, fell back on Pascalian fideism; Leibniz was too much of a Platonist to abandon reason.

35. Leibniz, letter to Hansch (May 1712), in Dutens v, 167. See also Leibniz, *Theodicy*, trans. Huggard, II, 175–178, pp. 236–238.

36. Mulvaney, "Divine Justice in Leibniz' 'Discourse on Metaphysics,' " pp. 61ff.

37. Leibniz, "Suite des réflexions sur le livre intitulé *Loix civiles*," in *Textes inédits*, II, 652.

38. Leibniz, *Theodicy*, trans. Huggard, I, 6, p. 127: "Our end is to banish from men the false ideas that represent God to them as an absolute prince employing a despotic power, unfitted to be loved and unworthy of being loved."

39. Schneider, *Justitia universalis*, pp. 477–478.

40. Leibniz, *Theodicy*, trans. Huggard, III, 416, pp. 372–373; Leibniz, letter to Wedderkopf (1671), in Loemker I, 226–227.

41. Leibniz, *Theodicy*, trans. Huggard, II, 145, p. 214.

42. Leibniz, letter to Antoine Arnauld (1671), in Ger. I, 73–74.

43. Ibid.

44. Plato, *Republic*, bk. x, 614b ff., in *Collected Dialogues*, pp. 838ff.

45. Leibniz, letter to Antoine Arnauld (1671), in Ger. I, 73–74.

46. Here I paraphrase the remarks of Ursula Goldenbaum (Humboldt Universität, Berlin), presented in response to my paper at the Berlin-Brandenburg Akademie der Wissenschaften (February 28, 1995), "Leibniz' Universal Jurisprudence: Justice as 'the Charity of the Wise.' " Dr. Goldenbaum's naturalistic reading of Leibniz' ethics ties him closely to Spinoza—as she freely grants. (Her remarks will be published in the Proceedings of the Akademie.)

47. Michael Oakeshott, "On Being Conservative," in *Rationalism in Politics*, pp. 194–196.

48. Michael Oakeshott, *The Voice of Liberal Learning*, ed. Timothy Fuller (New Haven, 1989), pp. 66–67.

49. Ibid. For Leibniz' notion of "living mirrors," see Laurence Bonquiaux, *L'harmonie et le chaos: Le rationalisme Leibnizien et la "nouvelle science"* (Louvain, 1994), pp. 182ff.

50. See, inter alia, Oakeshott, "Rational Conduct," in *Rationalism in Politics*, pp. 96–97.

51. Michael Oakeshott, "The Masses in Representative Democracy," in *Rationalism in Politics*, enl. ed., ed. Timothy Fuller (Indianapolis, 1991), pp. 330ff.

52. Oakeshott, *The Voice of Liberal Learning*, pp. 43–44.

53. Even though Hegel's view of Leibniz was not very favorable, he at least thought that his Hanoverian predecessor had avoided a mindless empiricism in which "reason is a bone."

54. Paul Janet, *Histoire de la science politique* (Paris, 1896), ii, 248.

55. Gareth Stedman-Jones, manuscript on the history of socialism, chapter on Marx and his German predecessors (especially Leibniz and Kant). Dr. Stedman-Jones, of King's College, Cambridge, kindly sent this chapter to me at Oxford in January 1995.

56. Ibid., pp. 1, 24–25. When the Stedman-Jones manuscript is published, it will be invaluable in setting Marx in his German context.

57. Ibid., pp. 25ff.

58. This has been most persuasively done by Lucien Goldmann in *Immanuel Kant*, trans. R. Black (London, 1971), pp. 176–177—a remarkable study.

59. See, for example, Leibniz, letter to Morrell (September 1698), in *Textes inédits*, i, 136ff.

60. Aristotle, *Politics* 1295 b28, trans. Barker.

61. Machiavelli, *The Prince*, ch. 18.

62. Hobbes, *Leviathan*, ed. Oakeshott, ch. 15.

63. Rousseau, *Lettres écrites de la montagne*, 1764 ed., pp. 34–37.

64. Hegel, *Philosophy of Right*, trans. T. M. Knox (Oxford, 1942), pp. 105ff.

65. Nietzsche, *Twilight of the Idols*, pp. 498ff.

66. Freud, "Thoughts for the Time on War and Death" (1915), in his *Civilisation, War and Death*, ed. J. Rickman (London, 1968), pp. 5ff.

67. Pascal, *Pensées*, trans. Trotter, no. 792 (Brunschvicg numbering), pp. 326–327.

68. Leibniz, letter to Queen Sophie-Charlotte of Prussia, cited in Robinet, *Le meilleur des mondes*, p. 309 (also in Acad. Ed. i, ii, 166).

69. W. H. Barber, *Leibniz in France* (Oxford, 1953), chs. 3–5.

70. Hegel, *Philosophy of Right*, preface, pp. 12–13.

71. Leibniz, *De Tribus Iuris Naturae et Gentium Gradibus*, in *Voraus Edition zur Reihe VI*, ed. Schepers, Faszikel 7 (Münster, 1988), p. 1387: "Justitia [est] caritas sapientis, sive virtus quae hominis affectum erga hominem ratione moderatur."

Index